ATLAS OF 20th CENTURY WARFARE

ARCTURUS

Arcturus Publishing Limited
26/27 Bickels Yard
151–153 Bermondsey Street
London SE1 3HA

Published in association with
foulsham
W. Foulsham & Co. Ltd,
The Publishing House, Bennetts Close, Cippenham,
Slough, Berkshire SL1 5AP, England

ISBN 0-572-03042-8

This edition printed in 2005

British Library Cataloguing-in-Publication Data: a catalogue record for this book is available from the British Library

Printed in China

CONTENTS

WORLD WAR I

WORLD WAR II: EUROPE

WORLD WAR II: THE PACIFIC

THE KOREAN WAR

THE VIETNAM WAR

THE ARAB-ISRAELI CONFLICT

WORLD WAR I

CHAPTER 1: THE EUROPEAN WAR

Wilhelm II, emperor of Germany 1888-1918, proved unequal to the task of wisely governing his inherited empire.

Irregular Macedonian fighters guard a highway leading to Salonika during the First Balkan War, 1912.

World War I, fought between 1914 and 1918, was a vast conflict that involved most of the world's major powers. Two grand alliances confronted one another: Britain, France, Russia, Italy, the USA and others on one side, and Germany, Austria-Hungary, Turkey and Bulgaria on the other. The war was fought on land, at sea, and, for the first time, in the air. Advances in technology had produced powerful and deadly new weapons which changed the nature of warfare forever. It began in Europe. In 1871 the large and industrially developed German Empire had replaced France as the continent's major power. Needing support, France had reached an agreement ('entente') in 1904 with its old enemy Britain, which was also anxious about German ambitions.

For many years Britain had enjoyed good relations with most of the states that made up Germany. The British royal family were of German descent and related to the Emperor of Germany. By the 1900s, however, this traditional Anglo-German friendship was breaking down. The British feared that their enormous overseas empire, covering one quarter of the world's surface, was threatened by German ambitions in Africa and elsewhere. Secondly, there was serious industrial and commercial competition between the two empires. Thirdly, Britain saw the construction of a large German Navy as a direct threat to Britain's worldwide naval supremacy. By 1910 Britain and Germany were in an arms race as they tried to outdo one another in warship construction.

THE BALKAN QUESTION For centuries the Balkan peninsula in south-east Europe had been part of the Turkish Ottoman Empire. In the nineteenth century Turkish power declined and the Balkans divided into small, independent states. The most politically influential were Greece, Romania, Bulgaria, Bosnia, and, especially, Serbia. In 1912-3 the intense rivalry between the Balkan states flared into two wars.

The neighbouring Russian and Austro-Hungarian Empires competed with each other for influence among the Balkan states. In 1908, for example, the Russians were furious when the Austro-Hungarians annexed the provinces of Bosnia and Herzegovina.

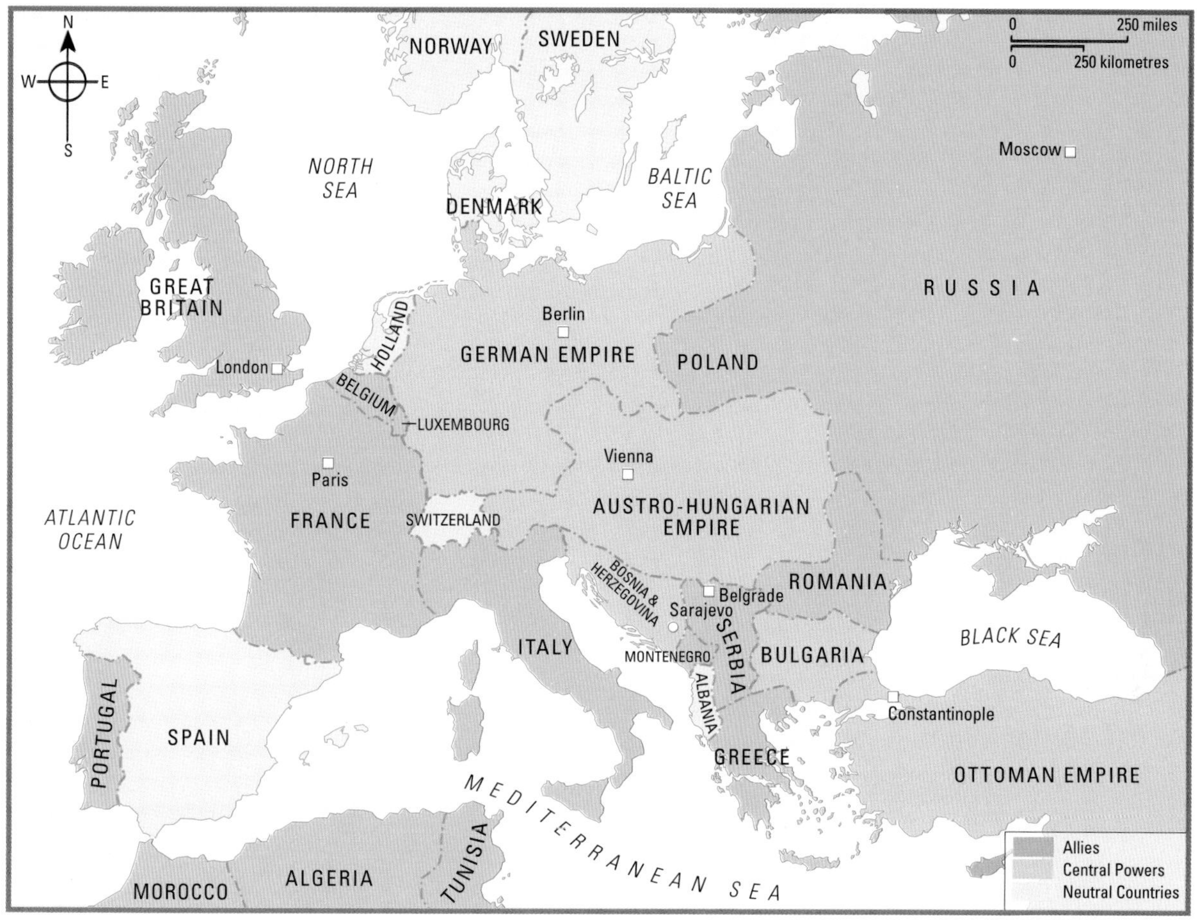

A continent divided – how the states of Europe lined up to fight during World War I. Many had aligned with one side or another long before the fighting broke out in August 1914

The chief bone of contention between them was Serbia, allied to Russia but distrusted by Austria-Hungary.

By 1914 Europe's dangerous international rivalries were backed up by a series of military alliances and agreements. On one side were the countries bound together by the Triple Entente (France, Britain and Russia) – the Allies. Ranged against them were the Central Powers of Germany and Austria-Hungary, linked by a Dual Alliance and supported with reservations by Italy (the Triple Alliance). Although

MANPOWER OF THE MAIN EUROPEAN RIVALS

Allies		**Population**	**Armed forces at outbreak of war**
Triple Entente:	Russia	167 million	5 million
	France*	39.6 million	3.78 million
	Britain*	46.4 million	733,500
Central Powers			
Dual Alliance:	Germany	67 million	4.5 million
	Austria-Hungary	49.9 million	3.35 million
Serbia (with Allies, 1914)		5 million	460,000
Italy (with Allies, from 1915)		35 million	875,000
Turkey (with Central Powers, 1914)		21.3 million	300,000?

* France and Britain could also draw on the considerable manpower of their overseas colonies.

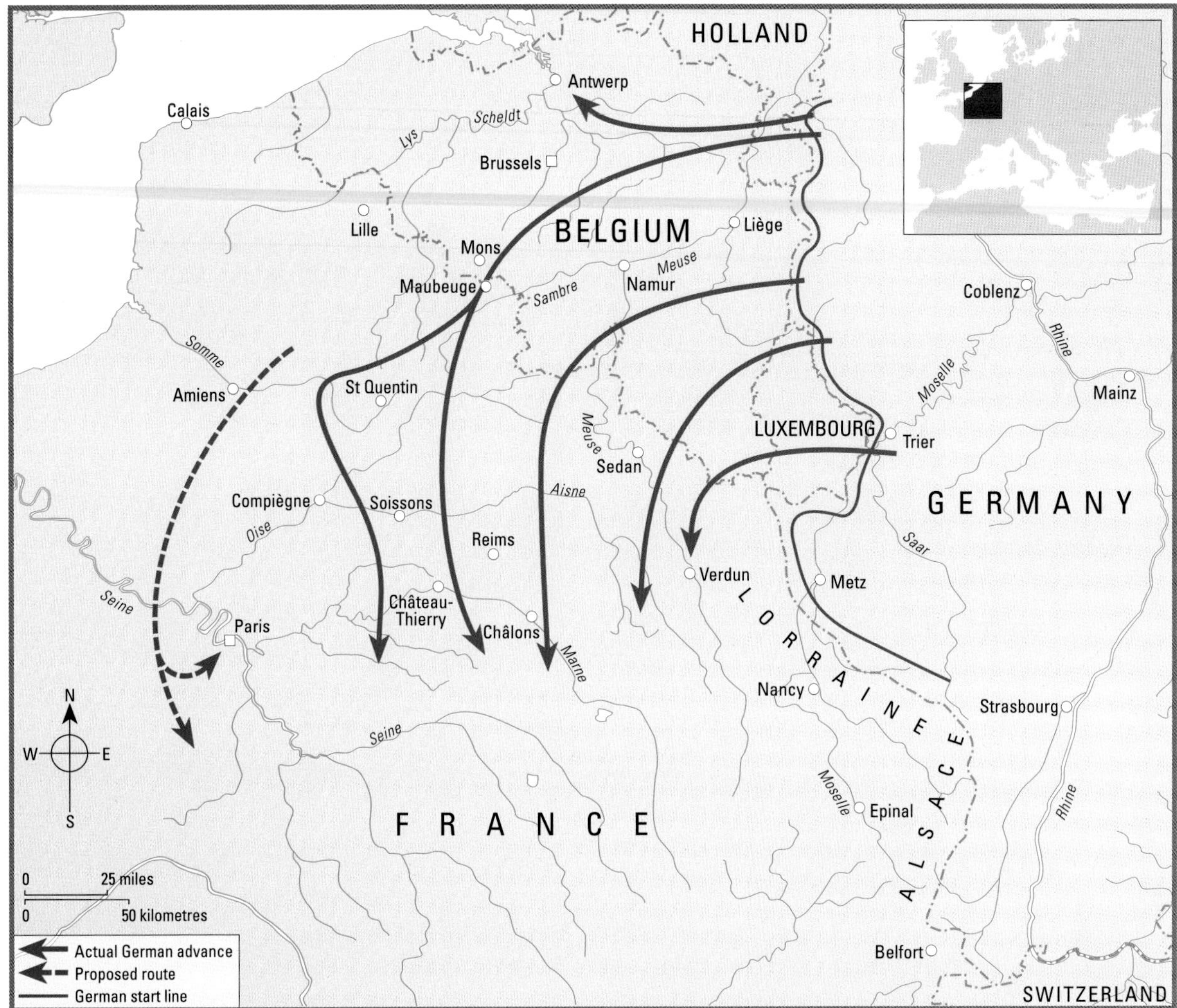

Excellent on paper ... the German Schlieffen Plan envisaged a swift knock out blow in the west by driving through neutral Belgium and then surrounding Paris.

these alliances were theoretically defensive, they meant a small conflict might well spread over the entire continent – and beyond.

WAR PLANS The outbreak of war in 1914 was not unexpected, and each side had made careful plans in advance. France, for instance, arranged to attack east into Alsace and Lorraine, provinces that Germany had seized in the war of 1870-1. Predicting such a move, in 1905 the German Chief of Staff General Count Alfred von Schlieffen had planned a swift attack on northern France through neutral Holland and Belgium. He believed this would quickly knock France out of the war and enable Germany to turn on Russia.

The Schlieffen Plan was altered, and weakened, by his successor, General Helmuth von Moltke. He reduced the force attacking from the north and bypassed Holland. Nevertheless, Germany's assault on Belgium brought Britain into the war because it had guaranteed Belgian neutrality.

In the tense atmosphere of the early twentieth century, the European powers were terrified of being caught unawares. If one country increased the size of its armed forces, as Germany did in 1912, its rivals immediately did the same: Russia responded to Germany's 170,000 increase by swelling its army by half a million. This in turn frightened the Germans into further increases, so quickening the arms race. To meet these military requirements, all the major states except Britain obliged young men to undertake military service.

THE ARMS RACE

Sir Edward Grey, Britain's foreign secretary at the outbreak of war, outlined the process of the arms race: *'One nation increases its army and makes strategic railways towards the frontiers of neighbouring countries. The second nation makes counter-strategic railways and increases its army in reply. The first nation says this is very unreasonable, because its own military preparations were only precautions, and points out ... that the first nation began the competition; and so it goes on, till the whole Continent is an armed camp covered by strategic railways.'*

[From *Twenty-five Years, 1892-1916,* Viscount E. Grey]

Helmuth von Moltke, the German commander whose failure to execute the Schlieffen Plan led to his dismissal in 1914.

The gigantic Russian army had the reputation of being a 'steamroller' – slow to get going but unstoppable once on the move. Furthermore, it was growing larger by the day, and Russia itself was developing mass-produced weapons. The German command feared that the longer war was delayed, the less chance they had of winning. Consequently, when Austria-Hungary threatened war with Serbia in July 1914, the German Emperor Wilhelm II gave his ally his full backing: if war was to come, his generals argued, then the sooner the better.

Britain's iron shield: headed by the battleship HMS *Neptune*, the Royal Navy displays its power at the 1911 Spithead Fleet Review.

INTO BATTLE The outbreak of war was sparked by the assassination of Archduke Franz Ferdinand, heir to the throne of Austria-Hungary, on 28 June 1914. The Austro-Hungarians blamed Serbian terrorists for the outrage, and declared war on Serbia on 28 July. This started a domino effect. When Russia prepared to help Serbia, Germany declared war on it (1 August). France, Russia's ally, mobilized its troops so Germany declared war on it too. This launched the Schlieffen Plan, bringing Britain into the conflict (4 August). The Schlieffen Plan very nearly succeeded. The Germans drove back the French in the east and moved through Belgium to within 50 km of Paris by late August. The French, with British support, halted the offensive on the River Marne, ending German hopes of a swift victory.

The Battle of the Marne, 5-9 September 1914, was the first in which aircraft played a vital role. The Schlieffen Plan called for the German armies to encircle Paris from the west. However, finding his enemy in disarray, the commander of the German First Army, General Alexander von Kluck, advanced across the Marne to the east of the capital. This was spotted by Allied aircraft. The French commander, Marshal Joseph Joffre, responded with an attack on Kluck's unguarded right flank – and the Germans were obliged to withdraw.

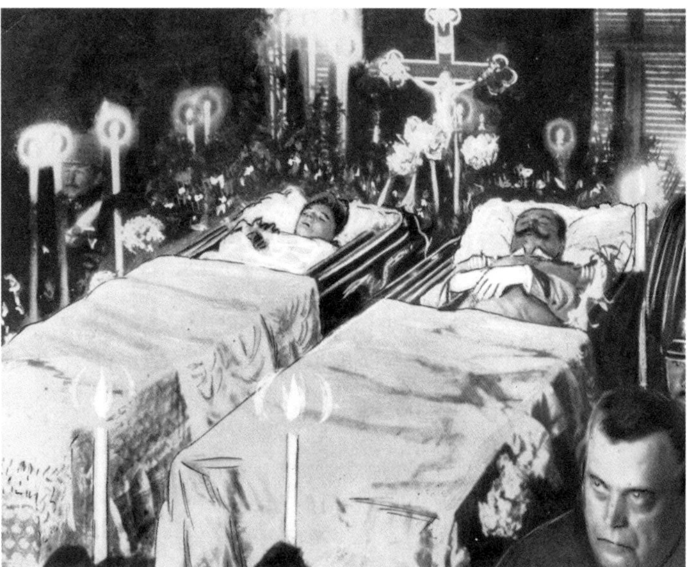

Two deaths that led to millions more ... the bodies of the Austrian Archduke Franz Ferdinand and his wife Sophie lie in state.

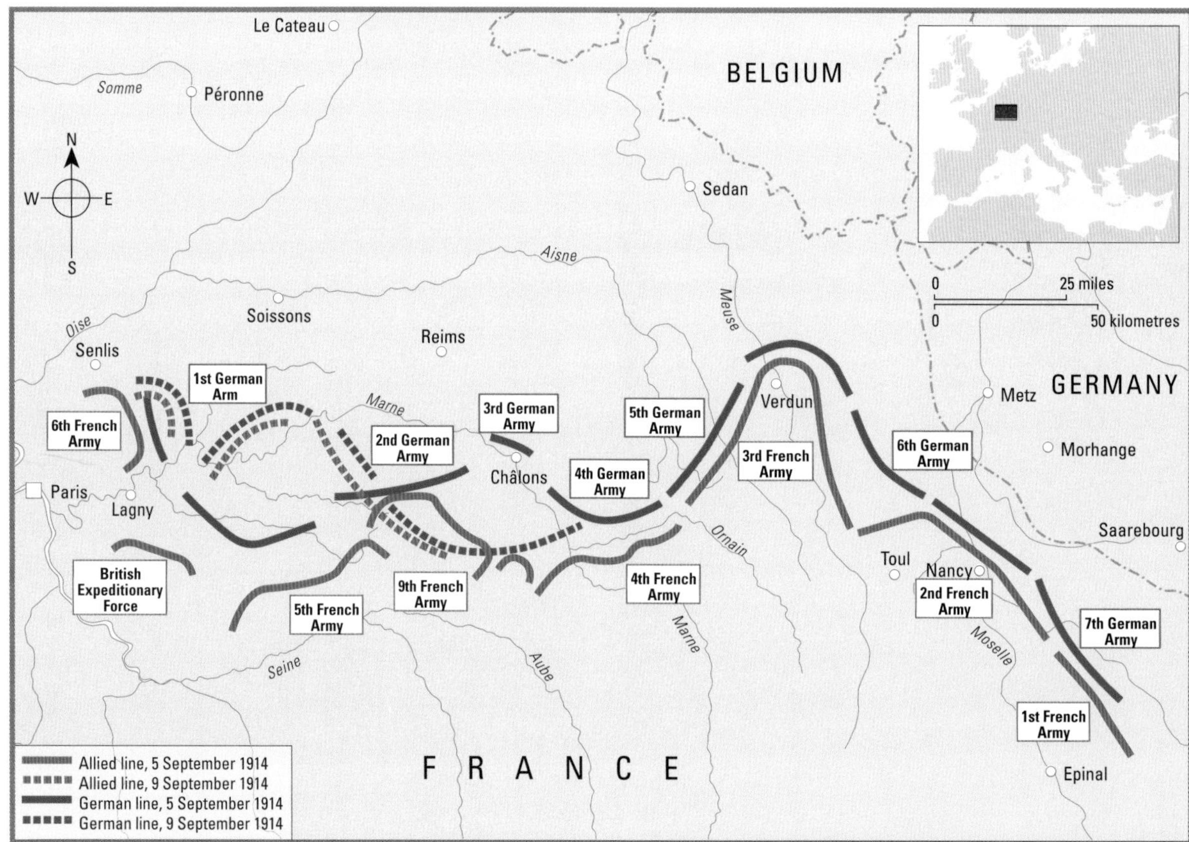

The Battle of the Marne, September 1914. By halting the German advance, the Allies ensured a long and bitter conflict.

The battle turned out to have been one of the most decisive of modern history. The failure of the Schlieffen Plan forced Germany to fight on two fronts, in the west against Britain and France, and in the east against Russia. In the end this proved more than it could stand. Moreover, the battle virtually ended the war of movement in Western Europe. Unable to out-manoeuvre each other, the two sides swiftly settled to long-drawn-out and costly campaigns of trench warfare (see pages 10-11).

TRENCH WARFARE The classic strategy of armies facing one another is to seek to outflank (get round behind) their enemy. This is precisely what the

TIMETABLE OF THE BATTLE OF THE MARNE

14-25 August	Germans advance on all fronts towards Paris.
31 August	Germans within 50 km of Paris.
4 September	General Kluck moves south-east of Paris, crossing River Marne. This is seen by Allied spotter planes.
6 September	French and British counterattack on Kluck's right flank.
6-8 September	Fierce fighting all along the line.
9 September	Kluck orders his army to withdraw. German commander-in-chief, General von Moltke, orders withdrawal to the River Aisne, north of Paris.

French soldiers in action during the Battle of the Marne, September 1914. At this early stage of the war soldiers were not equipped with either camouflaged uniforms or steel helmets.

Temporary shelters that became home – German soldiers in hastily-constructed trenches, 1914.

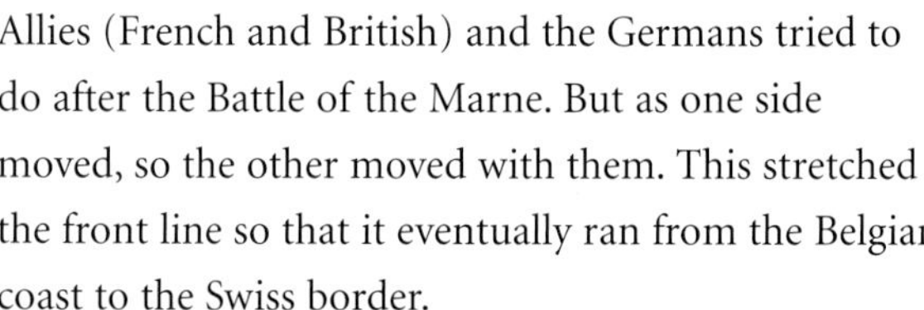

TROUBLE WITH WATER

One of the great problems of trench warfare, as Captain J.I. Cohen wrote from Ypres in 1915, was drainage,

'This horrible country is made of mud, water and dead Germans. Whenever water is left in a trench it drags the earth down on either side and forms a fearfully sticky viscous matter that lets you sink gently down and grips you like a vice when you're there. ... Cover is got by building ... dug-outs, behind the trench. Two walls of sandbags with a sheet of corrugated iron on top and an oil-sheet under it to make the whole waterproof.'

[Quoted in *The Imperial War Museum Book of the First World War*, edited by Malcolm Brown]

Allies (French and British) and the Germans tried to do after the Battle of the Marne. But as one side moved, so the other moved with them. This stretched the front line so that it eventually ran from the Belgian coast to the Swiss border.

Improved military technology – in particular, barbed wire, machine guns and heavy artillery – made a frontal attack almost impossible. To protect themselves, troops on either side dug lines of trenches, usually three deep. These filthy, dangerous holes became the hallmark of the war, both on the Western Front and elsewhere.

World War I was the first to be fought between large industrialized nations. Power depended as much upon industrial output – ships, artillery, rifles, and so forth – as on human muscle. Pinned down by barbed wire, and at the mercy of streams of quick-fire bullets and bombardment by high-explosive shells, the individual soldier became just a statistic: categorized as either able-bodied, wounded, or dead. The war they fought had little to do with glory or valour; it was about 'attrition', grinding the enemy down until they (or you) could take no more.

The trench line from Switzerland to the Channel was complete by the beginning of winter. At the time, it was not seen as in any way permanent. On 30 October, for example, the Germans began a series of attacks on a salient [bulge] in the Allied line around

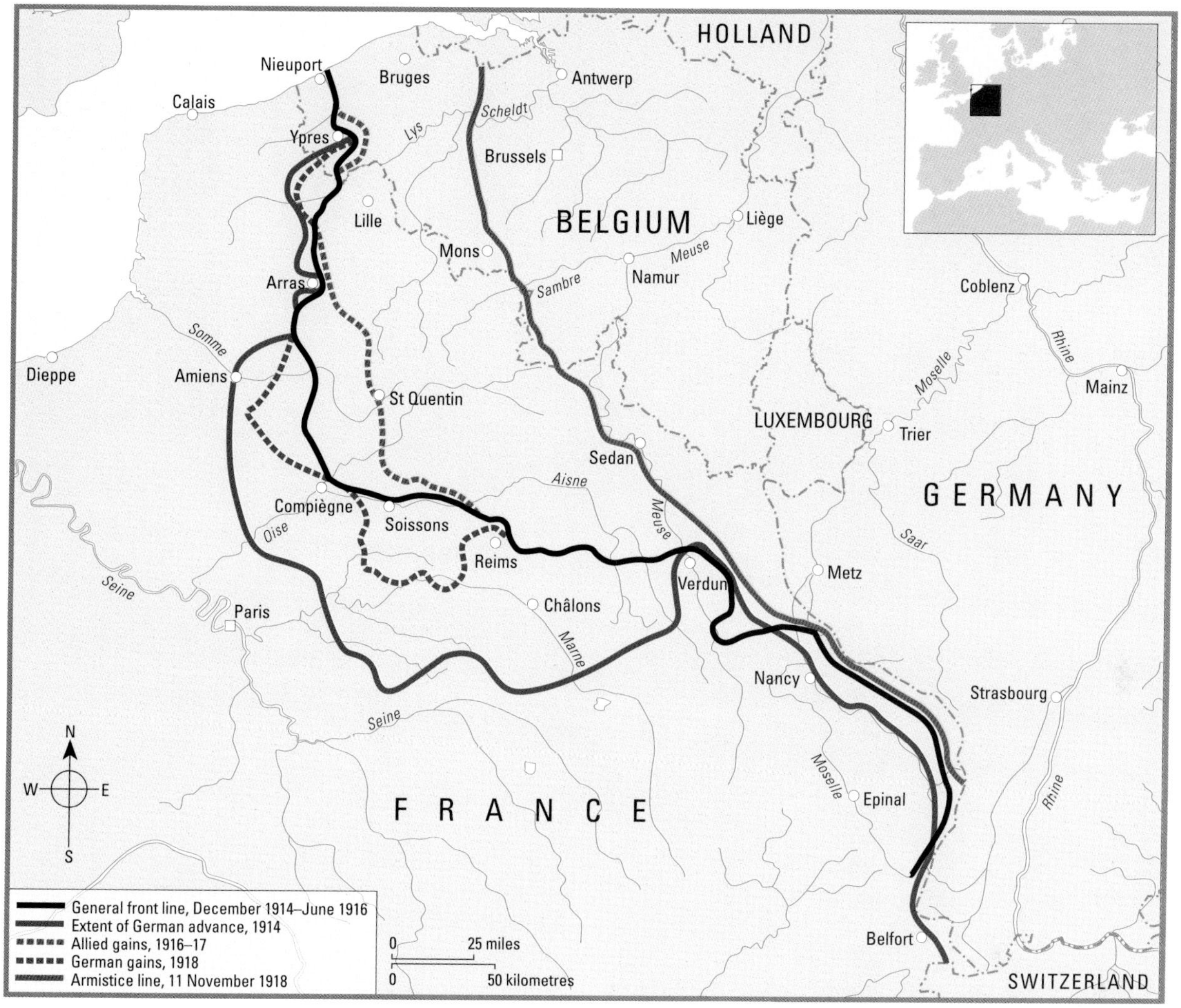

The Western Front, 1914-18. The dominance of defensive technology meant that the line moved little in over four years of fighting.

the town of Ypres in Belgium. The fighting lasted until 24 November. Although very little ground was gained, the casualties were shocking: 58,200 British, some 50,000 French, and 134,300 Germans. The full horror of mechanized [trench] warfare had begun to be seen.

THE EASTERN FRONT, 1914-15

The Russian Empire entered the war with enthusiasm. Loyalty to the all-powerful emperor, Nicholas II, swelled and his massive armies assembled quicker than anticipated. By mid-August 1914 two armies, commanded by Generals Pavel Rennenkampf and Alexander Samsonov, were advancing into Prussia, in north-east Germany. However, although moving less

French soldiers operate a captured German machine gun. Weapons like this took a terrible toll of human life in the war of attrition on the Western Front.

Splendid-looking but redundant – as all cavalry, these Russian Cossacks were easy targets for machine gun and artillery fire.

The Eastern Front along which the mighty Russian Empire battled against the empires of Germany and Austria-Hungary.

slowly than expected, they also proved easier to halt.

The Russian commanders did not get on, making communication between their two armies at best patchy. Furthermore, the German commanders, Generals Paul von Hindenburg and Erich Ludendorff, managed to pick up uncoded Russian radio signals. These gave invaluable information about enemy troops numbers and movements.

In late August the Germans split the Russian armies and

CASUALTIES ON THE EASTERN FRONT, 1914

	Killed or wounded	Taken prisoner
Russian	617,000	182,000
German	115,000	–
Austro-Hungarian	400,000	100,000

These remarkable statistics reveal that in just five months of fighting well over a million soldiers had been lost and over one quarter of a million taken prisoner. The Russians alone had lost almost 800,000 (killed, wounded and captured).

crushed Samsonov's isolated force around the town of Tannnenberg in East Prussia. After the battle (26-30 August) the disgraced Russian commander committed suicide. The Germans then turned on Rennenkampf, outmanoeuvred him, and defeated him at the Battle of Masurian Lakes (9-14 September). By the autumn the Russians were once more back behind their own frontiers.

Further south, in Galicia, the Russians faced the armies of the Austro-Hungarian Empire. Ruled since the thirteenth century by the Habsburg family, the Austro-Hungarian Empire was one of the oldest in Europe. Its territory stretched from Bohemia (modern-day Czech Republic) to Bosnia in the Balkans.

The idea behind this European empire of many peoples and cultures was somewhat out of date. Held together by a vast bureaucracy and loyalty to Emperor Franz Joseph I, it was less well-suited to industrial war than Germany. In Galicia, after initial setbacks, the Russians pushed the multi-national Austro-Hungarian forces back and advanced along a wide front until halted by the rugged terrain of the Carpathian Mountains.

By Christmas 1914, the situation on much of the Eastern Front was similar – thought less rigid – to that in the West. Millions of men, sheltered within frozen trenches, faced each other across barely 100 metres of barren 'no-man's-land'.

Too young to die? Russian prisoners of war after the decisive Battle of the Masurian Lakes, September 1914, included this very young soldier.

THE BALKANS Given the region's troubled history (the mixture of peoples of different ethnic backgrounds and religious beliefs had led to many conflicts in the past), it is little surprise that the fighting in the Balkans was as ferocious and costly as anywhere. It began in 1914 with a massive Austro-Hungarian attack on Serbia. Fighting to defend their native land, the Serbs proved fierce fighters. Out of a population of some five million, they raised an army of half a million and even drew on the services of women. The invaders were repeatedly driven back with heavy losses.

In 1915 the tide turned. Bulgaria joined the war on the side of the Central Powers and Germany sent 300,000 troops to assist its ally. Utterly overwhelmed, the Serbs fought on to the end of year and some escaped to join Allied forces elsewhere. Nevertheless, by 1916 Serbia was out of the war and Austria-Hungary's power now reached to the frontiers of Greece and Albania.

Romania, wooed by both sides, eventually joined the war on the side of the Allies in August 1916. It proved a costly mistake. Russia was by this time exhausted, leaving the 500,000-strong Romanian army exposed to an attack by a combined force of Austro-Hungarians, Bulgarians, Turks and Germans. By the end of the year Bucharest, the capital city, had fallen. Four hundred thousand men and three-quarters of the country's territory were lost.

Another area of fighting in the Balkans was at Salonika, a port in neutral Greece. Here, in an attempt

KNOWING THE TERRAIN

A British journalist describes how the Serbian commander General Mishitch used his local knowledge to defeat the Austro-Hungarian attack of December 1914:

'He suddenly advanced in a general attack, on the morning of December 3rd, 1914, and completely surprised the Austro-Hungarians. He caught them leisurely moving along the valley paths. Capturing the overlooking hills, the Serbs shot the hostile columns down, while the Austro-Hungarians were still wondering where they should place their artillery. Naturally, the Serbs knew every rise and fall of the ground, for Mishitch himself had been born and bred [there].'

[Quoted in *The Great War*, edited by H.W. Wilson and J.A. Hammerton]

British soldiers in a cheerful mood after landing at Salonika in Greece on their way to reinforce their hard-pressed Serbian allies to the north.

to assist Serbia in 1915, the Allies landed a force of British and French troops which moved north towards Serbia. It came too late to help the Serbs, however, and was too small to do much on its own. Relatively secure behind their barbed wire, the Allied troops made no notable advance until September 1918. By then the war was almost over. Extraordinarily, the maintenance of the Salonika Front cost almost 500,000 casualties, 18,000 from the war and the rest from disease.

To the surprise of many, Serbia held out against the numerically superior Austro-Hungarians and fell to the Central Powers only when German troops joined the invasion in 1915.

A Serbian howitzer prepares to fire on the invading Austrians, 1915. With no direct link to the sea, Serbia could not easily receive Allied munitions.

CHAPTER 2: THE FIGHTING SPREADS

In vain seeking the Gallipoli break-out: an Allied heavy field gun in action at Helles Bay on the tip of the Gallipoli peninsula, 1915.

The Turkish Ottoman Empire, a friend of Germany before the war, entered the conflict on the side of the Central Powers in November 1914. This had little immediate impact on the conflict, other than threatening British-held Egypt and forcing Russia to open yet another front to the east of the Black Sea. The following year, however, Turkey was involved in a major campaign that, had it succeeded, might have altered the whole course of the war.

In February and March 1915 British and French warships tried to force their way through the Dardanelles, the narrow neck of water that links the Mediterranean to the Black Sea. The aim, strongly backed by Britain's Winston Churchill, the First Lord of the Admiralty, was to seize Constantinople (modern-day Istanbul) and open a sea route to Russia. Had this been achieved, there was a possibility that the Allies would be able to threaten the Central Powers from the east.

LANDING AT GALLIPOLI The naval operation was a failure. Three ships were sunk by Turkish mines and the heavy shore guns remained intact. Undaunted, the Allies turned to a different strategy: a landing on the Gallipoli Peninsula than runs up the western side of the Dardanelles. In April 75,000 British, French and Anzac (Australia and New Zealand Army Corps) men went ashore on different points of the toe of the peninsula. Some met almost no resistance and, had they pressed inland, might have quickly secured a sound base.

The Allied commanders were too hesitant or simply incompetent, and the important advantage was lost. The Turkish resistance, well organized by the German General Liman von Sanders, kept the Allies pinned down on

0 5 miles
0 5 kilometres
Royal Naval Division
Turkish 7th Division
Gallipoli
AEGEAN SEA
GALLIPOLI PENINSULA
Suvla Bay
Second British landings
Anzac Cove
ANZAC
Dardanelles
Maidos
Turkish 9th Division
Chanak Kale
TURKEY
Krithia
First British landings
Cape Helles
French
Kum Kale
N
W
E
S
Allied landings
Allied feint attacks
Area captured by Allies
Turkish fort
Turkish batteries
Turkish minefield

The Gallipoli Campaign, 1915-16. Although daring and original in concept, the Allied plan failed through gross mismanagement on the ground and because of the courage of the Turkish resistance.

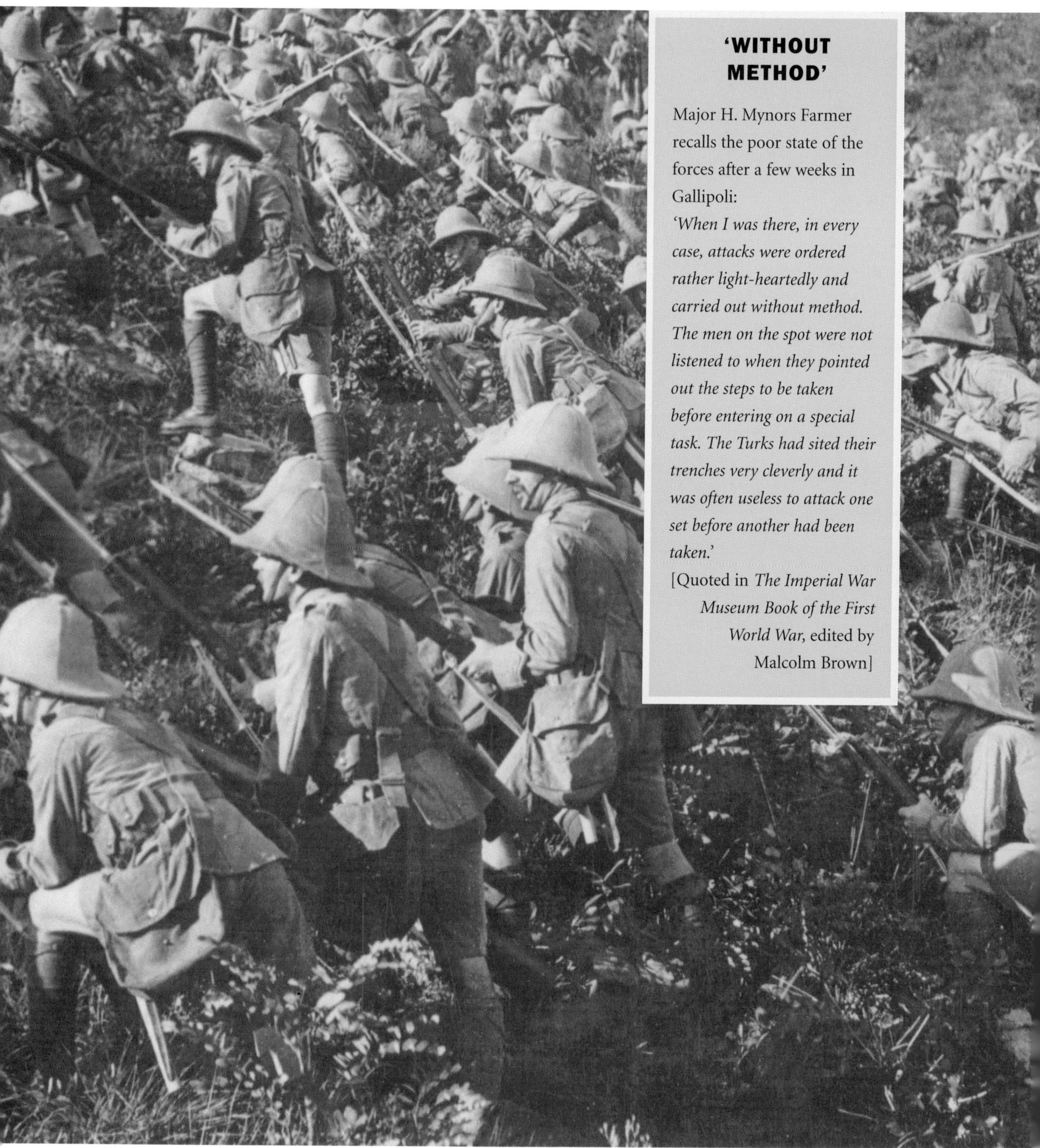

'WITHOUT METHOD'

Major H. Mynors Farmer recalls the poor state of the forces after a few weeks in Gallipoli:

'When I was there, in every case, attacks were ordered rather light-heartedly and carried out without method. The men on the spot were not listened to when they pointed out the steps to be taken before entering on a special task. The Turks had sited their trenches very cleverly and it was often useless to attack one set before another had been taken.'

[Quoted in *The Imperial War Museum Book of the First World War*, edited by Malcolm Brown]

Going nowhere – British troops at Gallipoli try to advance beyond the beaches, August 1915. Time and again they were thrown back by the well-organized Turkish defences.

the beaches. A second landing in August was equally ineffective.

In October the decision was taken to withdraw, an operation completed by January 1916. So ended one of the major fiascos of the war, a dismal catalogue of poor planning and incompetent leadership that produced some 250,000 casualties on either side.

NORTHERN ITALY Italy's agreements with Germany and Austria-Hungary did not oblige it to enter the war on their side in 1914. This was just as well because at the time its armed forces were in poor shape – there were only 600 machine guns in the entire country, for example. Nevertheless, the temptation to join the war proved too great to resist, and the following year (May 1915) it sided with the Allies in the hope of gaining territory from Austria-Hungary.

The war did not go well for the Italians. They remained short of weapons and munitions, both of which were supplied in large quantities by Britain and France. Furthermore, as is clear from a glance at the map, the Austro-Hungarians held the key strategic positions in the mountains overlooking the Italian lines.

Fighting the enemy – and the weather. Troops of the Italian Alpine Regiment prepare for action in the snowy Alps, 1915.

The American novelist Ernest Hemingway served as a volunteer with an ambulance unit on the Italian Front. He based his novel *A Farewell To Arms* (1929) directly on his experiences. This is how he describes the scene in the first chapter of the book:

'There were mists over the river and clouds on the mountain and the trucks splashed mud on the road and the troops were muddy and wet in their capes; their rifles were wet …

At the start of the winter came permanent rain and with the rain came cholera. But it was checked and in the end only seven thousand died of it in the army.'

[From *A Farewell To Arms*, Ernest Hemingway]

withdrawal halted only on the River Piave, 110 km from the Isonzo. Around 275,000 Italians had been captured. On the Piave the Italians managed to dig in and rebuild. Assisted by Allied reinforcements, the new commander, General Armando Diaz, launched a final offensive in October 1918 against an enemy that was by now dispirited and exhausted from sustaining years of fighting on two fronts. The Allies advanced swiftly along a broad

Austrian troops armed with flame-throwers advance along the Isonzo River, 1916.

The front in north-east Italy. The easy gains that Italy hoped for when it joined the war in 1915 were not forthcoming.

Austria-Hungary found it hard enough managing its long front with Russia, so to begin with it was content to resist Italian assaults. Between 1915-17 the Italians launched eleven full-scale offensives in the region, none of which managed to seize more than a few kilometres of ground. After the last, made in the late summer of 1917, the Italian commander General Luigi Cadorna decided to build up his defences to face an expected attack by German as well as Austro-Hungarian forces.

The Central Powers' attack of 24 October-12 November 1917, known as the Battle of Caporetto, was a total disaster for the Italian Army. German forces advanced 23 km on the first day, and the Italian

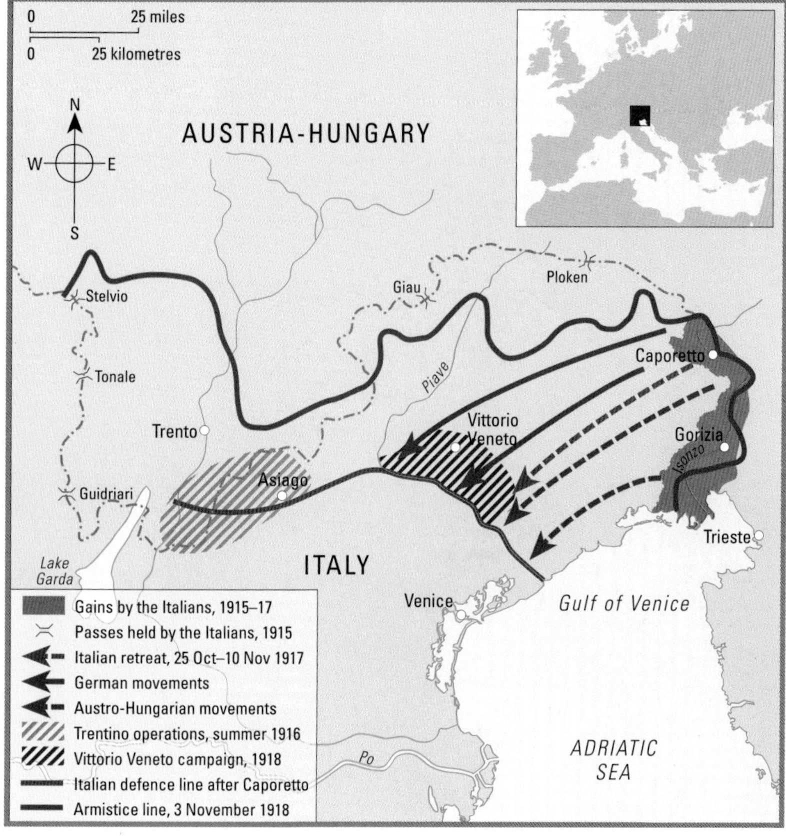

Hail the victor! The British General Allenby rides into Jerusalem after driving the Turks from the city, December 1917.

front until Austria-Hungary signed an armistice on 3 November 1918, bringing hostilities between that country and the Allies to a close (see also page 50).

MIDDLE EAST The war extended into the Middle East when the fleet of the Turkish Ottoman Empire bombarded Russian Black Sea ports without warning on 29 October 1914. Declarations of war soon followed. In alliance with the Central Powers, who provided officers and munitions for the depleted Turkish Army, Turkey fought on four fronts. On only one, Gallipoli (see pages 14-15), did it achieve success.

In the north the Turks launched an attack on southern Russia (the Caucasus) in an attempt to seize the region's oilfields. At the Battle of Sarikamish (29 December 1914 to 3 January 1915) they were roundly defeated, suffering 30,000 casualties and losing much of the remainder of their army as prisoners of war.

TROUBLE AHEAD

Eager for support, British politicians made conflicting offers to their allies. They promised the Arabs independence, and the Jews a national homeland in Palestine. Foreign Minister Lord Balfour's letter to Lord Rothschild, the leader of Britain's Jews, proved to be one of the seeds of the modern Arab-Israeli conflict.

'His Majesty's Government view with favour the establishment in Palestine of a national home for the Jewish people, and will use their best endeavours to facilitate the achievement of this object, it being clearly understood that nothing shall be done which may prejudice the civil and religious rights of existing non-Jewish communities in Palestine, or the rights and political status enjoyed by Jews in any other country.'

2 November 1917.

[Quoted in *Arab-Israeli Conflict and Conciliation: A Documentary History,* edited by Bernard Reich]

In the eastern corner of their empire, in the region of Mesopotamia (modern-day Iraq) at the head of the Persian Gulf, the Turks faced an invasion by an Anglo-Indian army sent from British-held India. At first the invaders made swift progress, taking the region's oilfields. The Turks regained the initiative in 1916 when they took 8,000 Anglo-Indian prisoners at Kut al Imara. By the time hostilities ended, however, the British had again moved forward, capturing Baghdad (March 1917) and advancing further up the Tigris and Euphrates rivers.

The Suez canal in Egypt, a key route between Britain and India, the jewel in its imperial crown, was an obvious target for the Turks. Knowing this, the British built up strong defences, resisted Turkish assaults in 1914-15, and pressed on into Sinai in 1916-17. They were assisted by a widespread revolt among the Arab peoples, eager to be rid of their Turkish overlords.

Held up for a while at Gaza, at the end of 1917 the Allies seized Jerusalem in Palestine. The large Anglo-Arab force, commanded by the able General Sir

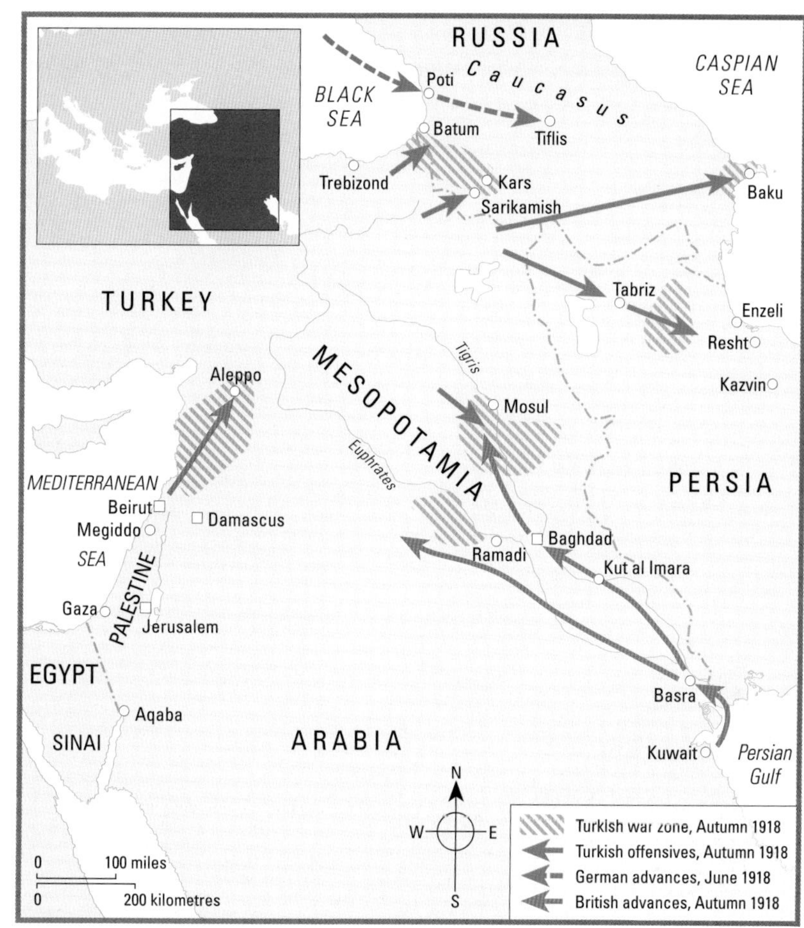

Fighting in the Near and Middle East, where the Turkish Ottoman Empire fought the Russians and the British, and also struggled to hold down a revolt of the Arabs.

Battling for the Empire – Indian gunners defend the British-held Suez Canal against a Turkish attack.

Edmund Allenby, then destroyed the remaining Turkish forces in the region at the Battle of Megiddo, and moved forward to occupy Damascus in Syria on 1 October 1918.

AFRICA The Middle East was not the limit of the fighting. The conflict became truly global as early as 1914, when Japan, an ally of Britain, seized German colonies in the Pacific Ocean and in mainland China. There was fighting in Africa, too. Here Allied forces from Britain, France and their colonies assaulted the four German colonies in Africa: Togoland (Togo), the Cameroons (Cameroon), German South-West Africa (Namibia), and German East Africa (Tanzania). The aim was to seize territory and shut down the powerful German radio stations that were monitoring Allied shipping.

Togo fell swiftly to French and British troops in 1914. The same two countries gradually occupied the Cameroons, 1914-17. On the outbreak of war South Africa offered to undertake the capture of German South-West Africa. This was achieved by four columns, totalling 50,000 men, over a period of ten months.

In contrast, German resistance in East Africa continued throughout the war. This was largely due to the leadership of General Paul von Lettow-Vorbeck, a brilliant guerrilla commander. In 1914 he had a mere 2,750 men (of whom 2,500 were Africans) to hold a territory the size of France. Later this rose to 14,000 (11,000 Africans). Against him were ranged almost the entire South African Army and many European and local troops and assistants, totalling at their peak 350,000 men. This was precisely what Lettow-Vorbeck wanted – to divert as many

LOSSES IN AFRICA

Cameroons	
Britain	2,300 killed, wounded and captured
France	3,900 killed, wounded and captured
Germany	6,575 killed, wounded and captured
South-West Africa	
South Africa	1,760 killed, wounded and captured
Germany	4,580 killed, wounded and captured
East Africa	
Allies	51,600 killed or died of disease
	8,800 wounded
	1,900 captured
Germany*	5,000 killed and wounded
	6,000 captured

* Figures no more than estimates

War East African style! A British soldier seated on an ox during the long campaign to hunt down the brilliant German General Paul von Lettow-Vorbeck.

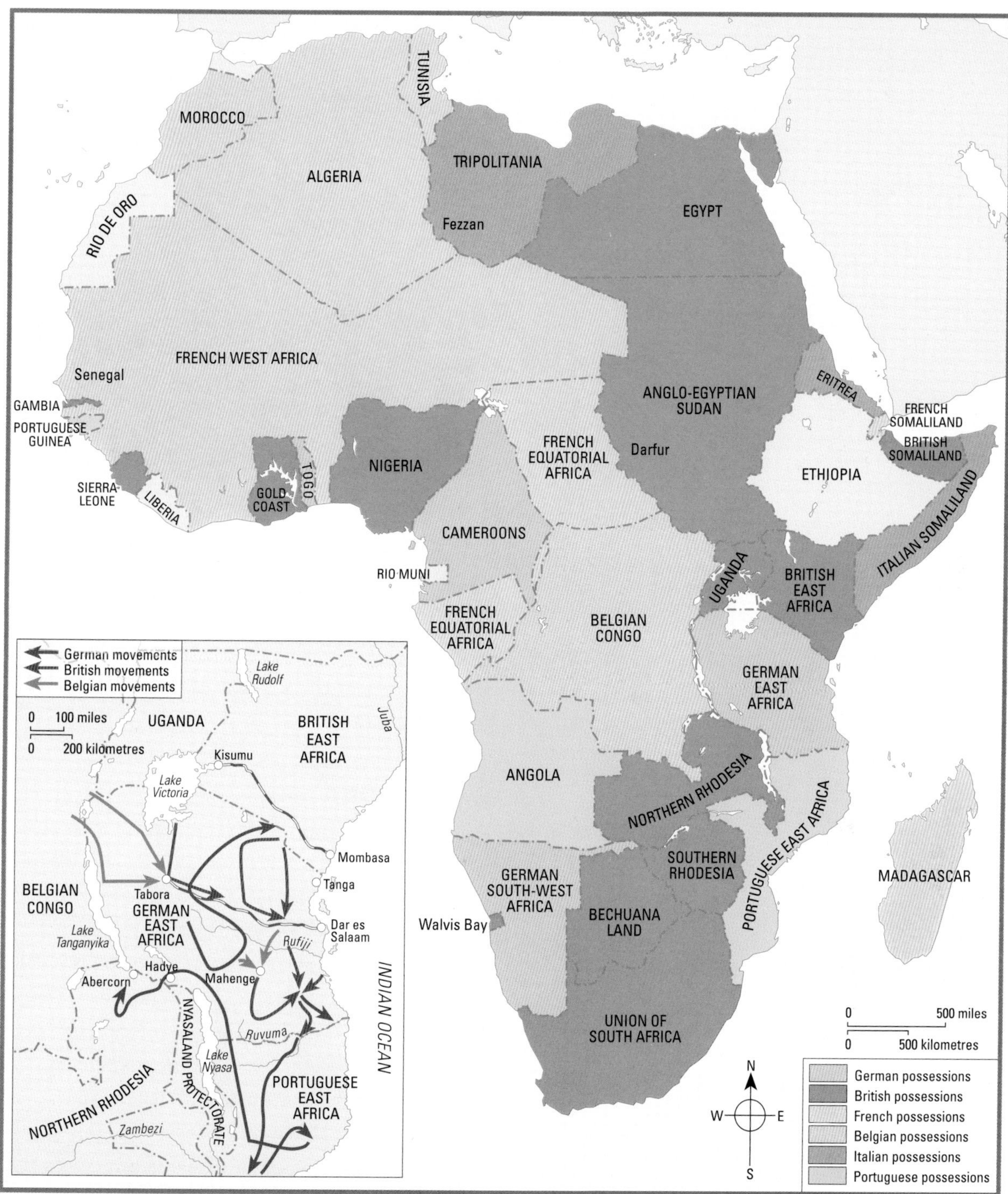

Africa during World War I. The continent was drawn into the fighting because during the previous century it had been carved up by the imperial European powers. The inset shows the campaign in German East Africa.

Allied soldiers as possible from the battles in Europe (see statistics panel).

After a successful but costly attack early in 1915, Lettow-Vorbeck decided to stick to hit-and-run guerrilla tactics. He used local conditions and speed of movement to great effect. A successful tactic was to build up a strong defensive position, hold it for a while in order to inflict maximum casualties on the attackers, then slip away before the final assault. Only when he heard of the Armistice (see page 49) did the

COMPARATIVE NAVAL STRENGTHS, 1914

Allies	Britain	France	Russia	Italy	Japan	USA*	Totals
New-style battleships (dreadnoughts)	22	8	0	3	2	10	45
Old-style battleships	40	14	10	7	10	23	104
Cruisers	130	28	12	21	34	34	259
Destroyers	221	81	25	33	50	50	460
Torpedo boats	109	187	72	80	0	23	471
Submarines	73	70	22	23	12	18	218

* By the time the United States entered the war in 1917, all fleets were larger.

Central Powers	Germany	A-Hungary	Turkey	Totals
New-style battleships (dreadnoughts)	15	6	0	21
Old-style battleships	22	6	2	30
Cruisers	57	7	2	66
Destroyers	90	18	8	116
Torpedo boats	115	65	9	189
Submarines	31	5	0	36

The foredeck and main guns of the German battleship *Braunschweig* pictured at the start of the war in 1914.

undefeated Lettow-Vorbeck finally surrender on 23 November 1918.

WAR AT SEA Naval warfare had been revolutionized during the fifty years before 1914. Huge steel battleships, driven by steam turbines and armed with massive shell-firing guns in turrets, had made all other large warships obsolete. However, these remarkable vessels were vulnerable to mines (as we saw in the Dardanelles, pages 16-17) and torpedoes. The latter could now be delivered with great accuracy by submarines. Finally, the use of spotter aircraft and radio enabled commanders to know their enemy's precise location and movements.

Essentially, the naval war developed into one of blockades – the Allies seeking to cut Germany and Austria-Hungary's overseas supplies of food and raw materials, while the Germans tried to do the same to Britain and France. In the end, it was the Allied blockade that succeeded, bringing Germany to its knees in the autumn of 1918.

Germany' chief hope of breaking the Allied blockade lay in sailing its High Seas Fleet past the British Grand Fleet into the open oceans. After some

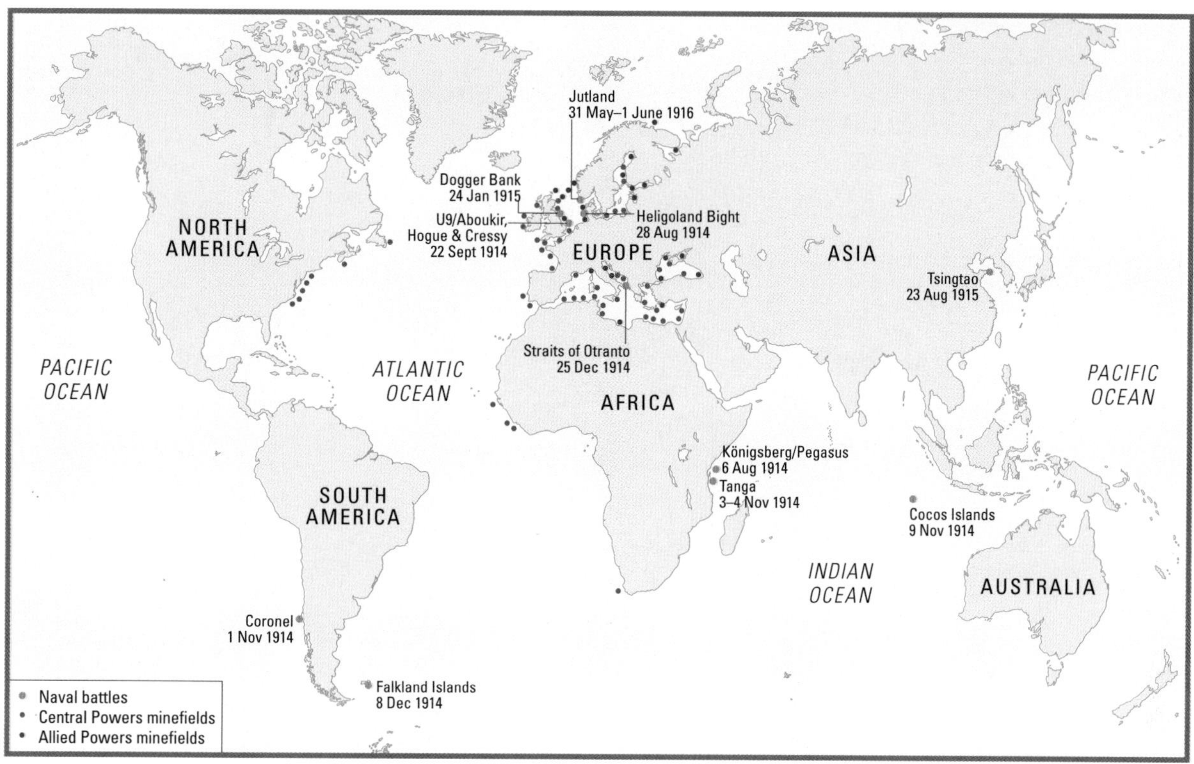

The naval war. Apart from the major engagement between the British and German fleets at Jutland, 1916, conflicts were small scale, involving no more than a handful of vessels on either side.

early naval encounters at Coronel, the Falkland Islands (both 1914), and in the North Sea (1914-15), in May 1916 Admiral Reinhard Scheer decided to attempt this full-scale break-out. The German High Seas Fleet met the British Grand Fleet at the Battle of Jutland, the only major naval engagement of World War I. The British suffered greater losses but drove the Germans back to port, where they remained for the rest of the war. After Jutland the Germans relied on submarines, known as U-boats, to sever Allied supply lines. For an effective blockade, U-boats needed to attack all shipping – neutral or Allied – destined for Britain and France. This tactic infuriated the US and helped bring it into the war on the Allied side in April 1917. By 1918 the use of convoys and improved anti-submarine weapons (for example, the depth charge, 1916) had finally broken the U-boat's dangerous stranglehold.

WAR IN THE AIR The wartime development of aircraft technology was dramatic, driven mainly by the need to conduct aerial observation of enemy artillery, and to prevent the enemy from doing this themselves. In 1914 warplanes were slow, fairly unreliable, incapable of carrying heavy loads, and used

A Fairey F.17 seaplane, 1917. The emergence of such aircraft enabled fleet commanders to keep track of the enemy with much greater accuracy.

A German naval Zeppelin airship taking off from its base. Although capable of flying huge distances, Zeppelins were slow and vulnerable to enemy fire.

Early bombing – a British aircrew prepares to drop its aircraft's lightweight bombs by hand. Inevitably, the accuracy of the bombing was rather hit and miss.

largely for reconnaissance work. By 1918 they had become much more powerful and reliable, and were designed with specific tasks in mind. They were also organized as a separate branch of the armed forces, such as the Royal Air Force (1918), and were seen as a vital element in any military or naval operation. Air superiority, which the Allies had achieved by 1918, was key to success on the ground. The major Allied offensive of September 1918, for example, took place under cover provided by over 450 aircraft.

One of the first specialist aircraft to appear was the fast and manoeuvrable fighter, designed to shoot down enemy aircraft in 'dogfights'. A popular example was the British Sopwith Camel. The French Breugets were among the earliest bombers. The Italian SIA 7 was intended specifically for reconnaissance, the German Halberstadt CL11 for attacking troops on the ground, and the Short 184 for carrying torpedoes.

A German speciality was the gas-filled airship, known as the Zeppelin, used for long-range bombing. Able to rise to 6,700 m (higher than any aircraft before 1916) and carry 1,000 kg of bombs, they killed 550 civilians in raids on Britain. Once aircraft could reach the same height as a Zeppelin, however, the cumbersome 'sausages' (as they were known) became easy targets.

In 1918 two aircraft appeared that signposted the future. One was Germany's sleek and rapid Junkers D1,

The war in the air. This map shows how the use of aircraft as bombers meant that no one on the ground, neither soldier nor civilian, was safe from attack.

the world's first all-metal warplane. The other was Britain's Handley Page V/1500, a four-engined bomber capable of carrying 2,000 kg of bombs and staying airborne for fourteen hours. With aircraft such these, no one, neither soldier nor civilian, was safe. Thus World War I saw the emergence of the 'home front' – war waged against the civil population of a country – alongside the traditional battle front.

THE GROWTH OF AIR FORCES

Number of aircraft	France	Britain*	Italy	USA	Russia	Germany	A-Hungary
1914	150	50	120		145	250	80
1915	390	153	240		553	800	112
1916	1,420	410	430		724	1,550	144
1917	2,335	997	660	55	579	2,270	296
1918	3,222	1,799	720	740	260	2,710	616

* Western Front only

Note that not all of these aircraft were of military use. Of the 55 aircraft available to the United States in April 1917, for instance, 51 were obsolete.

CHAPTER 3: DEADLOCK, 1915-17

During 1915, particularly after the failure of the Allied Gallipoli expedition (see pages 16-17), it was generally recognized that the fighting on the Western Front was now critical and that the war would be won or lost there. Here, at the direct interface between Germany, France and Britain where the front lines confronted one another, the fighting became more and more costly.

At the start of the year commanders on both sides, especially the Allied one, hoped that a quick breakthrough would end the stalemate on the Western Front and bring the war to a rapid conclusion. However, as they found time and time again, while seizing three lines of enemy trenches was difficult enough, co-ordinating an advance after that proved just about impossible. In March 1915, for instance, the British broke through at Neuve-Chapelle in northern France but, after advancing 2 km, the attack ground to a halt. The story was similar the next month, when the Germans, using poison gas for the first time, broke through at Ypres in Belgium. When the battle stopped

One of the millions of victims – a French soldier killed in the 1915 campaign in the Champagne region.

Walking through hell: German reinforcements move up to the front line during the Champagne offensive of 1915.

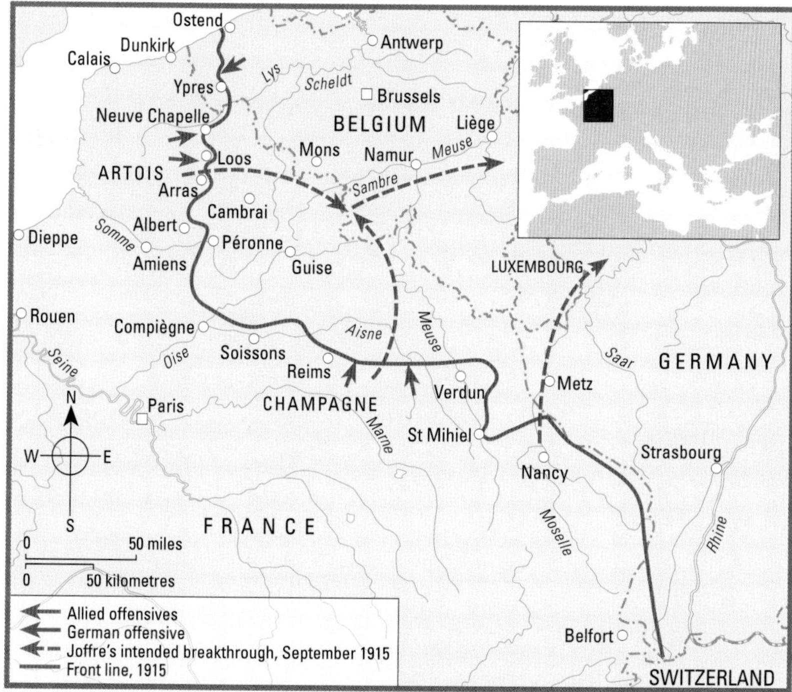

The breakthrough that never came: the Allied plan for the spring offensive of 1915 that it was hoped would win the war at a stroke.

on 25 May they had done no more than flatten out the Ypres salient. German and Allied casualties totalled 103,000.

In May the British and French went on the offensive again, this time in the Artois region. As before, in some places the attackers managed to break through the enemy lines but they made little progress after that. September saw the launching of a massive offensive that was to smash through the German lines in Champagne and allow the French to sweep north into Belgium. After a 2,500-gun bombardment, 500,000 French troops attacked along a 24-km front. The same pattern emerged: some initial gains, then stagnation, and horrific casualty rates. By 28 September the French had lost 145,000 men.

As the Champagne offensive was grinding to a halt, an Anglo-French offensive started further north in the Artois region of France. The French lost 48,000 men for negligible gains, while the incompetent leadership of Sir John French, commander of the British army in France, bungled the promising British breakthrough around the village of Loos (25 September to 4 November).

THE BATTLE AT VERDUN Unknown to each other, both sides planned even bigger offensives for 1916. They hoped for breakthrough, of course, but there was a growing recognition that this might not be possible. In its place came the concept of attrition (see pages 10-11) – a war that would be won only when the enemy were either too depleted or too exhausted to fight on.

While the Allies planned a summer offensive near the River Somme,

IN THE FRONT LINES

Although it is a novel, *All Quiet on the Western Front* by the German soldier Erich Remarque is widely recognized as one of the finest accounts of life on the Western Front. This is his description of bombardment:

'An uncertain red glow spreads along the skyline from one end to the other. It is in perpetual movement, punctuated with bursts of flame from the nozzles of the batteries ... French rockets go up, which unfold a silk parachute to the air and drift slowly down. They light up everything as bright as day ... "Bombardment," says Kat. The thunder of the guns swells to a single heavy roar and then breaks up again into separate explosions. The dry bursts of the machine guns rattle. Above us, the air teems with invisible swift movement, with howls, pipings, and hisses ...'

[From *All Quiet On the Western Front*, Erich Remarque]

at the junction of the French and British armies, the German commander General Erich von Falkenhayn hoped to break France's spirit by continual assault on a narrow front that was difficult to defend. His target was Verdun, a city that for historical reasons he knew the French would defend

Counterattack! French troops defending their line in the Verdun region go over the top in a counteroffensive against the encircling Germans in 1916.

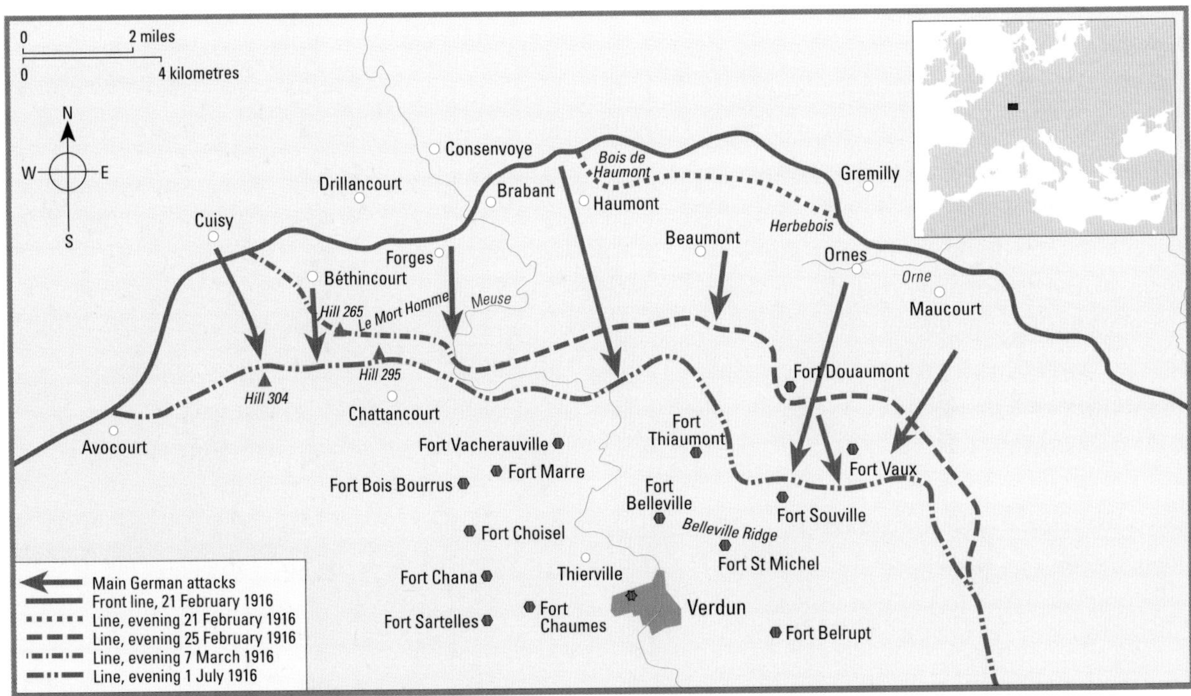

The Verdun campaign of 1916. Although the Germans made some significant gains, they failed to break through or crush the spirit of the French Army.

VERDUN IN PERSPECTIVE

French and German losses in just one battle in 1916 exceeded those of all major combatant nations during fighting in the previous year.

Losses in 1915

	French	British	German	Total
Neuve-Chapelle -		13,000	7,000	20,000
Ypres	10,000	59,000	35,000	104,000
Artois	102,000	28,000	49,000	179,000
Champagne	143,000		85,000	228,000
Artois-Loos	48,000	61,000	56,000	165,000
	303,000	**161,000**	**232,000**	**696,000**

Losses in the Battle of Verdun, 1916

French	378,000
German	337,000
	715,000

to the last man. Here, he undertook to 'bleed' the French army to death. The German attack on Verdun began on 21 February 1916. One million men launched themselves on a network of forts that had been left undermanned and under-gunned. Within seventy-two hours, after the Germans had pushed forward more than five kilometres, it looked as if they might well take Verdun and its surrounding defences. As Falkenhayn had predicted, however, the French were determined to hold out. They poured men and munitions into the line, and resolved that the German forces should not be allowed to pass.

Happy to be out of it – German prisoners taken at Verdun are paraded through the streets under mounted guard on their way to captivity.

What became known as the 'hell of Verdun' raged on for the rest of the year. The French lost perhaps 378,000 men, but their army was not quite bled white. The Germans, on the other hand, lost almost as many themselves. Since they were also fighting on the Eastern Front, where they had to support Austria-Hungary, as well as supplying troops to other theatres

OVER THE TOP

British private soldier Roy Bealing remembers going over the top of his trench during an attack on the Somme:

'When the whistle went, I threw my rifle on top of the trench and clambered out of it, grabbed the rifle and started going forward. There were shell-holes everywhere. I hadn't gone far before I fell in one. … I must have fallen half a dozen times before I got to the first line, and there were lads falling all over the place. You didn't know whether they were just tripping up, like me, or whether they were going down with bullets in them, because it wasn't just the shells exploding round about, it was the machine guns hammering out like hell from the third German line because it was on slightly higher ground.'

[Quoted in *Somme*, Lyn Macdonald]

of war, such as Africa and the Middle East, the losses were harder for them to bear. Moreover, in July their assault on Verdun had drawn a massive British counter-assault on the Somme.

THE SOMME As we saw on page 29, in late 1915 the Allies had planned a joint attack on the Somme for the late summer of 1916. This plan was altered when the Verdun offensive pinned down the bulk of the French Army. In response, the main weight of the Allied attack, which at the request of the French was brought forward by several weeks, would now be borne by the British.

Fix bayonets! British troops prepare to go over the top on the first day of the Battle of the Somme, 1 July 1916. For many this was their first experience of battle; for most of the 60,000 killed and wounded it was also their last.

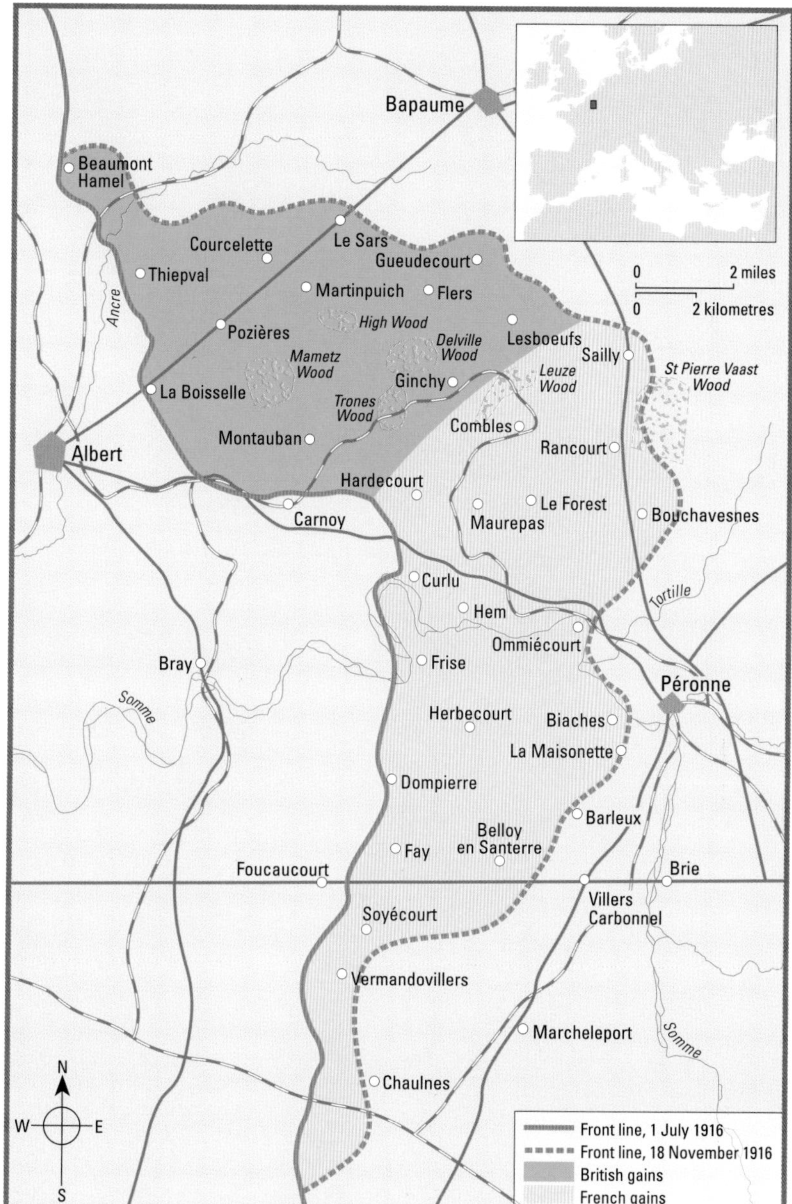

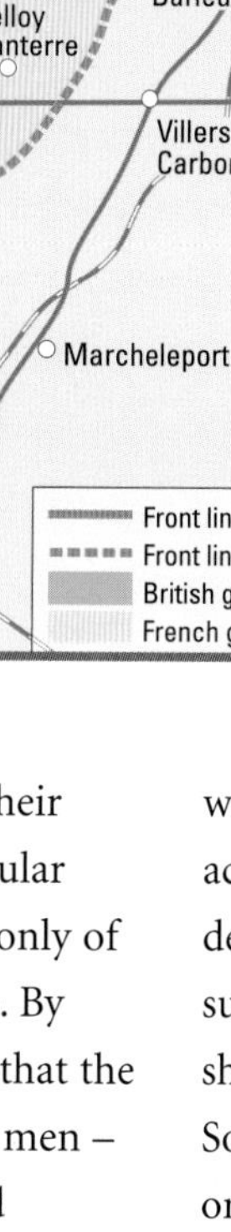

Field Marshal Sir Douglas Haig (1861-1928), friend of King George V and commander-in-chief of the British forces in France 1915-18.

The Battle of the Somme, 1916. The choice of battleground was made not for strategic reasons but because it was where the French and British lines met.

Before 1914 the British had concentrated their military spending on the Royal Navy. Their regular army ready for European action had consisted only of the 150,000-strong British Expeditionary Force. By 1916 this had been all but wiped out, meaning that the hugely expanded army – now over two million men – was largely made up of eager but inexperienced volunteers. They were joined by the small but highly efficient contingents provided by Canada, South Africa, New Zealand and Australia. It was with these forces, domestic and colonial, that the new British commander, Sir Douglas Haig, hoped to break through the well-arranged German defences on the Somme.

Despite careful preparation and a gigantic eight-day preliminary bombardment of the enemy lines, the first day of the offensive – 1 July 1916 – was the worst ever experienced by a British army. Walking across no-man's-land into intact barbed wire and the deadly fire of machine guns, most of which had survived the artillery bombardment in deep concrete shelters, the attackers were mown down like grass. Some 58,000 men were lost for negligible gains. Only on the southern flank and in the neighbouring French sector was much headway made.

The battle raged on until November, by when the Allies had advanced no more than 16 km at a cost of 613,000 men killed and wounded (419,000 British). Even so, the German Army had suffered equally heavily and, combined with the effects of Verdun and the Brusilov Offensive (see below), by the end of the year was no longer in a fit state to launch an offensive.

RUSSIA'S LAST CAST

As the British were attempting to take pressure off the French by attacking on the Somme, so the Russians had gathered themselves for one final offensive on the Eastern Front. It was also planned to help their Italian allies by drawing Austro-Hungarian divisions away from the Alps. The general responsible for planning and launching the attack was Alexei Brusilov, probably the most able Russian commander of the war.

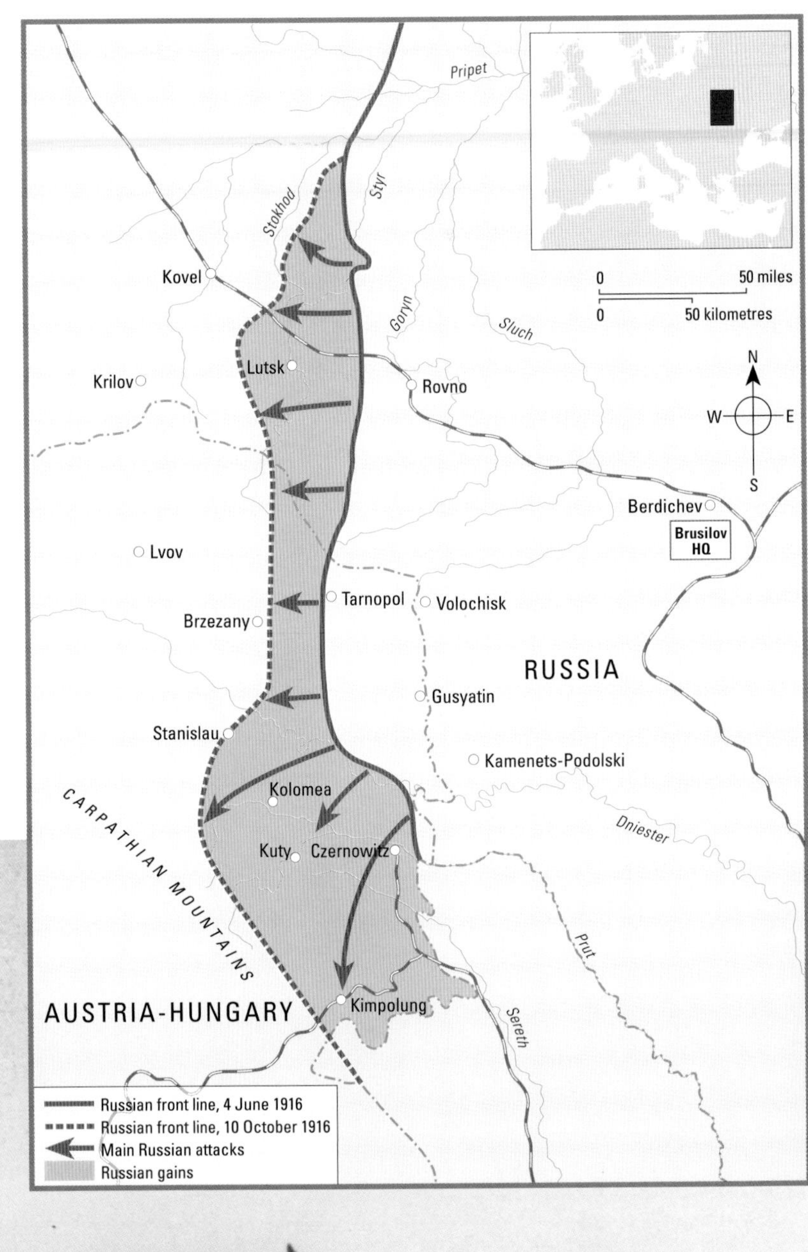

Russia's Brusilov Offensive in 1916 forced the Germans to switch troops from the Western Front but brought the Russian army to its knees.

Enough is enough – tired of official incompetence and senseless slaughter, Russian soldiers surrender in 1917.

The last tsar of Russia, Nicholas II, sits alone after being forced to abdicate his throne in 1917.

What is now called the 'Brusilov Offensive' began on 4 June 1916. The Russians moved forward in the valleys of the Rivers Prut and Dniester, and further north towards the town of Lutsk. Brusilov placed himself between the two points of attack. His enemy, mostly Austro-Hungarian, were taken somewhat by surprise and fell back in disarray. Within a fortnight the Russians had advanced 80 km and taken almost 100,000 prisoners.

Realizing the danger, both German and Austro-Hungarian reinforcements were rushed to the front, and the Russian advance halted for a while. Twice that summer it was resumed. It met with considerable success against the Austro-Hungarians in the south, where the Russians reached the Carpathian Mountains, but less against the Germans in the north. Finally, in mid-September, Brusilov called off the entire operation. His army had fought itself to a standstill, having lost perhaps 1.4 million men as casualties and prisoners. The figure for his opponents was only slightly less.

Brusilov had been let down by his support services, not by his troops. Sometimes attacks were halted because the ammunition ran out. On other occasions reinforcements came too late because of the inefficiency of the Russian railway system. Supplies of food and new weapons were at best unreliable, sometimes non-existent. To cap it all, the country's military leadership, from Supreme Commander Tsar

THE MAKE-UP OF THE RUSSIAN ARMY

The Brusilov Offensive was launched with the Russian 3rd, 7th, 8th, 9th and 11th armies. Their strengths and varied make-up were as follows:

3rd Army
6 infantry divisions
6 cavalry divisions (5 of Cossacks)
1 reserve division

7th Army
9 infantry divisions
2 divisions of Finnish troops
2 cavalry divisions (1 of Cossacks)
3 reserve divisions, including 1 of Turks

8th Army
10 infantry divisions
2 divisions of Turkish troops
3 cavalry divisions (1 of Cossacks)
1 division of Finnish troops
2 reserve divisions

9th Army
9 infantry divisions
5 cavalry divisions (4 of Cossacks)
1 reserve division

11th Army
8 infantry divisions
4 cavalry divisions
1 division of Finnish troops
3 reserve divisions

Total initial strength of all armies: 57 infantry divisions (570,000 men approx.) and 20 cavalry divisions (200,000 men approx.) (Note: These figures do not include reinforcements who were brought up later.)

Nicholas II downwards, failed to co-operate or co-ordinate their activities. In short, after the Brusilov Offensive the entire Russian military machine was beginning to fall apart.

FRANCE GRINDS TO A HALT The most interesting development on the Western Front during 1917 was the German withdrawal to the Hindenburg Line (*Siegfried Stellung*) that ran south in France from Arras to near Soissons. This was a pre-prepared defensive arrangement of barbed wire entanglements, trenches, machine-gun posts and concrete bunkers that proved exceptionally difficult to penetrate by conventional means. Having given up any idea of launching an offensive in this part of the front, the Germans retired to it between 23 February and 5 April. In contrast, the Allies still hoped for the elusive breakthrough. The new French commander, General Robert Nivelle, well-known for his offensive strategies, believed he could break through the German lines in the region of the River Aisne. His subordinates, including Marshal Philippe Pétain, strongly advised him to reconsider. He refused.

Germany's Hindenburg Line, 1916, peppered with many shell craters.

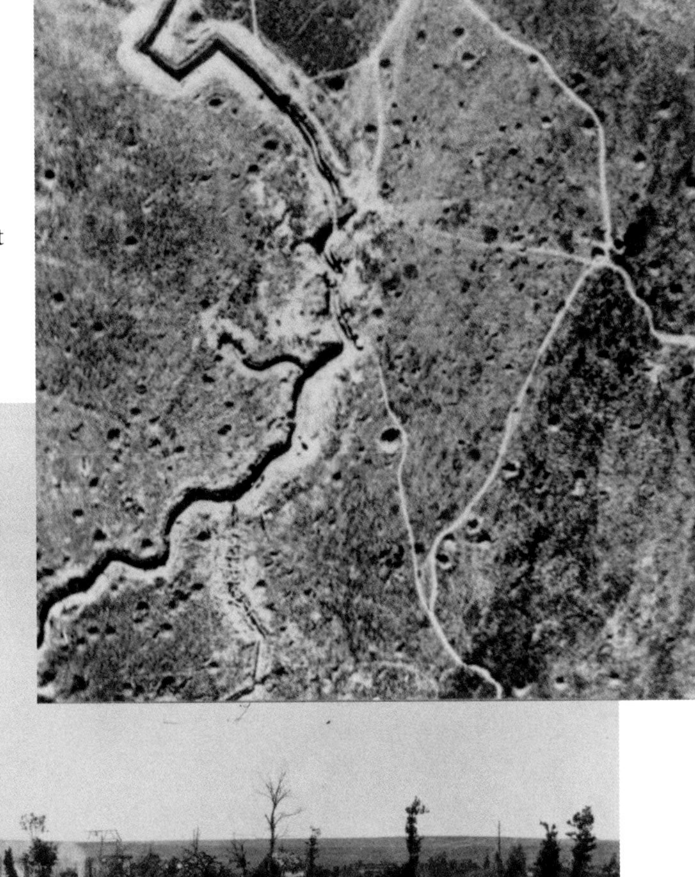

An army falls apart – French deserters run towards the German lines, Spring 1917. News of events such as this mutiny by serving soldiers was not revealed to the general public.

By way of a diversion, in April the British under Haig attacked near Arras. After the usual bombardment, they made the biggest single-day advance of the war by British forces thus far – five and

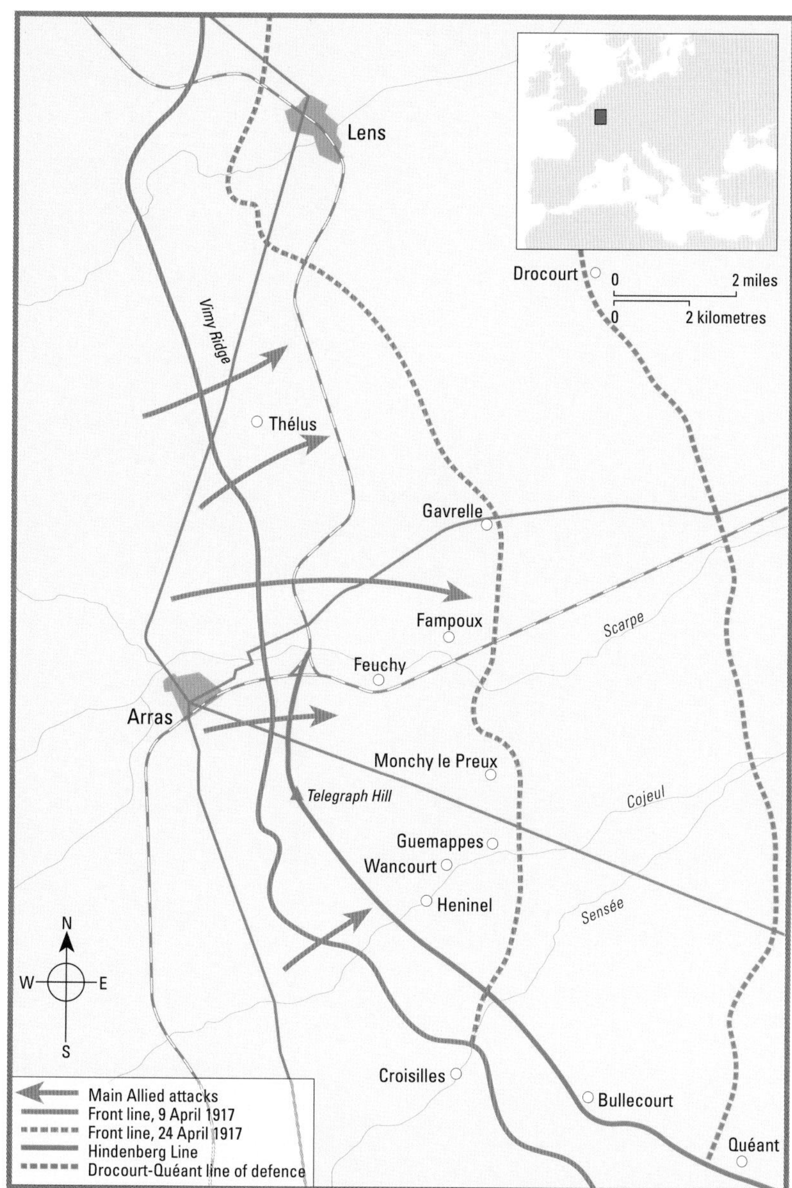

The Battle of Arras, 1917. The seizure of Vimy Ridge by Canadian forces was one of the most gallant actions of the entire war.

GASSED

Harold Clegg recalls the effects of a German attack in July 1917 using a new form of gas – mustard gas – that burned away at the organs with which it came into contact.

'Our eyes now began to feel irritated. The tea was instrumental in making all and sundry commence to vomit. After being violently sick I received instructions to prepare myself to join a [guard] party … I began to scrape the … mud from my [equipment] …

'While doing so I heard several men complain about pain in their eyes, some even complaining of going blind.'

July 1917.

[Quoted in *The Imperial War Museum Book of the First World War*, edited by Malcolm Brown]

a half kilometres! Although the fighting continued to mid-May, further gains were very limited before the offensive was called off.

Meanwhile, the French had launched their offensive between Soissons and Reims (positions shown on map on page 29). Yet again, despite the use of tanks (first seen on the Somme), a decisive breakthrough that could release the cavalry over open ground was not achieved. After some early gains, including the capture of 20,000 German soldiers and a section of the Hindenburg Line, the advance floundered to a halt. The casualty rate had been as high as ever – in less than a month Nivelle lost 187,000 of the 1.2 million men under his command. The Germans figure was about 163,000.

The morale of many French troops now broke: a large number simply refused to take part in any further attacks. For a while (April to June 1917) the mutiny threatened to force France out of the war, making a German victory highly probable. Nivelle was promptly sacked and, with great skill, Pétain began the difficult task of pulling his shattered forces together again.

The war of attrition goes on ... and on. Heavily laden British troops moving up to the front line, October 1917.

THE ONLY ONE

Private R. Le Brun, a Canadian machine gunner, remembers fighting in the deep November mud around the village of Passchendaele.

'There was nothing between us and the Germans across the swamp. Three times during the night they shelled us heavily, and we had to keep on spraying bullets into the darkness to keep them from advancing. The night was alive with bullets. By morning, of our team of six, only my buddy Tombes and I were left. Then came the burst that got Tombes. It got him right in the head. ... It was a terrible feeling being the only one left.'

[Quoted in *They Called it Passchendaele*, Lyn Macdonald]

THE GERMAN LINE HOLDS 1917 was the crucial year of the war. Russia was in turmoil (see pages 40-1). Austria-Hungary crushed the Italians (see pages 18-19), who were more and more disillusioned with the war. The bulk of the French were in no fit state to do more than hold their line. The German command sensed that victory in the east was near, and a sustained attack on the demoralized French line might, at last, achieve breakthrough. Field Marshal Douglas Haig, the British commander-in-chief, still believed he could pierce the German line with a massive frontal assault.

On top of this came the dramatic development of 6 April 1917 – the United States of America joined the war on the Allied side. Two factors in particular persuaded Congress to take this momentous step. First, early in the year Germany reintroduced unrestricted submarine warfare, which threatened the shipping of the neutral United States. Second, the British intercepted a German telegram offering part of the southern US to Mexico if it would side with the Central Powers. When

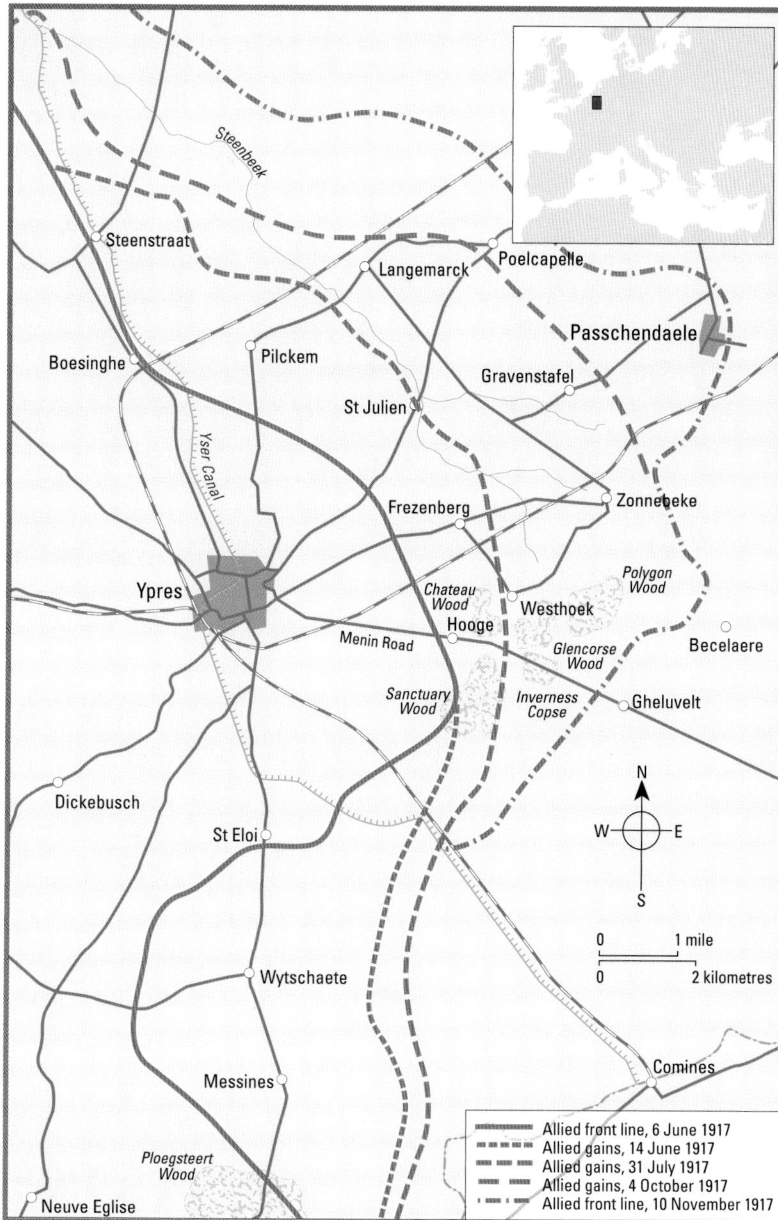

The Third Battle of Ypres, 1917. British soldiers commonly named it after the small, smashed village they eventually managed to capture – Passchendaele.

US President Woodrow Wilson led his country into the war in April 1917.

this information reached the US government, war with Germany was inevitable.

Although US naval forces made an immediate difference in the Atlantic, on land the US intervention had no immediate impact. Its army was tiny and inefficient, and it was almost eighteen months before a large modern force could be raised, equipped, trained, and brought to bear on the enemy. In the meantime, the British made one last effort to win the war on their own.

Haig had spent eighteen months planning his Ypres offensive of July 1917. The Germans had spent almost as long preparing to meet it. The result was a titanic struggle akin to that which had taken place at Verdun the previous year. No breakthrough came, although the British did manage to take the high ground that overlooked Ypres, including the village of Passchendaele. However, the 310,000 casualties that it cost hurt the British much as the French had been hurt the previous spring.

THE COLLAPSE OF RUSSIA By unwisely assuming overall command on the Eastern Front in September 1915, Tsar Nicholas II of Russia sealed his own fate. Henceforward all failures

– and there were many – would ultimately be laid his feet. By the end of 1916 the country's railway system had collapsed, and millions of city-dwellers faced starvation. The armed forces were in chaos. The tsar and his government were thoroughly discredited.

Food riots in March 1917 brought matters to a head. The tsar abdicated and was replaced by a Western-style republican government that promised to hold free elections. It did not, however, take Russia out of the war. In July 1917, at the request of his hard-pressed allies in the west, Prime Minister Alexander Kerensky called for yet another offensive. It lasted nineteen days. Faced with fierce counterattacks by the Central Powers, along broad stretches of the front the Russian soldiers simply threw down their arms and fled. A further German offensive in September pushed closer to Petrograd (St Petersburg).

Kerensky's unelected Provisional Government staggered on until November, when it was overthrown in a communist coup in Petrograd.

The collapse of Russia on the Eastern Front, 1917-18. The German advance brought them vast industrial and agricultural wealth.

THE TREATY OF BREST-LITOVSK

Russia surrendered the following to the Central Powers:

Territory	Ukraine, Finland, Baltic Provinces (Estonia, Lithuania, Latvia), the Caucasus, Belorussia (White Russia), Poland.
Population	33 per cent
Railway network	53 per cent
Arable land	25 per cent
Coal fields	70 per cent
Total industry	40 per cent

Trotsky and Stalin, key members of the communist Bolshevik party, address crowds of supporters in Moscow, October 1917.

Trotsky hoped the communist revolution would spread from Russia to Germany and other countries, so he put off reaching an agreement with the Germans. They responded by advancing rapidly towards Petrograd. This forced Trotsky's hand. On 3 March 1918 Russia formally made peace, surrendering to the Germans vast territories, including the Ukraine, Finland and Poland, and much of its industrial capacity. Germany was now free to concentrate all its resources on the Western Front in an attempt to win the war before American power could make itself felt.

The communists rapidly extended their rule to Moscow and other cities, attracting support with their slogan, 'Peace! Bread! Land!' To provide the promised peace, the country's new leaders, Vladimir Lenin and Foreign Minister Leon Trotsky, signed an armistice with the Germans on 3 December 1917. Negotiations soon followed.

Alexander Kerensky, Russia's liberal premier who alienated his countrymen by continuing the war with Germany.

CHAPTER 4: VICTORY AND DEFEAT

General Erich von Ludendorff, the German commander who masterminded his country's final offensive in the spring of 1918. He is pictured here after the war in around 1924.

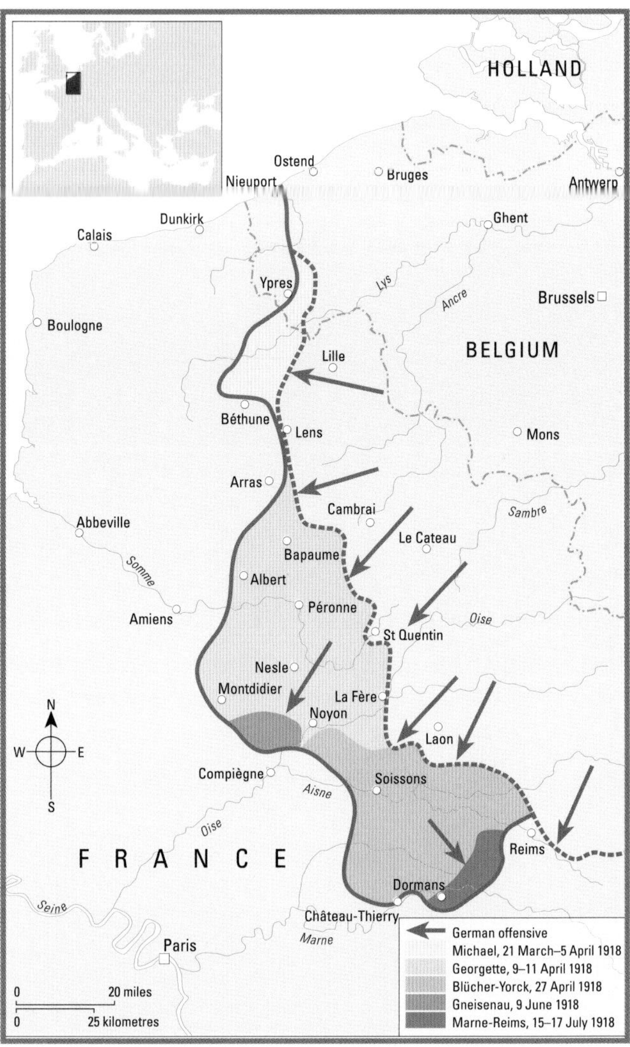

Germany's spring offensives, 1918. A series of dramatic offensives in early 1918 managed to recapture in weeks territory that had been lost over the previous years.

The final German offensives that would win or lose the war were masterminded by General Erich von Ludendorff. For this first attack, and the one about which he was most optimistic, he chose his ground carefully. His target was the lightly-held British front on the old Somme battlefield, perhaps the weakest point in the enemy line. By mid-March he had transferred thousands of troops from the Eastern Front, assembling three German armies (sixty-three divisions or some 630,000 men) to face twenty-six divisions of the British Third and Fifth Armies.

The German assault began in thick fog on 21 March. First came a 6,000-gun bombardment, many firing mustard gas shells, then an advance all along the line. Overwhelmed, the British fell back. For a time it looked as if the two armies might be split apart, leaving the Germans free to sweep into the heart of France. To cope with the crisis, the French soldier Marshal Ferdinand Foch was appointed supreme commander of all Allied forces on the Western Front. Co-ordinating the resistance, he rushed French reinforcements to the front. Finally, having fallen back eighty kilometres in places (the greatest movement of the trench war), the Allied line held fast. On 5 April Ludendorff called the operation off.

THE COST OF THE LUDENDORFF OFFENSIVES, MARCH-JUNE 1918

Casualties (killed and wounded)

	German	French	British	Total
Somme/Lys	348,000	112,000	343,000	803,000
Aisne	130,000	96,000	28,000	254,000
Oise	45,000	35,000		80,000
Total killed in four offensives	124,000	220,000	61,000	405,000

One of many thousands of British soldiers killed during the German offensives of 1918. This man died covering the retreat of his comrades.

Having failed to break through on the Somme, Ludendorff turned his attention to the line further north. Here he had located another weakly-defended British sector, this time south of Ypres on the River Lys. Launching another gigantic attack, the Germans came extremely close to breaking through. Indeed, if Ludendorff had been less cautious in following up early progress, the Lys Offensive (9-29 April) might have led to a German victory.

Abandoning the Lys offensive, Ludendorff turned his attention to the French on the River Aisne (27 May-2 June) and in the Oise Valley (Noyon-Montdidier, 9 to 13 June). As before, neither offensive made the anticipated progress. Despite suffering enormous casualties, the Allied line remained intact. Ludendorff's time was running out.

ALLIED ADVANCE

Ludendorff next planned a huge summer offensive for the Flanders

The Frenchman Marshal Ferdinand Foch was given overall command of the Allies on the Western Front in 1918.

Blinded by an attack with poison gas during the Second Battle of the Marne (July 1918), two French soldiers are led to a field hospital by their comrades.

region, where the line was held by the British and Belgians. To tie down the French and prevent them from sending reinforcements north, on 15 July 1918 he launched an attack along the River Marne. Here, on the site of the first major battle of the war, three German armies advanced on either side of the famous Champagne city of Reims (see page 29).

A familiar pattern emerged. The Germans made some progress but were halted when the Allies managed to bring up reinforcements. On this occasion, however, the fighting did not stop there. To the Germans' surprise, on 18 July Foch ordered a counterattack. Backed by 350 tanks, the French drove the Germans back over the ground they had captured and beyond. Ludendorff urgently brought up reinforcements of his own and had stopped the Allied advance by early August. Nevertheless, an attack had become a serious defeat, and plans for a further German offensive were cancelled.

It was now the turn of the Allies to go on the offensive. Putting into effect Haig's plan, Foch's first aim was to eliminate the salients in the Allied line that

CROSSING THE OLD BATTLEFIELD

In the autumn of 1918 Major P.H. Pilditch cycled across the Somme battlefield searching for the grave of a friend killed in 1914:

'On the way back we spent some time in the old No Man's Land of four years' duration … It was a morbid but intensely interesting occupation tracing the various battles among the hundreds of skulls, bones and remains scattered thickly about. The progress of our successive attacks could be clearly seen from the types of equipment on the skeletons, soft caps denoting 1914 and early 1915, then respirators, then steel helmets marking attacks in 1916. … There were many of these poor remains all along the German wire.'

[Quoted in *The Imperial War Museum Book of the First World War*, edited by Malcolm Brown]

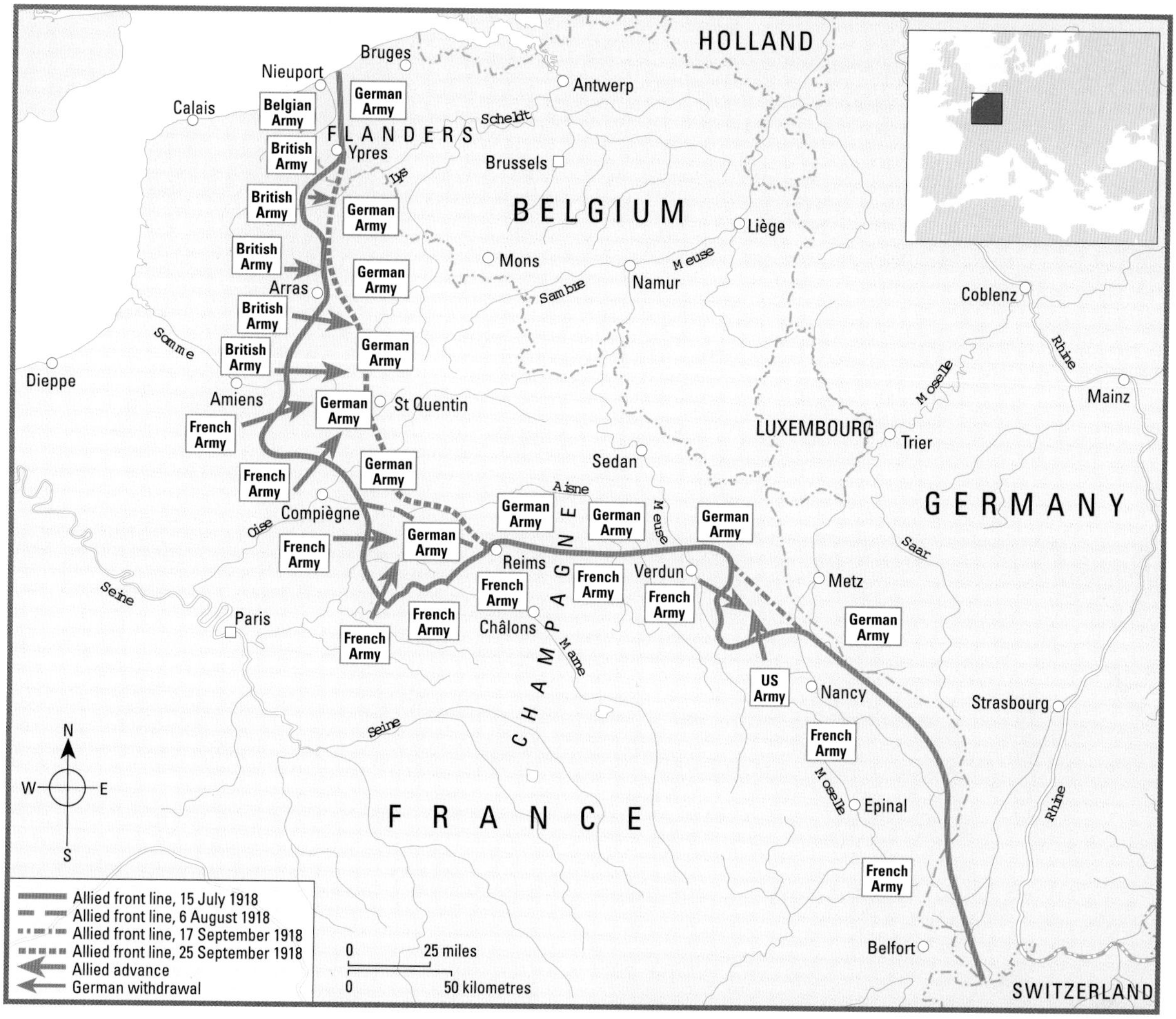

'Salient busting': the Allied campaigns that pushed back the Germans and reduced the salients (bulges) in the front line on the Western Front, July-September 1918.

had been created by the Ludendorff offensives. By 5 August the Aisne salient had been recovered. Then, on 8 August, a large-scale attack was launched to the east of Amiens to recapture the lost Somme battlefield. On a remarkable first day – the 'black day of the German army' – British, French and Canadian troops advanced 16 km. Six thousand prisoners were taken and 100 guns captured. In some places the Germans, for the first time in the war, fled in disarray before the overwhelming onslaught of tanks, aircraft, artillery and infantry.

Some of the many thousands of German soldiers captured by the Allies during August 1918.

The Allies pressed forward until early September, by which time the Germans had abandoned all the ground gained earlier and withdrawn to the Hindenburg Line. Thousands more prisoners had been taken and many more guns seized. As summer turned to autumn, the outlook for the German Army was looking bleaker by the day.

IMPACT OF AMERICA Having entered the war in April 1917, General John Pershing, the commander of the US forces in France (the American Expeditionary Force, AEF) set about building an American Army. By the end of the war there were some two million US troops in France, where they were trained and equipped.

First to see action was the US First Division, which on 28 May 1918

AMERICAN CASUALTIES ON THE WESTERN FRONT

Cantigny	1,600
Belleau Wood	8,800
Marne	40,000
St Mihiel	7,000
Meuse-Argonne	117,000

Total in all theatres 281,000

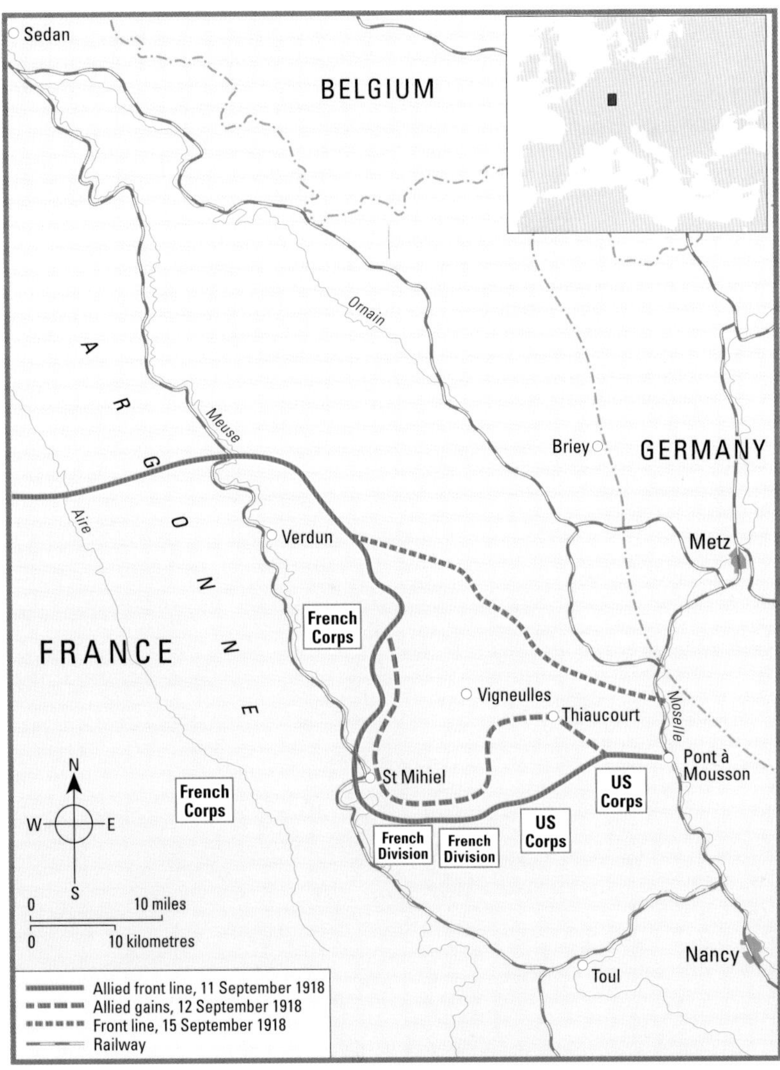

Enter the USA – the St Mihiel battlefield where American forces made their first major contribution to the Allied victory.

US troops of the 18th Infantry Machine Gun Battalion advance towards the front line near St Mihiel, 13 September 1918.

The transatlantic alliance – US General John Pershing (right), the commander of the American Expeditionary Force, with the Allied commander-in-chief Marshal Foch of France.

successfully captured the village of Cantigny during the German Aisne River offensive. A week later the Second Division withstood a German attack and captured Belleau Wood near Château-Thierry. By the time of the Marne attack and counterattack (see pages 44-45), the US had over a quarter of a million men in the field. The American First Army, however, was not ready for independent action until the end of the month.

The full impact of the US intervention was finally felt in September, during the Allied salient-busting operations. The US First Army was given the task of reducing the St Mihiel salient south-east of Verdun. Attacking on 12 September with 600 aircraft in support, the Americans caught the Germans in the process of withdrawing and cleared most of the salient in a single day. The message to the Allies and foe alike was obvious – the Americans were now a force to be reckoned with.

From St Mihiel Pershing moved north of Verdun to work with the French in the massive Meuse-Argonne offensive that lasted to the end of the war (see pages 48-49). After good progress when the attack began, the Americans became bogged down in October and suffered heavy casualties. With more and more troops ready for battle each day, the AEF was now divided into two armies. By the time of the Armistice on 11 November, they were once again making rapid progress, and even beat the French in the 'race to Sedan'. As many had predicted in 1917, once the US had managed to mobilize its manpower all hopes of a German victory had disappeared.

CHAPTER 5:

THE END OF THE WAR

Armistice at last. Joyful Parisians celebrate the end of hostilities on the streets of the French capital on 11 November 1918.

THE FINISH OF THE WAR

British soldier James Bird wrote home describing the day the war stopped.

'The Saturday afternoon was very exciting, the band of the Canadians played in the square, and during the afternoon two of our planes did all sorts of tricks and stunts, flying very low, this simply made the inhabitants go mad with delight …

[Monday.] This was the day of the finish of the war. I walked into Mons in the afternoon, we were mobbed and nearly lost all our buttons. It was indeed a great day for Britain, as well as France. It made one feel glad to be alive, and to think that after four years hard fighting we had at last reached the place where our troops were in 1914 …'

[Quoted in *The Imperial War Museum Book of the First World War*, edited by Malcolm Brown]

Having removed the dangerous salients from their line, on 26 September the Allies began their final onslaught. Foch's master plan involved three offensives: a small Belgian attack forward of Ypres, larger forces of French and Americans in a pincer movement on the River Meuse swinging north of Verdun, and the British and French, in the largest attack, driving towards Cambrai and St Quentin.

The southern Franco-American offensive was the first to begin. With overwhelming force, including air

The German High Seas Fleet surrenders to the British at Scapa Flow, Orkney, Scotland on 21 November 1918.

superiority and large contingents of tanks, the Allies drove the Germans steadily back, capturing Sedan on 6 November. The armistice was signed as they prepared to move south over the German border to Metz. At the other end of the line the Belgians (with some support from other nations) advanced equally rapidly to Ostend and on towards Antwerp. To their south the British, supported by French and American divisions, took Cambrai, forced the Germans to abandon the Hindenburg Line on 4 October, and were pushing on towards Charleroi when hostilities ceased.

Hindenburg and Ludendorff had been virtually running Germany since early 1918. When their armies were pushed back so dramatically in the autumn, Ludendorff put out feelers for a ceasefire. The terms were unacceptable – Germany was asked to surrender all land occupied since 1870, dismantle its armed forces, surrender much of its martial equipment, and set aside its treaties with Russia and Romania. As the war dragged on, Germany's allies began to desert. Bulgaria signed an armistice on 29 September. At home mounting starvation and discontent led to strikes and riots. When the navy mutinied, revolution became a real possibility. Ludendorff accepted the inevitable. On 26 October he resigned and fled to Sweden. Hindenburg remained at his post. Turkey signed an armistice on 30 October, and Austria-Hungary on 3 November. Finally, at 11 am on 11 November, Germany too accepted the Allies' terms and the guns finally fell silent.

The final Allied advance, autumn 1918. After the war the Germans took pride in the fact that no foreign soldier had set foot on their soil.

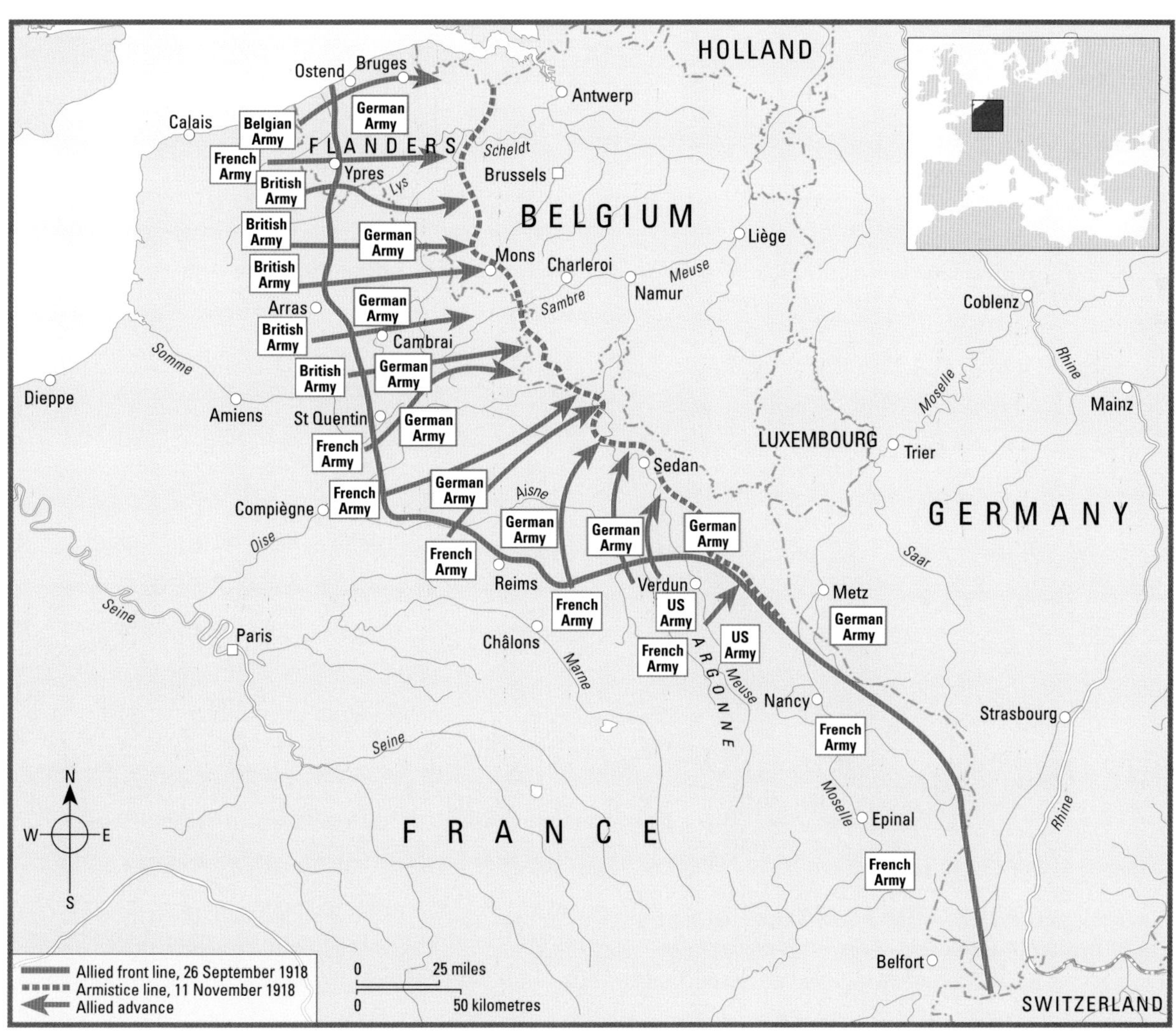

MAKING PEACE A series of long-negotiated treaties turned the various short-term armistices into what was hoped would be lasting peace. The Treaty of St Germain organized the break-up of the Austro-Hungarian Empire, creating the separate states of Austria, Hungary, and Czechoslovakia (the Balkan peoples had already established themselves as Yugoslavia). As with the other treaties, it also limited the military capacity of the former Central Powers. At Neuilly (27 November 1919) Bulgaria's frontiers were established. The terms of Hungary's surrender were sealed at Trianon on 4 June 1920. The Treaty of Trianon (10 August 1920) broke up the Ottoman Empire, leaving the much smaller state of Turkey.

WHAT MIGHT HAVE BEEN ...

In introducing his Fourteen Points to the US Congress on 8 January 1918, President Wilson spoke of the world he hoped would emerge after the war:

'What we demand in this war ... is that the world be made fit and safe to live in; and particularly that it be made safe for every peace-loving nation which, like our own, wishes to live its own life, determine its own institutions, be assured of justice and fair dealings by the other peoples of the world, as against force and selfish aggression. All the peoples of the world are in effect partners in this interest ...'

[Quoted in *Great Issues in American History: From Reconstruction to the Present Day, 1864-1969*, edited by Richard Hofstadter]

By far the most important treaty was that dealing with Germany. Signed at Versailles, France, on 28 June 1919, it was an extremely harsh document that the Germans had no option but to accept. This was not what some peacemakers had envisaged in 1918. For instance, in his Fourteen Points (January 1918), US President Woodrow Wilson had set out a reasonable and moderate set of peace aims. At Versailles these were overridden by the demands of French Prime Minister Georges Clemenceau and, to a lesser extent, British Prime Minister David Lloyd George. Both were driven by public opinion at home demanding vengeance after four-and-a-half years of slaughter.

(Left to right) Prime Minister David Lloyd George of Great Britain, President Georges Clemenceau of France and US President Woodrow Wilson on their way to the Versailles peace talks, June 1919.

By the Treaty of Versailles Germany lost all its colonies and some territory in Europe. It was obliged to accept total responsibility for the war, disband most of its armed forces, and pay the Allies an impossible 200 million gold marks (£6,600 million) in reparations [compensation] for war damage. Britain and France also took possession of the former Central Powers' colonies. As the popular cry ran, Germany had been squeezed 'until the pips squeaked'.

As many recognized at the time, the Versailles settlement was no recipe for long-term peace. It left the once proud Germany humiliated, weakened and impoverished – ideal soil in which extremists might plant their wicked seeds of revenge. In this way the ground was prepared for World War II, which broke out just over twenty years after the end of this 'War to End All Wars',

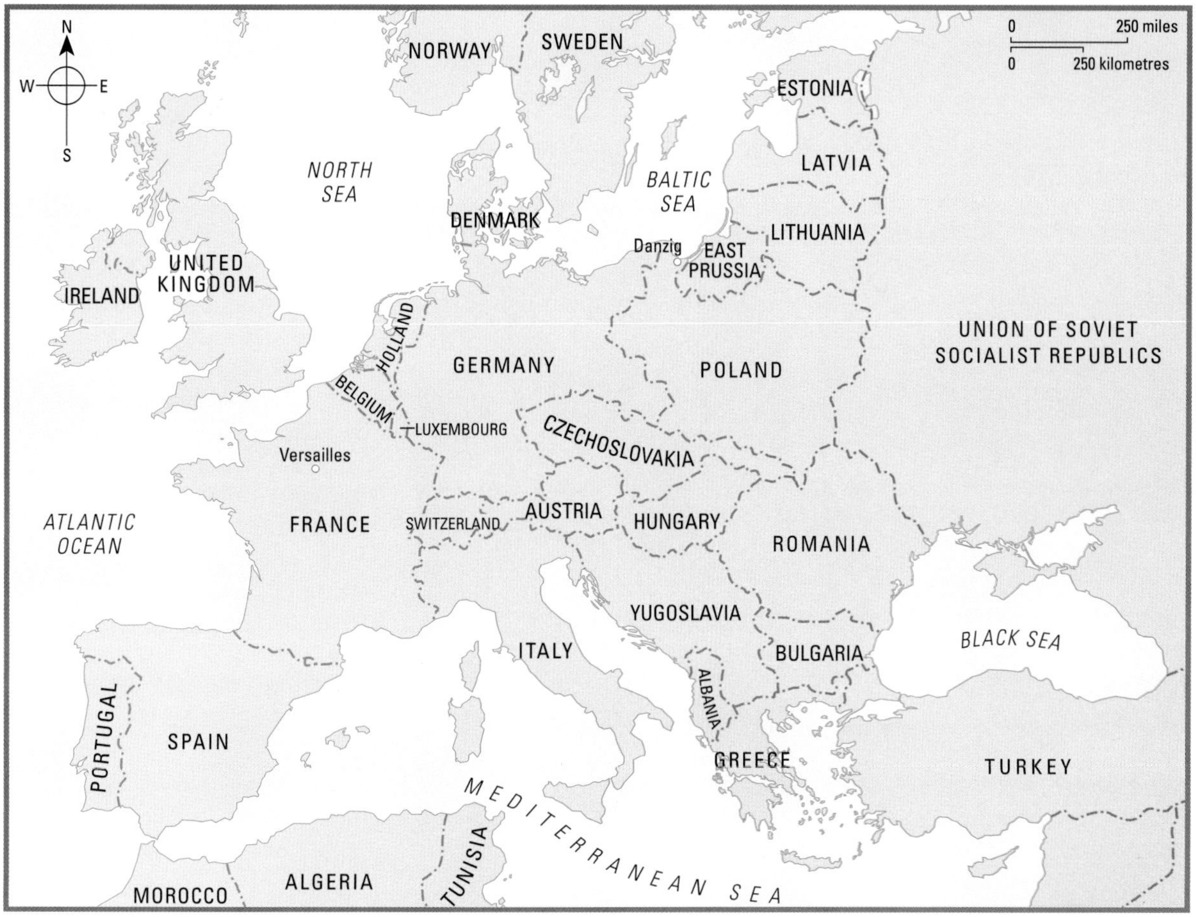

N
W
E
S
0 250 miles
0 250 kilometres
NORWAY
SWEDEN
ESTONIA
LATVIA
NORTH SEA
BALTIC SEA
DENMARK
Danzig
EAST PRUSSIA
LITHUANIA
UNITED KINGDOM
IRELAND
HOLLAND
GERMANY
POLAND
UNION OF SOVIET SOCIALIST REPUBLICS
BELGIUM
LUXEMBOURG
CZECHOSLOVAKIA
Versailles
ATLANTIC OCEAN
FRANCE
SWITZERLAND
AUSTRIA
HUNGARY
ROMANIA
YUGOSLAVIA
ITALY
BULGARIA
BLACK SEA
ALBANIA
PORTUGAL
SPAIN
GREECE
TURKEY
MEDITERRANEAN SEA
TUNISIA
MOROCCO
ALGERIA

Post-war Europe, showing the much reduced Austria, Germany, Russia and Turkey, and the host of new states, such as Czechoslovakia and Yugoslavia. Danzig was termed a Free City under League of Nations protection.

Into the Roaring Twenties – thousands of delighted citizens turn out for a victory parade on New York's Fifth Avenue, 1919.

PROFILES OF MILITARY AND POLITICAL LEADERS

THE GENERALS

GENERAL ALEXEI BRUSILOV (1853-1926)
Unlike most World War I commanders, the energetic Alexei Brusilov showed both flair and imagination. Having made a name for himself in Russia's war with Turkey, 1877-8, he was key to his country's advance into Galicia in 1914. His finest moment was the spectacular but ultimately unsuccessful offensive of 1916 which greatly helped his hard-pressed French allies on the Western Front. After the war he served with the communist Red Army.

MARSHAL FERDINAND FOCH (1851-1929)
Having lived under occupation in Lorraine, a province that France had surrendered to Germany after military defeat in 1871, Ferdinand Foch needed no motivation in his quest to drive out the invader. An author of two books on strategy, he distinguished himself at the Battle of the Marne (1914). For much of the war he had called for all Allied forces to be under a single command. When the idea finally became reality in 1918, the task fell to him. Showing great skill, insight

and tact, he masterminded the successful Allied offensives of the final months of the war.

FIELD MARSHAL DOUGLAS HAIG (1861-1928)
Douglas Haig is one of the most controversial military commanders in British history. His supporters refer to his steely character, his determination to succeed against all odds (a man of powerful faith, he seemed to have believed that God was guiding him), and his skilful offensives of 1918. Opponents accuse him of being rigid in strategy and insensitive to human losses, particularly during the British Somme, Arras, and Passchendaele offensives, 1916-17.

FIELD MARSHAL PAUL VON HINDENBURG (1847-1934)
The aristocratic Paul von Hindenburg went to army cadet school at the age of eleven and served with distinction until retirement in 1911. On the outbreak of war, he was recalled and sent, with the more able second-in-command Ludendorff, to meet the Russian attack on Prussia. His reputation was made by victories at Tannenberg and Masurian Lakes. Placed in overall command of Central Powers strategy in 1916, he concentrated, unsuccessfully, on defence. He was elected president of Germany in 1925, and appointed Adolf Hitler chancellor in 1933.

GENERAL FRANZ CONRAD VON HOTZENDORF (1852-1925)
Having been put in charge of the Austrian Army in 1906, Franz Conrad was eager for war with Serbia and Italy. When war came, however, he found it more testing than he expected, especially against Serbia. In the end, his most likely chance of success – against Italy in 1916 – was cut short by the Brusilov Offensive. He was put under Hindenburg's overall command in September 1916 and dismissed the following year.

MUSTAFA KEMAL (1881-1938)
Known in later life as the 'father of the Turks' (Ataturk), Kemal played a vital role in resisting the Allied landings in Gallipoli in 1916. He then fought with distinction in the Caucasus, remaining the only undefeated Turkish commander. First president of the new Turkish Republic (1924), he crowned his military career with an even more successful one as a modernizing politician.

GENERAL ERICH VON LUDENDORFF (1865-1937)

Extremely able but occasionally flawed in judgement, von Ludendorff helped re-arrange the Schlieffen Plan (see pages 6-7) and guided Hindenburg in the key victories against Russia in 1914. Thereafter, Hindenburg and Ludendorff worked closely together, becoming virtual masters of Germany by 1918. Having almost won the war with his Spring 1918 offensives, Ludendorff's fortunes declined rapidly. He fled to Sweden in disguise in 1918, re-emerging after the war as a Nazi politician.

GENERAL HELMUTH VON MOLTKE (1848-1916)
Nephew of one of Prussia's greatest generals, Helmuth von Moltke (sometimes known as 'von Moltke the Younger') is principally remembered for working with Ludendorff to alter the Schlieffen Plan to attack western France. By weakening the German right flank, which was to sweep down to the west of Paris, he was partly responsible for the failure of the German strategy at the Battle of the Marne, 1914. He was dismissed two days later.

GENERAL JOHN JOSEPH PERSHING (1860-1948)
John Pershing's military experience, gained in small-scale encounters such as chasing bandits in Mexico, hardly fitted him for what he was to meet on the Western Front. However, appointed to command the AEF in 1917, he built it up into an effective fighting force. Although Clemenceau called for his dismissal after a poor showing in the Argonne Forest, the idea was rejected and Pershing's armies played an important part in the Allies' last offensives of 1918.

MARSHAL PHILIPPE PÉTAIN (1856-1951)
Philippe Pétain, a keen student of war, realized earlier than most experts that offensives against artillery, barbed wire, and machine guns would be virtually impossible. His advice was ignored. Not until the Germans threatened breakthrough at Verdun in February 1917 did he get the chance to put his ideas to the test. The dramatic defence of Verdun made him a national hero, and he was made commander-in-chief of the French Army in May 1917. Tragically, the 'hero of Verdun' ended his life in prison for treacherous co-operation with the Nazis in World War II.

THE POLITICIANS

GEORGES CLEMENCEAU (1841-1929)
French Prime Minister
A tough and energetic man of peasant stock, the seventy-six-year-old Clemenceau (nicknamed 'the Tiger') took over the leadership of France in the grim days of 1917. His speeches and single-minded dedication lifted the nation, and guided it to victory the following year. A keen admirer of the USA, he was always eager for it to join the Allies.

DAVID LLOYD GEORGE (1863-1945)
British Prime Minister
Lloyd George had doubts about going to war, but changed his mind after the German invasion of Belgium. Thereafter, as Minister of Munitions and Prime Minister (December 1916 onwards), he used his considerable skills to gear the nation's industrial might to winning the war. As a radical, he did not always see eye to eye with high-born military commanders.

NICHOLAS II (1868-1918)
Tsar of Russia
Russia could hardly have had a less suitable leader during World War I. Nicholas, the hereditary tsar, was blessed with neither intelligence, nor steadfastness, nor insight. He chose poor ministers and generals, and allowed his court to become a nest of scandal. Having abdicated in 1917, he and his family were executed by the communists the following year.

WILHELM II (1859-1941)
Emperor of Germany
Rather out of his depth in the world of international politics into which he had been born, on several occasions Wilhelm II (emperor or kaiser from 1888 onwards) upset relations with Britain through his tactless statements and actions. Having offered to support Austria-Hungary against Serbia in 1914, thereby making war likely, his influence declined. He abdicated on 9 November 1918 and fled the country.

WOODROW WILSON (1856-1924)
In some ways the most attractive of the war leaders, the idealistic Wilson worked as an academic before being elected US president in 1912. He reluctantly took his country to war in 1917, then worked tirelessly for a better world once victory had been achieved. Sadly, having moderated his allies' calls for vengeance at Versailles, illness prevented him from taking his plans further.

STATISTICS CONCERNING COMBATANT NATIONS

All statistics taken from John Ellis and Michael Cox, eds., *The World War I Databook*, Aurum Press, 1993.

AGGREGATE MILITARY CASUALTIES AND CIVILIAN DEATHS OF THE BELLIGERENTS 1914-18

Country	**Population (millions)**	**Number Served in Forces (millions)**	**Force Casualties**				
			Killed and Missing	**Wounded**	**P.O.W.**	**Total Killed, Wounded & Missing**	**Total Civilian Deaths**
Australia	4.87	0.42	53,560	155,130	3,650	208,690	–
Austria-Hungary	49.90	7.80	539,630	1,943,240	2,118,190	2,482,870	?
Belgium	7.52	0.27	38,170	44,690	10,200	82,860	30,000
Bulgaria	5.50	1.20	77,450	152,400	10,620	229,850	275,000
Canada	7.40	0.62	58,990	149,710	2,820	208,700	–
France	39.60	8.66	1,385,300	4,329,200	446,300	5,714,500	40,000
Germany	67.00	13.40	2,037,000	5,687,000	993,800	7,724,000	700,000
Greece	4.80	0.28	5,000	20,000	c.1,000	25,000	130,000
India	316.00	1.68	62,060	66,690	11,070	128,750	–
Italy	35.00	5.90	462,400	955,000	530,000	1,417,400	?
Japan	67.20	0.80	?	?	–	1,970	–
New Zealand	1.05	0.13	16,710	41,320	500	58,030	–
Portugal	6.00	0.20	7,220	13,751	6,680	20,971	–
Romania	7.51	?	219,800	120,000	c.60,000	339,800	265,000 to 500,000
Russia	167.00	12.00	1,800,000	4,950,000	3,910,000	6,750,000	2,000,000
Serbia	5.00	0.71	127,500	133,150	70,000	260,650	600,000
South Africa	6.00	0.23	7,120	12,030	1,540	19,150	?
Turkey	21.30	0.99	236,000	770,000	145,000	1,006,000	2,000,000
United Kingdom	46.40	5.70	702,410	1,662,625	170,389	2,365,035	1,386
United States	92.00	4.35	51,822	230,074	4,434	281,896	–

AGGREGATE NAVAL LOSSES OF THE MAJOR POWERS, BY TYPE OF SHIP, AND AGGREGATE PERSONNEL LOSSES 1914-18

	UK	**France**	**Russia**	**Italy**	**Japan**	**USA**	**Total**	**Germany**	**Austria-Hungary**	**Turkey**	**Total**
Battleship	13	4	2	3	1	–	23	1	3	2	6
Battlecruiser	3	–	–	–	1	–	4	1	–	–	1
Cruiser	13	5	2	3	–	1	24	6	2	1	9
Light Cruiser	12	–	1	–	2	–	15	18	–	–	18
Monitor	5	–	–	2	–	–	7	–	3	–	3
Torpedo Gunboat	5	3	–	–	–	–	8	–	–	–	–
Sloop	18	–	3	–	–	–	21	–	–	9	9
Destroyer	67	15	6	8	1	2	99	}109	6	1	}126
Torpedo Boat	11	10	9	4	1	–	35		8	2	
Aircraft Carrier	3	–	–	–	–	–	3	–	– –	–	–
Minelayer	2	2	5	–	–	–	9	–	–	1	1
Minesweeper	–	–	30	2	–	1	33	29	–	2	31

	UK	France	Russia	Italy	Japan	USA	Total	Germany	A-Hungary	Turkey	Total
Submarine	54	14	12	11	–	–	91	178	7	–	185
Personnel:											
killed	34,650	15,650	?	3,170	?	8,106	?	78,300	980	?	?
wounded	4,510		?	5,250	?		?		310	?	?

ANNUAL GERMAN U-BOAT LOSSES BY LOCALITY 1914-18

	North Sea, Orkneys and Shetlands	English Channel and Belgian Coast	North Channel, Irish Sea, Bristol Channel	North Atlantic	South Atlantic (south of Scilly Isles)	Baltic	Mediter-ranean	Black Sea and Bosphorous	Unknown	Total
1914	3	2	–	–	–	–	–	–	–	5
1915	10	2	1	1	2	1	–	1	1	19
1916	8	2	1	4	–	1	1	3	2	22
1917	13	13	4	25	5	1	2	–	–	63
1918	13	9	9	14	10	–	12	–	2	69
Total	47	28	15	44	17	3	15	4	5	178

MONTHLY TOTALS OF BRITISH, ALLIED AND NEUTRAL MERCHANT SHIPPING LOST THROUGH ENEMY ACTION 1914-18 (GROSS TONNAGE)

	British	Allied and Neutral	Total
1914 August	44,692	18,075	62,767
1914 September	89,251	9,127	98,378
1914 October	78,088	9,829	87,917
1914 November	9,348	10,065	19,413
1914 December	26,815	17,382	44,197
TOTAL	**248,194**	**64,478**	**312,672**
1915 January	32,276	15,705	47,981
1915 February	36,372	23,549	59,921
1915 March	71,768	9,007	80,775
1915 April	24,383	31,342	55,725
1915 May	89,673	30,385	120,058
1915 June	91,315	40,113	131,428
1915 July	57,274	52,366	109,640
1915 August	151,354	34,512	185,866
1915 September	102,135	49,749	151,884
1915 October	54,156	34,378	88,534
1915 November	94,655	58,388	153,043
1915 December	74,490	48,651	123,141
TOTAL	**879,851**	**428,145**	**1,307,996**
1916 January	62,645	18,614	81,259
1916 February	75,928	41,619	117,547
1916 March	99,696	67,401	167,097
1916 April	141,409	50,258	191,667
1916 May	64,722	64,453	129,175
1916 June	36,976	71,879	108,855
1916 July	85,228	32,987	118,215
1916 August	45,026	117,718	162,744
1916 September	109,263	121,197	230,460
1916 October	177,386	176,274	353,660
1916 November	170,409	141,099	311,508
1916 December	182,728	172,411	355,139
TOTAL	**1,251,416**	**1,075,910**	**2,327,326**
1917 January	155,686	212,835	368,521
1917 February	316,964	223,042	540,006
1917 March	357,064	236,777	593,841
1917 April	551,202	329,825	881,027
1917 May	353,737	242,892	596,629
1917 June	419,267	268,240	687,507
1917 July	367,594	190,394	557,988
1917 August	330,052	181,678	511,730
1917 September	196,457	155,291	351,748
1917 October	276,359	182,199	458,558
1917 November	173,647	115,565	289,212
1917 December	253,500	145,611	399,111
TOTAL	**3,751,529**	**2,484,349**	**6,235,878**
1918 January	180,348	126,310	306,658
1918 February	227,582	91,375	318,957
1918 March	199,751	142,846	342,597
1918 April	215,784	62,935	278,719
1918 May	192,938	102,582	295,520
1918 June	163,629	91,958	255,587
1918 July	166,004	130,963	296,967
1918 August	147,257	136,558	283,815
1918 September	137,001	50,880	187,881
1918 October	59,229	59,330	118,559
1918 November	10,220	7,462	17,682
TOTAL	**1,699,743**	**1,003,199**	**2,666,942**
GRAND TOTAL	**7,830,733**	**5,056,081**	**12,886,814**

SIGNIFICANT DATES

1830
Greece gains independence from the Turkish Empire.

1839
Treaty of London guarantees the neutrality of Belgium.

1859-70
Kingdom of Italy created.

1861
Romania formed.

1870-1
Franco-Prussian War.

JANUARY 1871
German Empire proclaimed at Versailles.

MAY 1871
Treaty of Paris. France cedes Alsace and Lorraine to Germany.

1878
Congress of Berlin. Serbia, Bosnia-Herzegovina, Bulgaria, Montenegro and Romania granted independence from Turkey.

1879
Austro-German Dual Alliance.

1882
Italy agrees Triple Alliance with Germany and Austria-Hungary.

1888
Wilhelm II becomes Kaiser (emperor) of Germany.

1894
Franco-Russian Alliance signed.

1898
Germany begins its naval build-up.

1902
Anglo-Japanese Alliance.

1904
Anglo-French *entente cordiale.*

1905
Schlieffen Plan drawn up.

1907
British Expeditionary Force formed.
Anglo-Russian entente.

1908
Austria-Hungary annexes Bosnia and Herzegovina.

1912
Woodrow Wilson elected president of the USA.

1912-3
Two Balkan Wars.

JANUARY 1914
German officer commands Constantinople garrison.

28 JUNE 1914
Archduke Franz Ferdinand assassinated in Sarajevo, Bosnia.

28 JULY 1914
Austria-Hungary declares war on Serbia. Russia mobilizes.

1 AUGUST 1914
Germany declares war on Russia. France mobilizes.

3 AUGUST 1914
Germany declares war on France.

4 AUGUST 1914
German troops enter Belgium. (Midnight) Britain declares war on Germany.

12 AUGUST 1914
Britain and France declare war on Austria-Hungary.

23 AUGUST 1914
Japan joins Allies.

26-30 AUGUST 1914
Germans defeat Russians at Tannenberg (above).

5-9 SEPTEMBER 1914
German advance on the Western Front stopped at the Battle of the Marne.

9-14 SEPTEMBER 1914
Germans defeat Russians at Masurian Lakes.

14 SEPTEMBER 1914
Falkenhayn becomes German commander-in-chief.

29 OCTOBER 1914
Turkey joins Central Powers.

30 OCTOBER-4 NOVEMBER 1914
First Battle of Ypres.

NOVEMBER 1914
Russian advances in Galicia.

29 DECEMBER 1914-3 JANUARY 1915
Russians defeat Turks at Sarikamish.

FEBRUARY 1915
Germany begins unrestricted submarine warfare (to September). Allied naval forces fail to pass through the Dardanelles.

MARCH 1915
Allied offensive at Neuve-Chapelle.

25 APRIL 1915
Allies land at Gallipoli.

APRIL-MAY 1915
2nd Battle of Ypres – first use of poison gas.

MAY 1915
Italy joins Allies.
Allied offensive in Artois.
Germans making gains on Eastern Front.

AUGUST 1915
Germans capture Warsaw (Poland).
Nicholas II takes command of Russian armies.

SEPTEMBER 1915
French offensive in Champagne.
Allied Artois-Loos offensive (to November).
Bulgaria joins Central Powers.
Serbia overwhelmed.

OCTOBER 1915
Allies land at Salonika in Greece.

DECEMBER 1915
Joffre becomes French commander-in-chief. Haig becomes British commander in chief.

21 FEBRUARY 1916
German attack on Verdun begins (to December). Pétain ordered to defend Verdun.

31 MAY-1 JUNE 1916
Battle of Jutland (foot of page).

4 JUNE 1916
Brusilov offensive begins (to September).

1 JULY 1916
British Somme offensive begins (to November) (right).

AUGUST 1916
Romania joins Allies.
Hindenburg replaces Falkenhayn as German commander-in-chief.

DECEMBER 1916
Lloyd George becomes British prime minister.
Nivelle becomes French commander-in-chief.

JANUARY 1917
Zimmerman telegram urging Mexico to attack United States in alliance with Germany intercepted.

FEBRUARY 1917
Germans begin to fall back to Hindenburg Line. Germany reintroduces unrestricted submarine warfare.

MARCH 1917
Nicholas II abdicates after revolution in Russia.
British take Baghdad in Mesopotamia.

6 APRIL 1917
USA declares war on Germany.

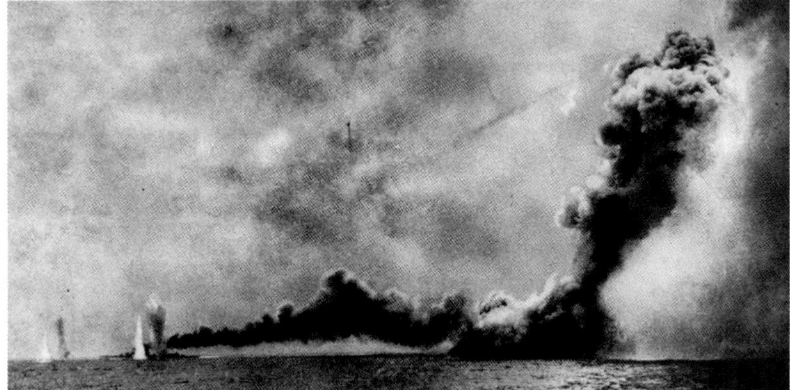

9 APRIL-16 MAY 1917
British offensive at Arras.

16 APRIL-9 MAY 1917
Nivelle's disastrous offensive on River Aisne.

MAY 1917
Allies introduce convoys to protect merchant shipping.
Pétain becomes French commander-in-chief.

JUNE 1917
First US troops land in France.

JULY 1917
Kerensky offensive on Eastern Front.

31 JULY 1917
Third Battle of Ypres (Passchendaele) begins (to November).

SEPTEMBER 1917
Germans advance on Petrograd.

24 OCTOBER-12 NOVEMBER 1917
Italians defeated at Caporetto.

NOVEMBER 1917
Communist revolution in Russia.
Clemenceau becomes prime minister of France.

DECEMBER 1917
British take Jerusalem.

1918
Civil War in Russia (to 1921).

JANUARY 1918
Wilson puts forward his Fourteen Points.

3 MARCH 1918
Germany and Russia sign Treaty of Brest-Litovsk (right).

21 MARCH-5 APRIL 1918
Ludendorff offensive on Somme. Foch appointed to be supreme commander of Allied forces.

9-29 APRIL 1918
Ludendorff's Lys offensive.

27 MAY-2 JUNE 1918
Ludendorff's offensive on River Aisne.

28 MAY 1918
US forces see action at Cantigny.

9-13 JUNE 1918
Ludendorff's offensive on the River Oise.

15 JULY-5 AUGUST 1918
Ludendorff's last offensive, on the Marne, met by Foch's counterattack.

8 AUGUST-4 SEPTEMBER 1918
Allied Amiens offensive.

12-16 SEPTEMBER 1918
US offensive at St Mihiel.

26 SEPTEMBER 1918
Allies launch Meuse-Argonne offensive (foot of page).

27 SEPTEMBER 1918
Allies launch Cambrai-St. Quentin and Flanders offensives.

29 SEPTEMBER 1918
Bulgaria signs an armistice.

1 OCTOBER 1918
British take Damascus in Syria.

4 OCTOBER 1918
Germans abandon Hindenburg Line.

23 OCTOBER-NOVEMBER 1918
Austro-Hungarians overwhelmed on Italian Front.

30 OCTOBER 1918
Turkey signs armistice.

3 NOVEMBER 1918
Austria-Hungary signs armistice.

6 NOVEMBER 1918
Allies take Sedan.

11 NOVEMBER 1918
Armistice on Western Front.

JANUARY 1919
Paris Peace Conference opens at Versailles.

28 JUNE 1919
Germany signs Treaty of Versailles.

10 SEPTEMBER 1919
Austria signs Treaty of St Germain en Laye.

27 NOVEMBER 1919
Bulgaria signs Treaty of Neuilly.

4 JUNE 1920
Hungary signs Treaty of Trianon.

10 AUGUST 1920
Turkey signs Treaty of Sèvres.

WORLD WAR II:

EUROPE

CHAPTER 1: THE WAR BEGINS

German dictator Adolf Hitler shakes hands with army officers at a Nazi Party rally in 1934. Hitler rapidly expanded Germany's armed forces through the 1930s.

World War II is generally said to have started on 1 September 1939, when Germany, ruled by the Nazi dictator Adolf Hitler, invaded its neighbour Poland. But conflict in Europe had been building up for several years before that date.

Hitler had come to power in Germany in 1933. He was publicly committed to the overthrow of the Versailles Treaty, the peace treaty imposed by the victors on a defeated Germany in 1919 at the end of the Great War (now known as World War I). Under the terms of the treaty, Germany was only allowed a small army with limited armaments and no air force. It was not allowed to have troops in the Rhineland, the part of Germany bordering on France. The borders of Germany set by the treaty left many German-speaking people outside the country's frontier. Austria, whose population was mostly German-speaking, was forbidden to become part of Germany.

Hitler challenged the Versailles settlement step-by-step. He rapidly set about rebuilding Germany's armed forces, including its air force. Rearmament was already well under way by the time it was officially announced in 1935. The following year German troops marched into the demilitarized Rhineland. Britain and France, the two powers mainly responsible for the Versailles Treaty and with a major interest in upholding it, protested but did nothing.

THE AXIS ALLIANCE In 1936 Hitler formed the Axis alliance with another dictator, Italy's Benito Mussolini, who had angered Britain and France in 1935 by his invasion of the independent African country of Abyssinia (Ethiopia). When civil war broke out in Spain in July 1936, Germany and Italy sent military forces to support General Francisco Franco's Nationalist rebels against the Republican government. Franco eventually triumphed in 1939.

Meanwhile, emboldened by his success in remilitarizing the Rhineland, in March 1938 Hitler annexed Austria – this was known as the Anschluss ('joining together'). Hitler's army faced no resistance and he was greeted by cheering crowds in the Austrian capital, Vienna. Once again, Britain and France did nothing.

Next Hitler's attention turned to Czechoslovakia, a well-armed democratic country and an ally of France. Czechoslovakia had a large German-speaking minority living in the Sudetenland area, bordering on Germany. Hitler threatened to invade Czechoslovakia to 'liberate' the Sudeten Germans. This seemed certain to lead to war with Britain and France. But in September 1938, at a conference held in Munich, Britain and France agreed to join with Germany and Italy in ordering the Czechs to hand over the Sudetenland to Germany. British prime minister Neville Chamberlain returned

0 200 miles
0 200 kilometres
N
W E
S

Germany
Saarland, incorporated 1935
Rhineland, remilitarized 1936
International boundary, 1937
Austria, annexed by Germany, March 1938
Sudetenland, annexed by Germany, September 1938
To Hungary, November 1938
Bohemia & Moravia, annexed to Germany, March 1939
Slovakia, as a client state of Nazi Germany, nominally independent from September 1938

NORWAY
Oslo
SWEDEN
Stockholm
FINLAND
ESTONIA
LATVIA
LITHUANIA
Moscow
SOVIET UNION
NORTH SEA
DENMARK
BALTIC SEA
EAST PRUSSIA
IRELAND
GREAT BRITAIN
London
NETHERLANDS
Berlin
GERMANY
Warsaw
POLAND
SUDETENLAND
BELGIUM
LUXEMBOURG
Paris
Maginot Line
CZECHOSLOVAKIA
SLOVAKIA
RUTHENIA
BOHEMIA & MORAVIA
Vienna
AUSTRIA
HUNGARY
FRANCE
SWITZERLAND
ROMANIA
Bucharest
BLACK SEA
Belgrade
YUGOSLAVIA
BULGARIA
Sofia
ITALY
ADRIATIC SEA
Rome
ALBANIA
PORTUGAL
Madrid
SPAIN
CORSICA
SARDINIA
TURKEY
GREECE
Gibraltar
MEDITERRANEAN SEA
SICILY
CRETE

HITLER'S ACHIEVEMENTS

In April 1939, German Nazi dictator Adolf Hitler looked back triumphantly over his successes. He declared: *'I have … endeavoured to destroy sheet by sheet that Treaty [of Versailles] which … contains the vilest oppression which peoples and human beings have ever been expected to put up with. I have brought back to the Reich provinces stolen from us in 1919; I have led back to their native country millions of Germans who were torn away from us and were in misery…'*

[Quoted in *Hitler*, Joachim Fest]

The Saarland voted to rejoin Germany in 1935. The rest of Germany's expansion was achieved by the threat of military action.

Hitler drives triumphantly through the streets of the Austrian capital, Vienna, after the annexation of Austria – the Anschluss – in June 1938.

Danzig – now Gdansk – on the Baltic provided Hitler with a pretext for invading Poland in September 1939. Once the Soviet Union also invaded from the east, the Poles had no chance. The partition of Poland had secretly been agreed between Germany and the Soviet Union before the war began.

to Britain claiming 'peace with honour', while German forces occupied the Sudetenland without a shot being fired.

Chamberlain and other 'appeasers' believed that if Hitler was allowed to overturn the Versailles Treaty, gathering all German-speaking people within Germany's borders, he would be satisfied and peace would be maintained. But in reality Hitler's ambitions went much further. His ultimate goal, as he told his generals in 1939, was to obtain 'living space [*Lebensraum*] in the East'. This meant that Germany must conquer Slav peoples such as the Czechs, Poles and Russians to create a German-ruled empire that would dominate Europe. This would also allow Hitler to crush other groups he hated and feared, especially communists and Jews.

Hitler had declared the Sudetenland his 'last territorial claim in Europe'. But in March 1939 German troops marched into the Czech capital, Prague, and Czechoslovakia ceased to exist. In the same month, Germany took over Memel on the Baltic and Italy invaded Albania. Then the focus shifted to Poland. The Poles were in dispute with Germany over the port of Danzig (Gdansk). Although it had mainly a German population, the peace treaty had made Danzig a 'Free City' linked to Poland. Hitler demanded the return of Danzig to Germany and a 'corridor' through Poland to link Germany with East Prussia.

THE SOVIET ALLIANCE Now shamed by their failure to defend Czechoslovakia, in April 1939 Britain and France signed a treaty with Poland, committing themselves to go to war if the Poles were attacked. The crucial issue then was the position of the Soviet Union, led by the communist dictator Josef Stalin. The British, French and Polish governments disliked and distrusted Stalin. But in the summer of 1939 Britain and France rather half-heartedly sought an alliance with the Soviet Union, aware that only the Soviets were in a position to give the Poles immediate military assistance in case of a German invasion.

Hitler and Stalin were, on the face of it, implacable enemies. Nazism was an explicitly anti-communist

DEVASTATING DEFEAT

During the fighting in Poland in 1939, the death toll was high and many more were taken prisoner. The estimated figures are:

60,000	Poles killed in action
25,000	Polish civilians killed
694,000	Polish prisoners in German hands
217,000	Polish prisoners in Russian hands

German losses, although substantial, were far lighter:

14,000	German soldiers killed

movement. The Soviets had sent military aid to the Republican side in the Spanish Civil War. Yet in August 1939, while the British and French dithered, Hitler sent a delegation to Russia which swiftly struck a ruthless deal with the Soviets. Publicly this Nazi-Soviet Pact was a non-aggression treaty – an agreement that Nazi Germany and the Soviet Union would not attack one another. But secretly the two powers agreed to partition Poland between them.

On 1 September 1939 German troops invaded Poland. The Poles had a large army, but with out-of-date equipment. Germany, by contrast, used its most modern tank formations and aircraft in the invasion. The tanks moved fast, punching holes in the Polish lines and penetrating deep inside Poland. They were supported by Stuka dive-bombers, acting as 'aerial artillery'. The German *Luftwaffe* (air force) also bombed Polish cities, terrorizing the population.

The Polish forces were already in disarray when, on 17 September, the Soviet Union invaded eastern Poland. The Polish government fled

German soldiers pull down a barrier on the Polish border on 1 September 1939. In response to the invasion of Poland, Britain and France declared war on Germany two days later.

Soviet commisar for foreign affairs Vyacheslav Molotov signs a non-aggression pact with Nazi Germany on 23 August 1939, watched by German foreign minister Joachim von Ribbentrop (left).

the country the next day. Warsaw, the Polish capital, surrendered on 28 September. The defeat of Poland had taken four weeks.

WAR ON GERMANY The German invasion of Poland led Britain and France to declare war on Germany on 3 September. But the British and French government had no enthusiasm for war and did nothing effective to help the Poles. Britain was in no position to help Poland militarily, and France, which could have launched an offensive against Germany, was committed to a defensive strategy. A British Expeditionary Force was sent to France but the Allied forces stayed on the defensive – even though, with the best German troops occupied in Poland, Germany's western border would have been vulnerable to a swift attack. Once Poland was defeated, Britain and France felt even less inclined to go on the attack.

Finnish soldiers wearing winter camouflage man a machine-gun during the war between Finland and the Soviet Union in 1939-40.

The Finns used troops on skis to launch counter-offensives after the Soviet invasion.

Germany and the Soviet Union duly carved up Poland between them. The Soviet Union also bullied the independent Baltic states, Estonia, Latvia and Lithuania, into allowing Soviet troops to be stationed on their territory. But another of the Soviet Union's neighbours, Finland, was not so accommodating.

The Soviet Union proposed changes to its border with Finland which would have improved the Soviet defensive position in case of an attack from the west. The Finns refused. On 30 November 1939 the Soviet Red Army invaded Finland. To their surprise, they met fierce resistance. In harsh winter weather, over 120,000 Soviet soldiers died attempting to breach the Finnish defences. As Finnish resistance held the Soviet army at bay, Britain and France discussed sending an expeditionary force to support the Finns – an action which would have put them simultaneously at war with the Soviet Union and Germany.

In February 1940, however, the Red Army broke through and the following month the Finns were forced to accept a peace agreement that gave the Soviet Union rather more territory than it had originally asked for. In the summer of 1940, Stalin went on to absorb Estonia, Latvia and Lithuania into the Soviet Union, and took the province of Bessarabia from Romania. But by then momentous events in Western Europe had distracted attention from the East.

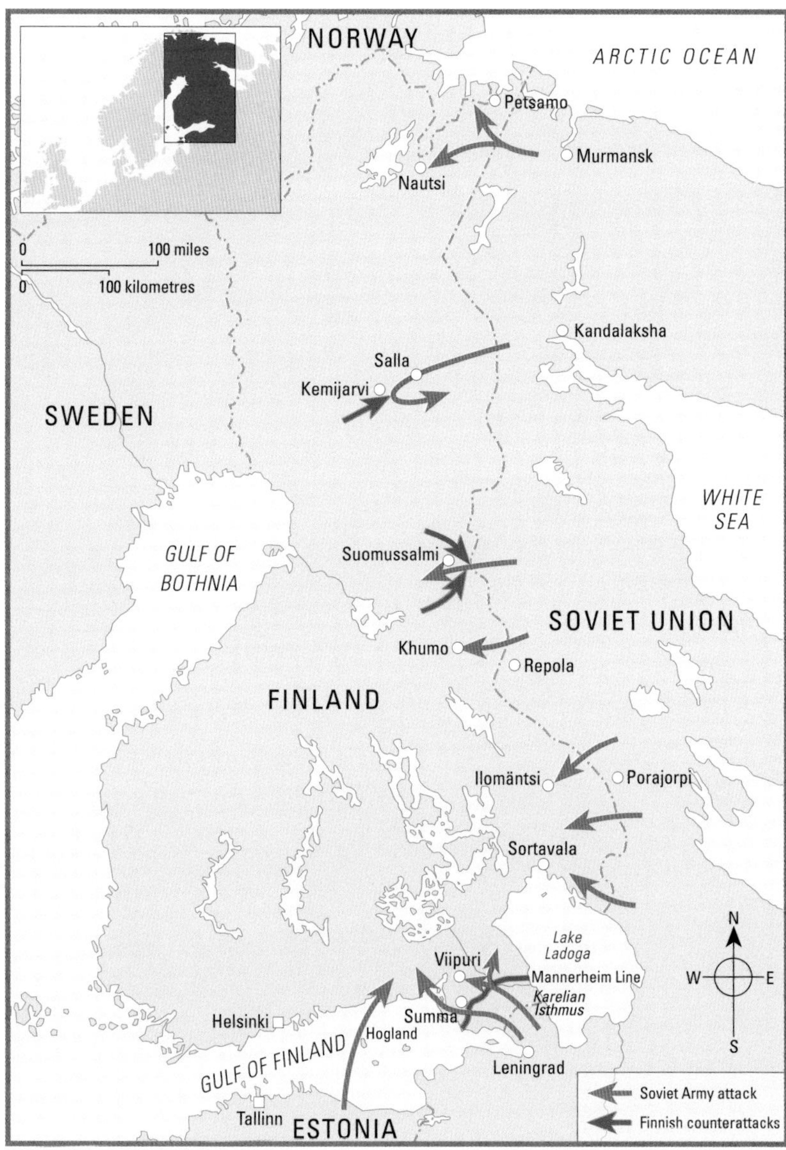

INCAPABLE REDS

The events of the Winter War led many people to underestimate Soviet military strength. In a radio broadcast in January 1940, Winston Churchill, then Britain's First Lord of the Admiralty, said that Finland *'had exposed, for the world to see, the incapacity of the Red Army.'*

[Quoted in *History of the Second World War*, B.H. Liddel Hart]

The Mannerheim Line, a strong defensive position named after Finland's senior military commander, was the key to the war between the Soviet Union and Finland in 1939-40. After the Soviets broke through the Line in February 1940, the Finns soon had to agree to a negotiated peace.

CHAPTER 2: BLITZKRIEG

The Junkers Ju-87 dive-bomber, known as the Stuka, was a crucial weapon in Germany's 'Blitzkrieg' offensives in the early years of the war.

The period between September 1939 and April 1940 in western Europe was dubbed the 'Phoney War'. The British Expeditionary Force (BEF) in France numbered over 350,000 troops by the spring of 1940, and France had mobilized an army almost five million strong. But there was no significant fighting. The Allied forces passively awaited a German offensive, manning the Maginot Line (see map on page 5), a powerful concrete fortification along France's frontier with Germany that spread out along the border with neutral Belgium.

In April 1940, partly in response to criticism of the lack of military action, Britain and France decided to move to cut off supplies of iron ore that were being exported to Germany from mines in neutral Sweden. The iron ore was being shipped chiefly through Narvik, a port in another neutral country, Norway. On 8 April the Allies sent ships to mine Norwegian coastal waters. They also prepared to land troops at key Norwegian ports.

GERMANS ATTACK NORWAY But the Germans had been planning their own invasion of Norway. On 9 April, German troops seized control of neutral Denmark and moved on to attack Norway. In a series of lightning moves, they occupied coastal

German troops drag a gun up a beach during the Norwegian campaign in the spring of 1940.

towns from Oslo in the south to Narvik in the far north. Airborne troops were parachuted in to capture key airfields – the first use of parachutists in war – but most of the German soldiers arrived by ship.

THE ROYAL NAVY The British Royal Navy was unable to stop German ships delivering and then resupplying troops, because the British warships could not operate effectively while within range of German land-based aircraft. The Royal Navy did succeed in sinking a fair number of German warships, especially in fierce battles at Narvik. But most of Norway was in German hands by early May.

In Britain, the defeat in Norway undermined confidence in Chamberlain's leadership. On 10 May Winston Churchill replaced Chamberlain as prime minister. On Churchill's first day as prime minister, the Germans launched their long-awaited offensive on the western front.

The German army was easily outnumbered by the British and French. It even had less tanks than its opponents, though more aircraft. But the Germans

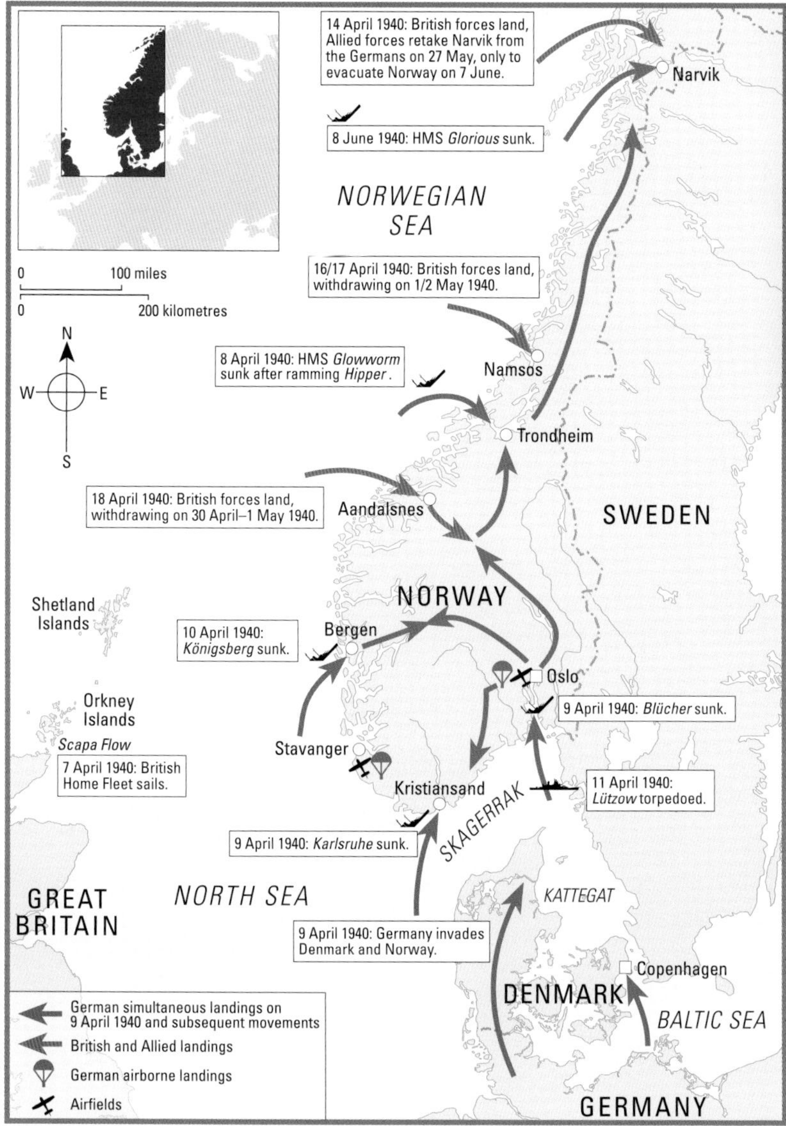

The German invasion of Norway in April 1940 was resisted by Britain and France, who also sent ships and landed troops.

A German tank rolls unchallenged along a country road during the occupation of Denmark in April 1940. The Danes were powerless to resist the German invasion.

LOSSES IN NORWAY

The level of combat losses in the Norway campaign was quite low compared with battles later in the war. The estimated death toll was:

German	5,500
British	4,500
Norwegian	1,800
French	500

triumphed through the use of the 'Blitzkrieg' ('lightning war') tactics first employed against Poland – fast-moving armoured columns breaking through or outflanking enemy defences, with aircraft supporting the armour and causing panic and terror behind the lines.

The Germans began their offensive by invading Belgium and the Netherlands, both neutral countries. In a series of surprise attacks, German airborne troops seized bridges, airfields and the key Belgian fortress of Eben Emael, allowing armoured forces quickly to penetrate deep into enemy territory. Within five days the Dutch surrendered, but not before the port city of Rotterdam had been devastated by German bombers. Meanwhile the best elements of the British and French armies advanced into Belgium to meet the advancing Germans. This was a fatal mistake.

CHURCHILL DEFIANT

On 4 June 1940, Prime Minister Winston Churchill told the House of Commons: '*We shall defend our island, whatever the cost may be, we shall fight on the beaches, we shall fight on the landing grounds, we shall fight in the fields and in the streets, we shall fight in the hills; we shall never surrender.*'
[Quoted in *The Most Dangerous Enemy: A History of the Battle of Britain*, S. Bungay]

The Germans had originally planned to launch their main thrust through northern Belgium. But during the winter of 1939-40 Hitler had instead adopted a plan proposed by General Erich von Manstein. This called for a major attack by armoured divisions much further south, through the Ardennes region. Since the Ardennes was rough country, considered almost impassible, Allied defences in this sector were weak. Commanded by General Heinz Guderian, the spearhead of the German panzers (armoured vehicles) crossed the Meuse River near Sedan on 13 May. They broke through the Allied lines and sped north-west towards the Channel coast, which they reached on 20 May. The Allied forces in Belgium were cut off from behind.

The only option open to the hard-pressed BEF and its Allies inside Belgium was to escape by sea. Fortunately from an Allied point of view, the German armour temporarily halted its rapid advance on 23 May, leaving one Channel port still in Allied hands: Dunkirk. Between 26 May and 3 June, under constant bombardment from the air, some 338,000 men were evacuated from the port and beaches of Dunkirk. Most were carried by Royal Navy or merchant navy vessels, although a range of fishing vessels, yachts, tugs and barges crewed by civilian volunteers also played their part.

Allied troops wait to be evacuated from the beach at Dunkirk. Men formed queues into the sea, where small boats took them on board.

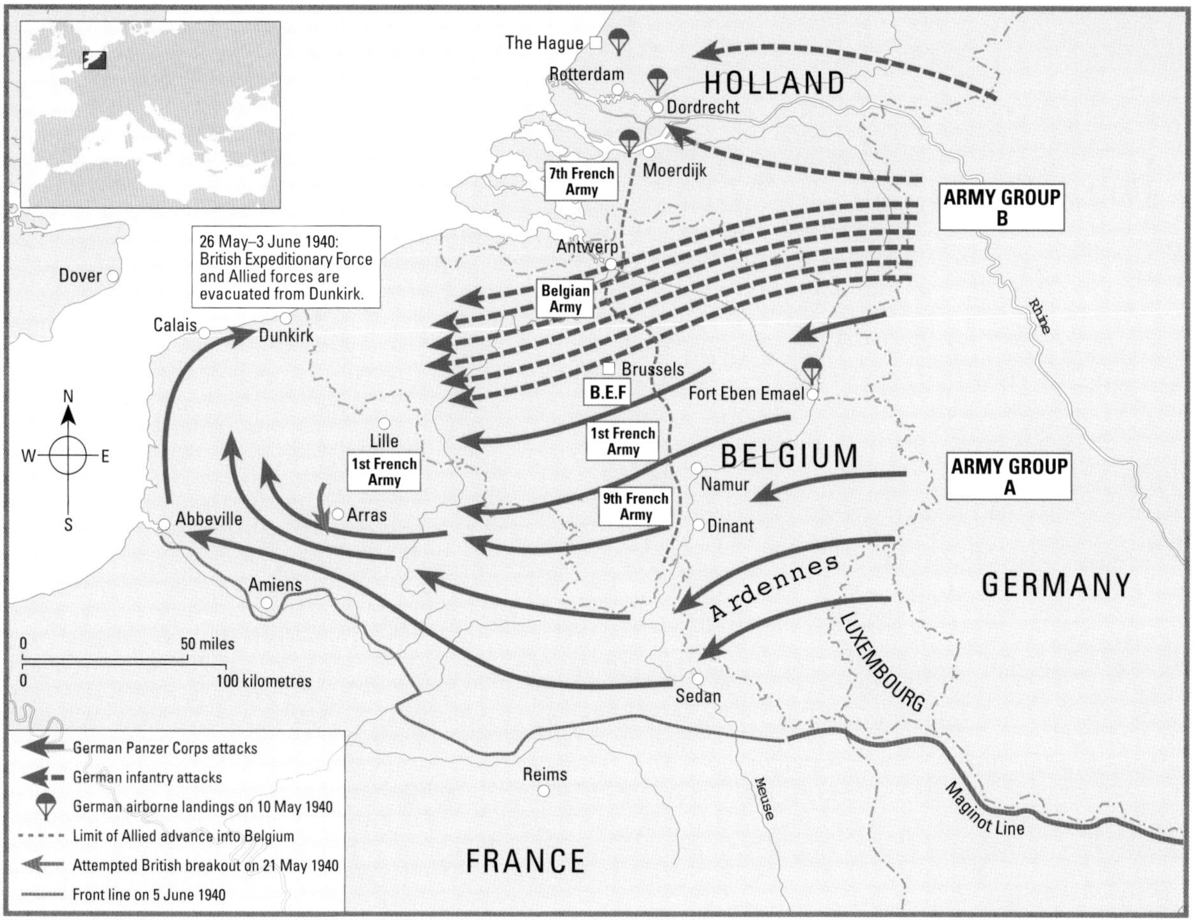

The Hague
Rotterdam
HOLLAND
Dordrecht
Moerdijk
7th French Army
ARMY GROUP B
26 May–3 June 1940: British Expeditionary Force and Allied forces are evacuated from Dunkirk.
Dover
Antwerp
Belgian Army
Calais
Dunkirk
Brussels
B.E.F
Fort Eben Emael
Rhine
1st French Army
Lille
1st French Army
BELGIUM
ARMY GROUP A
Namur
9th French Army
Arras
Abbeville
Dinant
Ardennes
GERMANY
Amiens
LUXEMBOURG
0 50 miles
0 100 kilometres
Sedan
Reims
Meuse
Maginot Line
FRANCE

- German Panzer Corps attacks
- German infantry attacks
- German airborne landings on 10 May 1940
- Limit of Allied advance into Belgium
- Attempted British breakout on 21 May 1940
- Front line on 5 June 1940

The breakthrough of German Panzers at Sedan and their rapid progress to the Channel coast cut off the Allied armies which had advanced into Belgium further north. Dunkirk provided the only escape route from the encirclement.

Dunkirk was a great escape, but the scale and speed of the German victory was still astonishing. On 5 June the Germans resumed their offensive, driving south and west into France. The French army was swept aside. On 14 June the Germans entered Paris and two days later a new French government, headed by the elderly Marshal Philippe Pétain, asked for an armistice. The fighting stopped on 25 June. The Germans occupied the north and west of France, while Pétain was left to govern the south of the country from the town of Vichy.

Although Britain had brought most of its soldiers back safely from Dunkirk, they had lost almost all their tanks, artillery and other heavy equipment. Hitler hoped that Britain, like France, would accept defeat and ask for peace terms. Some of the British government wanted to do this. But Churchill was determined to fight on. Reluctantly accepting that the British would not make peace, on 16 July Hitler ordered his generals to prepare an invasion of Britain, Operation Sealion. He also ordered an air offensive. The *Luftwaffe* –

German tanks advance through Belgium in May 1940. The German army's used panzer formations as a shock attack force, creating a new form of mobile warfare.

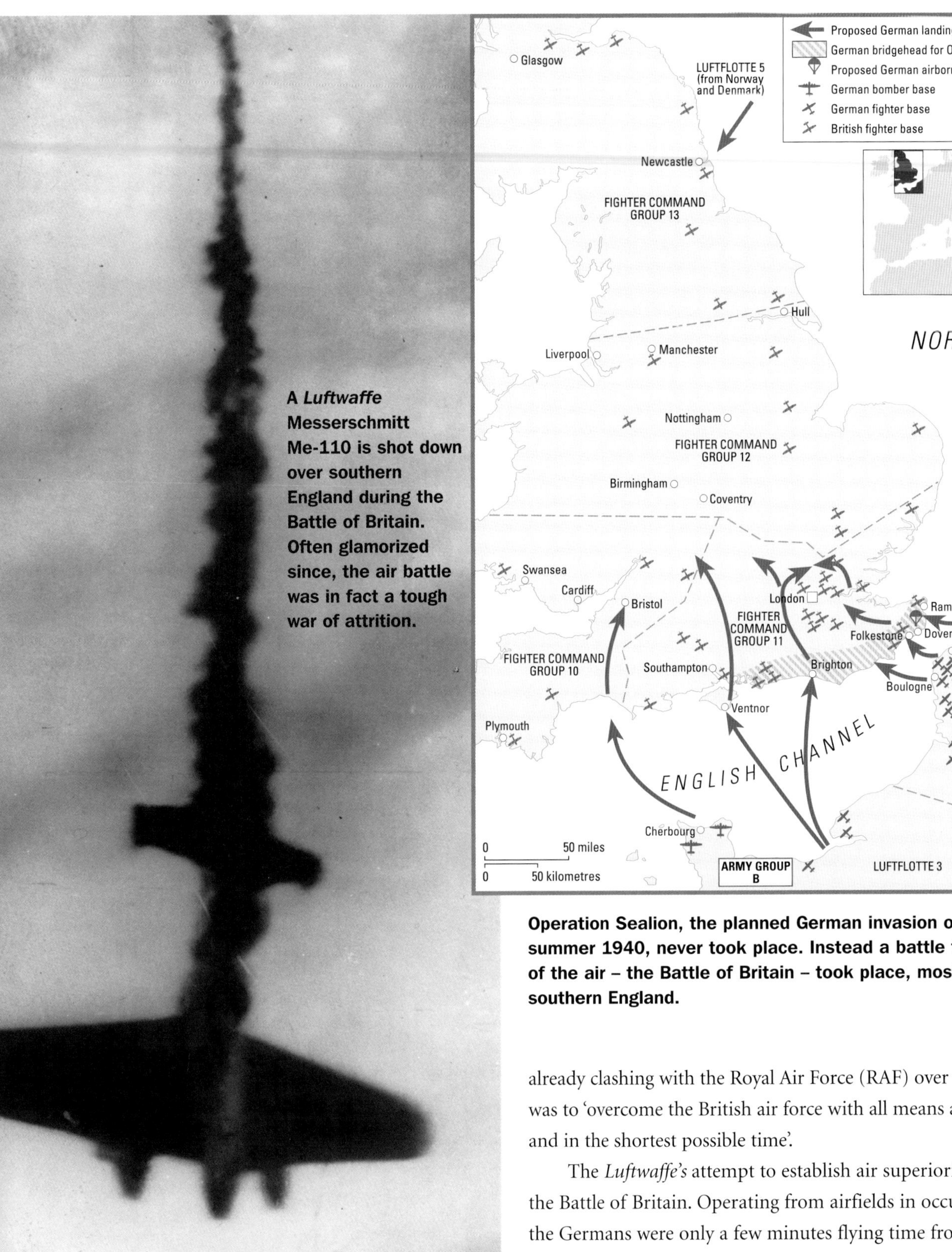

A *Luftwaffe* Messerschmitt Me-110 is shot down over southern England during the Battle of Britain. Often glamorized since, the air battle was in fact a tough war of attrition.

Operation Sealion, the planned German invasion of Britain in summer 1940, never took place. Instead a battle for command of the air – the Battle of Britain – took place, mostly over southern England.

already clashing with the Royal Air Force (RAF) over the Channel – was to 'overcome the British air force with all means at its disposal and in the shortest possible time'.

The *Luftwaffe's* attempt to establish air superiority is known as the Battle of Britain. Operating from airfields in occupied France, the Germans were only a few minutes flying time from southern England. Britain's air defences were, however, the best organized in the world. Radar stations and ground observers radioed warning of approaching enemy planes to operations rooms, from where orders were sent to airfields to 'scramble' the Hurricanes and Spitfires of

RAF Fighter Command – flown by Canadians, New Zealanders, South Africans, Australians, Poles and Czechs as well as British pilots. Some of these fighters engaged the German Messerschmitt fighters in 'dogfights' while others took on the German bombers.

THE BLITZ From mid-August through the first week in September, the *Luftwaffe* carried out repeated attacks on airfields, aircraft factories and radar installations in an attempt to wear down resistance by the RAF. But led by Sir Hugh Dowding, Fighter Command looked after its resources well, steadily inflicting damage on the *Luftwaffe* while minimizing its own losses. On 7 September the *Luftwaffe* switched to bombing London. Mass daylight raids led to some major air battles – almost 1,000 German aircraft were involved on 15 September – but they did not bring the *Luftwaffe* any closer to achieving command of the air. By October German plans for invading Britain had been abandoned and the *Luftwaffe* was concentrating on bombing Britain's cities by night.

Dubbed 'the Blitz', the intensive night bombing campaign lasted from September 1940 to May 1941. Although London was the main target, many other cities were hit, including Liverpool, Coventry, Bristol, Plymouth, Belfast and Cardiff. At first air defences were almost powerless against night attacks and the bombers met little resistance. Only gradually did the development of radar-guided night fighters and anti-aircraft guns begin to allow the defenders to hit back. Bombing was a terrifying experience for the civilian population – some 43,000 people were killed in the Blitz. But it failed either to destroy Britain's industries or frighten the British into surrender.

It has often been said that during this period Britain 'stood alone'. But this was never altogether true. Britain had the support of her Commonwealth and also, increasingly, of the United States. When war broke out in Europe, most US citizens strongly opposed getting involved in the conflict. The spectacle of the Battle of Britain and the Blitz, however, helped to swing US opinion behind Britain. This was of great help to US President Franklin D. Roosevelt, who was personally convinced

THE BATTLE OF BRITAIN

The *Luftwaffe*'s overall losses in the Battle of Britain were far higher than the RAF's, but the RAF had more fighters downed. The *Luftwaffe* lost far more airmen because many of its aircraft shot down were bombers with a crew of four.

Luftwaffe losses:
1,887 aircraft, of which 873 were fighters; 2,698 airmen

Fighter Command losses:
1,023 aircraft; 544 airmen

RAF fighter pilots run to their aircraft to meet an attack. Every second counted, as it was vital to gain sufficient altitude before meeting the enemy.

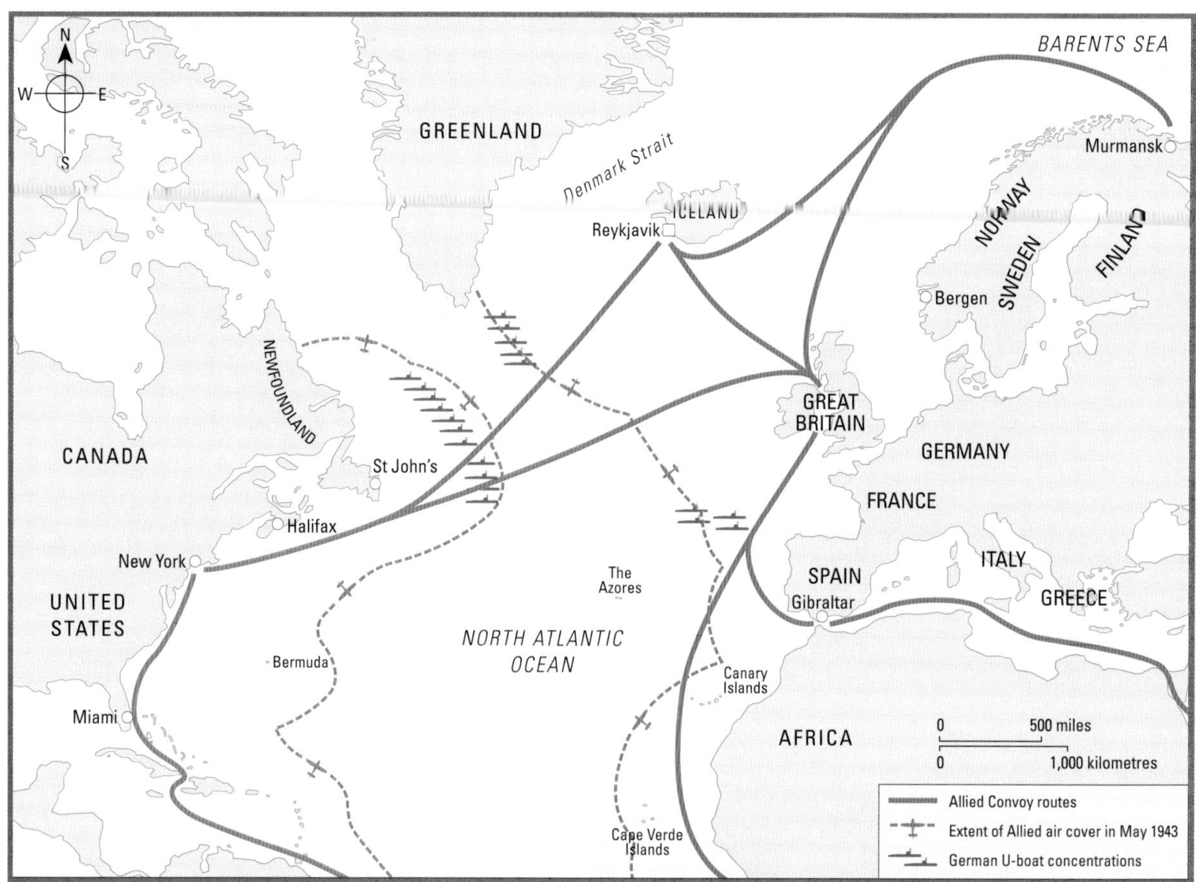

The Allied supply lines across the Atlantic from the US and Canada to Britain, and north to the Soviet port of Murmansk, were crucial to Britain's survival.

that the survival of Britain was essential to the defence of the United States.

Roosevelt at first hoped to keep the United States out of the fighting by giving Britain the tools to do the job – the USA would be 'the arsenal of democracy'. Under the Lend-Lease programme, approved by the US Congress in March 1941, the United States provided Britain with arms without immediate payment. The programme was later extended to other allies of the United States, including the Soviet Union.

President Roosevelt (left) and Prime Minister Churchill meeting on a warship in August 1941. This led to an Anglo-American declaration of principles, the Atlantic Charter.

THE BATTLE OF THE ATLANTIC The only way to get US-manufactured armaments and other supplies to Britain, however, was by ship. This led to the Battle of the Atlantic – a long struggle against German surface raiders and, above all, U-boats (German submarines) which sought to cut Britain's ocean supply line. Through 1941, the United States was drawn into this conflict at sea step-by-step. By the second half of the year, without being officially at war with Germany, US naval vessels were escorting merchant convoys part way across the Atlantic.

In August 1941, Churchill and Roosevelt met on board warships off the Newfoundland coast of Canada

German U-boats line up with their crews on deck.

and agreed a joint declaration of principles, the Atlantic Charter. The United States was thus already thoroughly committed to the British side in the war when Germany's Asian ally Japan attacked the US Pacific naval base at Pearl Harbor on 7 December 1941. Hitler then put an end to any further American hesitations by declaring war on the United States.

THE CODE IS BROKEN Still US involvement in the European war would come to nothing if the Allies were unable to ferry men and equipment across the Atlantic. In 1942 U-boat 'wolf packs' sank 7.8 million tons of Allied shipping. This meant that the Allies were losing more ships than they could build. If this had continued, Britain might have had to surrender for lack of food, fuel and other essential supplies.

In 1943, however, the situation was transformed by a combination of factors, including the use of long-range aircraft on anti-submarine patrols and the cracking of German naval codes by British codebreakers. Almost 100 U-boats – a quarter of the entire German submarine force – were destroyed in the first five months of the year. They never again threatened to cut the link between the USA and Europe.

IT MUST BE DONE

In May 1941, although the United States was not yet at war with Germany, US President Franklin D. Roosevelt told the American people: *'The delivery of needed supplies to Britain is imperative. This can be done. It must be done. It will be done.'*

[Quoted in *The Second World War*, Martin Gilbert]

A depth charge explodes, watched by the crew of an Atlantic convoy escort vessel. Depth charges were used to attack submerged U-boats.

CHAPTER 3: WAR IN THE MEDITERRANEAN

Swordfish biplanes fly over HMS *Illustrious*. Swordfish from *Illustrious* devastated the Italian fleet at Taranto in November 1940.

CYNICAL DICTATOR

In June 1940, Italian dictator Benito Mussolini cynically expressed why he thought it was necessary for Italy to fight: *'I need several thousand dead in order to take my place at the table with the victors.'*

[Quoted in *The Second World War*, Henri Michel]

Despite the Axis alliance with Nazi Germany, Italian dictator Benito Mussolini did not go to war in September 1939. He was only too aware of the weaknesses of his armed forces. Instead he waited until a German victory seemed assured, declaring war on Britain and France on 10 June 1940. He hoped to exploit this opportunity to extend Italy's empire in North and East Africa and take effective control of the Mediterranean at little military cost.

Britain's position in the Mediterranean certainly looked precarious in the summer of 1940. There were British bases at Gibraltar on the southern tip of Spain, and on the island of Malta, south of Sicily. British troops were also stationed in Egypt to defend the Suez Canal, a vital communications link with the British Commonwealth, and in Palestine and Cyprus. Most of the rest of the Mediterranean was in hostile hands. Italy controlled Libya in North Africa and some of the Greek islands. Spain under General Franco was neutral but well-disposed towards Hitler and Mussolini. The French government at Vichy, which controlled southern France, collaborated with the Germans.

Britain had hopes that the French colonial authorities ruling Syria, Lebanon and French North Africa would side with General Charles de Gaulle's Free French movement, which fought alongside the British. But instead they stayed loyal to Vichy. The hostility of Vichy France to Britain was confirmed in July 1940 when the Royal Navy sank French warships in the Algerian port of Mers-el-Kebir, in order to stop them falling into the hands of the Germans.

THE ITALIANS IN AFRICA Despite the apparent weakness of Britain's position in the Mediterranean, however, it was Italy that at first suffered disaster after disaster. In North Africa, the Italian army advanced into Egypt only to be trounced by a far smaller British and Commonwealth force, which then pushed deep into

Above: In 1940, much of the Mediterranean zone was in the hands of powers hostile to Britain – Vichy France and Italy. Malta was a key staging post for the British navy between Gibraltar and Egypt.

Libya, taking 130,000 Italian prisoners. Further south, Britain evicted Italy from its recently won colony of Abyssinia, now Ethiopia. In November 1940 Swordfish biplanes from the Royal Navy aircraft carrier HMS *Illustrious* crippled three battleships and a cruiser in a daring raid on the Italian port of Taranto. The Italian navy took another battering in an encounter with the British fleet at Cape Matapan five months later. A further setback for Mussolini came in Greece, where an Italian invasion in October 1940 stalled in the face of stiff Greek resistance.

The weakness of the Italians forced the Germans to come to their aid. The arrival of German forces in the Mediterranean theatre quickly turned the situation around. *Luftwaffe* units stationed in

Italian soldiers who have surrendered to the British prepare a meal in a prisoner-of-war camp in Libya, North Africa. The Italian troops were generally poorly trained, badly led and lacking up-to-date equipment.

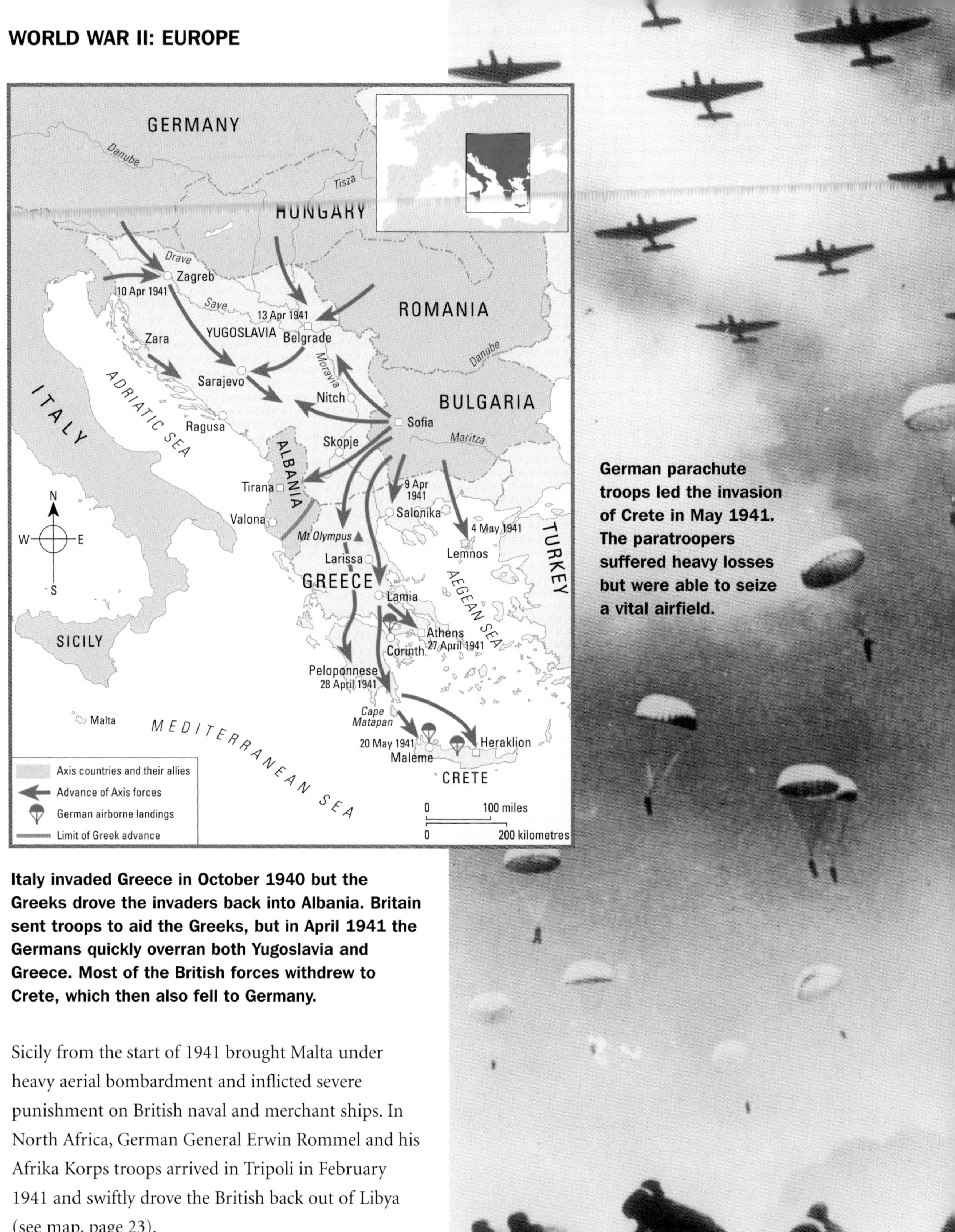

German parachute troops led the invasion of Crete in May 1941. The paratroopers suffered heavy losses but were able to seize a vital airfield.

Italy invaded Greece in October 1940 but the Greeks drove the invaders back into Albania. Britain sent troops to aid the Greeks, but in April 1941 the Germans quickly overran both Yugoslavia and Greece. Most of the British forces withdrew to Crete, which then also fell to Germany.

Sicily from the start of 1941 brought Malta under heavy aerial bombardment and inflicted severe punishment on British naval and merchant ships. In North Africa, German General Erwin Rommel and his Afrika Korps troops arrived in Tripoli in February 1941 and swiftly drove the British back out of Libya (see map, page 23).

One reason for Rommel's instant success was that some 60,000 British, New Zealand and Australian troops had been transferred from North Africa to Greece, in anticipation of German intervention there in support of the Italians. However, before the Germans could invade Greece, another crisis erupted in the region. In Yugoslavia, an uprising in late March 1941 overthrew the pro-German government and replaced it by a pro-British regime. Hitler immediately decided to invade Yugoslavia as well as Greece.

ONE-SIDED FIGHT

Germany's triumphs in Yugoslavia and Greece were overwhelming. The German army took prisoner: 90,000 Yugoslavs, 270,000 Greeks, 13,000 British and Commonwealth troops Germany lost some 5,000 men killed or wounded.

YUGOSLAVIA CONQUERED Beginning on 6 April, the Germans, aided by Italian and Hungarian troops, carried out another astonishingly swift and effective campaign, routing their enemies in just three weeks. Yugoslavia was conquered and broken up, the largest single part becoming the state of Croatia, closely tied to Italy and Germany. Greece was also overrun. Some 50,000 British, Commonwealth and Greek soldiers were evacuated from southern Greece by sea, most of them being taken to the Greek island of Crete.

There followed one of the boldest military operations of the entire war. On 20 May, exploiting the fact that they had complete command of the air, the Germans launched an invasion of Crete by airborne troops, floating down by parachute or landing in gliders. British codebreakers had provided precise information about enemy plans from intercepted messages, and German losses in the initial attack were heavy. But the Germans were allowed to seize control of an airfield at Maleme on the north of the island, after which they were able to fly in more troops and equipment in transport aircraft. By the end of the month the island was in German hands.

The British feared that the Germans might go on to capture other islands, especially Malta. But although Malta was put under siege – hammered by continual *Luftwaffe* bombing raids and almost starved into submission by the sinking of ships carrying food and fuel to the island – it was never invaded.

Once Germany had attacked the Soviet Union in June 1941 (see page 25), Hitler viewed the Mediterranean as a sideshow. Rommel had to fight on

The war in Yugoslavia was the occasion for large-scale massacres of civilians, especially Serbs killed by the Germans, Italians and Croatians.

General Bernard Montgomery was appointed commander of the British Eighth Army in North Africa in August 1942, three months before the victory at El Alamein.

in the North African desert with often inadequate resources. From the summer of 1941 to the summer of 1942, the fighting swung back and forth. Rommel generally had the better of the tank battles, but was never quite able to break through to Cairo and the Suez Canal. His last offensive was stopped at Alam Halfa, in the Egyptian desert, in August-September 1942.

The war in the desert was far more important to Britain than to the Germans because it was at the time the only place where British troops could engage the enemy in battle. The same logic dictated that the United States become involved in North Africa. In 1942 it was essential that the US Army, in the war since December 1941, should do some actual fighting against Germany and Italy. The US chiefs of staff favoured an invasion of German-occupied France, but the British persuaded them that this was too risky. The United States then opted for an invasion of French North Africa to attack Rommel's forces from the rear.

THE BATTLE OF EL ALAMEIN

The forces engaged at Alamein in October-November 1942 were:

Axis	
men	104,000
tanks	489
artillery	1,219
aircraft	350
Eighth Army	
men	195,000
tanks	1,029
artillery	2,311
aircraft	530

EL ALAMEIN, EGYPT On 23 October 1942 the British Eighth Army, commanded by General Bernard Montgomery, launched a large-scale offensive against a well-prepared Axis defensive line at El Alamein, Egypt. By 4 November the Eighth Army had broken through, forcing Rommel to retreat towards Tunisia. This victory was followed on 8 November by

British infantry advance in the desert. Such 'action' photos were almost always posed for the cameras.

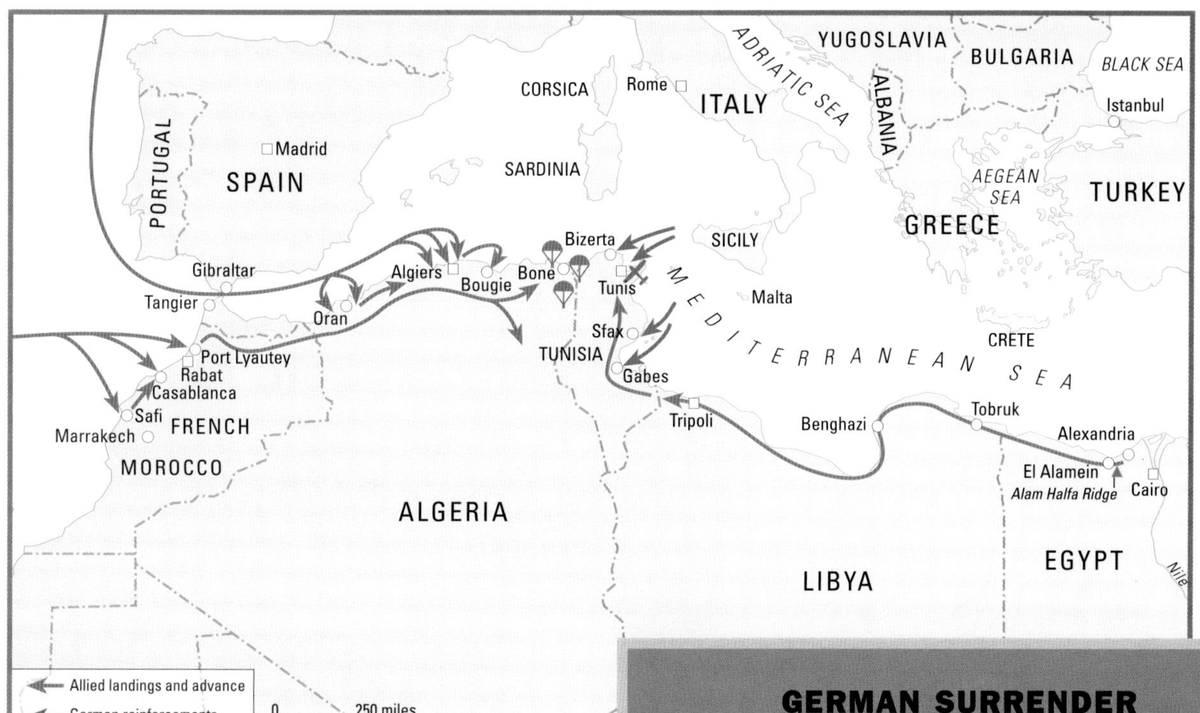

After its victory at El Alamein in October-November 1942, the British Eighth Army advanced across North Africa to Tunisia.

GERMAN SURRENDER

British journalist Alan Moorhead witnessed the Axis surrender in Tunisia. He wrote: *'We rode back ... to Tunis, past the prisoners who now stretched in a procession reaching from the tip of Cap Bon far into Tunisia. Weeks were going to elapse before a final count revealed the total at over a quarter of a million prisoners... In all the Axis had lost close to a million men in Africa. Now they had nothing, absolutely nothing to show for it.'*

[From *African Trilogy,* Alan Moorhead]

General Erwin Rommel was an inspired German tank commander in North Africa.

Operation Torch, the landing in French North Africa of Allied forces commanded by General Dwight D. Eisenhower.

The last stages of the North African campaign did not go smoothly for the Allies. Unwilling to accept defeat anywhere, Hitler gave higher priority to the desert war and rushed reinforcements into Tunisia. Allied hopes that the Axis forces could be defeated by the end of 1942 were dashed. But the troops that Hitler poured into North Africa were being sacrificed in a lost cause. When the Axis forces were finally forced to surrender in May 1943, some 200,000 Germans and Italians were taken prisoner. The Allies could now use North Africa as a jumping-off point for an invasion of Italy.

CHAPTER 4:
CLASH OF GIANTS

German troops advance through the ruins of a Russian village in July 1942. The devastation of the Soviet Union by the German invaders followed Hitler's order to carry out 'a war of annihilation'.

RUTHLESS WARFARE

German army commanders accepted Hitler's view that the war with the Soviet Union would be of a different nature from the war in the west. One tank commander, General Erich Hoepner, told his men: *'This struggle has to have as its aim the smashing of present-day Russia and must consequently be carried out with unprecedented severity. Every military action must ... be led by the iron will mercilessly and totally to annihilate the enemy.'*

[Quoted in *Hitler*, Vol 2., Ian Kershaw]

After the Nazi-Soviet Pact of August 1939, Soviet dictator Josef Stalin behaved as a loyal ally of Hitler, supplying Germany with food and raw materials, including oil. But as early as July 1940 Hitler informed his generals of his intention to invade the Soviet Union. Planning for the invasion, which was codenamed Operation Barbarossa, began the following December.

Hitler felt contempt and hatred for the Soviet people, both because they were communists and because they were Slavs – regarded by Hitler as an inferior sub-human race. He told his generals that they were embarking on a 'war of annihilation [total destruction]'. Victory would, Hitler believed, make Germany unbeatable, with control of vast supplies of food and raw materials. There would be no country left in Europe capable of challenging German power.

The Germans had a low opinion of the Soviet Red Army, despite its huge size, and confidently expected to achieve total victory in one to three

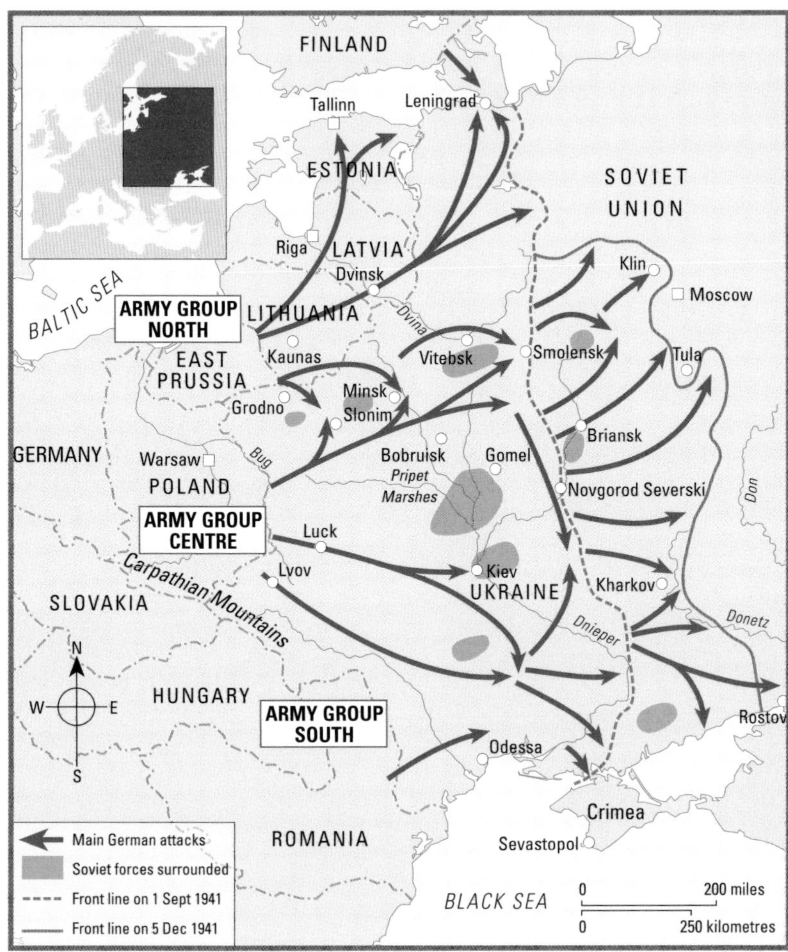

Invading the Soviet Union in June 1941, German forces advanced rapidly and captured millions of Soviet soldiers. Leningrad was put under siege, but the German advance ground to a halt in December without reaching Moscow.

months. They intended to launch their offensive in May 1941 and win well before the dreaded Russian winter closed in. The start of Barbarossa was delayed, however, partly because of the events in Yugoslavia and Greece which required the Germans' attention in the spring (see pages 20-1). The launch of the offensive was finally set for 22 June.

For the invasion, an army over three million strong was assembled along the border with the Soviet Union, from the Baltic in the north to the Black Sea in the south. It included not only Germans but also soldiers from Romania, Hungary, Italy, Finland, Slovakia and Spain. Only a small part of this huge force consisted of armoured divisions, however, and much of the army did not even have motorized transport – there were 3,550 tanks involved in the offensive, but 700,000 horses.

Stalin received precise warnings of the coming offensive both from his own spies and from Britain, which was reading German coded messages, but failed to place his forces on full alert. As a result, the Soviet forces were taken by surprise and their shallow defensive lines were easily broken.

The Soviets had more tanks and aircraft than their enemies and Soviet

German soldiers found the fighting in the Soviet Union a far tougher task than earlier campaigns. They came to fear a posting to the Eastern Front as almost the same as a death sentence.

soldiers fought fiercely in defence of their homeland. But they were poorly organized and poorly led. The first month of the campaign was an total disaster for them. The German Army Group Centre advanced rapidly, taking Minsk and Smolensk by mid-July (see page 25). Had they continued to advance towards Moscow, they might have taken the Soviet capital. In August, however, Hitler ordered them to turn aside to help Army Group South conquer the Ukraine. By the end of September, the encircled Soviet forces in the south had been forced to surrender at Kiev, while the German Army Group North was on the outskirts of Leningrad.

By the time the advance on Moscow resumed at the beginning of October, however, the weather was already worsening. Heavy rains were followed by snow and bitter cold. By the end of November the Germans were within 20 km of the centre of Moscow, but without clothing or equipment for a winter war, they faltered in the face of fanatical Soviet resistance. On 5 December the Soviets counterattacked in force. Freezing cold and worn down by five months of hard fighting, for the first time in the war the Germans retreated. Moscow was saved.

THE FATE OF LENINGRAD

Unquestionably 1941 had been a catastrophic year for the Soviet armed forces. They had lost probably a million men killed and 3.5 million taken prisoner. But German losses had also been extremely heavy – around a million killed, wounded or taken captive.

The sufferings of the Soviet people were typified by the fate of Leningrad, which was kept under

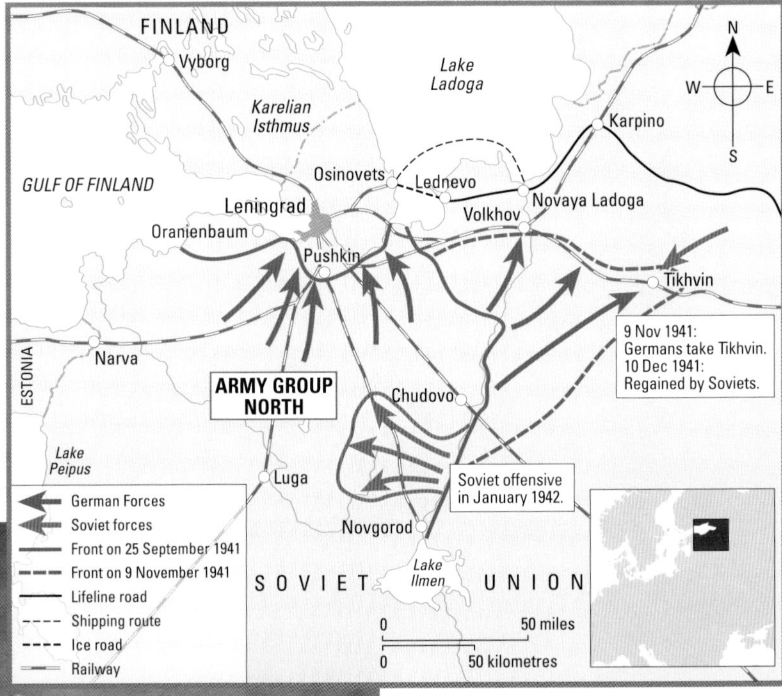

The only lifeline to besieged Leningrad was across Lake Ladoga, by boat in summer and by a road across the ice in winter.

A Soviet propaganda photograph shows snipers in snow camouflage fighting on the Leningrad front in 1943. Soviet troops generally coped better with fighting in severe winter weather conditions than their German enemy.

Cossack cavalry, from the Don region of the Soviet Union, ride out on patrol. Despite the use of tanks and trucks, horses played an important role in warfare on the Eastern Front.

OVERWHELMED BY DEATH

A Leningrad resident, Vera Inber, writing in her diary in December 1941, described how people were overwhelmed by the scale of the deaths in the besieged city: *'The mortuary itself is full. Not only are there too few trucks to go to the cemetery, but, more important, no gasoline to put in the trucks and the main thing is – there is not enough strength left in the living to bury the dead.'*

[Quoted in *Russia's War,* Richard Overy]

blockade by the Germans for 900 days from September 1941 to February 1944. The city's only lifeline to the outside world was across Lake Ladoga – by boat in summer and over the ice in winter. Around a million of the Leningrad population died either under bombardment or of starvation and disease. The terrible brutality of German rule in the occupied areas ensured that, even among people who had suffered injustice and oppression under Stalin, there were very few inclined to collaborate with the invaders.

German artillery shells a factory in Stalingrad in 1942. Named after the Soviet dictator, the city became a prize neither side felt they could afford to lose.

The survival of the Soviet Union came as a huge relief to Britain and the United States, who desperately needed Stalin as an ally against Hitler. Stalin equally need the Western Allies, who provided a generous flow of modern military equipment, delivered to the Red Army via the Arctic port of Murmansk. But in factories relocated to safety beyond the Ural mountains, the Soviets were also soon producing their own armaments in vast quantities, including tanks and aircraft that were a match for anything the Germans had.

In 1942, however, it still looked as if Hitler might win the war in the Soviet Union. In the first half of the year the Soviets exhausted their strength in a series of costly and largely unsuccessful counterattacks. The Germans then launched a devastating offensive in the south that carried them to the Caucasus mountains, threatening the vital Baku oilfields. At the same time, the German Sixth Army advanced on Stalingrad, a city on the Volga river.

The Germans reached the suburbs of Stalingrad in mid-September, but the Soviets defended the city building by building and street by street. Two months later, elements of the Red Army were still holding out in the city with their backs to the river. Then, on 19 November, Soviet forces counterattacked north and south of Stalingrad. They formed a noose around the city, with the German Sixth Army trapped inside. All efforts to break the iron ring around Stalingrad failed. Despite an impressive effort to supply the Sixth Army by air in terrible weather conditions, the German troops ran short of food and ammunition. On 31 January 1943 German Sixth Army commander Field Marshal Friedrich Paulus finally surrendered.

Stalingrad was a crushing defeat for Hitler and marked the turning point of the war. The Germans had reached the limits of their power. From then onwards, the forces ranged against Hitler would only get stronger, as the Soviet Union and the United States brought their vast reserves of manpower and industrial productivity to bear on the war.

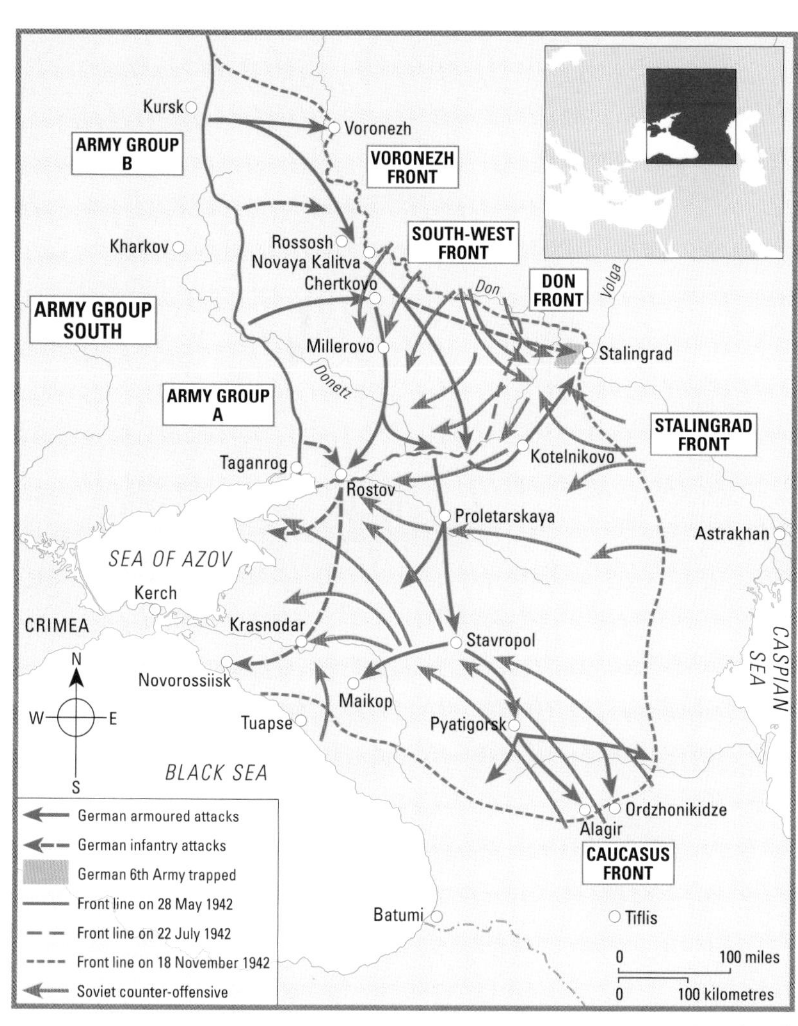

In the summer of 1942 the Germans advanced to Stalingrad and towards the oilfields in the Caucasus. The Soviet counter-offensive in November cut off the German army in Stalingrad.

Below: Some of the 91,000 German soldiers taken prisoner by the Soviets in the battle of Stalingrad: most would die in captivity.

LOSSES AT STALINGRAD

Although Stalingrad was a defeat for the Germans, it is generally accepted that Soviet casualties were heavier. They could afford such losses; the Germans could not. The majority of the German prisoners taken at Stalingrad died in captivity.

German losses: 147,000 dead, 91,000 prisoners

Soviet losses: c.500,000

CHAPTER 5: OCCUPIED EUROPE

At the peak of its success in the war, Nazi Germany controlled a vast area of Europe from the Atlantic to the Caucasus and from Norway to the Mediterranean. Every country on the European mainland except the Soviet Union had either been conquered, or was allied with Germany, or was a neutral that made itself useful to the Nazis.

Throughout German-occupied Europe there were shortages of food and other life essentials. Here French people search through refuse in the hope of finding scraps to eat.

At the end of 1942, German domination of Europe was at its fullest extent. The Wehrmacht had recently occupied Vichy France and pushed deep inside the Soviet Union.

> **MASTER RACE**
>
> Many Poles were deported to Germany for use as slave labour. Instructions issued by the Nazis to Germans who found themselves working alongside Poles stressed German racial superiority: *'Germans, the Pole is never your friend. He is inferior to every German on your farm or in your factory. Remember that you belong to the master nation.'*
>
> [Quoted in *The Second World War*, Henri Michel]

A French Resistance fighter is prepared for execution by a German firing squad. The Germans on many occasions executed groups of prisoners in retaliation for the killing of German officers or soldiers by the Resistance.

In most countries that the Nazis occupied (Poland was one exception) they found political movements that were keen to imitate Nazi policies and that collaborated enthusiastically with the occupiers. The Vichy French government of Marshal Pétain, for example, actively collaborated with the Nazis even before the area of France it governed was occupied by German troops, which did not happen until the end of 1942. Collaborators were often known as 'Quislings', after the Norwegian Nazi leader Vidkun Quisling, head of government in Occupied Norway.

STARVATION AND NEGLECT The scale of suffering under Nazi rule was almost unimaginable. Within Nazi-occupied Europe, many millions of people died in the course of the war – systematically or casually slaughtered by the Germans and their allies, or allowed to die of starvation or neglect.

The immediate demands of the war effort led the Germans to exploit conquered territories ever more intensely as the war became more desperate. For conquered peoples, this led to hardship and malnutrition. A growing labour shortage in Germany was met by forcibly importing hundreds of thousands of foreign workers, or using prisoners of war and inmates of concentration camps as slaves who were forced to work in factories and on building projects.

But the way the Nazis behaved was also based on their long-term aim to create a 'New Order' on the continent. The Nazi New Order was to be a Europe based on the domination of the so-called Aryan race – Germans and other blond, blue-eyed people – over the rest. The Slavs, regarded as sub-human, were to be either reduced to slavery or exterminated to make room for German settlers in the east. The Poles (a Slav people) lost about one in five of their population in the course of the war. Soviet prisoners of war (also Slavs) died in their millions in German camps, and further millions of Soviet citizens perished during the occupation. The Roma and Sinti (Gypsy) people of Europe also suffered grievously under Nazi rule.

THE JEWS The only people worse treated than the Slavs were the Jews. German military successes brought around eight million Jewish people under Nazi rule. There was no room for them in the Nazi New Order. Europe was to be 'cleansed' of Jews, strangely regarded by Hitler as a demonic race responsible for Germany's and the world's ills. From 1941 onwards, the Nazis embarked upon a 'Final Solution' of the 'Jewish problem'. They set out systematically to exterminate the Jewish people – men, women and children. At first, hundreds of thousands were killed by firing squad or gassed in the back of vans. Then death camps were established at sites inside occupied Poland – Majdanek, Chelmno, Treblinka, Sobibor, Belzec, Auschwitz – where Jews were killed in purpose-built gas chambers. The Nazis devoted massive resources to organizing the transportation of Jews from all over Europe to the death camps. It is estimated that about six million Jews were killed in the Holocaust.

The brutality of Nazi rule inevitably led to resistance. Secret movements were set up in all occupied countries. Their activities ranged from organizing acts of passive resistance such as strikes or the concealment of Jews from their persecutors, to sabotage, assassinations, uprisings and full-scale guerrilla warfare. The largest armed resistance movements were in the occupied areas of the Soviet Union and in Yugoslavia, where two mutually hostile guerrilla armies, one led by the communist Josip Broz Tito and the other by the Royalist Colonel Draza Mihailovic, fought the Germans, Italians and Croats. Other substantial partisan groups included those in the south of France and in northern Italy towards the end of the war.

Resistance movements pinned down considerable numbers of German troops which could have been used elsewhere in the war. In Poland, for example, when the underground Home Army staged an armed insurrection in Warsaw in 1944, more than 20,000

These ovens at the Dachau concentration camp in Germany were used to cremate the bodies of prisoners killed by the Nazis.

Jewish people deported to Auschwitz by the Germans wait to discover their fate. Many, including almost all children, were gassed to death within hours of arrival at Auschwitz.

German troops, backed by airpower, were engaged for two months in putting down the uprising. But resistance groups were never strong enough to drive out the occupation forces unaided.

Britain tried to encourage resistance through the Special Operations Executive (SOE), set up in 1940, later helped by the American Office of Strategic Services (OSS). The SOE and OSS sent secret agents into Occupied Europe, as well as delivering arms and equipment to resistance groups. These perilous operations cost many brave people their lives but had limited effect.

As well as encouraging resistance movements, between

The Nazi camps dedicated to the extermination of Jews were situated in the Polish General Government – German-occupied Poland. Concentration camps, used mostly to provide slave labour, were mainly in Germany. Auschwitz was both a concentration camp and an extermination camp.

A German soldier supervises the burial of massacred Polish Jews, probably in late 1941. The men digging would then also be killed.

SAVED BY SLAVERY

The lives of many Jews and Slavs were saved by the German need for slave labour in their factories, which led the Nazis reluctantly to keep them alive. Hitler's propaganda chief Joseph Goebbels wrote in his diary in March 1941: *'We have to go easy on the 30,000 Jews who work in armaments production; we need them – who would have thought this could ever become possible?'*

[Quoted in *The Holocaust*, R.G. Grant]

1940 and 1943 the Western Allies carried out a few scattered coastal raids on German-occupied Europe. The largest of these, a landing at Dieppe, northern France, by Canadian troops in August 1942, was a disaster, with over 3,000 of the 5,000 troops involved either killed or taken prisoner.

THE BOMBING OFFENSIVE

There was one way, however, in which the Allies could strike at the very heart of Germany. This was through air attack. From 1940 onwards RAF Bomber Command carried out raids on Germany and in 1942 the

US daylight bombing raids were at first launched from East Anglia in Britain. From 1943 onwards, bases in North Africa and Italy brought targets such as the Ploesti oilfields in Romania within range.

The scene in Hamburg after the devastation of the city by bombing in 1943. American bombers attacked Germany by day and the RAF did the same by night.

PROFIT AND LOSS

The effectiveness of the Allied bombing campaign has been much disputed. Huge resources were devoted to it – the RAF alone dropped almost a million tons of bombs on Germany. The RAF and USAAF also paid a heavy price in lost lives. Yet, as well as the damage it caused, the bombing offensive forced the Germans to devote major resources to homeland defence – it occupied the cream of their air force. The death toll among bomber crews and civilians was:
RAF Bomber Command aircrew 55,500 killed
USAAF Eighth Air Force aircrew 26,000 killed
German civilians killed 600,000

American B-24 Liberator bombers turn for home after raiding a German airfield.

US Army Air Force (USAAF) joined in the bombing campaign. Based in eastern England, the USAAF carried out its bombing raids by day, depending on the firepower of its high-flying bombers to hold off German fighter aircraft. The RAF bombed by night, relying on the cover of darkness to get through the enemy defences.

The bombing offensive was on a massive scale. In mid-1942 the RAF carried out raids with over a thousand bombers in the sky at the same time. The night raids were often inaccurate and the bombers suffered heavy losses, but they could have a devastating effect on cities. In one night in July 1943, an RAF raid on Hamburg is reckoned to have killed over 40,000 German civilians. Bombing by day, the Americans sought to be more accurate, aiming to hit specific factories or other economic or military targets. Bad weather and the intensity of German anti-aircraft defences meant, however, that the US bombers also often missed their targets and paid a high price. In August 1943, for example, the USAAF lost 60 bombers in a single day.

As the war went on, Allied bombing became increasingly effective. Allied advances in the Mediterranean meant that bombers were able to operate from North Africa and Italy as well as England. The introduction of the P-51 Mustang long-range fighter as a bomber escort in 1944 at last gave day bombers a real defence against German fighters. Improvements in navigation and tactics made even night bombers reasonably accurate. Although German factories never ceased to function, the bombing of sources of fuel supplies, especially the Ploesti oilfields in Romania, had a crippling effect on the German war machine in the last year of the war.

There was no let up in the air offensive as the war drew to a close. The Allied bombing of the city of Dresden in February 1945 may have killed over 50,000 people. By then most German cities, including the capital Berlin, had been reduced to ruins.

CHAPTER 6: THE TIDE TURNS

British troops wade ashore during the Allied invasion of Sicily in July 1943. This was the start of long hard fight up the Italian peninsula which continued for the rest of the war.

MONASTERY DESTROYED

One of the most controversial decisions of the war was made by Allied commanders in February 1944 when they ordered the bombing of the 1400-year-old monastery of Monte Cassino.

Commenting on the decision, General Eisenhower said: *'If we have to choose between destroying a famous building and sacrificing our own men, then our men's lives count infinitely more, and the buildings must go.'*

[Quoted on the Texas Military Forces Museum website]

By 1943 Britain and the United States were keen to invade mainland Europe to create a 'Second Front' that would bring relief to the Soviet Union, which was doing the bulk of the fighting against Germany. At a meeting held in Casablanca, Morocco, in January of that year, Roosevelt and Churchill chose Sicily as the target for their troops to re-enter Europe – a much easier option than attempting landings on the north coast of Occupied France.

North Africa was cleared of Axis forces in May 1943 (see page 23). The following July Allied troops – American and British Commonwealth in almost equal numbers – crossed the Mediterranean. With supremacy both in the air and at sea, the Allies carried off the landings fairly smoothly, but they had to overcome some stubborn resistance from German forces on the island. Sicily was in Allied hands by mid-August.

The invasion of Sicily was the final blow to the prestige of Italian dictator Benito Mussolini. He was deposed and replaced by an Italian army officer, Marshal Pietro Badoglio. Although Badoglio assured the Germans that Italy would carry on fighting, he secretly sought peace with the Allies. An armistice between Italy and the Allies was announced in early September, while the Allies invaded mainland Italy across the Straits of Messina from Sicily and by landing on the beaches at Salerno.

But the Germans, commanded by Field Marshal Albert Kesselring, were swift to disarm Italian troops and take over the defence of the Italian peninsula. The Salerno landings were fiercely resisted by German Panzers. Eventually forced to withdraw, the Germans pulled back in good order and stood firm along the Gustav Line, centred on the famous monastery of Monte Cassino. The advance of the Allied army – a multinational force including, among others, Poles, Indians, New Zealanders and French North African troops – ground to a halt. Cassino did not fall until mid-May, three months after the bombing of the monastery (see box above), after a lot more hard fighting to clear the Allied advance.

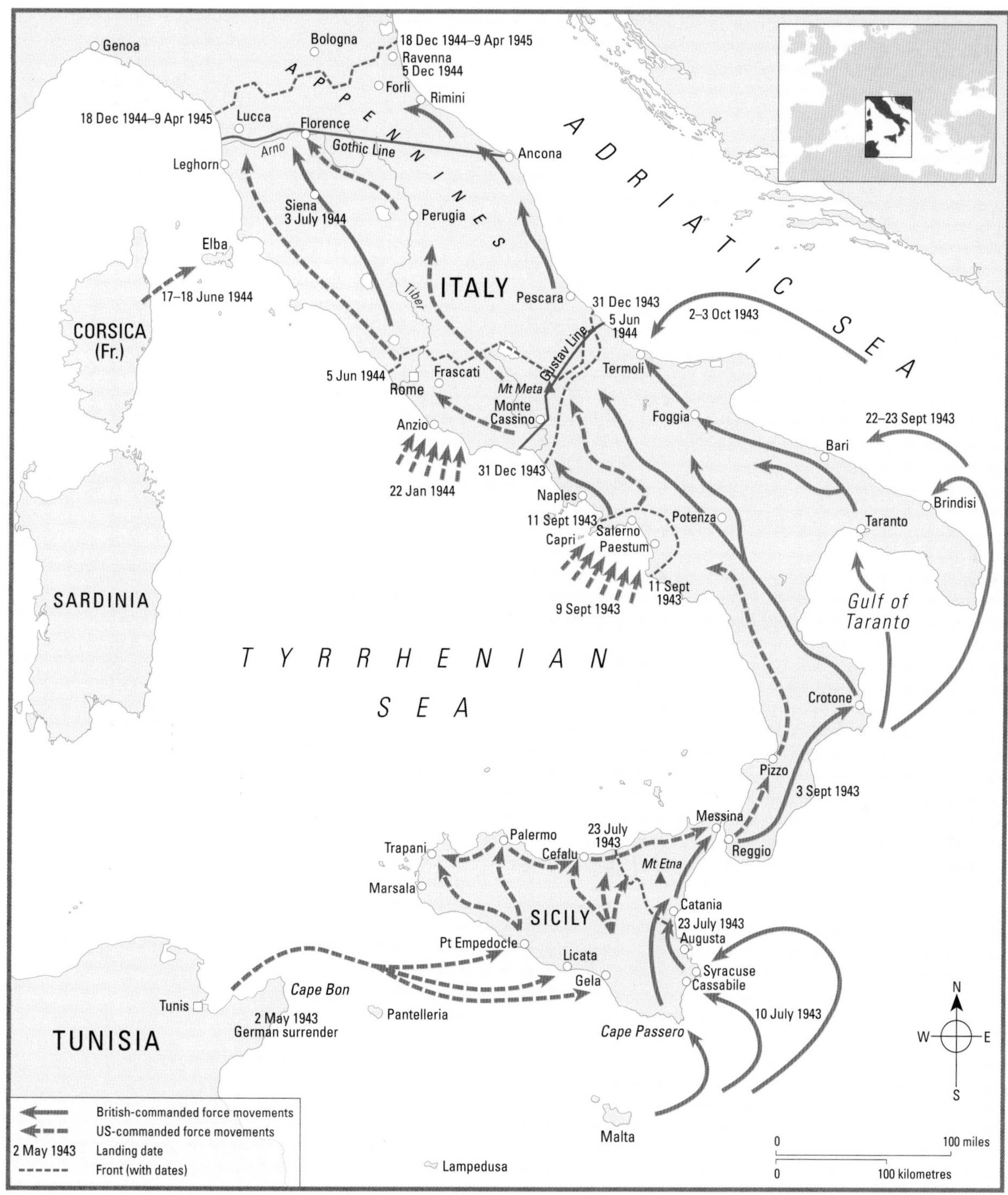

THE 'SOFT UNDERBELLY OF EUROPE' In an attempt to get the advance moving again, in January 1944 the Allies landed a force at Anzio, between the Gustav Line and Rome, but the Germans reacted swiftly and hemmed in the landing force. The Allies did not enter Rome until the following June – and they still faced a further series of German defensive lines to the north. Once optimistically described by Churchill as the 'soft underbelly of Europe', Italy had proved to be nothing of the sort.

The Allied occupation of Sicily and then the invasion of mainland Italy in September 1943 brought hopes of swift progress. But the advance stalled in front of Cassino, and despite the Anzio landings in January 1944, two years of fighting were needed to reach northern Italy.

Soviet Katyusha multiple rocket launchers – popularly known as 'Stalin's Organs' – prepare to fire during the Soviet counter-offensive against the German invaders. Fired in volleys, the rockets could deliver a devastating artillery barrage.

Soviet troops advance through a Polish city in 1944. Around one fifth of the Polish population died during the war, either killed in the fighting or massacred by one side or the other.

Although the fighting in Italy was fierce, it was dwarfed by the scale and savagery of the conflict on the eastern front. There the Soviet offensive of the winter of 1942-3, which had brought victory at Stalingrad, had carried the Red Army forwards to a line that pushed out west of the city of Kursk. In July 1943, the Germans launched an armoured counterattack against the Kursk salient, hoping for a crushing victory that would once more give them the upper hand. But for the first time the German armour and its air support had met their match. In the largest armoured battle ever seen, with more than 2,000 tanks committed on each side, the German offensive was repulsed and a Soviet counterattack forced the Germans to retreat.

BACK TOWARDS GERMANY From that point onwards, the tide of war on the eastern front flowed in only one direction – back towards Germany. The Soviets now had tanks and aircraft as good as, or better than, those of the Germans, and their commanders used them with flair and intelligence. In September 1943 the Red Army reached the Dniepr River, and the following November they took the Ukrainian capital, Kiev. Soviet casualties were consistently much higher than those suffered by the Germans, but the Germans were increasingly outnumbered. About three million Axis troops faced over six million Soviet soldiers at the end of 1943, and the Soviets had a similar superiority of numbers in tanks and aircraft.

The siege of Leningrad was lifted in February 1944 and by May most of the Ukraine and Crimea were back in Soviet hands. The greatest remaining obstacle to the Red Army's advance was German Army Group Centre, which continued to occupy Belorussia. In June 1944 the Soviets

After the victory at Kursk in the summer of 1943, the Soviet Red Army drove the Germans out of the Soviet Union. In the centre their advance came to a halt just short of Warsaw.

SEEING THE ENEMY

Journalist Alexander Werth saw German prisoners paraded through Moscow in the summer of 1944. He described the reaction of the people who gathered to see their enemies in the flesh:

'The Moscow crowd was remarkably disciplined. They watched these Germans walk, or rather shuffle past, in their dirty green-grey uniforms. … I heard a little girl perched on her mother's shoulder say, "Mummy, are these the people who killed Daddy?" And the mother hugged the child and wept.'

[Cited in the *Faber Book of Reportage*, ed. John Carey]

launched Operation Bagration, a vast and complex offensive that in five weeks drove Army Group Centre hundreds of kilometres back across the pre-war Soviet border into Poland.

At the end of July the Red Army's advance in Poland stopped on the east bank of the Vistula, the river that runs through the Polish capital, Warsaw. The Soviets took no action to help the Polish Home Army's uprising in the city (see pages 32-3), which was put down by the Germans with such ferocity that over 200,000 Polish civilians were killed. The Soviet advance continued further south, however. In the second half of 1944 Soviet forces entered Romania, Hungary and Yugoslavia, reaching the outskirts of the Hungarian capital, Budapest, by the end of the year.

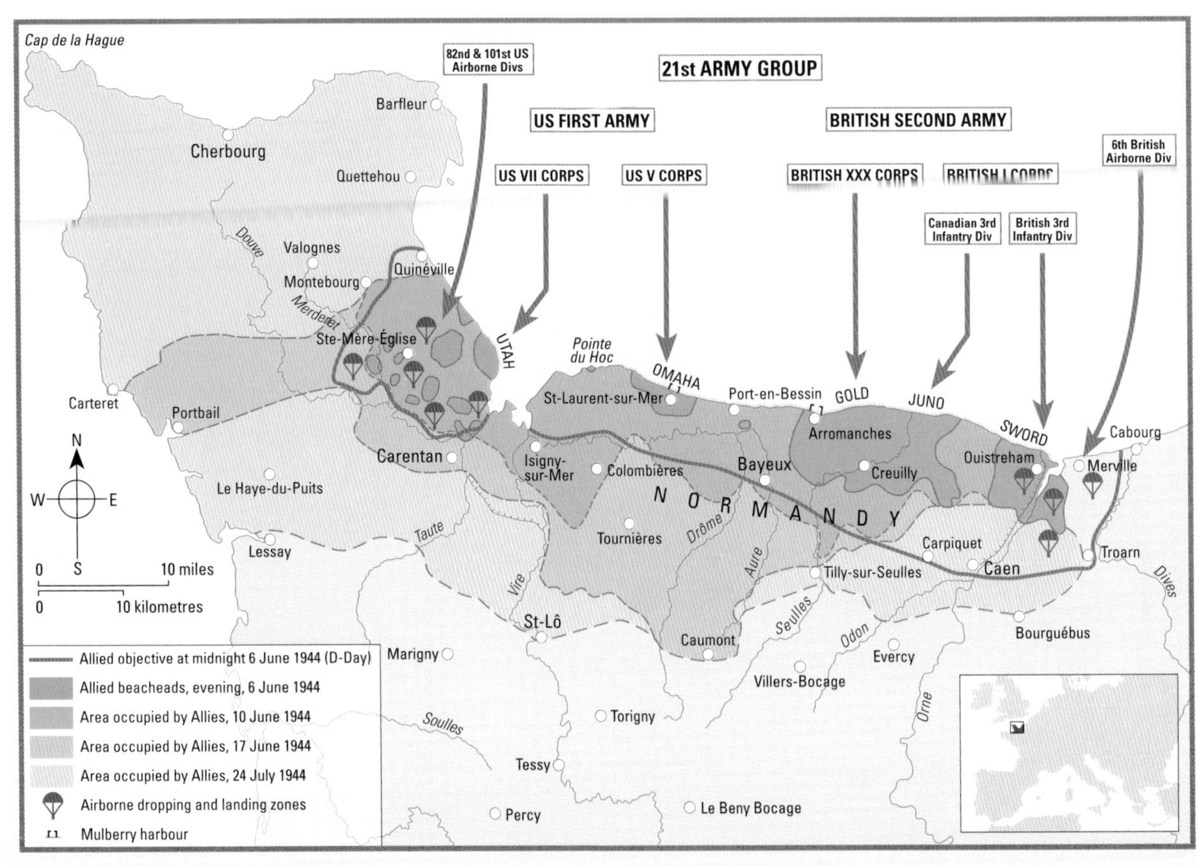

D-DAY LANDINGS

Landing over 130,000 men on fortified beaches, the Allies expected heavier casualties on D-Day, 6 June 1944, than they actually suffered:

Troops landed

75,215 British and Canadian

57,500 American

Casualties

4,300 British and Canadian

6,000 American

The beaches chosen for the D-Day landings were code-named Utah, Omaha, Gold, Juno and Sword.

American troops wade ashore on Omaha beach during the Normandy landings.

Allied Supreme Commander Dwight Eisenhower talking to men of the US 101st Airborne Division in advance of the D-Day Normandy landings.

The desperate situation of the Germans on the eastern front was matched by the situation in the west. On 6 June 1944 – known as D-Day – the Western Allies began the long-awaited invasion of France with landings on the coast of Normandy. Carefully planned under the direction of Allied Supreme Commander General Dwight Eisenhower, Operation Overlord was the largest seaborne invasion ever launched, involving 1,200 warships, 5,000 landing craft and troop transports, and 10,000 aircraft. Two artificial harbours ('Mulberries') were towed across the Channel, so the army could be supplied and reinforced once ashore.

UTAH, OMAHA, GOLD, JUNO AND SWORD All the careful preparation was almost undone by the weather, which was so rough it seemed the invasion would have to be abandoned. Gambling on a brief break in the storms predicted by weather forecasters, however, Eisenhower embarked his US, British and Canadian troops in southern England for a night-time crossing to France. Airborne troops were dropped into Normandy under cover of darkness, and at dawn the seaborne troops landed on five beaches – codenamed Utah, Omaha, Gold, Juno and Sword.

The invaders had some key advantages. Their command of the air and the sea was such that the German air force and navy barely interfered. A clever deception plan had convinced Hitler that the invasion would come in the area around Calais (a port about 250 km north-east along the coast), so that even when news of the landings came through, he remained convinced that it was only a diversionary attack. The destruction of communications links by Allied bombers in any case made it hard for the Germans to move reinforcements swiftly to Normandy.

Yet the success of the landings was a close-run affair. The coast was heavily fortified. On Omaha beach, the American 1st Infantry Division suffered heavy casualties and was very nearly driven back into the sea. When a beachhead was established, progress was still slow. Montgomery's British and Canadian troops took over a month to capture Caen, a town they had hoped to occupy on the first day of the invasion. The weather remained a problem, with low cloud blocking air operations and storms wrecking one of the Mulberry harbours in the third week of June. The capture of the port of Cherbourg at the end of the month was a step forwards, but the failure to break through encircling German defences meant that

A French woman takes a close look at a knocked out German tank in a Normandy town. The German panzers fought skilfully and tenaciously, but they were vulnerable to Allied air attack.

US paratroopers advance as shells explode around them during Operation Market Garden in 1944.

growing numbers of Allied troops and quantities of supplies were bottled up in north-west Normandy.

In late July, while Canadian and British forces engaged the bulk of the German armoured divisions, US forces at last made the long-awaited breakout from Normandy, fanning out from Avranches west into Brittany and east towards the River Seine. The Germans launched a counterattack against Avranches, but suffered heavy losses and were threatened with encirclement as Canadian troops from the north prepared to link up with Americans swinging up from the south near the town of Falaise. Many of the Germans managed to escape eastwards before the 'Falaise Gap' was closed on 20 August, but nothing could now stop the Allies' rapid progress. On the same day, the spearhead of the US forces crossed the Seine.

On 15 August a new front had been opened by Allied landings in Provence on France's Mediterranean coast. The French Resistance was in open armed revolt, taking on the German army in many parts of France, including Paris. A Free French armoured division was allowed the honour of liberating the city on 25 August, preparing the way for Free French leader General Charles de Gaulle to form a new government to replace the discredited Vichy regime.

SUMMER 1944 In the heady days of summer 1944 it was easy to imagine that the war in Europe would be over by the end of the year. Two million Allied troops, 60 per cent of them from the USA, were advancing on Germany from the west while the largest part of the German army was still forced to remain facing the Soviets in the east. Montgomery's British Second Army liberated the Belgian capital, Brussels, in the first week of September, by which time General George Patton's US Third Army had reached the Moselle River, only 160 km from the Rhine.

At this point, though, the Allies lost momentum. In Belgium, they captured the major port of Antwerp intact, with the help of the Belgian Resistance, but were unable to use it immediately because the

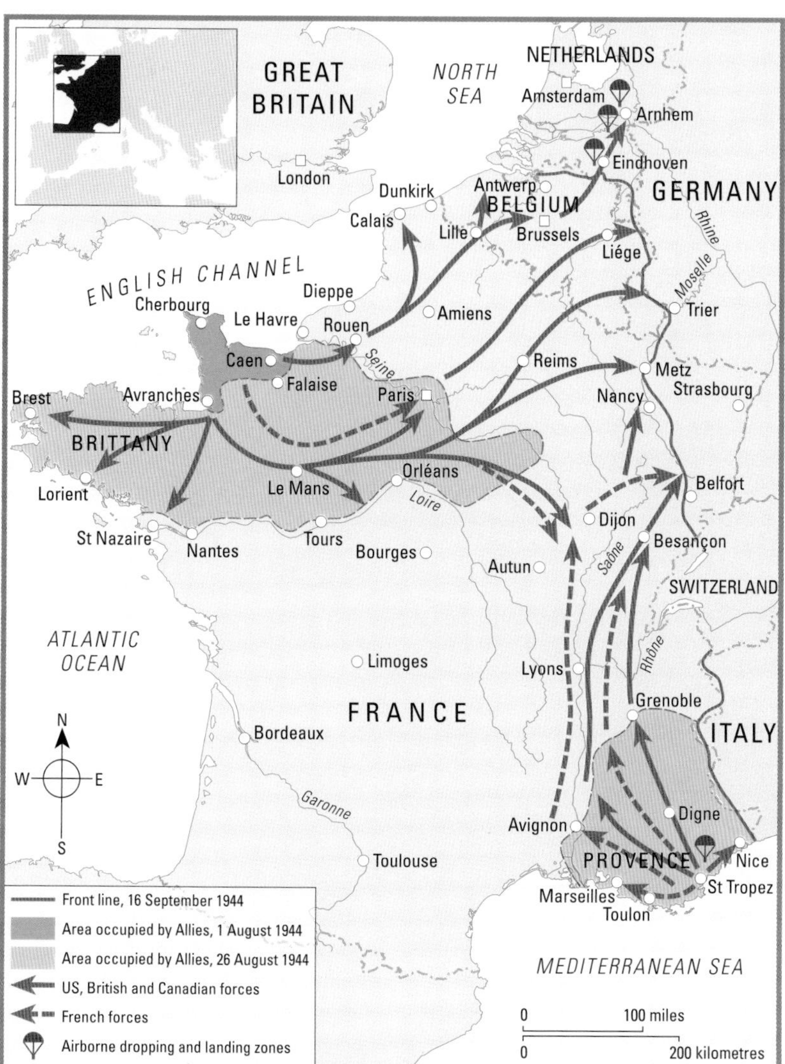

The liberation of France was achieved in August-September 1944, but the attempted breakthrough into Germany via Arnhem was a failure.

GERMAN WEAKNESS

It has often been debated whether a more vigorous offensive strategy could have allowed Allied troops to break through into Germany in the autumn of 1944. A German officer, General Westphal, wrote after the war: *'The overall situation in the West was serious in the extreme... Until the middle of October [1944] the enemy could have broken through at any point he liked with ease, and would have then been able to cross the Rhine and thrust deep into Germany almost unhindered.'*

[Quoted in *History of the Second World War*, B. H. Liddel Hart]

Germans remained in control of the River Scheldt leading into the port. It became increasingly difficult to keep the Allied armies supplied via now distant Normandy ports, and the advance ground to a halt.

In a bold attempt to end the war quickly, on 17 September Montgomery launched Operation Market Garden. Some 20,000 Allied airborne troops were dropped into the Occupied Netherlands by parachute and glider. They were to seize and hold a series of key bridges, allowing Allied tanks to drive across the Netherlands and into the Ruhr, Germany's industrial heartland. But the final river crossing, at Arnhem, proved 'a bridge too far'. British paratroops could not hold it and the armoured column failed to reach it in time. This failure condemned the Allies to continue fighting through the winter into 1945.

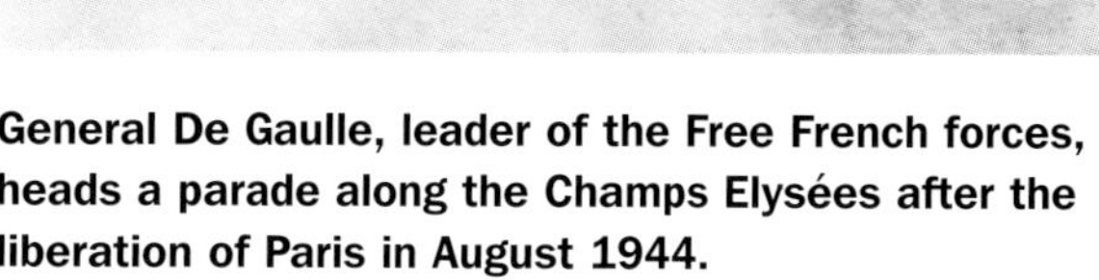

General De Gaulle, leader of the Free French forces, heads a parade along the Champs Elysées after the liberation of Paris in August 1944.

CHAPTER 7:
THE ROAD TO BERLIN

American tanks struggle to cope with the weather conditions in northern France during the Battle of the Bulge in the winter of 1944-5.

By the summer of 1944 many senior German army officers were desperate to end the war before it resulted in the total destruction of their country. They led a plot to assassinate Hitler, overthrow the Nazi regime and sue for peace. On 20 July 1944 the conspirators planted a time bomb at Hitler's headquarters in East Prussia. But although the explosion injured the dictator, he survived. Almost all those who had plotted against him were arrested and cruelly executed.

It was far from certain that a non-Nazi German regime could have negotiated a peace deal, since the Allies had adopted a policy of 'unconditional surrender' – meaning that the Germans must simply accept defeat and allow the victors to do with them what they pleased. It was certain, though, that with Hitler alive peace was out of the question. Hitler would never agree to surrender, so the total conquest of Germany was the only sure path to end the war.

Faced with an apparently hopeless situation, Hitler put his faith in German 'secret weapons' which entered the war in 1944. One of these, the first jet aircraft, had only a marginal effect on the conflict. Of more impact

FAITH IN VICTORY

Hitler's generals felt that the December 1944 Ardennes offensive was absurdly over-ambitious. According to Field Marshal Gerd von Rundstedt, ordinary German soldiers did not share this scepticism: *'The morale of the troops taking part was astonishingly high at the start of the offensive. They really believed victory was possible – unlike the higher commanders, who knew the facts.'*

[Quoted in *History of the Second World War*, B. H. Liddel Hart]

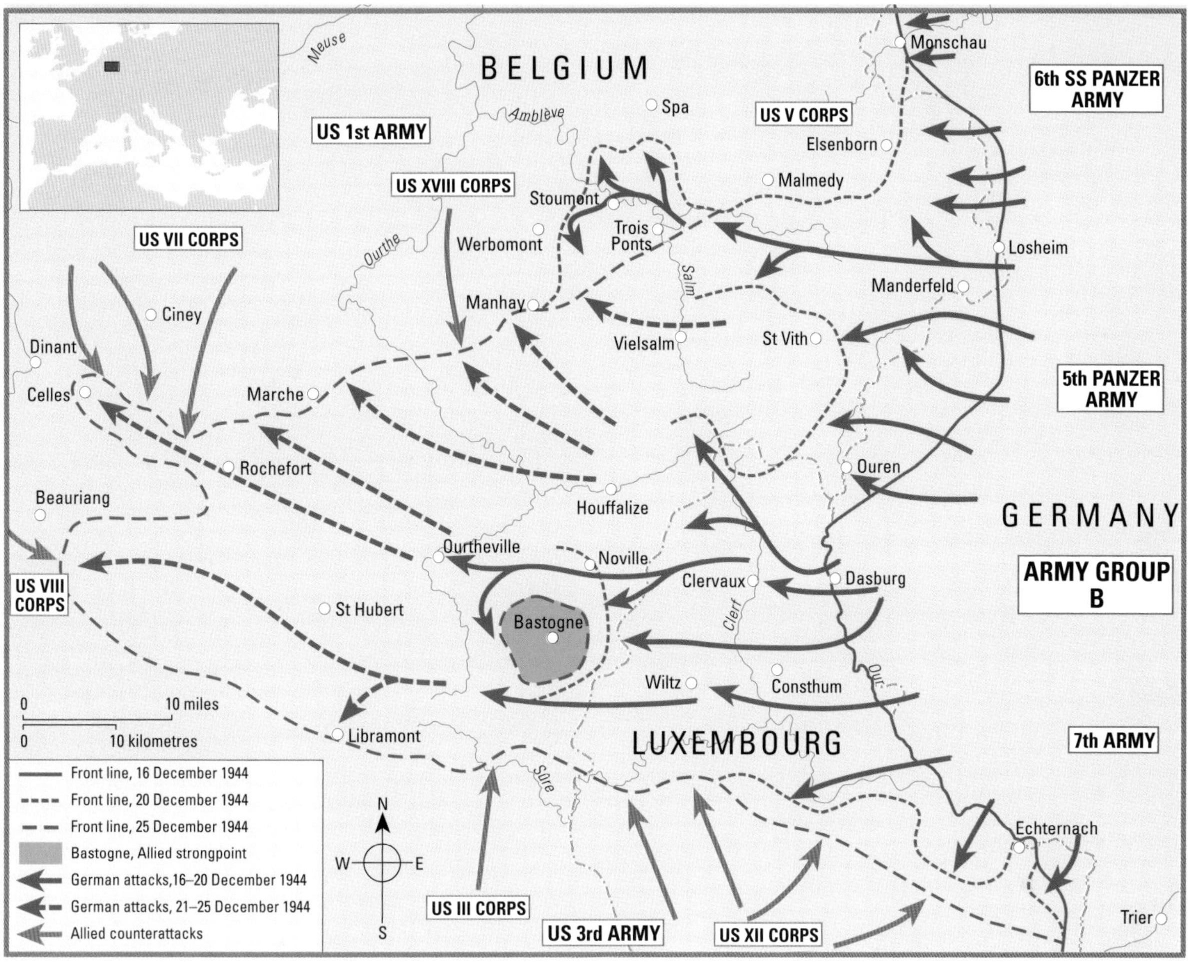

The German offensive of winter 1944 is known as the Battle of the Bulge because of the way it pushed into Allied-held territory.

were the 'V weapons'. The V-1 was a pilotless aircraft packed with explosives. The V-2 was the world's first supersonic ballistic missile – the forerunner of all today's space rockets. Fired chiefly at London and Antwerp, the V-1s and V-2s did a lot of damage. Together they killed almost 9,000 people in England. But they fell far short of having a decisive effect – for that they would have needed a nuclear warhead.

A V-1 pilotless aircraft photographed over Britain in 1945. The V-1 would dive when its fuel ran out, exploding on contact with the ground.

ARMOURED OFFENSIVE – BATTLE OF THE BULGE Let down by his secret weapons, in December 1944 Hitler decided to gamble on a shock German counterattack. In virtually a repeat of May 1940, he ordered an armoured offensive through the Ardennes region of Belgium. The tanks were to break through the Allied lines and advance rapidly across the River Meuse to the coast, taking the vital port of Antwerp.

Launched on 16 December, the Ardennes offensive (popularly known as the Battle of the Bulge) at first had just the success Hitler must have hoped for. The Ardennes front was thinly held by American forces and surprise was complete. Allied aircraft, which could have countered the German advance, were grounded by severe winter weather.

The Americans, however, reacted swiftly. Reinforcements were rushed in, tripling the US forces in the Ardennes within four days. American soldiers, especially those encircled at Bastogne, fought with great bravery. The German forces never reached the Meuse. On 23 December the weather lifted and Allied aircraft struck against the exposed enemy forces. On 26 December Patton's armour, on the advance from Normandy, relieved Bastogne (see page 45). By then German tanks and aircraft were running out of fuel. Through January 1945, in deep snow, the Germans made a fighting withdrawal back into their homeland. They had suffered around 100,000 casualties, as well as losing hundreds of aircraft and most of their tanks. Hitler had made his last gamble and lost.

The only hope left to the German dictator was that the Western Allies and the Soviet Union would fall out. But in February 1945 Roosevelt, Churchill and Stalin, meeting at the Ukrainian port of Yalta in the Crimea (see page 25), reached broad agreement on the

NOBLE CRUSADE

The Allied advance revealed to the outside world the full horror of the Nazi death camps and concentration camps. For most people, this removed any doubts about whether the war was justified. British historian A.J.P. Taylor, who lived through World War II, wrote: *'No English soldier who rode with the tanks into liberated Belgium or saw the German murder camps at Dachau or Buchenwald could doubt that the war had been a noble crusade.'*

[From *English History 1914-1945*, A.J.P. Taylor]

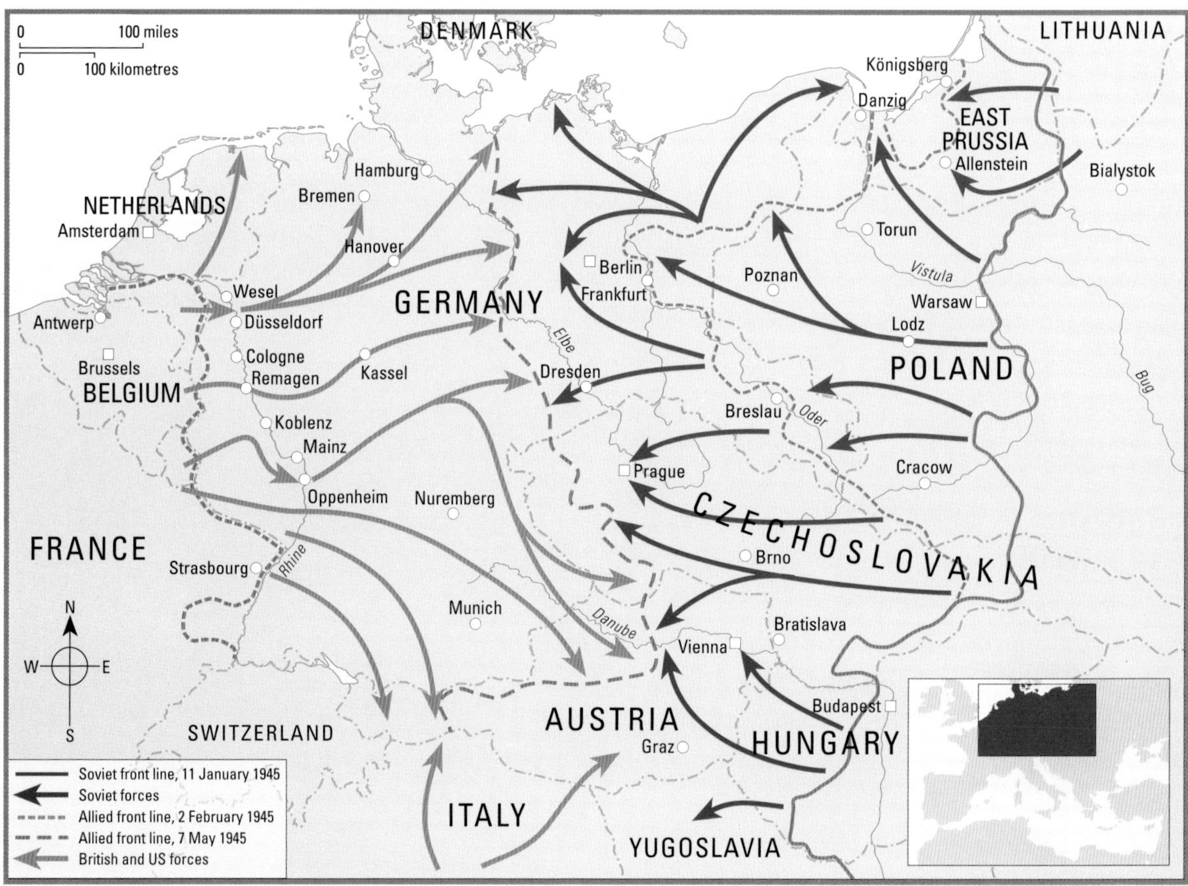

Germany was crushed between the Soviet forces advancing from the east and the Western Allies.

Hitler's last public appearance was in March 1945 when he distributed medals to members of the Hitler Youth movement.

immediate future of a conquered Germany.

On 12 January, the Red Army launched a massive offensive from the River Vistula, where they had halted five months earlier. They carried all before them, overrunning Poland and crossing into Germany by the end of the month, when their spearhead was only 65 km from Berlin. Further south, Soviet forces besieging Budapest in Hungary seized control of the city in mid-February, taking over 100,000 German prisoners.

ON THE WESTERN FRONT On the western front, Allied troops reached the banks of the Rhine in the first week in March. The Germans destroyed all the bridges across the river well in advance of the arrival of Allied forces, except at Remagen where the Americans found a single bridge intact and crossed it on 7 March. It was another fortnight before further Rhine crossings were made, by Patton in the south at Oppenheim and, shortly afterwards, by Montgomery in the north at Wesel.

Germany's situation was hopeless. Poorly armed members of the *Volkssturm*, Germany's Home Guard, were drafted into the front line to reinforce its vastly outnumbered and outgunned armies. German roads were crammed with refugees fleeing westwards in front of the advancing Soviet forces. Hitler, now installed in

Survivors in Dachau camp cheer their liberation by the US Army on 3 May 1945.

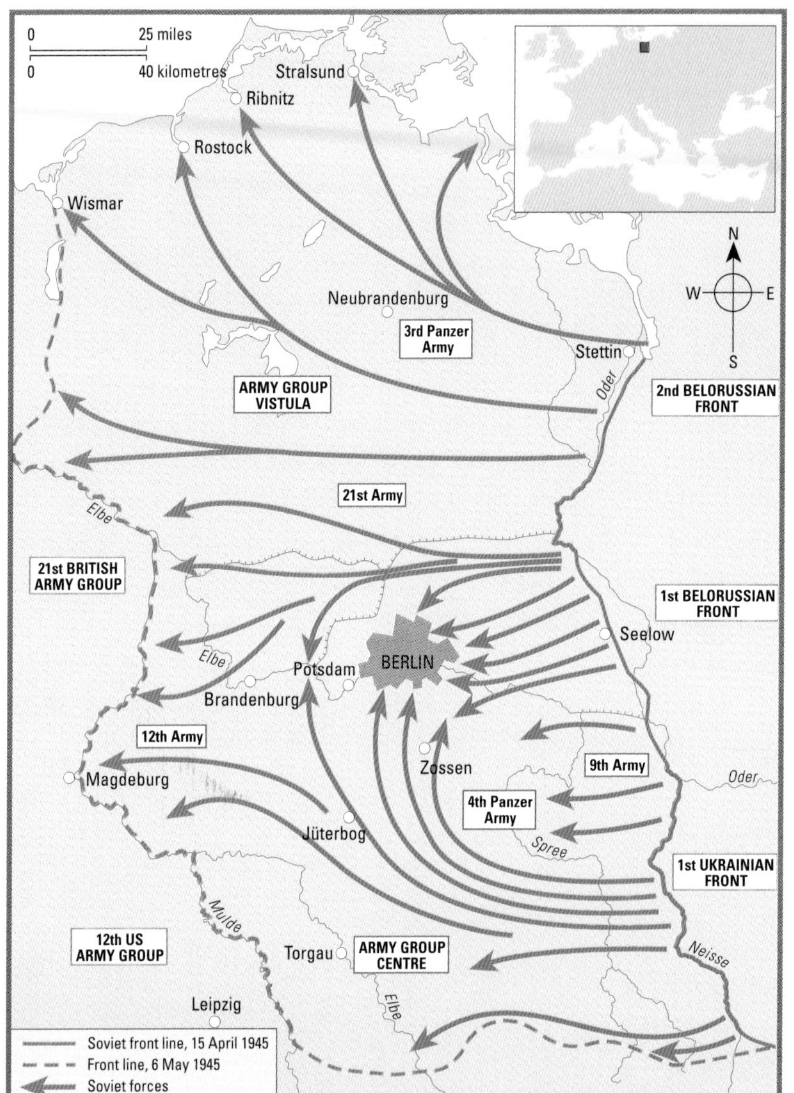

The First Belorussian Front, commanded by Marshal Zhukov, attacked Berlin directly from the east, while other Soviet forces joined in from south and north.

THE NATION WILL PERISH

Hitler was determined that if he was to go down, Germany would be destroyed with him. He gave orders to lay the country waste in the path of the invaders, saying: *'If the war is lost the German nation will perish. So there is no need to consider what the people require for continued existence.'*

[Quoted in *History of the Second World War*, B.H. Liddel Hart]

a bunker in Berlin, still clutched at straws. The death of President Roosevelt on 12 April was seized upon by the Nazis as a possible miracle that might save their skins – but Allied policy did not change.

Refusing to be drawn into a race with his Soviet allies, General Eisenhower decided to allow the Red Army to take the honour – and the heavy casualties – involved in the capture of Berlin. The Western Allies concentrated on mopping up in central Germany, accepting the surrender of over 300,000 German soldiers in the Ruhr in mid-April. On 25 April Soviet and US forces advancing from east and west met at Torgau on the Elbe River. By that time troops commanded by Russian Marshal Georgi Zhukov were fighting their way into the Berlin suburbs. The battle raged from street to street ever deeper into the heart of the city. As the sound of gunfire drew near to his bunker, Hitler committed suicide on 30 April.

Hitler's death did not immediately halt the fighting, which stuttered on until ended by a series of separate local surrenders. In Italy Mussolini, who had been running a puppet government under German control since his fall from power, was captured by Italian partisans and shot on 28 April. The following day the German commanders in Italy signed an unconditional surrender. German forces in Berlin surrendered on 2 May – taking the city had cost the Soviets around 300,000 casualties – and the armies in north-west Germany followed suit on 4 May. Finally, on 7 May General Alfred Jodl signed a general unconditional surrender of all German forces, to take effect the following day.

WHEN THE FIGHTING STOPPED

Despite the vast scale of the war, it was not followed by any great peace conference setting out to redraw the map of Europe. When the leaders of the victorious Allies met at Potsdam, west of Berlin, in July 1945, the main item on the agenda was the still continuing war with Japan. Most questions regarding Europe were either settled according to agreements that had been made in the course of the war or resolved by whoever was in military control of a given place when the fighting stopped.

As they had agreed during the war, the Allies divided the defeated Germany into four occupation zones – American, British, French and Soviet. Berlin was deep inside the Soviet zone, but it too was divided between the four Allied powers, each occupying a sector of the city. Austria, once more separated from Germany, was similarly divided into occupation zones.

The western border of the Soviet Union remained what it had become in 1941, so the Soviets kept the gains they made early in the war, including the takeover of the Baltic Republics and of eastern Poland. In compensation, Poland was allowed to take land from Germany in the west – so Poland in effect physically shifted westwards. Otherwise, changes of borders in Europe were quite small. Czechoslovakia, Yugoslavia, Austria and Hungary were broadly returned to the shape they had been given after World War I – the largest change was that Yugoslavia took Istria from Italy.

American and Soviet troops meet at Torgau on the Elbe river on 25 April 1945. There was genuine warmth of feeling between soldiers of the Western Allies and their Soviet counterparts at this time.

The Soviet flag is raised over the Reichstag building in Berlin, 30 April 1945.

Nazi leaders on trial at Nuremberg in September 1945.

IMPOSING A SYSTEM

During World War II Stalin told a fellow communist: *'This war is not as in the past. Whoever occupies a territory also imposes on it his own social system. Everyone imposes his own system as far as his army can reach. It cannot be otherwise.'*
[Quoted in *Russia's War*, Richard Overy]

In the years immediately after the war, much effort was put into the 'de-Nazification' of Germany and the prosecution of Germans for war crimes (the Nuremberg Trials). The problem of German minorities outside the borders of Germany – the issue that Hitler had exploited so successfully in the 1930s – was settled crudely and brutally by driving them out of their homes. All the Sudeten Germans, for example, were expelled from Czechoslovakia. In total some ten million German refugees, who had fled or been deported from lands to the east, had to make new lives for themselves in Germany.

Victory in the war had carried Soviet armies deep into the heart of Europe. They did not go home for over forty years. The Soviet Union set about installing a communist political and social system in the countries under its military control – Poland, Romania, Hungary, Bulgaria and Czechoslovakia – while in Yugoslavia the wartime resistance leader Tito also established a communist regime.

The United States, under the leadership of President Harry S. Truman, was from 1947 committed to the task of resisting the spread of communism worldwide. The Americans took steps to prevent communist parties taking power in Western Europe, including funding the Marshall Plan, a programme to rebuild West European economies and thus encourage social stability. In 1949, through the North Atlantic Treaty Organization (NATO), the United States pledged to defend Western Europe against attack by the Soviet Union. Like the Soviets, the American forces had come to stay.

Because of the rift between the wartime allies, in Germany the military occupation zones solidified into a political divide. The American, British and French zones became West Germany (the German Federal Republic) and the Russian zone became communist-ruled East Germany (the German Democratic Republic). The Soviets tried but failed to force the Western powers to withdraw from Berlin by a blockade in 1948-9, and West Berlin was left as a western outpost deep inside East Germany. The dividing line between communist-ruled Eastern Europe and the West – a physical barrier of concrete, barbed wire, armed guards and minefields – was dubbed the 'Iron Curtain'. A durable legacy of World War II, the curtain was not lifted until 1989.

The results of World War II were by no means entirely negative, however. The experience of destruction on such a massive scale was a major motive for Britain, France, Germany and Italy to sink their old differences and become partners in the European Union and NATO. A war between them became unthinkable. Remarkably, the people of Europe and their governments really had learned a lesson from history.

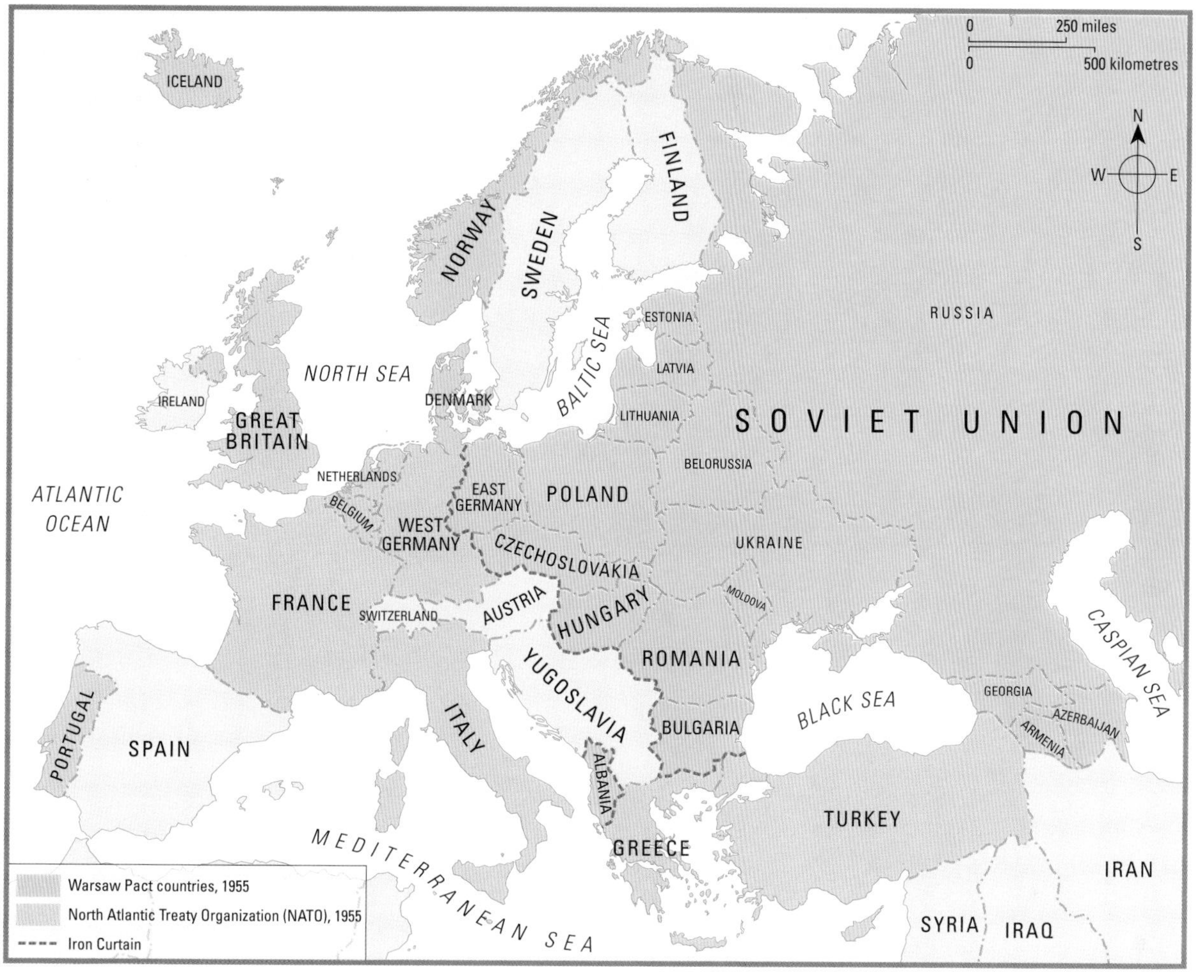

By the mid-1950s, Europe was divided between a Western alliance headed by the United States and the countries east of the Iron Curtain dominated by the USSR.

The wall that divided Berlin from 1961 to 1989 – the most visible symbol of the division of Europe that followed World War II.

PROFILES OF MILITARY AND POLITICAL LEADERS

FIELD MARSHAL SIR HAROLD ALEXANDER (1891-1969)
Alexander commanded the British rearguard which held off the Germans during the evacuation of Dunkirk in June 1940 – he was the last British officer to leave France. In August 1942 he was appointed British Commander-in-Chief in the Middle East. He oversaw the victories in North Africa from Alamein to Tunisia, the invasion of Sicily and the Italian campaign. By the end of the war Alexander was Allied Supreme Commander in the Mediterranean.

GENERAL OMAR BRADLEY (1893-1981)
After distinguishing himself as a corps commander in Tunisia and Sicily in 1943, Bradley commanded the American forces at the D-Day landings in Normandy. During the campaign in Europe that followed, he commanded Twelfth US Army Group. His swift decision-making was to a large degree responsible for the defeat of the German Ardennes offensive in December 1944.

WINSTON CHURCHILL (1874-1965)
As a Member of Parliament in the 1930s, Churchill led opposition to Prime Minister Neville Chamberlain's policy of appeasing Germany. He joined the government as First Lord of the Admiralty at the outbreak of war

and in May 1940 replaced Chamberlain as prime minister, heading a coalition government including both Conservative and Labour politicians. In the summer of 1940 his policy of no-surrender carried the day against defeatists in the government and his defiant speeches helped sustain British morale. He travelled widely during the war, at considerable personal risk, to maintain personal contact with Britain's Soviet and American allies. Two months after victory in Europe, he was defeated in a general election.

GENERAL MARK CLARK (1896-1984)
Clark was US Deputy Supreme Commander, under Eisenhower, for the November 1942 landings in North Africa. He subsequently commanded the Fifth Army in the Italian campaign, from the Salerno landings in September 1943 to the German surrender in Italy at the end of April 1945.

GENERAL CHARLES DE GAULLE (1890-1970)
Before the war, de Gaulle was a modernizing French officer who vainly urged the French Army to adopt mobile warfare using tanks and aircraft. After fighting in the campaign of May-June 1940 in France, he fled to Britain and established the Free French movement as a rallying point for those opposed to the pro-German French government at Vichy. When France was liberated in 1944, de Gaulle headed a provisional government. Largely as a result of his efforts, France was recognized as one of the victorious allies in 1945, alongside Britain, the US and the Soviet Union.

ADMIRAL KARL DOENITZ (1891-1980)
Doenitz was appointed head of the German U-boat force in 1935. He masterminded the use of submarines in 'wolf packs' – coordinated groups hunting down merchant ships. Commander-in-Chief of the German Navy from 1943, Doenitz was chosen by Hitler to succeed him as German head of state, a position he briefly held until arrested by the Allies in May 1945.

SIR HUGH DOWDING (1882-1970)
Commander-in-Chief of RAF Fighter Command from 1936, Dowding played a large part in

organizing Britain's radar-based air defences before the war. In May-June 1940 he resisted pressure to send too many RAF fighter aircraft to join the battle in France. During the Battle of Britain in July-September 1940 he made masterly use of limited numbers of men and aircraft to deny the *Luftwaffe* air supremacy.

GENERAL DWIGHT D. EISENHOWER (1890-1969)

Eisenhower was given command of the Allied invasion of French North Africa in November 1942. He proved so adept at the difficult task of making British and American generals work together that he was made Supreme Commander for the Normandy landings in 1944. During the subsequent campaign in Europe he was sometimes criticized for his cautious approach, preferring an advance on a broad front and refusing to race the Soviets to Berlin. After the war Eisenhower entered politics, becoming US President from 1953 to 1961.

REICHSMARSHALL HERMANN GOERING (1893-1946)

An ace pilot in World War I, Goering joined Hitler's Nazi Party in its early days in 1922. A powerful figure in the Nazi regime after 1933, he took a special interest in building up the *Luftwaffe*. In 1940 he boasted that the *Luftwaffe* would bring Britain to its knees. The *Luftwaffe's* failure dealt a crushing blow to his prestige. After the war, he was condemned to death at the Nuremberg War Crimes Trial but committed suicide before he could be executed.

GENERAL HEINZ GUDERIAN (1888-1954)

A leading tank expert in the 1930s, Guderian helped develop the Blitzkrieg style of fast-moving armoured warfare. His panzer corps played a leading role in the German victory in France in May-June 1940. Guderian led the 2nd Panzer Group in the invasion of the Soviet Union, but he was sacked by Hitler in December 1941 for withdrawing against specific orders to the contrary. Restored to favour, he was chief of the army general staff in 1944 when he again quarrelled with Hitler. He was on indefinite sick leave when the war ended.

AIR CHIEF MARSHAL SIR ARTHUR HARRIS (1892-1984)

Harris became commander-in-chief of RAF Bomber Command in 1942. He believed that bombing German cities would be a sure way of winning the war if only enough resources were devoted to it. After the controversial bombing of Dresden in February 1945, he was criticized for having led a campaign that caused the deaths of hundreds of thousands of German civilians.

ADOLF HITLER (1889-1945)

As leader of the Nazi Party Hitler became German Chancellor in 1933 and Führer ('leader') in 1935. By 1938 he had effectively achieved total control over the German officer corps. In World War II he insisted on taking major military decisions himself. The swift successes of the first years of the war confirmed Hitler's view of himself as an infallible Man of Destiny. His subsequent mishandling of the war with the Soviet Union brought disaster on the German Army. After surviving an assassination attempt by German officers in July 1944, he killed himself in his Berlin bunker on 30 April 1945.

FIELD MARSHAL ERICH VON MANSTEIN (1887-1973)

As a German staff officer in the winter of 1939-40, Manstein suggested a new strategy for the invasion of France, in which the main thrust would pass through the Ardennes instead of through northern Belgium. He won backing for this idea from Hitler, who overruled the German High Command. The brilliant success of Manstein's strategy was matched by his skill in the command of troops in the field, both in the defeat of France and subsequently in the invasion of the Soviet Union. In March 1944 Hitler sacked him for retreating in the face of overwhelming Soviet forces. After the war Manstein was charged with war crimes and spent four years in prison.

GENERAL OF THE ARMY GEORGE C. MARSHALL (1880-1959)
Marshall was US Army chief of staff from 1939 to 1945 – he took up the post on the day the war in Europe began. He energetically pursued the expansion and modernization of the US Army before America's entry into the war in December 1941. Once the United States was at war, he consistently supported the view that the defeat of Germany had to be given priority over the war in the Pacific. He retired from the army in 1945 and became US Secretary of State from 1947 to 1949. During that time he helped promote the recovery of Europe through the Marshall Plan. For this he was awarded the Nobel Peace Prize in 1953.

FIELD MARSHAL SIR BERNARD MONTGOMERY (1887-1976)

After performing creditably during the disastrous campaign in France and Belgium in 1940, Montgomery was appointed to command the Eighth Army in North Africa in August 1942. The victory at El Alamein the following October made him a national hero. He fought in Sicily and Italy before becoming Allied Land Commander for the Normandy invasion in June 1944 and eventually leading Allied forces into northern Germany in 1945. A great believer in methodical planning and the crushing of the enemy through superior forces, Montgomery was often criticized by US generals for being slow and excessively cautious.

BENITO MUSSOLINI (1883-1945)
As Italian dictator ('Il Duce') from the 1920s Mussolini claimed to be recreating the glory of the ancient Roman Empire – but he was privately well aware of the weakness of his army and his country's economy. In June 1940 he declared war on Britain and France, hoping to sneak advantage from a war won by Germany. A string of military disasters led to his fall from power in July 1943. Rescued from prison by German paratroops the following September, Mussolini was set up as head of a puppet Italian government in northern Italy. In April 1945, he was captured by Italian partisans and executed.

GENERAL GEORGE PATTON (1885-1945)
America's most inspired commander of armoured formations, Patton played a leading role in the fighting in Tunisia and Sicily in 1942-3. In 1944 he commanded the 3rd US Army in Normandy and in the subsequent breakout across France. In December 1944, his swiftness of response was crucial to the defeat of the German Ardennes offensive. Patton was, however, a controversial figure, nearly losing his command because of his aggressive attitude towards soldiers suffering from combat fatigue.

FIELD MARSHAL ERWIN ROMMEL (1891-1944)
Rommel performed impressively as a tank commander in the fighting in France in May-June 1940 and was promoted to head the newly formed Afrika Korps in February 1941. He generally outthought and outfought the British in the Desert War – earning the nickname the 'Desert Fox' – until the balance of forces turned overwhelmingly against him. Rommel had left North Africa by the time of the Axis surrender there in 1943. In command of the defence of

northern France at the time of the Normandy landings, he was badly wounded in an air attack on his car. Rommel was then implicated in the plot to assassinate Hitler and killed himself rather than be arrested.

PRESIDENT FRANKLIN D. ROOSEVELT (1882-1945)
President of the United States from 1933, Roosevelt was publicly committed to keeping America out of the war until his re-election to the presidency in November 1940. After that, he became increasingly open in his support for Britain. When the United States entered the war in December 1941, Roosevelt helped ensure that its major effort was directed against Germany, not Japan. Wartime summit meetings in which he took part included ones with Chuchill and Stalin at Teheran in 1943 and Yalta in February 1945. At these meetings the leaders agreed, among other things, that a defeated Germany would be divided into zones, each occupied by one of the victorious powers; and that Poland's borders would change, with the Soviet Union taking areas in the east and Poland being compensated with German territory in the west. Roosevelt died on 12 April 1945. After the war ended, he was sometimes accused retrospectively of having 'delivered eastern Europe to communist domination', although it was never convincingly said what he could have done to prevent it.

JOSEPH STALIN (1879-1953)
As dictator of the Soviet Union, in the 1930s Stalin was responsible for the deaths of tens of millions of Soviet citizens, including most of the Red Army officer corps, who were executed in a 'purge' in 1937-8. His cynical non-aggression pact with Hitler in 1939 and his failure to prepare adequately for the German invasion of 1941 brought his country to the brink of ruin. Yet between 1941 and 1945 he was able to motivate his people to heroic efforts through a mixture of patriotic enthusiasm and terror. Suspicious and cunning, Stalin mostly got the better of Churchill and Roosevelt in wartime meetings and he ended the war in control of eastern and central Europe.

JOSIP BROZ TITO (1892-1980)
Born Josip Broz, Tito was a Croatian Communist who organized a band of partisan resistance fighters soon after the German occupation of Yugoslavia in 1941. He won the backing of Britain and the United States who supplied his forces with arms and material, at the expense of rival partisans led by Draza Mihailovich. The Germans devoted some thirty divisions to the effort to suppress the partisans but failed. After 1945, Tito and his Communist party ruled the Yugoslav Federal Republic.

MARSHAL GEORGI ZHUKOV (1896-1974)
The outstanding Soviet military commander of World War II, Zhukov won Stalin's confidence by leading first the successful defence of Leningrad against the Germans in September 1941 and then the defence of Moscow in the following winter. He took much of the credit for the encirclement of the Germans at Stalingrad and for the Soviet victories of 1943 and 1944, and led the forces that captured Berlin in May 1945.

SIGNIFICANT DATES

16 MARCH 1935
Germany announces that it rejects the disarmament clause of the Treaty of Versailles.

3 OCTOBER 1935
Italy invades the independent African state of Abyssinia [Ethiopia].

7 MARCH 1936
German troops march into the demilitarized Rhineland.

17 JULY 1936
Beginning of the Spanish Civil War.

12 MARCH 1938
German troops march into Austria; Austria becomes part of Germany (the Anschluss).

29-30 SEPTEMBER 1938
The Munich agreement between France, Britain, Germany and Italy forces Czechoslovakia to cede the Sudetenland to Germany.

15 MARCH 1939
German troops occupy the Czech capital Prague.

29 MARCH 1939
General Franco, backed by Italy and Germany, wins the Spanish Civil War.

31 MARCH 1939
Britain and France promise to come to the defence of Poland if it is attacked.

7 APRIL 1939
Italy invades Albania.

23 AUGUST 1939
The Nazi-Soviet Pact is signed, secretly providing for Poland to be divided between Germany and the Soviet Union.

1 SEPTEMBER 1939
Germany invades Poland.

3 SEPTEMBER 1939
Britain and France declare war on Germany.

28 SEPTEMBER 1939
Invaded by the Soviet Union as well as Germany, Poland surrenders.

30 NOVEMBER 1939
The Soviet Union invades Finland, starting the Winter War.

12 MARCH 1940
The Winter War ends; Finland cedes some territory to the USSR.

9 APRIL 1940
The Germans invade Denmark and Norway.

10 MAY 1940
Winston Churchill replace Neville Chamberlain as British prime minister.

10 MAY 1940
Germany invades the Netherlands, Belgium and Luxembourg.

13 MAY 1940
German tanks enter France through the Ardennes.

26 MAY–3 JUNE 1940
Over 300,000 Allied troops are evacuated by sea from Dunkirk.

10 JUNE 1940
Italy declares war on France and Britain.

14 JUNE 1940
German troops enter Paris.

22 JUNE 1940
France and Germany sign an armistice.

JULY–SEPTEMBER 1940
The Battle of Britain: the RAF defeats the *Luftwaffe's* efforts to establish air supremacy.

SEPTEMBER 1940
Beginning of the Blitz – the nighttime bombing of British cities (continues to May 1941).

11 NOVEMBER 1940
British carrier-borne aircraft cripple the Italian fleet at Taranto.

11 FEBRUARY 1941
General Erwin Rommel arrives in North Africa to command Axis forces in the Desert War.

11 MARCH 1941
US Congress approves the Lend-Lease Bill to provide armaments to Britain.

6 APRIL 1941
German forces invade Yugoslavia and Greece.

20 MAY 1941
The Germans launch an airborne invasion of the island of Crete.

22 JUNE 1941
Germany invades the Soviet Union in Operation Barbarossa.

8 SEPTEMBER 1941
Leningrad is cut off from the rest of the Soviet Union; it remains under siege until February 1944.

5 DECEMBER 1941
Soviet forces launch a counterattack against the Germans in front of Moscow.

7 DECEMBER 1941
The Pacific war begins with the Japanese attack on the US naval base at Pearl Harbor.

11 DECEMBER 1941
Hitler and Mussolini declare war on the United States.

30 MAY 1942
The first 1,000-bomber raid against Germany is flown by RAF Bomber Command.

19 AUGUST 1942
Canadian troops raid Dieppe on the coast of Occupied France, suffer heavy losses.

13 SEPTEMBER 1942
The battle for Stalingrad begins.

23 OCTOBER–4 NOVEMBER 1942
The (Second) Battle of El Alamein: British-led forces defeat Rommel's Axis forces and drive them into retreat.

8 NOVEMBER 1942
In Operation Torch American and other Allied troops invade French North Africa.

31 JANUARY 1943
Germans surrender at Stalingrad.

13 MARCH 1943
German and Italian forces surrender in Tunisia.

5-14 JULY 1943
The Soviet Union inflicts another defeat on the Germans at the battle of Kursk.

10 JULY 1943
Allied troops invade Sicily.

25 JULY 1943
Mussolini is deposed as Italian head of government.

27–28 JULY 1943
An RAF bombing raid on Hamburg kills around 40,000 people.

17 AUGUST 1943
Sixty US bombers are shot down during raids on German factories.

8 SEPTEMBER 1943
The Italian surrender is announced; Allied troops land at Salerno the following day.

6 NOVEMBER 1943
The Soviet army recaptures the Ukrainian capital Kiev.

22 JANUARY 1944
Allied forces land at Anzio, south of Rome.

18 MAY 1944
Allied troops in Italy at last break through the Gustav Line at Monte Cassino.

4 JUNE 1944
Allied forces enter Rome.

6 JUNE 1944
D-Day: Allied forces invade Normandy.

21 JUNE 1944
The Soviets launch Operation Bagration, a major offensive that drives the Germans back into Poland.

20 JULY 1944
An attempt by German officers to assassinate Hitler fails.

1 AUGUST 1944
The Polish Home Army launches an uprising against the Germans in Warsaw.

1 AUGUST 1944
American forces in Normandy break through at Avranches.

24 AUGUST 1944
Paris is liberated.

3 SEPTEMBER 1944
Brussels is liberated.

17 SEPTEMBER 1944
Allied airborne troops are dropped into the Netherlands in Operation Market Garden.

16 DECEMBER 1944
The Germans launch a surprise counterattack in the Ardennes, beginning the Battle of the Bulge.

12–31 JANUARY 1945
The Soviets resume their offensive from the Vistula and push into eastern Germany.

4–11 FEBRUARY 1945
Stalin, Roosevelt and Churchill meet at Yalta.

13 FEBRUARY 1945
Soviet troops capture Budapest after a lengthy siege.

13-14 FEBRUARY 1945
Allied bombers destroy the city of Dresden.

7 MARCH 1945
American troops cross the Rhine at Remagen.

12 APRIL 1945
Roosevelt dies; Harry S. Truman becomes president.

28 APRIL 1945
Mussolini is killed by Italian partisans.

25 APRIL 1945
Soviet and American troops meet at Torgau on the Elbe.

30 APRIL 1945
Hitler commits suicide in his Berlin bunker.

2 MAY 1945
Berlin surrenders to the Soviet army.

7 MAY 1945
German commanders sign a general surrender.

8 MAY 1945
VE (Victory in Europe) Day.

STATISTICS CONCERNING COMBATANT NATIONS

Casualties

Australia

Killed, excluding war against Japan:	Total 9,572 Army 3,552 Navy 903 Air Force 5,117
Total killed including war against Japan:	27,073

Britain

Military killed:	Navy: 50,758 Army: 144,079 RAF: 69,606 total: 264,443
Civilians killed:	62,974
Merchant seamen killed:	29,180

Canada

Total military killed:	42,042 Army: 22,917 Navy: 2,024 Air Force: 17,101
Merchant navy killed:	1,148

France

Deaths:

Military:	210,000 (of which 40,000 from Alsace-Lorraine fighting for Germans)
Civilians:	150,000 (bombings and resistance fighting)
Prisoners and deportees:	240,000

Germany

Military killed and missing (to Jan 1945):	Army: 3,269,000 Navy: 149,160 Air Force: 294,728 total: 3,712,765
Civilian dead:	780,000 (estimate)

Italy

Some 150,000 army dead (including fighting for Allies); 50,000 naval and air deaths; perhaps 100,000 civilians died as partisans, in bombing, or after being deported

India (including present-day Pakistan and Bangladesh)

Total: 36,092 killed, mostly fighting against Japan

New Zealand

War deaths total:	11,671
Army:	6,839
Navy:	573
Air Force:	4,149
Merchant Navy:	110

South Africa

War deaths: total c.9,000, of which Air Force deaths: 2,227

Soviet Union

Total military dead: 8,668,400 (including 3.3 million died as prisoners of war)

Total civilian dead: 17 million (lowest estimate)

USA

Total US dead (all theatres of war):

Total dead:	405,399
US Army:	318,274
US Navy:	62, 614
US Marines:	24,511

Other European Death Tolls (estimates)

	military	civilian
Belgium:	12,000	76,000
Czechoslovakia:	10,000	215,000
Denmark:	1,800	2,000
Finland:	82,000	2,000
Greece:	79,743	350,000
Hungary:	200,000	290,000
Netherlands:	7,900	200,000
Norway:	3,000	7,000
Poland:	123,000	5,675,000
Romania:	300,000	200,000
Yugoslavia:	305,000	1,200,000

WORLD WAR II:

THE PACIFIC

CHAPTER 1: JAPANESE VICTORIES

Japanese troops parading through the Chinese city of Shanghai, captured in November 1937 after more than four months of fighting.

After many centuries of isolation from most of the world, Japan was well on its way to becoming a modern country by the 1930s. With seventy million people to feed, Japan welcomed Western technology but lacked natural resources, like oil and rubber, which were vital for a modernizing country. Unlike nations such as Britain and France, Japan also lacked an overseas empire in Asia that could provide it with wealth and natural resources. To remedy this, Japan took aggressive action to occupy a region in northern China called Manchuria in 1931 and six years later extended its control by going to war with China. The invasion of China in 1937, however, did not lead to a complete victory.

When World War II started in 1939, it was at first a European war that mainly involved Germany fighting other western European nations. However, the outbreak of war in Europe encouraged those in Japan who

A WAR ECONOMY

During the 1930s, governments in Japan spent more and more on their military build-up. These statistics show Japan developing a war economy.

Military budget as percentage of total government spending:
1931 29 per cent
1932 38 per cent
1933 39 per cent
1934 44 per cent
1935 47 per cent
1936 48 per cent
1937 72 per cent
1938 75 per cent
1939 72 per cent
1940 66 per cent

[From *The Oxford Companion to World War II*, edited by I.C.B. Dear]

saw further military expansion as the only way to make their country rich. By 1941 France and the Netherlands had been defeated by Germany, and Britain seemed powerless to resist. This gave Japan an opportunity to take over the Asian colonies of these weakened European powers. The natural resources of these colonies would enable Japan to defeat China, build up its own empire and stop relying on imports from hostile foreign countries like the USA.

THE UNITED STATES The hostility of the United States was the major stumbling block to Japan's ambitions. Although only the Philippines and a few islands in the Pacific were under American control, the US had its own ambitions in the region. The US particularly wanted to influence events in China, and had no intention of sharing naval power in the Pacific with Japan. In 1941 Japan began to grow short of essential imports after the US restricted its trade. This economic war got more bitter when Japan moved into the south of French Indo-China. The USA and Britain froze all Japanese funds under their control and cut essential oil supplies to Japan.

Japan had either to back down, by withdrawing from Manchuria, China and French Indo-China, or seize control of the European colonies in Asia and their natural resources. This would bring armed conflict with the US – but one way of dealing with this threat would be to launch a surprise attack on the US Navy and destroy its Pacific fleet.

Admiral Isoroku Yamamoto, the Commander-in-Chief of the Japanese Navy, planned a surprise attack

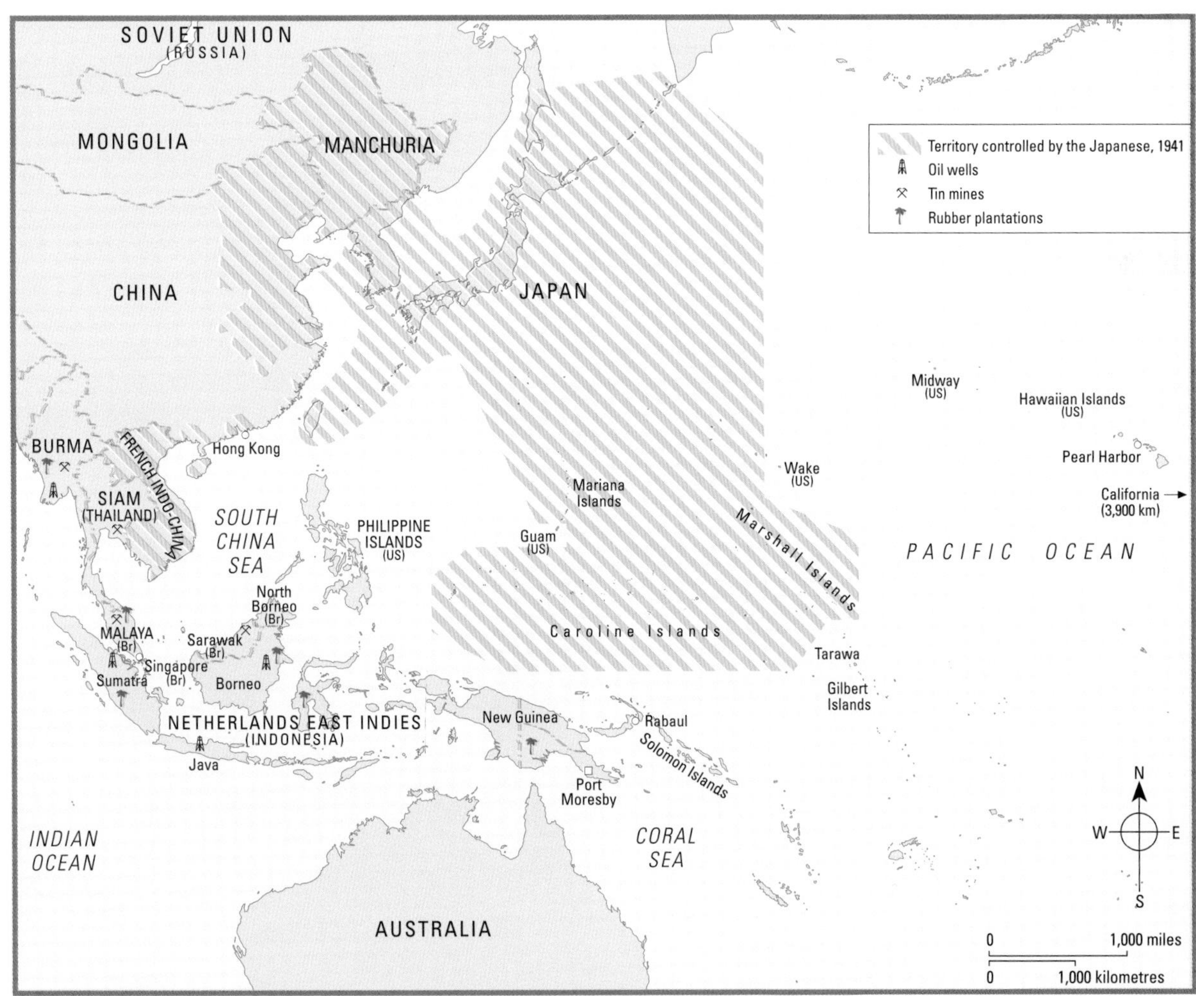

The countries in the Pacific region, showing British, Dutch (Netherlands), American and Japanese possessions, before war broke out in December 1941.

on Hawaii that was meant to destroy the American fleet that had been stationed there since the previous year. 'Climb Mount Niitaka' was the code sent by Yamamoto at the end of November 1941 for six Japanese aircraft carriers to set sail from the north-east of Japan and travel some 6,500 km to Hawaii, maintaining radio silence to avoid detection.

On 7 December, early in the morning, 183 Japanese planes gathered in a V-formation after taking off from the six aircraft carriers to the north of Hawaii. It took them over an hour to reach the island of Oahu, guided to their target by a local radio station playing music. Shortly before 8 am bombs began to rain down on the harbour and airfields. A second wave of attackers arrived at 8.40 am and inflicted more damage. American losses, in total, included eighteen sunk or badly damaged ships, including six battleships, 162 aircraft and the lives of 2,403 servicemen and civilians. The Japanese lost twenty-nine planes and their crews.

US naval power was not destroyed, however, mainly because the three aircraft carriers based at Hawaii were all out at sea at the time of the attack. A third Japanese attack, targeting the harbour's fuel tanks and repair facilities, was called off for fear of a counterattack from the aircraft carriers. If the fuel dumps had been destroyed, Pearl Harbor would have been permanently put out of action.

The US and Japan were now at war. Various claims have been made that advance warning of the attack was kept secret by US President Franklin D. Roosevelt and by Winston Churchill, Britain's wartime leader, because they wanted the United States to go to war. Historians have found no convincing evidence for this. There were intelligence reports indicating that something was to happen on 7 December but no-one put them together and drew the conclusion that Pearl Harbor was in danger of attack.

Unlike the Americans and Pearl Harbor, the British were expecting the Japanese to attack Malaya

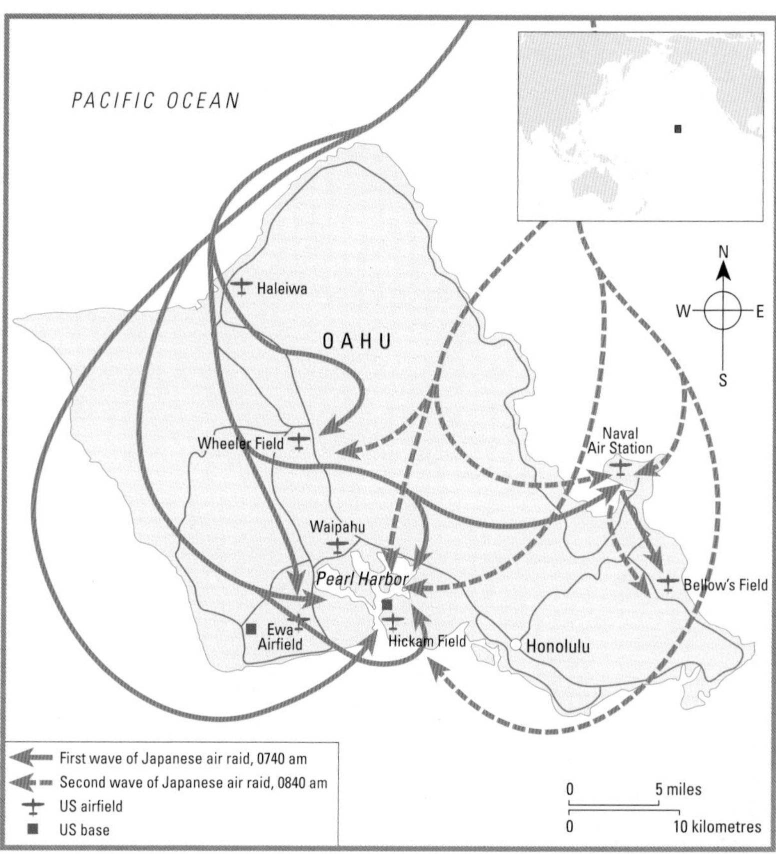

The Japanese bombing of Pearl Harbor was a complete surprise because no-one expected a long-distance attack from the north.

EYE WITNESSES

Leonard J. Fox, writing a letter home on board the USS *Helena* at the time, remembers what he saw on the ground: '*Torpedo planes swooped in from almost over my head and started toward "Battleship Row" dropping their lethal fish [torpedos]. First the* Oklahoma *... then it was the* West Virginia *taking blows in her innards ... and now it is the* Arizona *... Men were swimming for their lives in the fire-covered waters of Pearl Harbor.*'

[From *The Pacific Campaign*, Dan Van Der Vat]

US warships in Pearl Harbor proved an easy target because few of their guns were manned and ammunition was locked away.

Japanese forces at the southern tip of the Malayan peninsula.

The Japanese attack on Malaya, planned to begin at exactly the same time as the attack on Pearl Harbor on 7 December 1941, accidentally began a short while earlier. Siam was also attacked.

(W. Malaysia). They knew the Japanese would probably land on the beaches in the border area around north Malaya and south Siam (Thailand). This is what happened shortly after midnight on 8 December 1941. Local time in Hawaii was then 6 am on 7 December – it would be almost two hours before the first wave of planes reached Pearl Harbor – so the landings in south Siam and Malaya were Japan's first aggressive action in the Pacific war.

THE INVASION OF MALAYA Waiting for the Japanese was a large army of British-led troops, mostly Indians but also including Australians. They were continually pushed back as a smaller number of Japanese forces advanced at a blistering pace down the peninsula towards Singapore.

Most of the Japanese forces had no previous experience of jungle warfare but they were battled-hardened from fighting in China. Many of the troops they were fighting were inexperienced, and some of the Indian troops had never seen a tank until faced by some of the eighty transported by the Japanese. The Japanese also brought bicycles to travel down the well-maintained roads, and they used maps copied from school atlases. One Japanese tactic, when faced with enemy resistance, was often to go around the obstacle through the jungle or to use boats to bypass it along the coastline. The Japanese were also able to attack from the air, flying in from Indo-China and attacking British airfields. They quickly gained control of the skies over Malaya.

The defenders were not prepared for the well-trained and experienced Japanese who easily brushed aside attempts to hold them back. In only ten weeks, the Japanese had reached the southern tip of the peninsula. At this point only a narrow stretch of water divided the mainland from the island of Singapore, where the retreating Allied soldiers were now concentrated for a final battle with their enemy.

The islands of the Philippines – which served as a US military base in Asia – were around 11,000 km from the US West Coast, and 8,000 km even from Pearl Harbor, but only 2,000 km from Japan. General Douglas MacArthur, in overall military command of US forces in the Philippines, argued nevertheless

LOSS OF BATTLESHIPS

Two British battleships, HMS *Prince of Wales* and HMS *Repulse*, were dispatched from Singapore to intercept Japanese invasion forces. They were sunk off Malaya's east coast on 10 December 1941 in a land-based air attack; 840 men lost their lives. A war correspondent, O.D. Gallagher, was on the *Repulse*: '*... They were bombers. Flying straight at us. All our guns pour high-explosives at them, including shells so delicately fused that they explode if they merely graze cloth fabric. But they swing away, carrying out a high-powered evasive action without dropping anything at all. I realise now what the purpose of the action was. It was a diversion to occupy all our guns and observers on the air defence platform at the summit of the main mast. There is a heavy explosion and the* Repulse *rocks.*'

[From the *Daily Express*, 12 December 1941]

Before 1941, few thought that battlecruisers like HMS *Repulse* could be sunk from the air.

The controversial General Douglas MacArthur, admired as well as criticized by historians.

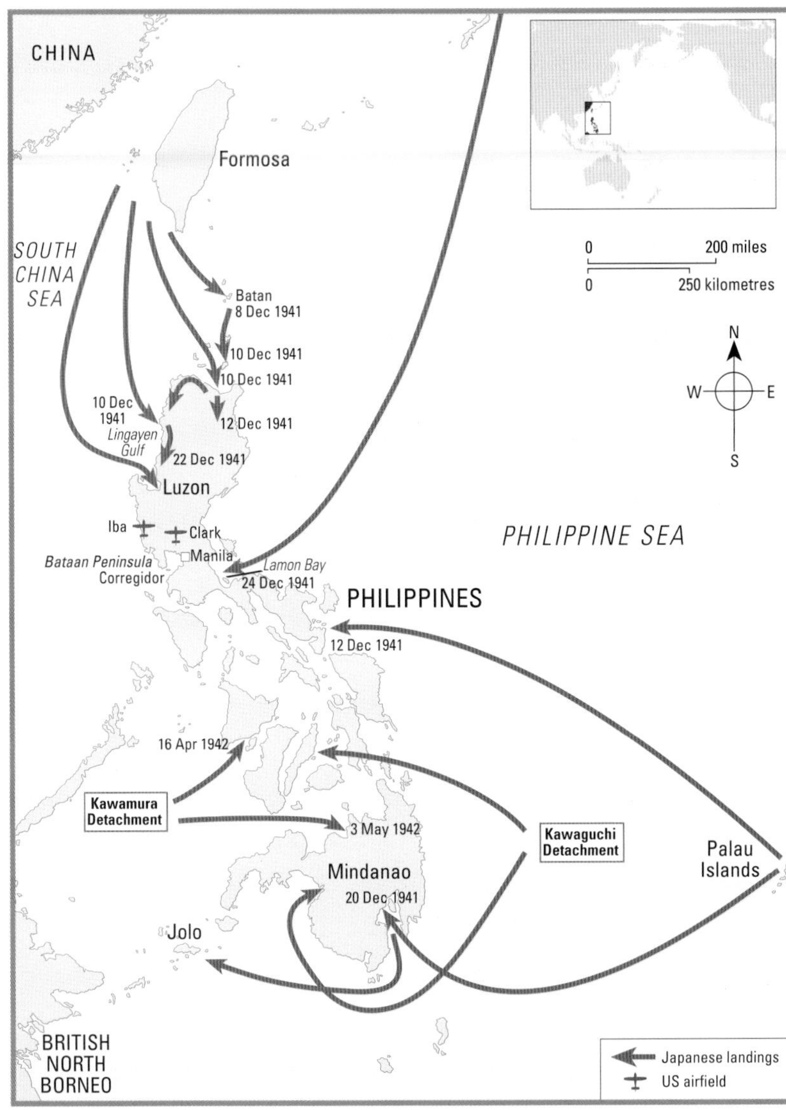

Unlike Pearl Harbor, an attack on the Philippines was anticipated but US forces were still defeated.

Japanese General Masaharu Homma sets foot on Philippine soil to oversee the capture of the islands.

that the islands could be defended and he built up a force of 30,000 American troops and over 100,000 Filipinos. The presence of B-17 bombers and over 100 P-40 fighter aircraft gave the Philippines the largest concentration of US air power in the Pacific.

Over nine hours passed between news of Pearl Harbor first reaching MacArthur's headquarters and the arrival of Japanese attack planes over Luzon. Historians are puzzled why nothing was done during this period, and why the Japanese attack was able to destroy B-17s and P-40s still on the ground at Clark airfield. A squadron of US aircraft, returning from a patrol at the time, was also taken by surprise and wiped out. MacArthur had lost half of his aircraft on the same day, 8 December 1941, that Japanese troops

Japanese soldiers celebrate the capture of a large American gun on Bataan; it took three months before they were finally able to capture the peninsula, early in April 1942.

began landing on Batan island to the north of Luzon.

Smaller landings took place over the next few days but the main Japanese invasion force arrived on 22 December in Lingayen Gulf on the west of Luzon. Two days later, more Japanese landed on the east coast in Lamon Bay and it became clear that General Masaharu Homma, commanding the Japanese, intended to trap the defending forces in a pincer movement. MacArthur, realizing this, decided to withdraw from around the capital city of Manila. Troops were ordered to retreat to the Bataan peninsula while the military command and the Philippine government withdrew to the island of Corregidor, south of the peninsula.

MacArthur needed reinforcements but US military commanders back in Washington D.C. did not want to

BOMBING MANILA

Carlos Romulo was working in Manila on 8 December when Japanese planes suddenly appeared in the sky: *'Fifty-four Japanese sky monsters, flashing silver in the bright noonday, were flying in two magnificently formed Vs. Above the scream of the sirens the church bells solemnly announced the noon hour.*

Unprotected and unprepared, Manila lay under the enemy planes – a city of ancient nunneries and chromium-fronted night clubs, of skyscrapers towering over nipa [palm] shacks, of antiquity and modernity, of East and West.

... Something pressed between my feet. It was Cola, the office cat, her feline instincts alarmed by the sirens. Their screaming stopped, and in their place we heard the throbbing of the planes.'

[Quoted in *How It Happened: World War II*, edited by Jon E. Lewis]

risk further losses at this stage. President Roosevelt told MacArthur to hold on for as long as was possible. A siege of the Bataan peninsula followed, as some 67,000 Filipino troops, over 12,000 Americans and 26,000 civilians squeezed onto a strip of land 40 km long and 32 km wide.

British General Arthur Percival (on the extreme right) on his way to sign a formal declaration of the surrender of Singapore in February 1942.

The year 1942 began with the Japanese driving forward into the Netherlands East Indies (Indonesia), the British falling back towards Singapore, and the Americans and Filipinos digging in on the Bataan peninsula.

Japanese troops, under the command of General Masaharu Homma, attacked early in January and broke through around Mt Natib in the Philippines. The US forces withdrew to a final line of defence, between Bagac and Orion, and forced Homma to call a halt to further attacks. The siege that followed lasted over two months.

By the beginning of February all the British-led troops were on Singapore island (see page 8) and another, shorter, siege began. With 70,000 soldiers at his disposal, the British general Arthur Percival made the mistake of trying to defend the entire length of Singapore's northern coastline and the Japanese were able to break through. Despite having only 35,000 troops, and with little ammunition left, the Japanese commander, General Tomoyuki Yamashita, waited to see what would happen. The city of Singapore was demoralized, some troops panicked and began to desert, and in the middle of February Percival surrendered to Yamashita. Churchill called it 'the worst disaster and largest capitulation in British history'.

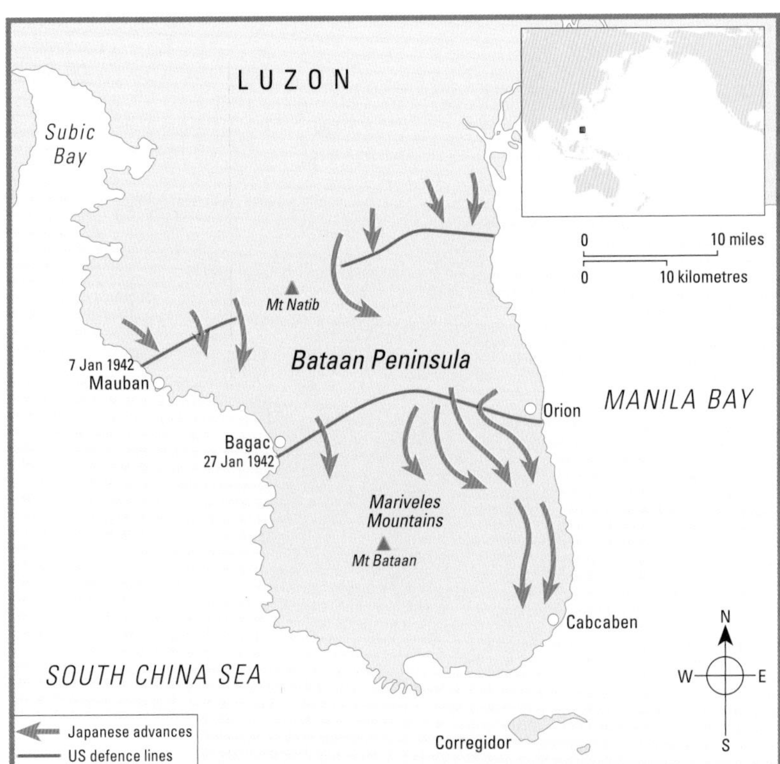

Such was the shortage of food, the defenders on Bataan were reduced to eating horses and water buffalo before surrender to the invading Japanese forces became inevitable.

Meanwhile, MacArthur had been instructed to leave Corregidor and seek safety in Australia. The troops he left behind were under orders not to surrender but this became increasingly difficult in view of what was happening. Food was in seriously short supply, malaria and other illnesses afflicted the besieged, and resistance became futile when the Japanese attacked once again in April. The American in charge, Major-General Edward King, disobeyed MacArthur and surrendered on 9 April to save unnecessary deaths. Nearly 80,000 survivors were

MORAL SURRENDER IN SINGAPORE

A Singaporean, Lee Kip Lin, and a British soldier, J.O.C. Hayes, were among those who witnessed scenes of indiscipline in the final days before the surrender of Singapore: '*We drove down Orchard Road and I remember very distinctly hundreds of these soldiers … sprawled all over the road, drunk. And they broke into the shops opposite the Orchard Road Market … the streets were full of obvious deserters. They loitered in twos and threes, armed and shouting the news that "they* [the Japanese] *won't be long now".*'

[From *Singapore*, Alan Warren]

marched out of the peninsula on what became known as the Bataan Death March (see pages 26-7).

THE WAR SPREADS By April 1942, the Japanese had not only conquered Malaya, Singapore and the Philippines, the greater part of the Netherlands East Indies had also been overrun, Hong Kong had surrendered, and the British were also defeated in southern Burma. Japan and the US were at war after the attack on Pearl Harbor and, following the invasion of Malaya, Britain and Japan were also at war. Germany had also declared war on the USA. World War II was now a truly global conflict.

The fortified island of Corregidor finally surrendered on 7 May 1942.

Jubilation breaks out when Japanese soldiers are told that the US and Filipino troops who were defending Bataan have surrendered.

CHAPTER 2: LAND AND SEA BATTLES

Japanese victories had secured for the country three-quarters of the world's natural rubber reserves, two-thirds of the tin, and vital supplies of oil. Japan now sought to protect its economic gains by reinforcing its perimeter to the south, capturing Port Moresby in New Guinea and cutting off Australia. US intelligence, having decoded Japanese messages, knew that an invasion force would pass through the Coral Sea. A task force of aircraft carriers and battleships was assembled to intercept and attack the Japanese convoys. The stage was set for the first naval battle in his-

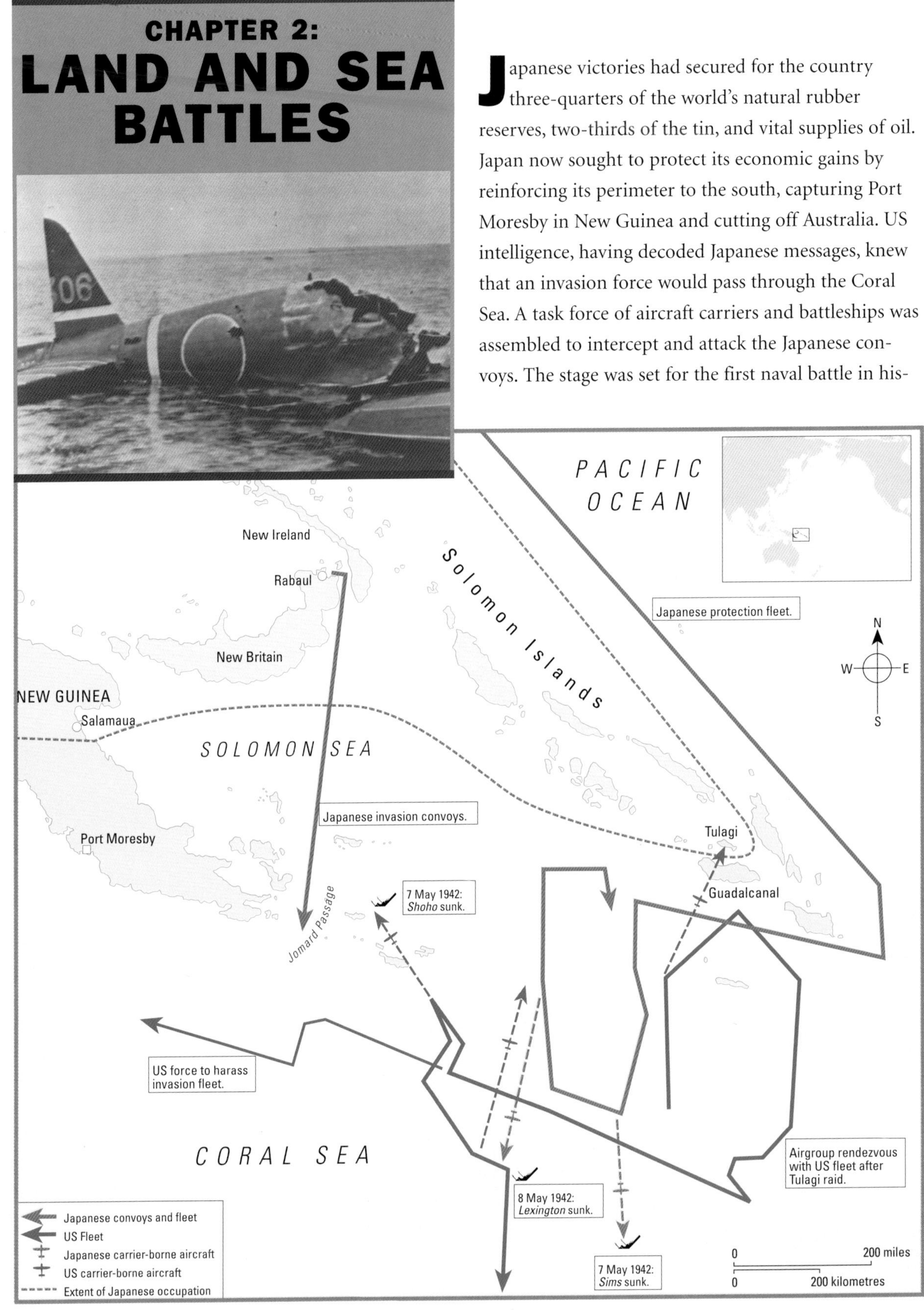

The battle of the Coral Sea was fought 4-8 May 1942 between US and Japanese navies.

tory in which the opposing sides never sighted one another, but relied on scout aircraft to direct attacks against one another's warships from the air.

The *Shokaku* and the *Zuikaku* were both Japanese carriers and, along with destroyers and cruisers, their job was to protect the invasion convoys aiming to land men at Port Moresby and Tulagi in the Solomon Islands. The convoys also had their own light carrier, the *Shoho*. On 5 May 1942, the US force assembled 650 km south of Guadalcanal. Two days earlier, Japanese ships landing at Tulagi had been attacked but the US plan now was to head for the Jomard Passage and to intercept the main Japanese invasion convoy.

BATTLE AT SEA

On 7 May 1942 US scout aircraft spotted the convoy, which then turned back to wait and see what would happen. The *Shoho* was attacked and sunk by aircraft from the USS *Lexington* and *Yorktown*. Japanese scout planes, like the American ones earlier in the day, were unable to find the enemy aircraft carriers, but they did find and sink a destroyer, USS *Sims*.

On 8 May, both sides located one another and launched full air strikes from their carriers. While equal in numbers, the Japanese had the superior Mitsubishi A6M Zero fighter and the *Lexington* was sunk after being hit by bombs and torpedoes. The *Yorktown* was damaged. The *Shokaku* was also damaged but the *Zuikaku* was never located.

In one sense, the result of the haphazard battle of the Coral Sea was a draw; both sides suffered losses but neither side was dealt a knock-out blow. In the long run, however, the USA could be pleased with the result: the enemy's attempt to capture Port Morseby was blocked and, with one carrier sunk and another badly damaged, the Japanese were weakened in advance of the next and more decisive sea battle that was about to take place.

BATTLE OF THE CORAL SEA

US aircraft carriers	2	Lost 1
Japanese aircraft carriers	3	Lost 1
US cruisers	5	Lost 0
Japanese cruisers	6	Lost 0
US destroyers	9	Lost 1
Japanese destroyers	7	Lost 0

[From *The Second World War in the East*, H.P. Willmott]

Opposite page: A Japanese fighter shot down during the battle of the Coral Sea and (below) the *Shokaku* on fire and taking evasive action during the same battle.

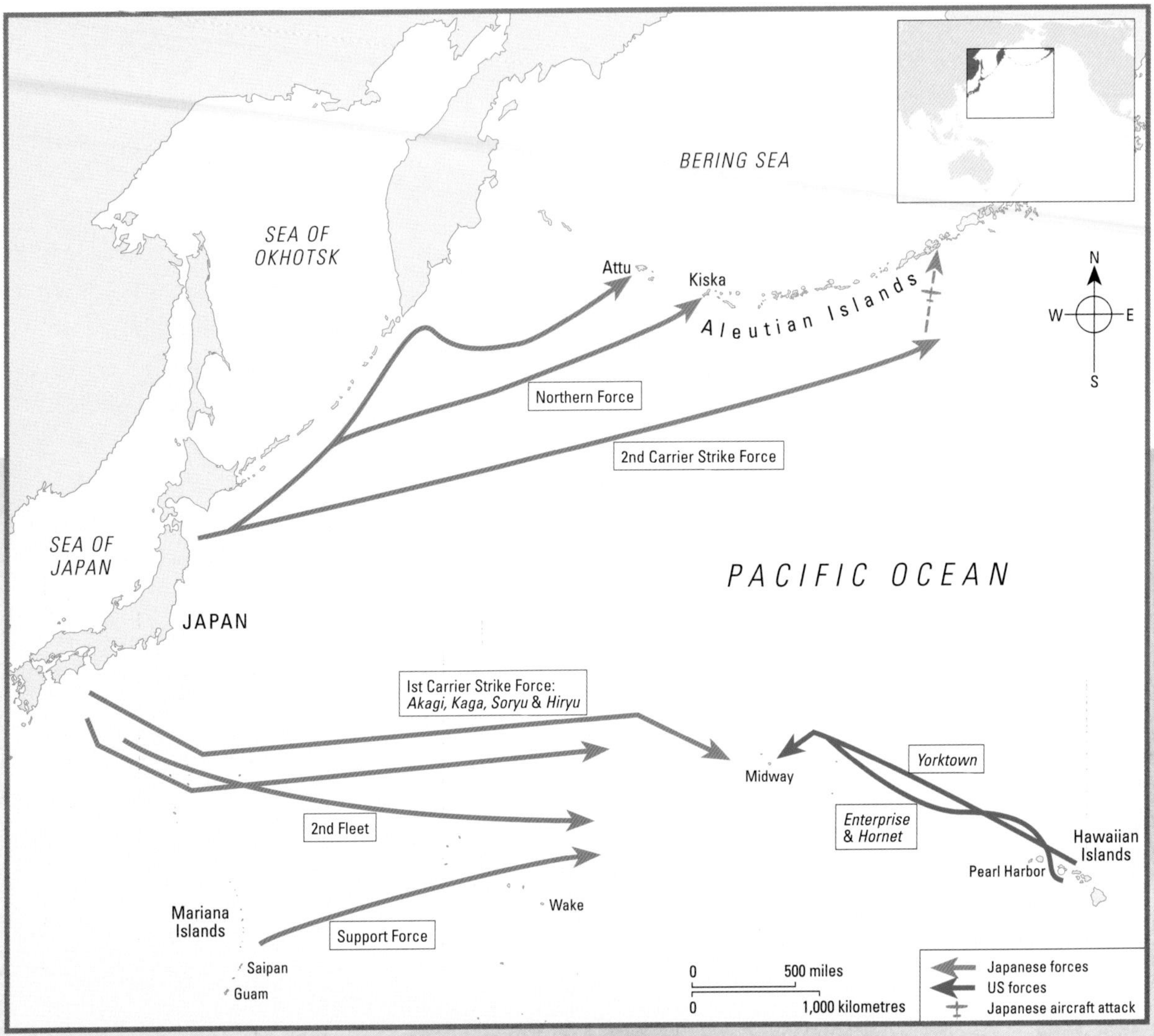

The scale for this map of the battle for Midway gives some idea of the enormous distances over which the battle was fought.

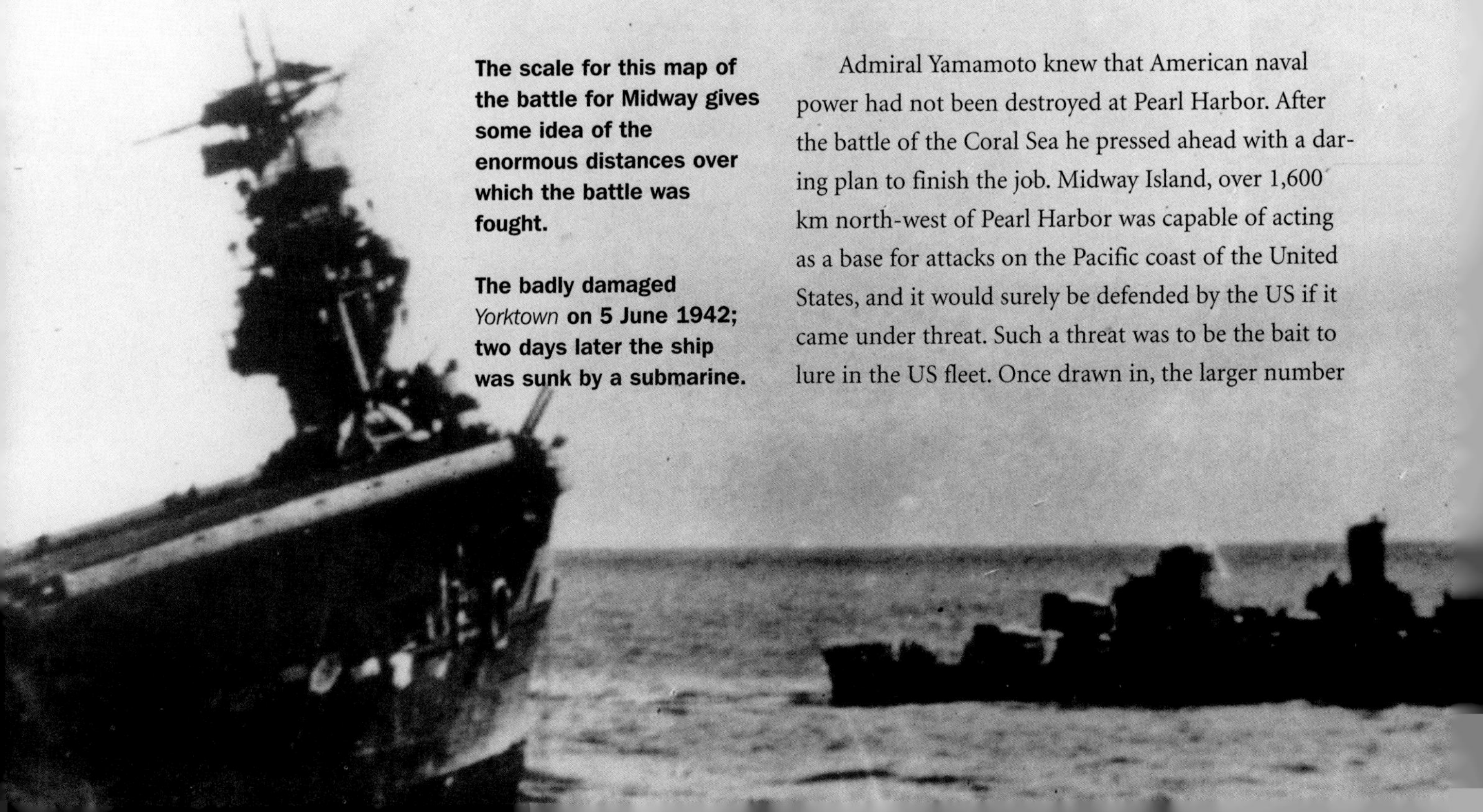

The badly damaged *Yorktown* on 5 June 1942; two days later the ship was sunk by a submarine.

Admiral Yamamoto knew that American naval power had not been destroyed at Pearl Harbor. After the battle of the Coral Sea he pressed ahead with a daring plan to finish the job. Midway Island, over 1,600 km north-west of Pearl Harbor was capable of acting as a base for attacks on the Pacific coast of the United States, and it would surely be defended by the US if it came under threat. Such a threat was to be the bait to lure in the US fleet. Once drawn in, the larger number of Japanese aircraft carriers, battleships and destroyers lying in wait could destroy the enemy fleet. The plan also called for a smaller attack on the Aleutian Islands, north of Midway, as a diversion to split the US fleet.

A Farewell Drink

Japanese Admiral Kusaka recalled the last moments on board *Hiryu*: *'When it was ascertained that the ship was in a sinking condition, Admiral Yamaguchi and Captain Kaku decided that they would go down with the ship. They all shared some naval biscuits and drank a glass of water in a last ceremony. Admiral Yamaguchi gave his hat to one of his staff officers and asked him to give it to his family; then there was some joking among them – the captain and the admiral – that their duties were finished when the ship sank.'*

[From *The Pacific Campaign*, Dan Van der Vat]

THE CODE HAD BEEN CRACKED

What Yamamoto did not know was that coded Japanese radio messages had been cracked, and Admiral Chester W. Nimitz, commander of the US Pacific Fleet, was aware of the plan. Early on 4 June 1942 Japanese carrier aircraft attacked Midway. Their carrier fleet was located by US aircraft from the *Yorktown* but their early attacks failed and thirty-five US planes were lost. Then US Admiral Raymond A. Spruance, with the *Enterprise* and *Hornet*, took the opportunity for a surprise attack. Three Japanese carriers were caught while they were refuelling after attacking Midway. A small group of American dive-bombers targeted the carriers. Their defenders were in disarray, and quickly the ships were turned into burning wrecks.

A fourth Japanese carrier, *Hiryu*, escaped and was able to join in an attack on the *Yorktown* on the afternoon of the same day. The *Yorktown* was seriously damaged, and would later be sunk by a Japanese submarine, but *Hiryu* was also damaged beyond repair. Spruance then chose to withdraw, which was just as well because there was another Japanese force advancing on Midway under Admiral Yamamoto.

The battle of Midway was the first decisive defeat in the Pacific of the Japanese. It signalled a shift in the balance of power in favour of the USA, although this was not recognized at the time. The Japanese lost four carriers, 225 aircraft and a cruiser; the Americans lost

Carrier-based torpedo bombers like these US Navy Avengers played an important part in the naval battles of the Pacific War.

one carrier, 146 planes and a destroyer. Hundreds of lives were lost on both sides.

The Solomon Islands (see page 14) stretch for about 1,000 km across the south Pacific. The Japanese had a base there at Rabaul, and a smaller presence on Tulagi and Guadalcanal. After the battle of Midway, neither side had gained control of the south Pacific and so the island of Guadalcanal became a battle-ground for the continuing struggle between Japan and the USA.

The battle started on 7 August 1942 when 10,000 US troops landed on Guadalcanal. Then unexpectedly, Japanese warships from Rabaul appeared nearby off Savo island and sank four cruisers sent there to protect the landings. Over 1,000 Allied seamen lost their lives in the Slot, in that part of the seaway between the Florida islands and Guadalcanal that

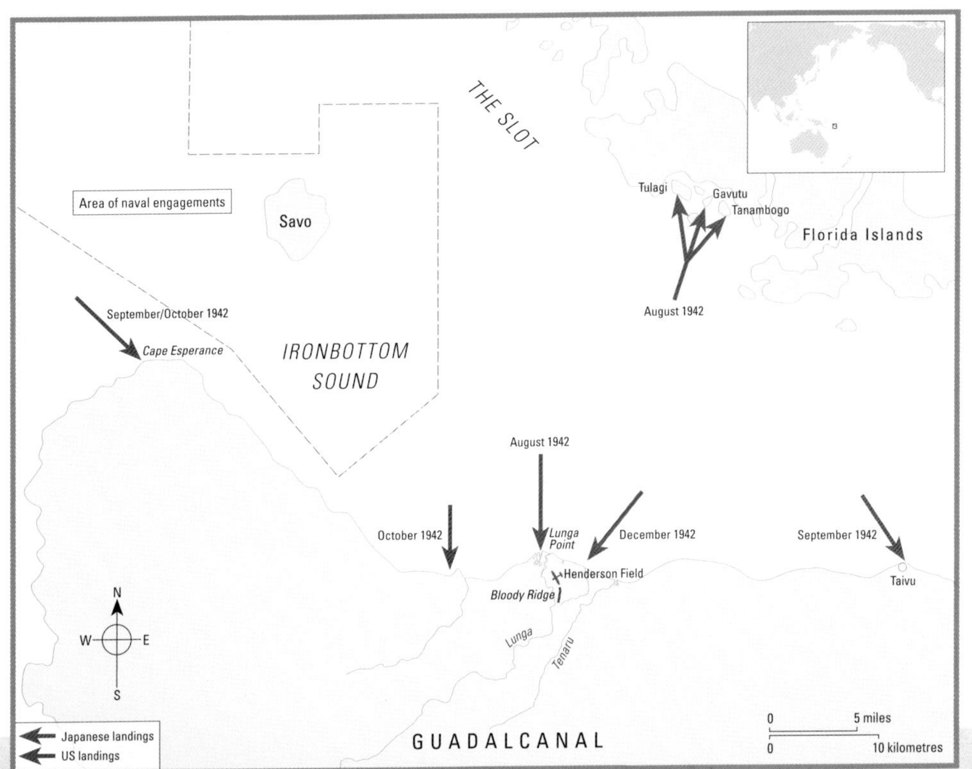

The land battle for Guadalcanal was mostly restricted to a relatively small area around Henderson Field airfield.

US Marines coming ashore from a landing craft to join the battle on Guadalcanal.

US Marines examine a Japanese machine-gun emplacement in the malaria-ridden jungle on the island of Guadalcanal.

became known as Ironbottom Sound because of all the ships that were sunk there. The Japanese then chose to withdraw rather than stay and attack the transport ships, to avoid the risk of counterattacks from the air.

THE BATTLE FOR GUADALCANAL The island of New Guinea (see page 20) and its capital Port Moresby, to the north of Australia, also became part of the struggle for control of the south-west Pacific. The troops on Guadalcanal were left unprotected and undersupplied, but they did complete an airfield that was left unfinished by the Japanese on the north coast. Named Henderson Field, it became a target for the Japanese when they landed their own troops on the island. Between September and November, each side was reinforced with thousands more soldiers who fought one another desperately in a series of engagements, with Japanese troops advancing to within 900 metres of the airfield in the battle of Bloody Ridge in September.

The land battles were accompanied by a series of seven naval engagements. In November, a three-day sea battle unfolded as the Japanese attempted to land fresh troops while aircraft from Henderson Field attacked them. No single engagement proved conclusive over five months of fighting but the US forces gradually took control. By January 1943 they had some 50,000 troops on the island. Finally the remaining Japanese, more than 10,000 of them, were evacuated from the island at night without being spotted by their enemy.

With the battle for Guadalcanal, close-combat fighting in tropical jungle conditions become a feature of the Pacific war. The island, in its own right, was not worth the losses that both sides suffered, but in the long run this was the first successful US land battle in the Pacific and it marked a turning point in the war. Australians became heavily involved in the fighting,

LOSSES AT GUADALCANAL

Naval engagements, 12-14 November 1942

US battleships	2	Lost 0
Japanese battleships	3	Lost 2
US heavy cruisers	2	Lost 0
Japanese heavy cruisers	2	Lost 0
US light cruisers	2	Lost 0
Japanese light cruisers	3	Lost 0
US destroyers	12	Lost 6
Japanese destroyers	19	Lost 3

Land engagements, August 1942-February 1943

US troops	60,000
Killed	1,600
Japanese troops	36,000
Killed/missing	15,000
Died of sickness	10,000

[From *The Second World War in the East*, H.P. Willmott]

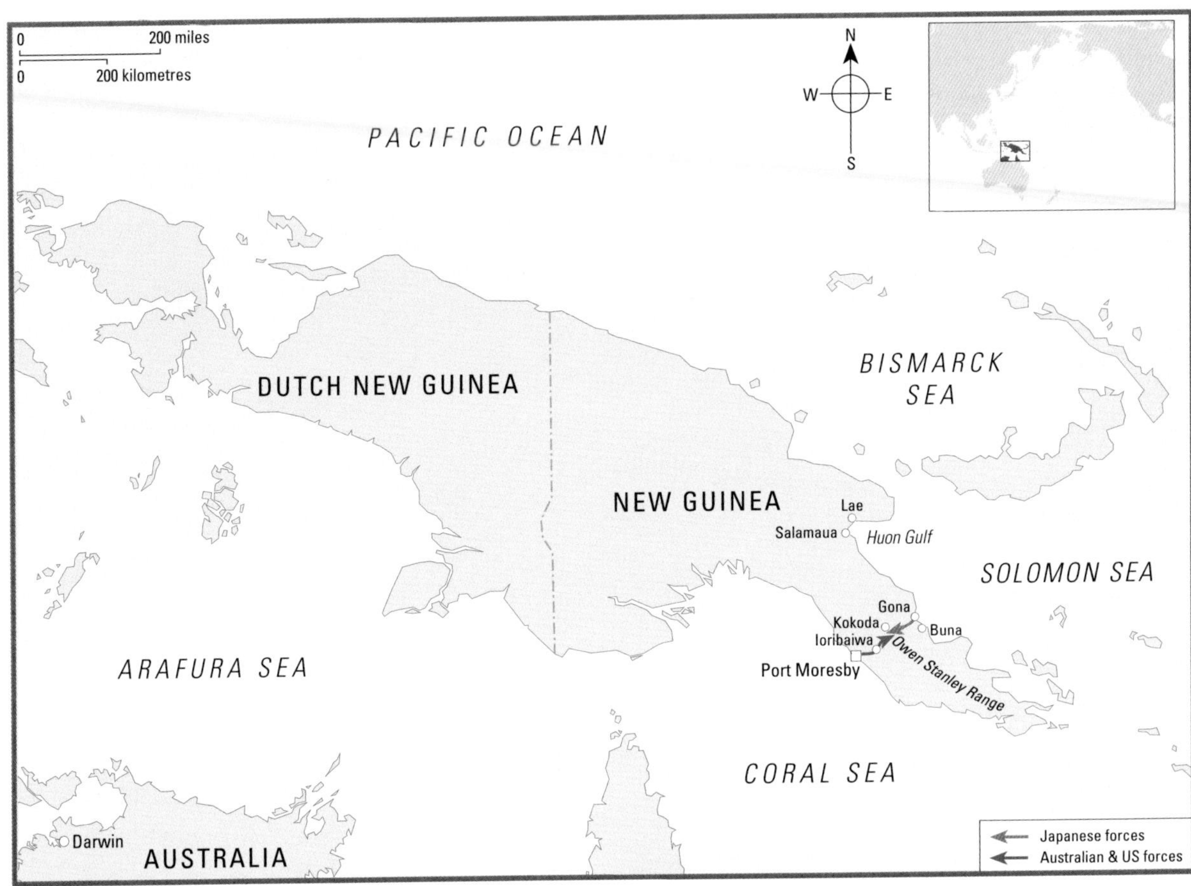

not least because their own country was coming under threat. By October 1943, there were nearly half a million Australian infantry in the Pacific, under overall US control, compared with fewer than 200,000 US land troops.

New Guinea was divided into a Dutch half, part of the Netherlands East Indies, and an Australian-controlled half.

Japanese forces had landed on the northern coast of New Guinea in March 1942. They intended to move overland and capture Port Moresby, but the battle of the Coral Sea interrupted this operation. After the battle of Midway, the US felt confident enough to try to clear this Japanese force. General MacArthur was in overall command as Australian troops moved north from Port Moresby to engage the enemy. Meanwhile, on 12 July 1942, more Japanese had landed on the northern coast and moved south. There was only one route across the 4,000-m high Owen Stanley mountains that divided Port Moresby from the north coast. It was an almost impassable mud track through jungle and over high ridges, known as the Kokoda trail. It became a desperate battleground as Japanese and Australian soldiers fought one another and struggled to survive in the jungle. Soldiers who lost the trail died and many Japanese also starved to death because of inadequate supplies of food.

General MacArthur passing Australian troops on their way to fight in the north of New Guinea.

Fighting over the Kokoda trail lasted until the Japanese withdrew in September. Australians and US troops then attacked Gona and Buna but it was not until January 1943 that the area was cleared of

MARCHING IN THE JUNGLE

Ogawa Masatsugu, a Japanese soldier, remembers the campaign in New Guinea and the terrible conditions that drove many soldiers to suicide: '*It rained for more than half a year straight. Our guns rusted. Iron just rotted way. Wounds wouldn't heal ... You slipped and fell, got up, went sprawling, stood up, like an army of marching mud dolls. It went on without end, just trudging through the muddy water, following the legs of someone in front of you ... All battlefields are wretched places. New Guinea was ghastly. There was a saying during the war: "Burma is hell; from New Guinea no one returns alive." ... In the army, anyone over thirty was an old man. Twenty-six or twenty-seven, that was your peak. The young soldiers, serving for the first time, didn't know how to pace themselves and died quickly, though there were many strong men, fishermen and farmers, among them.*'

[From *Japan At War*, Haruko Taya Cook and Theodore F. Cook]

The bodies of slain American soldiers lying on the beach at Buna on the north-east coast of New Guinea, January 1943.

Japanese. Meanwhile, from Lae and Salamaua on the north-west coast, another Japanese advance on Port Moresby got under way. By the end of February, it had been driven back. Japanese forces had been stretched in New Guinea because the battle for Guadalcanal was taking place at the same time.

CHAPTER 3: THE VICTIMS

Chinese civilians flee for their lives during a Japanese bombing raid on Canton in 1938.

Japan's rapid victories in the first half of 1942 established a new empire that stretched for thousands of kilometres, from mainland China to far-flung Pacific islands. It affected the lives of millions of ordinary citizens. Japan proclaimed the creation of a *Greater East Asia Co-Prosperity Scheme* that would liberate Asians from white colonial rule. At first, many people in the occupied countries welcomed this idea and saw the Japanese as liberators. In Sumatra, local people rose in rebellion against their Dutch rulers and arrested those

The Japanese, having conquered a vast area, were faced with the problem of keeping it under their control during the Pacific War.

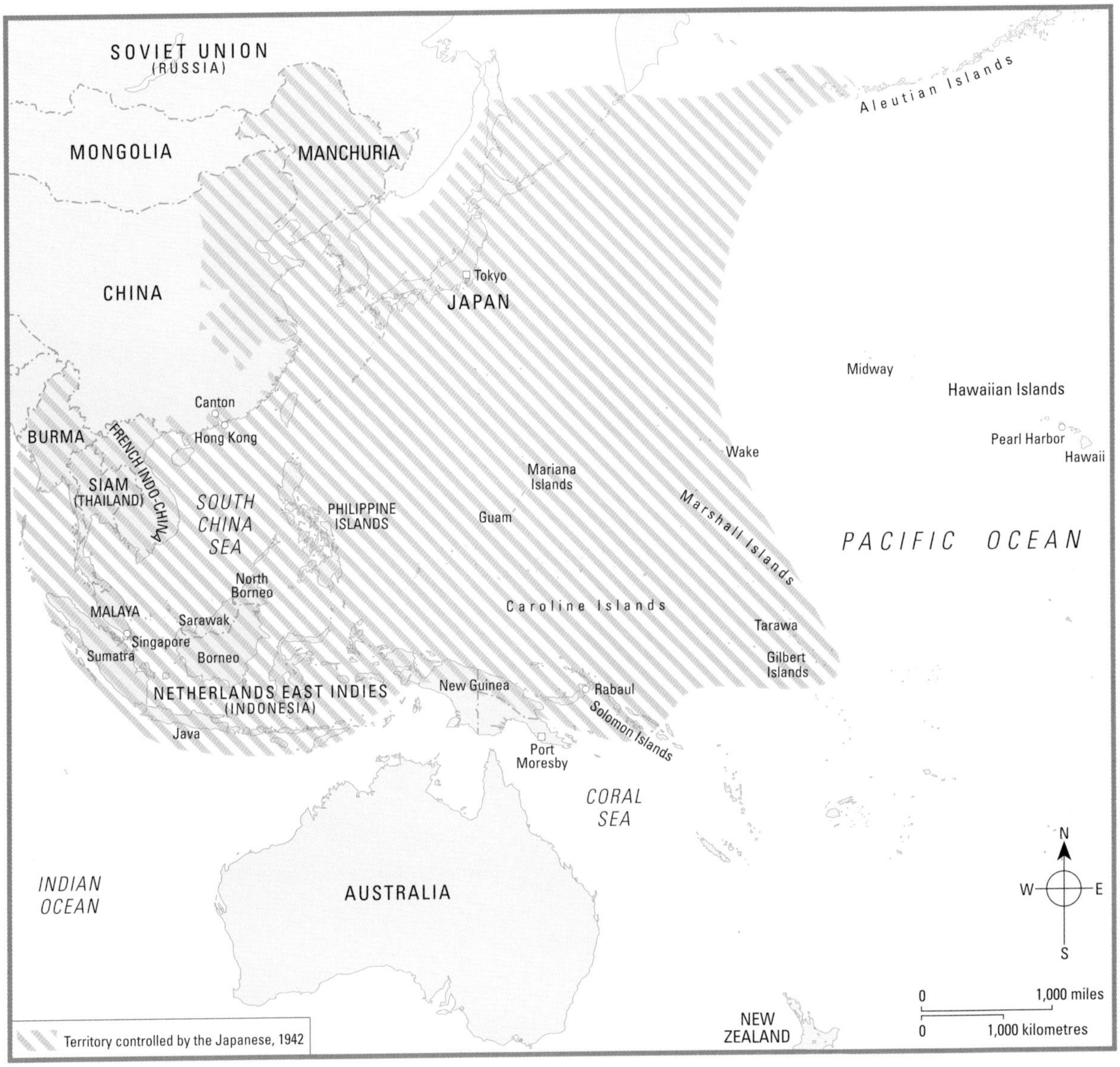

who tried to flee before the Japanese arrived. Later, peasants were forced into slave labour by the Japanese and an estimated four million people died as a result of the Japanese occupation of the Netherlands East Indies (Indonesia).

While the Japanese were fighting in China, they suspected Chinese living overseas of supporting their enemy. In Singapore, many thousands of Chinese were driven to beaches and machine-gunned by Japanese soldiers. It was not only the Chinese who were harshly treated. An estimated 200,000 women, mostly Korean but also Filipinos and some Dutch, were drafted into camps where they became 'comfort women', forced to provide sex for Japanese soldiers.

Neither the Japanese nor the Allies respected the culture of Pacific islanders and the islanders suffered terribly as a result. New Guineans, for example, died in tens of thousands as their land was bombed. Many were forced to work and fight for the opposing armies, meaning they could end up killing one another. Their traditional way of life came under severe stress as they struggled to cope: 'All the clans … who were once brave, courageous, and strong seemed to become like babies in their first day out of their mother's wombs. The landings of the Japanese, gun noises, and the actual sight of the ships … They could not run … It was a unique disaster beyond anybody's memory', recorded a New Guinean man.

Japanese victories between December 1941 and April 1942 led to huge num-

NOWHERE TO RUN TO

Pacific islanders had no choice but to endure the battles that erupted on their islands. One man describes how they tried to survive: *'All of us were in holes … We were hungry and thirsty, but no one could go out. If you travelled outside you would disappear … Then in their coming the [American] warriors were not straight in their working. They came to the shelter of ours, guns ready, and looked toward us inside. So great was our fear that we were all in a corner, like kittens. And then they yelled and threw in a hand grenade … When it burst, the whole shelter was torn apart … Earth fragments struck us, but the others in the other half, they died.'*

[From *The Second World War: A People's History*, Joanna Bourke]

Pacific islanders, like these on Guadalcanal helping US troops to build an airfield runway, became involved in the conflict in various ways.

The course of the Burma-Siam [Thailand] railway. It was built so that the Japanese did not have to send supplies to Burma by sea routes that would expose them to enemy attacks.

Allied prisoners-of-war awaiting internment after surrendering in the Philippines.

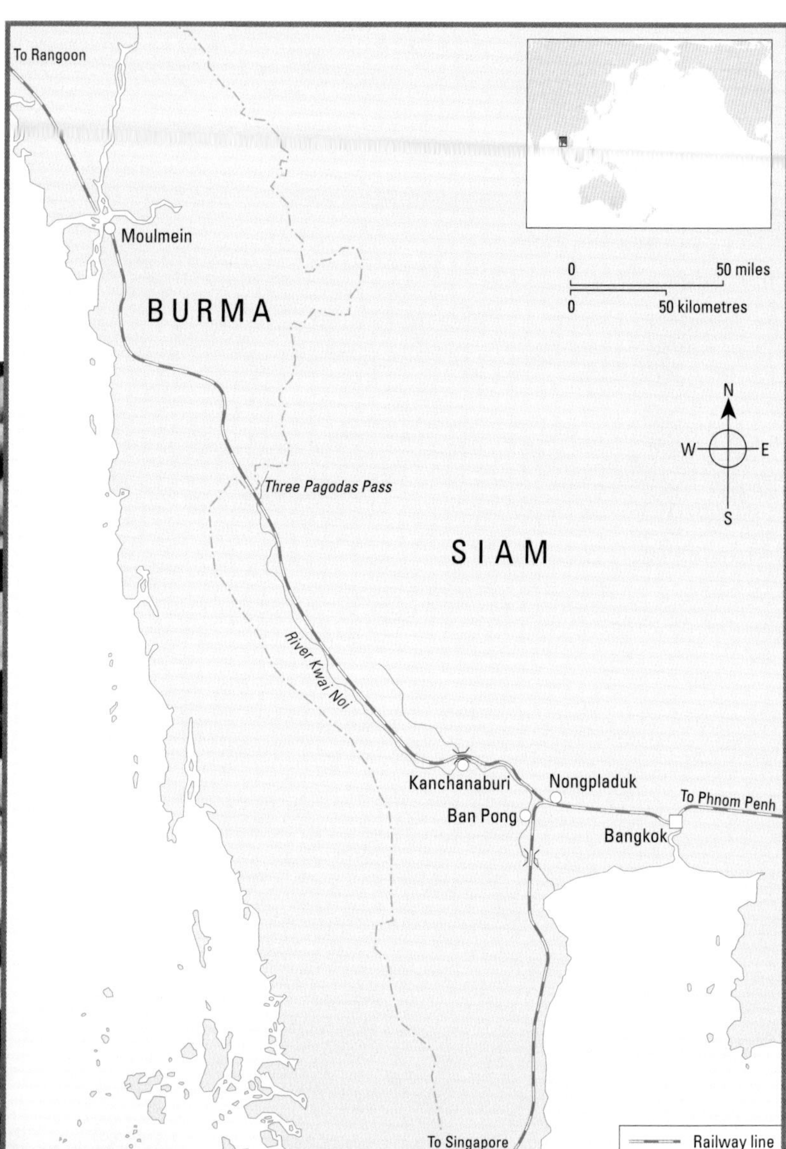

bers of soldiers and European civilians being taken prisoner. Around 70,000 troops surrendered in Singapore, plus 10,000 US soldiers and 62,000 Filipinos on the Bataan peninsula. There were a quarter of a million Dutch nationals in the Netherlands East Indies, 3,000 British in Hong Kong, 4,500 in Singapore, including about 300 children. Most of these people were interned and many did not survive the harsh conditions, poor diet and lack of medical facilities in the prison camps.

FORCED INTO SLAVE LABOUR

Food rations for prisoners kept them barely alive and they were forced to work on railway lines, coal mines, roads, docks and factories. Millions of peasants were forced into slave labour on Java, and in Siam the Japanese used prisoners of war (POWs) and civilians to dig a railway line to Burma through 420 km of mountainous jungle. Around 300,000 Asians from Malaya, Burma and the Netherlands East Indies were persuaded to work on the railway line, having no idea of the starvation diet and brutal conditions awaiting them. In addition, 60,000 Australian, British and Dutch POWs were transported to Siam to work on the railway. Conditions were awful for everyone, but

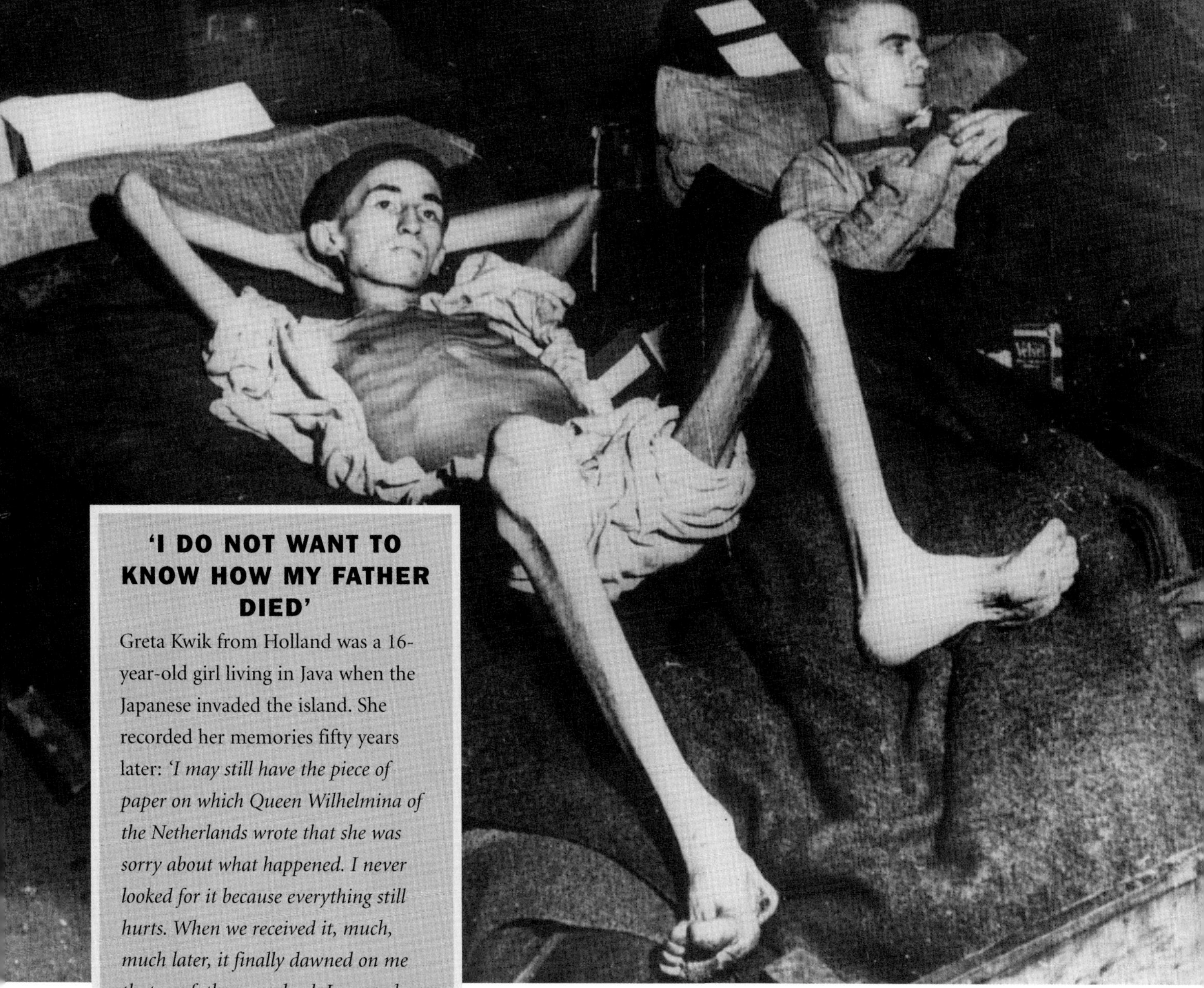

Many POWs in Japanese camps, kept alive with the barest minimum of food but still expected to work hard, never survived their ordeal.

'I DO NOT WANT TO KNOW HOW MY FATHER DIED'

Greta Kwik from Holland was a 16-year-old girl living in Java when the Japanese invaded the island. She recorded her memories fifty years later: '*I may still have the piece of paper on which Queen Wilhelmina of the Netherlands wrote that she was sorry about what happened. I never looked for it because everything still hurts. When we received it, much, much later, it finally dawned on me that my father was dead. I remember crying and banging my head against a wall in utter sorrow. I do not want to know how my father died. Was he standing, blindfolded, and shot? Did he have to kneel, hands bound behind his back, and have his head chopped off, to topple in a grave of his own digging? … I have waited for my father all my life … For most of the past 50 years, I have shed a tear every January 29, his execution date.*'

[From *The Second World War: A People's History*, Joanna Bourke]

Asians, very many of whom were women and children, suffered the worst. As many as one in three died; among the Allied prisoners of war, one in five died. Dr Hardie, a POW working on the Burma-Siam railway, kept a secret diary in which he recorded the plight of Asian prisoners: 'People who have been near these camps speak with bated breath of the state of affairs – corpses rotting unburied in the jungle, almost complete lack of sanitation, a frightful stench, overcrowding, swarms of flies.'

The Pacific War was an especially vicious conflict and part of the reason for this lies in a deep-rooted racism and nationalism that marked the attitudes of the countries fighting one another.

Allied prisoners-of-war during the Bataan Death March; of those who survived the march, another 16,000 died in the first few weeks at their destination camp.

BATAAN DEATH MARCH

William Dyess survived the death march but well understood what could have happened to him:

'Their ferocity grew as we marched on into the afternoon … I stumbled over a man writhing in the hot dust of the road. He was a Filipino soldier who had been bayoneted through his stomach. Within a quarter of a mile I walked past another. This soldier prisoner had been rolled into the path of the trucks and crushed beneath the heavy wheels.

The huddled and smashed figures beside the road eventually became commonplace to us. The human mind has an amazing faculty of adjusting to shock.'

[From *How It Happened: World War II*, edited by Jon E. Lewis]

The Japanese saw the US and Europe as wanting to make colonies out of the whole of Asia. They were seen as enemies in racial terms, hypocrites who would not admit to their own greed in wanting to control Asia. Racial attitudes took hold as Japan's own ambitions in Asia were blocked by the US. The views of military leaders who accused the United States and Britain of imperialism and of wanting to humiliate the Japanese race by not accepting them as equals gained influence in Japan.

RACISM AND THE BRUTALITY OF WAR The Japanese military code of conduct did not accept that a soldier could surrender honourably. Japanese soldiers were encouraged to think of themselves as noble warriors fighting a corrupt enemy, and an enemy who surrendered was next to worthless. Evidence of this brutal attitude came after the surrender of US and Philippine forces on the Bataan peninsula in 1942. Forced to march 105 km to a prison camp, the prisoners were clubbed and bayoneted along the way. Five to ten thousand Filipinos and over 600 Americans died on the trek, many from exhaustion and starvation.

The US forces and the Europeans and Australians had their own sense of racial superiority. The commander of British forces in south-east Asia, Air Chief Marshal Sir Robert Brooke-Popham, described how in 1940: 'I had a good close-up, across the barbed wire, of various sub-human specimens dressed in dirty grey uniform, which I was informed were Japanese soldiers.' An American general congratulated his troops on the capture of an island by speaking of: 'The sincere admiration of the entire Third Fleet is yours for the hill-blasting, cave-smashing extermination of 11,000 slant-eyed gophers.'

Many of the soldiers fighting in the Pacific War had no previous experience of battle. They were young men who had been conscripted or volunteered for service, and the reality of combat was a terrible experience. The death of friends and fellow soldiers was

A Japanese soldier, bayonet at the ready, guards Allied prisoners during their forced march up the Bataan peninsula.

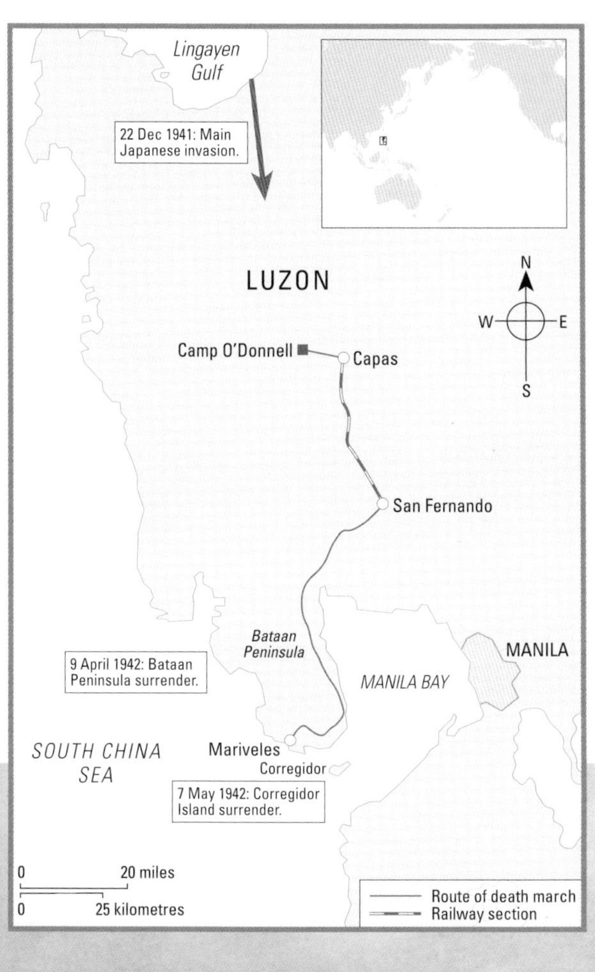

The course of the Death March up the Bataan peninsula to the former Philippine Army Camp O'Donnell, over a hundred kilometres to the north.

awful and it hardened attitudes towards the enemy. One American soldier, George Peto, remembered how, after the death of a friend, 'that sure put a different perspective on my part in the war'. Peto went on to say how it changed and hardened his attitude towards the enemy and, in a similar kind of way, after the surrender on the Bataan peninsula, one group of prisoners were told by a Japanese officer how 'we're going to kill you because you killed many of our soldiers.' For soldiers on both sides, the war became personal.

Atrocities against soldiers and civilians were committed by both sides. It was not unusual for captured

'A KILLING MACHINE'

Nelson Perry, an American soldier, remembers how the Pacific war turned ordinary individuals into something else: *'Men in combat cease being individuals; they become part of a machine that kills and that bayonets people, that sets fire to people, that laughs at people when they're running down the trail screaming in agony and you laugh at them. It's because you're no longer an individual, you're part of a machine, a killing machine.'*

Yamauchi Taeko, who surrendered on Saipan, made a similar observation: *'The American soldiers had been demons on the battlefield, ready to kill me in an instant. Now here they were, right in front of my eyes. Relaxed. Sprawled on top of jeeps, shouting, "Hey!" Joking with each other.'*

[From *Hell in the Pacific*, Jonathan Lewis and Ben Steele, and *Japan At War*, Haruko Taya Cook and Theodore F. Cook]

An American medic on Saipan; wounded soldiers were evacuated to hospital ships waiting offshore.

US soldiers remember and mourn their fallen comrades on Saipan.

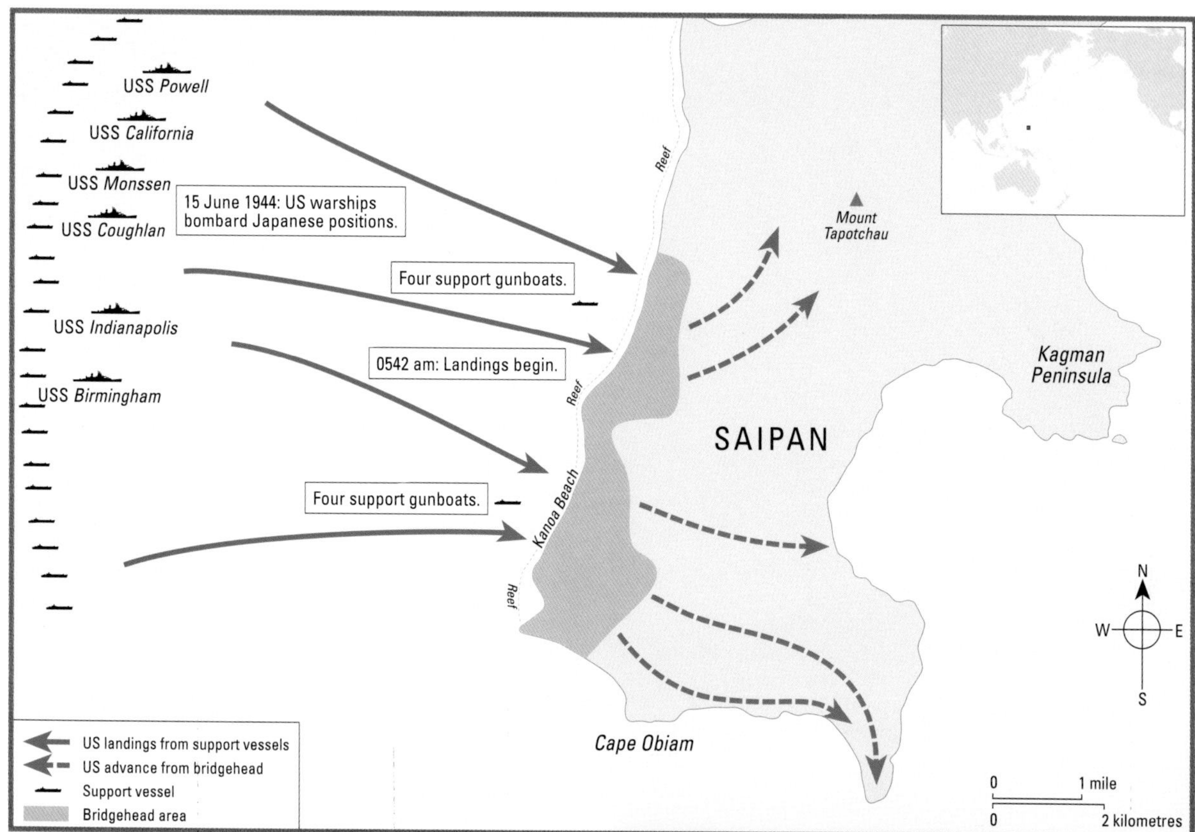

Japanese resistance on Saipan was fierce, despite intense bombardment by US battleships for two days before the landings.

Determined Japanese forces dug out defensive positions on Saipan which had to be destroyed one by one by US troops.

soldiers to be killed rather than taken prisoner. The capture of the Japanese-controlled island of Saipan in the Marianas involved ferocious fighting that illustrates just how vicious the Pacific war became. American troops landed on the island, 22 km long, in mid-June 1944. Three days had been planned for the island's capture but fierce Japanese resistance stretched this into three weeks. Some 4,000 Americans were killed or injured on the beaches in the first two days. The Japanese then withdrew to a rocky area around Mount Tapotchau.

One night early in July a desperate all-out attack, known as a banzai, was launched by Japanese infantry troops. Advancing in one massed group, regardless of the enemy's answering fire, the banzai turned into a suicidal attack. As many as 4,000 Japanese may have lost their lives in this one action. A few days later, in a state of mass hysteria, thousands of Japanese civilians living on the island jumped off the cliffs in defiance of American victory. Nearly 8,000 civilians died on Saipan, bringing total Japanese losses to over 30,000; American losses were 3,426 dead.

CHAPTER 4: FIGHTING BACK

Raising the flag on one of the Solomon Islands, symbolizing the successful expulsion of Japanese forces by US troops.

Early in 1943, with Guadalcanal captured and the enemy being forced off New Guinea, the Americans felt confident enough to push forward with their plan to capture the main Japanese base at Rabaul on New Britain. Troops landed on New Georgia at the end of June, but it was 5 August before the island's airfield was captured. There were battles at sea as well as fierce fighting on land that took their toll of inexperienced American troops who were not battle-hardened.

By the middle of August, flights from New Georgia's airfield supported new landings on the neighbouring island of Vella Lavella. Over a thousand Americans lost their lives taking the two islands and more than twice that number of Japanese died on New Georgia alone. By November, troops had landed on Bougainville and the following month saw landings on the Green Islands. Rabaul, however, was heavily defended by soldiers living in specially built tunnels. A land attack was put off and the island of New Britain was bombed heavily from the air until the Japanese garrison was put out of action.

Both the US Army under General MacArthur and the US Navy under Admiral Nimitz were in action against the Japanese. There was a certain amount of rivalry between the two forces, but it never became a

The map shows the main theatres of war as US and Japanese forces wrestled for control of the Solomons.

An assault boat carrying US Marines to land at Empress Augusta Bay on 1 November 1943, at the start of a hard-fought campaign to clear Bougainville island of its Japanese garrison.

US troops observe the bodies of Japanese soldiers killed on a Guadalcanal beach after an unsuccessful attempt to land reinforcements.

serious problem. Both commanders were helped by the fact that by the end of 1943 the American war economy had new aircraft, tanks and ships rolling off the production lines in record time. By early 1944, a new aircraft was being produced every 294 seconds. Also, American submarines, sailing from Pearl Harbor and Australian bases, achieved more and more success

TORMENTS OF WAR

Ogawa Tamotsu, a Japanese medic, was ordered to kill patients who were too ill to care for:

'I was at the front almost six years, in China, and then in the South Pacific. The final year was the most horrible. It was just a hell. I was a medic in a field hospital on New Britain Island … We were five or six medics with one to two hundred patients to care for … In the beginning it was hard to do it, then I got used to it and didn't cry any more. I became a murderer … Sometimes, when I look back, I even get a sense of fulfilment that I survived. Sometimes, though, it's all nothingness. I think to myself: I deserve a death sentence. I didn't kill just one or two. Only war allows this – these torments I have to bear until I die. My war will continue until that moment.'

[From *Japan at War*, Haruko Taya Cook and Theodore F. Cook]

An American Marine hurls a grenade at an enemy machine-gun post during the grim battle for Tarawa in November 1943.

against enemy shipping. The Japanese found it difficult to maintain supply lines and this seriously weakened their ability to keep fighting the war.

A KILLING ZONE The south-to-north advance on Japan, through New Guinea and eventually the Philippines, was under the command of General MacArthur. Admiral Nimitz preferred an 'island hopping' strategy, starting in the central Pacific and continuing through the Caroline Islands and the Marianas, before pushing close to Japan through Iwo Jima and Okinawa. After the decision to bypass Rabaul in the south-west, the initiative shifted to the central Pacific. Nimitz's campaign began with the tiny island of Tarawa.

Triangular in shape and nowhere rising more than 3.5 m above sea level, Tarawa is one of sixteen atolls forming the Gilbert Islands. It is made up of forty-seven coral islands, the largest of which, Betio, is only 4 km long. It was invaded in November 1943. The landing area, divided into zones called Red 1, 2 and 3 by the US, was expertly protected by nearly 5,000 elite troops under Japanese Rear-Admiral Shibasaki. A three-metre high barricade of coconut logs with steel clamps was constructed off the shoreline to channel the invaders into a killing zone. Here, they faced heavy gunfire from emplacements dug in behind timber and sand defences, while others were protected behind concrete. Tons of shells were fired at the island's defences but they had little effect, and the Japanese were able to

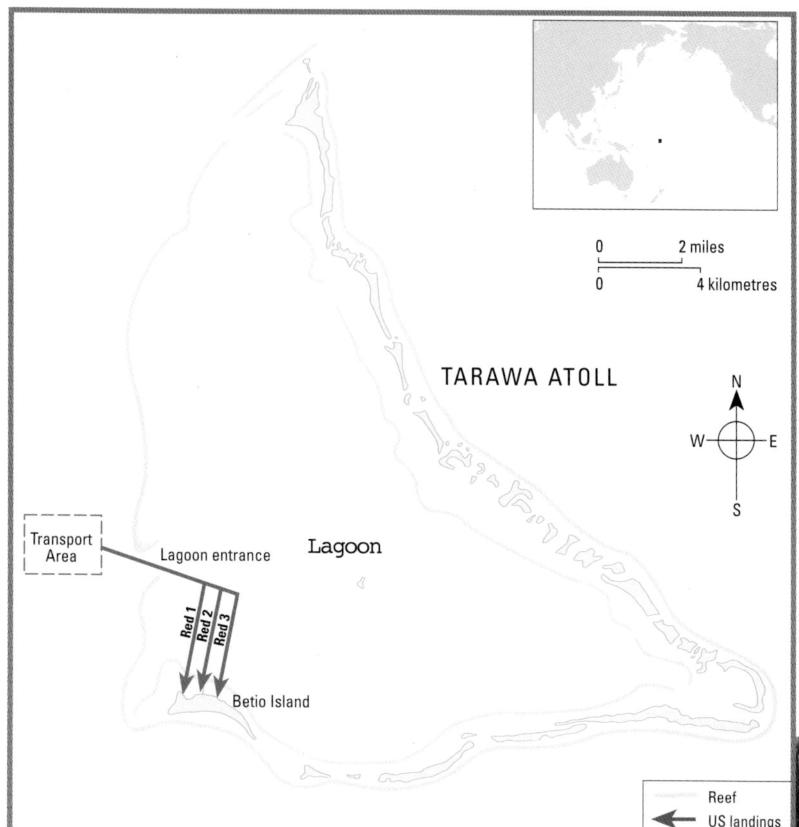

US troops and Japanese fought bitterly for possession of the coral island of Betio, part of Tarawa atoll. It is no larger than New York's Central Park.

fire at will at the troops wading ashore from landing craft unable to get through a coral reef that acted as a natural defence.

It was not until the second day, when American troops occupied part of the south shore and an area in the west, that reinforcements were able to land there. The Japanese eventually withdrew to the eastern end of the island and counterattacked with banzai charges, but by the end of the third day the island was taken. Casualty figures released by the US Army indicated that only 17 Japanese prisoners, out of a garrison force of 4,836, survived. American dead numbered over 800, with more than 2,000 injured.

US forces advancing in Tarawa, one of the most heavily fortified islands fought over during the Pacific War.

'Our only armour was the shirt on our backs'

Bob Libby should have landed on Red 1 but his launch hit the coral reef and he leaped overboard:
'The sound of screaming shells passed overhead, the unmistakeable crack of rifle fire zipped around our ears, heavy explosions on shore … the screams of the wounded were lost in this cacophony of sound – all the while we who survived so far still made our way to the beach to find some haven of safety, if such existed. … Every step of the way was a life and death situation; how anyone ever reached the shore is still mysterious to me as the enemy fire seemed to cover every inch between the reef and shore – there was no hiding place, no protection, our only armour was the shirt on our backs'.

[From *Tarawa – A Hell of a Way to Die*, Derrick Wright]

After Tarawa, the next objective was a group of thirty-six central Pacific atolls called the Marshall Islands. US intelligence had decoded messages that indicated the Japanese expected an attack on the outer atolls. These atolls was weakened by bombing attacks from Tarawa but they were bypassed, not surrendering until the end of the war. US troops landed on Majura atoll on 30 January 1944 – the first US occupation of pre-war Japanese land – and in mid-February the more heavily defended Eniwetok was successfully attacked from the air and by land. In February the navy attacked the Japanese base of Truk, one of the Caroline Islands, dropping thirty times as much explosives as the Japanese had dropped on Pearl Harbor.

General MacArthur, not to be outdone by Admiral Nimitz, captured the Admiralty Islands in the south-

A large transport vessel lands US troops in the Marshall Islands in April 1944.

After capturing the Marshall and Caroline Islands, the Mariana Islands were the next obvious target.

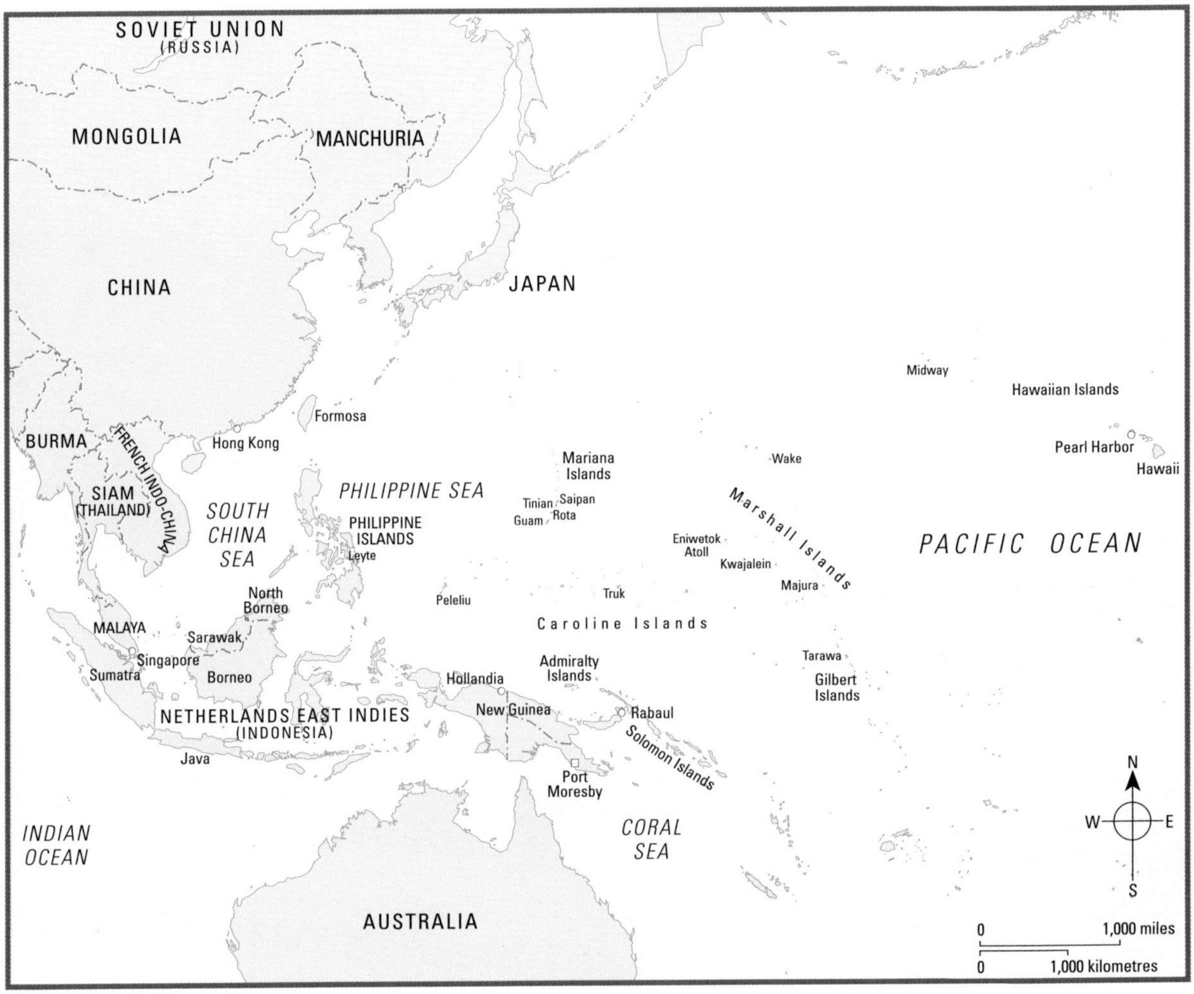

west and then seized Hollandia. The decoding of enemy messages allowed his forces also to leap over pockets of Japanese resistance, bypassing them and leaving them ineffective.

THE CENTRAL PACIFIC In the central Pacific, the way was open for an attack on the Mariana Islands: Saipan, Tinian, Rota and Guam being the main targets. Launching invasions in February 1944, Guam was the last of the islands to be taken in August. The Japanese mounted a strike force of nine aircraft carriers to repel the invaders in what became the battle of the Philippine Sea in June. It was the biggest carrier battle of the war. The Japanese were the first to locate their enemy but their pilots were outnumbered and out-matched by US fighters. The next day, the Japanese fleet was located; one carrier was sunk and three damaged; American submarines had already sunk two others.

After the capture of the Mariana Islands, there was a decision to be made: whether to move closer to Japan via Formosa, or take back the Philippines. MacArthur and Nimitz agreed on the Philippines and planned to seize the Japanese-occupied coral island of Peleliu as protection for landings on Leyte in the Philippines. The capture of Peleliu turned into one of the war's bloodiest engagements, starting on 15 September and not ending until the end of November.

The Japanese knew that it was important to try to prevent the capture of the Philippines

THE FORGOTTEN BATTLE

Equal in ferocity to the battle for Tarawa, the struggle for Peleliu received far less publicity during the war. Regarded as the Pacific War's 'forgotten battle', it is debatable whether it should ever have been fought because it made little difference to the capture of the Philippines. The human cost was terrible:

US
1,050 killed in action
150 died of wounds
5,450 wounded
36 missing

Japanese
10,900 killed
202 prisoners; 19 of which were Japanese, the rest being non-Japanese labourers

US soldiers celebrate the capture of Eniwetok atoll in the Marshall Islands, a useful staging post which brought American aircraft within range of the Caroline Islands.

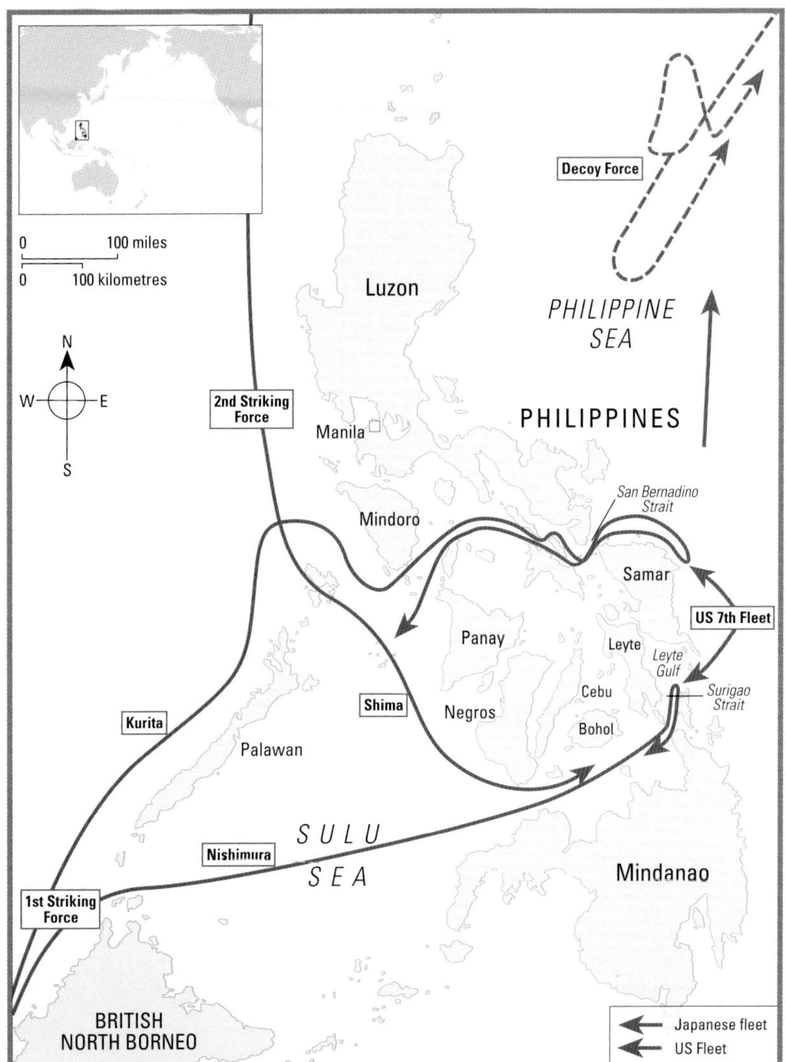

The Japanese 1st Striking Force split, with Nishimura heading east towards Leyte, and Kurita heading north-east.

Admiral Jizaburo Ozawa (1886-1963) played a successful part in the Leyte Gulf battle.

and so halt the US advance towards their home country. The plan was that Vice-Admiral Jizaburo Ozawa, in overall command of the operation, would divert the main US force by sailing four almost empty aircraft carriers to the north-east of the Philippines. The bulk of the Japanese naval force – comprising most of the warships Japan still had afloat – would be split between Vice-Admirals Kiyohide Shima and Takeo Kurita. Shima, aided by some of Kurita's ships under the command of Vice-Admiral Shoji Nishimura, would occupy Surigao Strait while Kurita would head for the San Bernardino Strait to the north. The American landing force would be caught in a pincer movement between the two of them and wiped out along with their support ships.

THE BATTLE OF LEYTE GULF

The plan failed, partly because Nishimura's force was virtually destroyed by American battleships and cruisers and Shima, who was following behind, withdrew without joining the fight. The other, stronger force, under Kurita, was met the following morning, and the ensuing battle was a close-run affair. For the first time, kamikaze pilots, suicidally crashing their aircraft on to their targets, sunk an American ship. The outcome of the battle seemed to be in doubt when Kurita withdrew, to the surprise and relief of the Americans.

Choosing to engage the enemy in the battle of Leyte Gulf, the largest naval battle in world history, was a worthwhile gamble for the Japanese. Without the Philippines, they would be cut off from their fuel supplies in the Netherlands East Indies. The gamble failed. The Japanese lost most of the major naval ships that they possessed and ten thousand Japanese lost their

Japanese kamikaze pilots preparing for their suicide attacks on US warships.

lives, as well as 1,500 US servicemen. Historians have credited the Japanese with a superior strategy and criticized Admiral William Halsey, in charge of the US forces, for falling for Ozawa's decoy and failing to prevent Kurita from reaching Leyte Gulf.

The US victory allowed MacArthur to land thousands of troops on Leyte and by the end of the year the general was ready to return to Manila, the capital city of the Philippines.

General Tomoyuki Yamashita, commander of Japanese forces in the Philippines, did not plan to fight in Manila. He left about 20,000 troops in the city, under Rear-Admiral Iwabuchi, and withdrew northwards to harass the enemy. He even planned to grow

BATTLE OF LEYTE GULF 24-5 OCTOBER 1944

US: Fleet carriers	9	Lost 0
Japanese: Fleet carriers	1	Lost 1
US: Light carriers	8	Lost 1
Japanese: Light carriers	3	Lost 3
US: Escort carriers	29	Lost 2
Japanese: Escort carriers	0	
US: Battleships	12	Lost 0
Japanese: Battleships	9	Lost 3
US: Heavy cruisers	5	Lost 0
Japanese: Heavy cruisers	15	Lost 6
US: Light cruisers	20	Lost 0
Japanese: Light cruisers	5	Lost 4
US: Destroyers	162	Lost 4
Japanese: Destroyers	35	Lost 4

[From *The Second World War in the East*, H.P. Willmott]

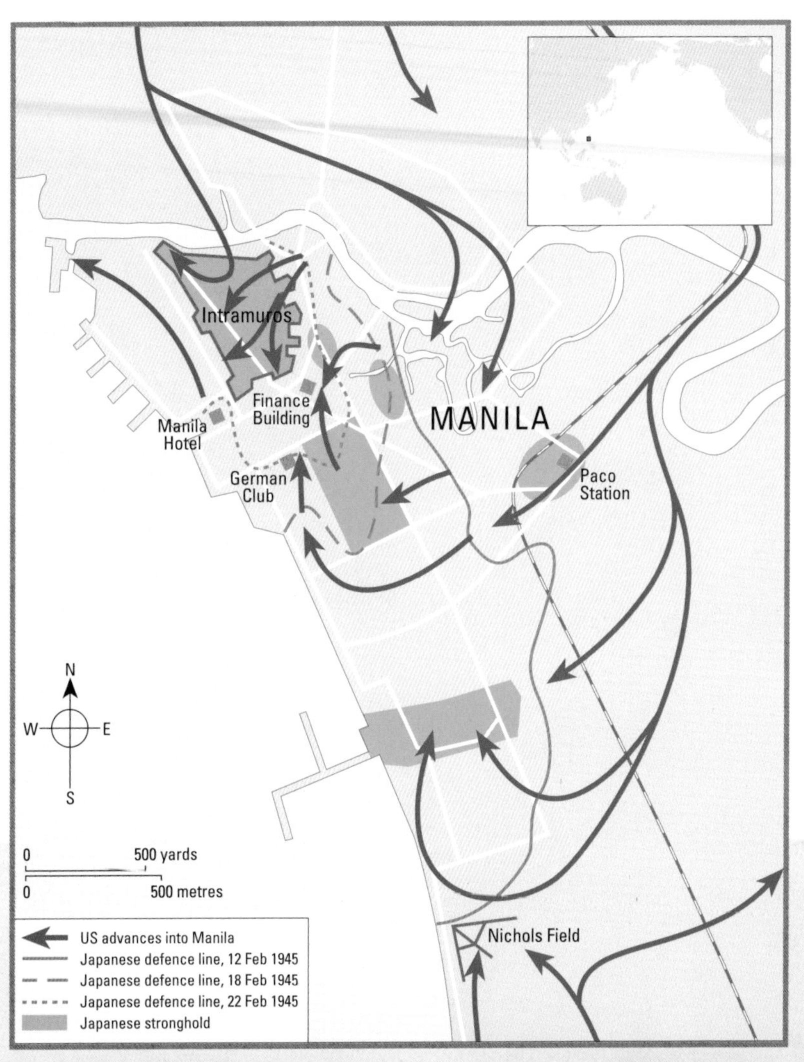

his own crops in the north of Luzon (see page 36) to feed his troops. Iwabuchi, however, chose to avenge his country's disastrous naval defeats by fighting to the bitter end in the city. The resulting battle was the Pacific War's only battle in which Americans and Japanese fought in a city.

The first US advance from the south was stopped at Nichols Field and suffered 900 casualties. An advance from the north turned into a grim battle around Paco station where 300 Japanese held out for two days at a cost of 335 American casualties. On 15 February, Iwabuchi rejected Yamashita's order to break out of the city and made his last stand in Intramuros, a square mile of stone-built buildings surrounded by a high wall.

For every soldier killed in the battle for Manila, which had a population of 800,000, six civilians lost their lives.

An historic moment: General Douglas MacArthur returning to the Philippines, wading ashore on Leyte on 25 October 1944.

The corpse of an American soldier is carried on a stretcher through the ruins of Manila.

The Americans decided to employ heavy artillery and most of the city was reduced to rubble. Around 100,000 Filipino residents of the city lost their lives amidst the fighting, fires and explosions. The Japanese, knowing they were to die, took to slaughtering civilians, especially European residents. They attacked the German Club, where 1,500 European refugees were sheltering, killing hundreds with bayonets and clubs.

THE BATTLE FOR MANILA WAS OVER In and around Intramuros, buildings were attacked and destroyed one by one. On 21 February the Manila Hotel was destroyed and four days later, with shells hitting his headquarters, Iwabuchi and others committed suicide. The last building in Japanese hands, the Finance Building, was reduced to rubble on 3 March. The battle for Manila was over.

The US, who lost 1,100 men, counted over 16,000 Japanese bodies. MacArthur, who knew he had nothing to be proud of, ordered that no public monuments commemorating the 'liberation' of the city should be erected in either the Philippines or the United States.

WAR TALK

'We are very glad and grateful for the opportunity of being able to serve our country in this epic battle. Now, with what strength remains, we will daringly engage this enemy. Banzai to the Emperor! We are determined to fight to the last man' Vice-Admiral Iwabuchi, 15 February 1945.

'People of the Philippines: I have returned. By the grace of Almighty God our forces stand again on Philippine soil – soil consecrated in the blood of our two people ... Rally to me.' General MacArthur, returning to the Philippines two and a half years after he had been forced to leave Corregidor.

[From *Atlas of World War II Battle Plans*, edited by S. Badsey, and *How It Happened: World War II*, edited by Jon E. Lewis]

CHAPTER 5: CLOSING IN

A moment in time: US Marines attack a Japanese position on Iwo Jima, 23 March 1945.

The 'island hopping' strategy of the Americans had proved remarkably successful and the final objectives in the advance towards Japan were the two islands of Iwo Jima and Okinawa. There were three airfields on Iwo Jima, 1,050 km south of Tokyo, which could be used to provide fighter cover for long-range B-29 bombers attacking Japan from the Mariana Islands.

Beginning in February 1945, 110,000 US soldiers were put ashore on Iwo Jima and some 800 warships were involved in an operation that lasted well over a month. The island's first airfield was taken within forty-eight hours and the second within a week but the Japanese were securely positioned in the north of the island and it was here that the fiercest fighting unfolded.

The geography of Iwo Jima, one of the Volcano Islands, helped to make it the most heavily fortified island that the Americans had yet attempted to capture. Mount Suribachi, an extinct volcano at the southern tip of the island, provided cover for defenders firing on the beach. Out of twenty-four US battalion commanders that came ashore in the first landing, nineteen were killed or wounded. Also, the volcanic ash on the beaches could be mixed with cement to make a hard concrete and the defenders used this to reinforce their positions across the island. The Marines fought hard to take the island – their courage symbolized by the famous photograph taken on 23 February of the Stars and Stripes being raised on Mount Suribachi.

The human cost of fighting for an island only eight kilometres long was appalling: over one in three of the US Marines, nearly 4,000 men, were killed; over 20,000 Japanese died. The casualty rate reached 75 per

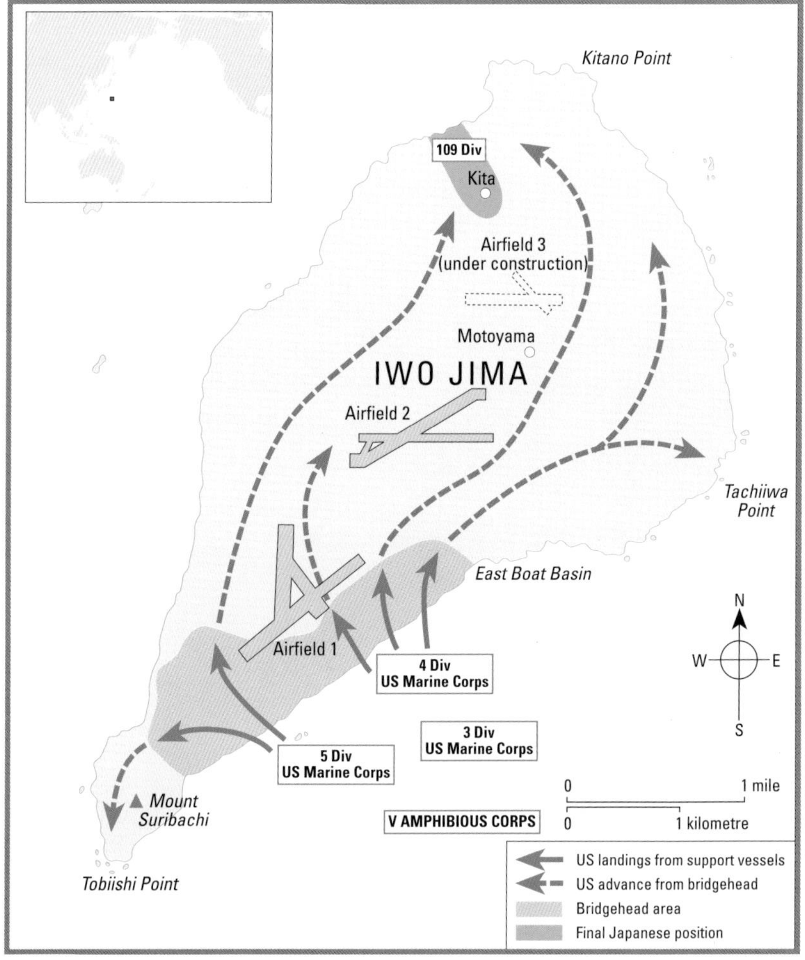

The Japanese dug in for stubborn resistance against US advances in the north of Iwo Jima.

cent in two US Marine divisions. The Japanese, desperately seeking to keep their enemy from their homeland, fought almost to the last man. They were led by Lt-General Tadamichi Kuribayashi, who conducted a very well-organized defence. In 1956, all American bodies were exhumed and returned to the United States.

A LETTER HOME

Lt-General Kuribayashi and his wife Yoshii had three children. He wrote home regularly, concerned for their welfare: '*Our officers and men know death very well. I am sorry to be fighting the United States of America, but I want to defend this island as long as possible, and to delay the enemy air raids against Tokyo. Ah, you have worked well for a long time as my wife and as a mother of three children. Your life will become harder and more serious. Be careful of your health, and live long. The future of our children will not be easy too. Please take care of them after my death.*'

[From *The Battle for Iwo Jima*, Derrick Wright]

This famous photograph, showing the US Stars and Stripes flag being raised on Iwo Jima's Mt Suribachi, came to symbolize the determination of the United States to defeat Japan in the Pacific War.

Fifty years after the battle, Japanese volunteers were still returning to Iwo Jima to look for the remains of missing soldiers to cremate and return the ashes to Japan.

The island of Okinawa was the final stepping-stone to Japan. The island, 96 km long, had safe harbours from which an invasion of Japan could be launched, as well as airfields. It was vital for the Japanese to defend it and the United States, aware of this, mounted the most complex operation in the Pacific War to secure its capture. The huge scale of the resources employed gives a good idea of just how inevitable it was that Japan would lose the war. More oil and petrol was supplied to the naval forces between March and June 1945 than Japan imported in the whole of 1944. Over half a million troops were involved and more than 1,200 warships. Over 90,000 missions were flown by carrier-based US aircraft in the course of the campaign and the carrier force remained at sea for a continuous period of three months. It has been calculated that one of the American divisions landed with enough food to supply the city of Colombus, Ohio, for a month.

The Japanese knew they could not win. The giant *Yamato* battleship and eight destroyers left Japan to join the battle with only enough fuel for a one-way voyage. Nearly 2,000 kamikaze missions attacked American shipping in waves of massed attacks called *kikusui* (floating chrysanthemums). They inflicted huge damage but, in a struggle between seamen fighting to live and pilots dying in order to fight, the island's capture could not be prevented.

A SOLDIER'S NIGHTMARE

In 1984, John Garcia recalled Okinawa. The Japanese woman he refers to was someone he shot in error, mistaking her for a soldier: '*I had friends who were Japanese and I kept thinking every time I pulled a trigger on a man or pushed a flamethrower down into a hole: What is this person's family gonna say when he doesn't come back? He's got a wife, he's got children, somebody … I'd get up each day and start drinking. How else could I fight the war? Sometimes we made the booze, sometimes we bought it from the navy…*
Oh, I still lose nights of sleep because of that woman I shot. I still lose a lot of sleep. I still dream about her. I dreamed about it perhaps two weeks ago.'

[From *'The Good War': An Oral History of World War II*, edited by Studs Terkel]

A wounded Japanese officer emerges from a cave and surrenders on Okinawa.

ON OKINAWA On Okinawa itself, it took three weeks to conquer the Motubo peninsula where Japanese defenders were concentrated. The other main area of fighting was south of a line between Naha and Yonabaru and it was 27 May before Naha was in US hands. Out of a garrison force of nearly 80,000 men, only 7,400 Japanese were taken prisoner. Over 7,500 soldiers died and nearly 5,000 seamen lost their lives on the US side.

The near-suicidal resistance of the Japanese to US advances made the idea of invading Japan itself a fearsome prospect. This led to a new policy of bombing Japanese cities, put into effect from March 1945 until the end of the war.

Major-General Curtis E. LeMay, in charge of the

Marines of the US 6th Division take cover during the advance on Naha, the capital of Okinawa, where Japanese forces were concentrated.

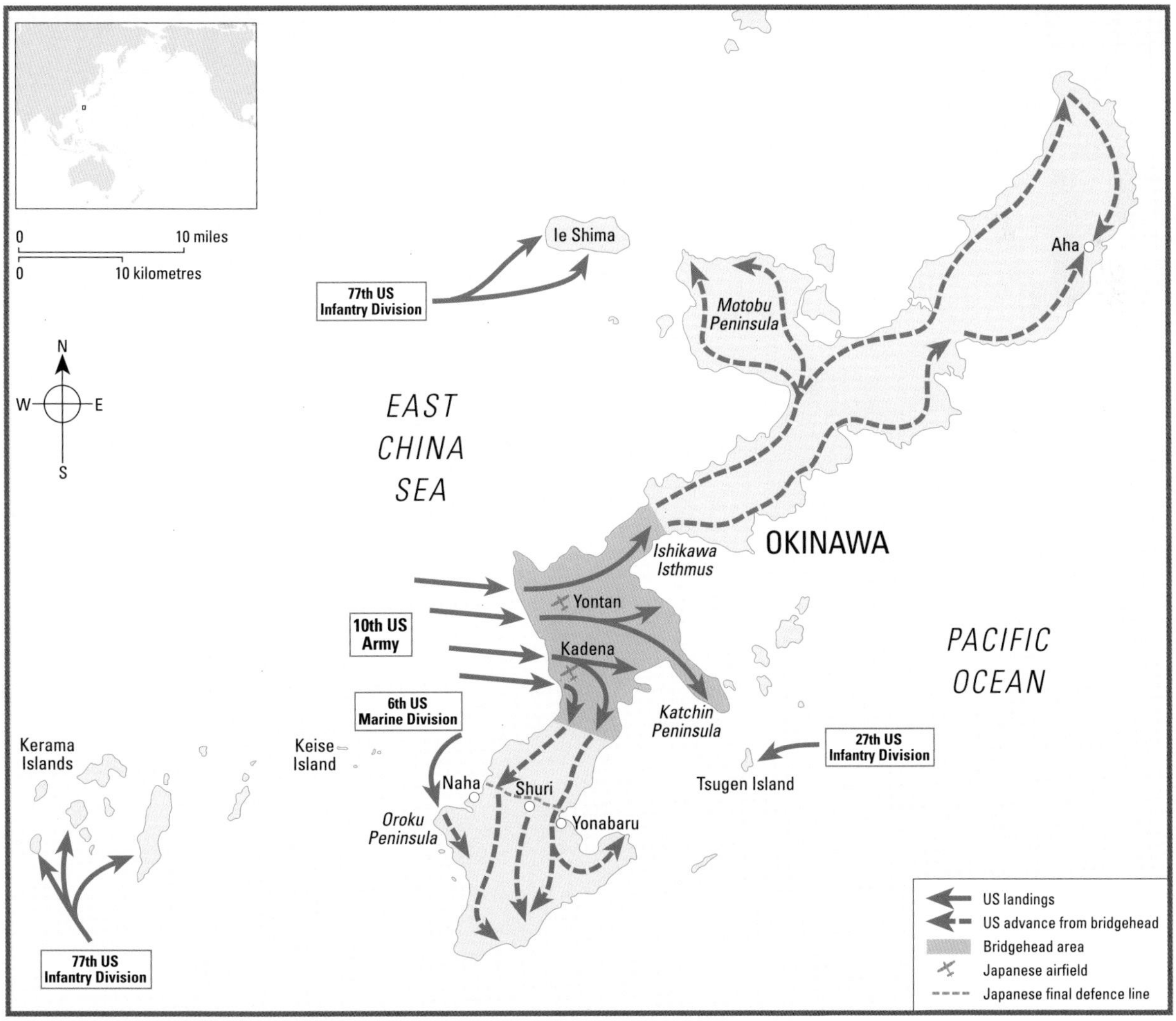

Lt-General Ushijima, the Japanese commander of Okinawa, committed suicide when the island was finally taken by US forces.

The bombardment of Japan was carried out by almost 600 bombers which eventually could attack almost any target they chose, encountering little resistance. The destruction was immense.

bombardment, began by abandoning the earlier policy of daytime, high-altitude raids that were meant to hit particular targets. This was not proving effective and the new policy involved night raids flying at far lower altitudes. Areas of cities were now subjected to bombing that caused fires rather than explosions. Densely packed Japanese cities had many wooden buildings and fires spread rapidly. All Japanese cities became targets and around ten million people were killed, injured or made homeless as a result.

Tokyo, the capital city, suffered especially from firestorms caused by intense bombing. Fires consumed more and more oxygen, turning the city into one large inferno, with temperatures rising to 800°C, fanned by hurricane force winds. In one raid on 9 March, 83,000 civilians died.

REDUCED TO RUINS Between mid-May and mid-June, six of Japan's major industrial cities were largely reduced to ruins by B-29 bombers. These huge aircraft also bombed during the day, protected by fighters from Iwo Jima. They shot down so many

Loading bombs onto one of the 3,970 B-29 Superfortress bombers built by the US for use only in the Pacific War. The aircraft was based on Saipan Island, in the Mariana Islands.

Japanese fighters trying to hit the B-29s that the Japanese grounded their remaining aircraft, keeping them for use against the expected land invasion. By August, Japan's economy had been largely disabled as a result of the bombing raids and over a quarter of a million civilians had been killed. Most Japanese now realized that their country could not win the war, although military leaders insisted that further resistance would force the United States to negotiate a peace that was not too unfavourable for Japan.

'Blown away'

Schoolgirl Funato Kazuyo, with her two brothers, Kōichi and Minoru, and her younger sister, Hiroko, were in a shelter [in Tokyo] when they realized a fire was heading towards them: *'When we went out, we could see to the west, in the direction of Fukagawa, everything was bright red. The north wind was incredibly strong. The drone of the planes was an overwhelming roar, shaking earth and sky. Everywhere, incendiary bombs were falling* ... [They ran from the fire and took shelter elsewhere] *'We lay flat on our stomachs, thinking we would be all right if the fire was gone by morning, but the fire kept pelting down on us. Minoru suddenly let out a horrible scream and leapt out of the shelter, flames shooting out of his back. Kōichi stood up calling, "Minoru!" and instantly, he too, was blown away. Only Hiroko and I remained.'*

[From *Japan At War*, Haruko Taya Cook and Theodore F. Cook]

Nearly half the entire urban area of Tokyo was flattened by US bombing raids between March and June 1945.

World War II was drawing to a close. A defeated Nazi Germany had surrendered to the Allies in May 1945 and the US advance towards Japan was reaching a climax. Meanwhile, war was still raging in another, less well-known theatre in China and Burma.

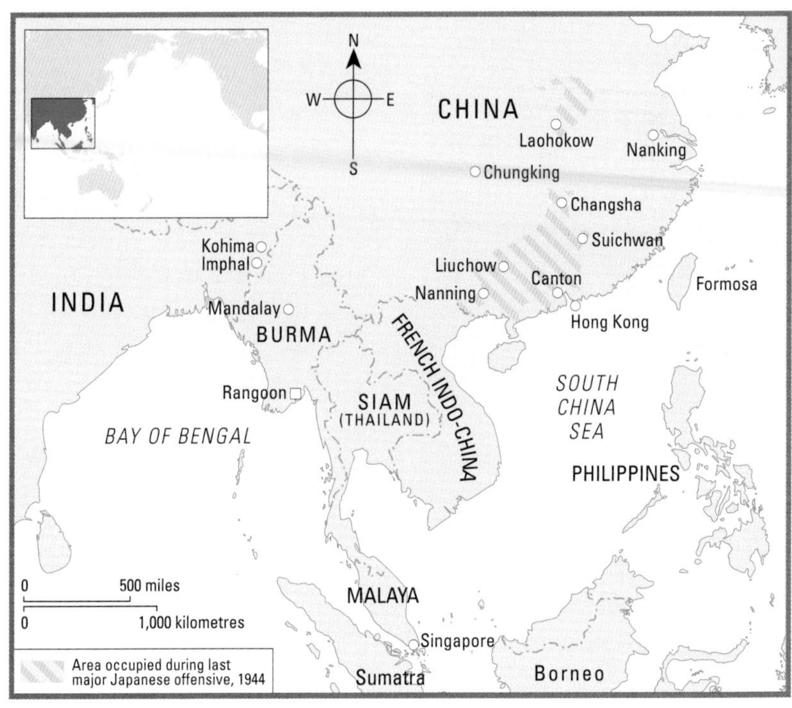

Fighting in China tied down around a million Japanese soldiers and saw Mao Tse-tung and his Communist army emerge as the future face of the country. The map shows the area occupied during Japan's last major offensive in China in 1944.

CHIANG KAI-SHEK

Chinese nationalists under Chiang Kai-shek, who had been fighting Japanese forces since the invasion in 1937, were supported by the Allies and supplied with arms and money. The Japanese invasion of Burma early in 1942 cut off the supply line to the nationalists and fighting developed for the control of Burma. The turning point in this war came in March 1944 when Allied troops, mostly Indians under the British General William Slim, were attacked by the Japanese at Imphal in India. The opposing armies battled it out for months but the Japanese were gradually worn down and by July they were forced to withdraw. General Slim pushed into Burma and captured Mandalay and then the capital, Rangoon.

The success of the US 'island hopping' strategy then made the fate of Burma less important to the Allies. Another reason was the realization that Chiang Kai-shek was not an effective ally. It was his communist rival, Mao Tse-tung, who was more useful in helping to tie up about a million Japanese troops in China.

Mao Tse-tung addressing a crowd in November 1944; the war against Japan helped bring about, in 1949, the creation of the People's Republic of China.

The success of Chinese troops against the Japanese, under the command of the US general Joseph Stilwell, only confirmed Chiang Kai-shek's ineffectiveness. Both Stilwell and Chiang Kai-shek were supplied from India, with US and British pilots flying over a series of mountain ridges to make the supply drops. As a result this route was nicknamed the Hump. The awful human cost of China's fight against Japan often tends to be forgotten in accounts of World War II. The number of Chinese nationalists who died fighting, and civilians who died through starvation and disease, is impossible to calculate but it certainly reaches into the millions.

'I DID IT FOR MY MOTHERLAND!'

Uno Shintaro, fighting in China, recalls a young Chinese prisoner called Cheng Jing who was proved to have stolen some guns: '... *He was only sixteen or seventeen. He looked so innocent and naïve that they brought him back without killing him. He soon learned our Japanese songs and some officers put him to work in the regimental armoury repairing weapons. Everyone trusted him.*

The regiment received twenty to thirty pistols each year. That year they went missing. Cheng Jing had stolen them and passed them along to the guerrillas ... When he realized he wouldn't be spared, his attitude changed ... As Cheng Jing passed by the door of my room on the way to his execution, he shouted at me, "I will avenge myself on you! I did it for my motherland!"'

[From *Japan At War*, Haruko Taya Cook and Theodore F. Cook]

General Slim's 14th Army, composed of British, Indian, Burmese, Chinese and African soldiers, advances towards Mandalay in Burma in March 1945.

CHAPTER 6: THE END OF THE WAR

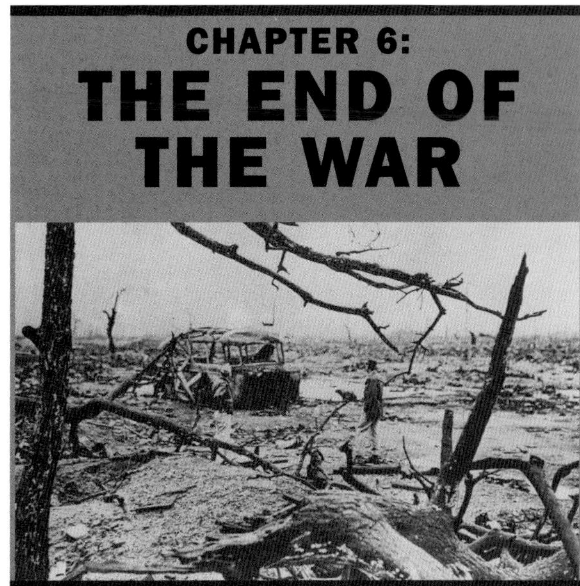

The city of Hiroshima flattened to the ground as the result of a single atomic bomb.

It was the possibility of Nazi Germany developing an atomic bomb that led to the United States developing its own weapon of mass destruction. When the new bomb was ready, it was used against Japan instead. Plans for the invasion of Japan, with its anticipated high costs in life, supplies and money, were no longer needed once the new type of bomb had been dropped on the cities of Hiroshima and Nagasaki. On 14 August, Japan's Emperor Hirohito announced on Japanese radio that the country had been defeated. Japan surrendered, bringing the Pacific War and World War II to an end.

The use of the atomic bomb remains probably the most controversial issue of the war, although it aroused no great disagreement in 1945. As it turned out, the long-term consequences of the use of the atom bomb were profound. It was the beginning of a horrific change in human history because the world would soon have to live with the fact that nuclear weapons could destroy civilization itself. Some of the scientists involved in the development of the atom bomb realized this and did not want the new weapon to be used. They were overruled, however, because the need to defeat the Japanese was seen as the priority.

HARRY S. TRUMAN Harry S. Truman, the president of the United States at the time, had been informed that between 25,000 and 46,000 Americans

A mushroom cloud over Nagasaki, a result of the atom bomb dropped on the city: 'When you deal with a beast you have to treat him as a beast,' wrote President Truman after the attack.

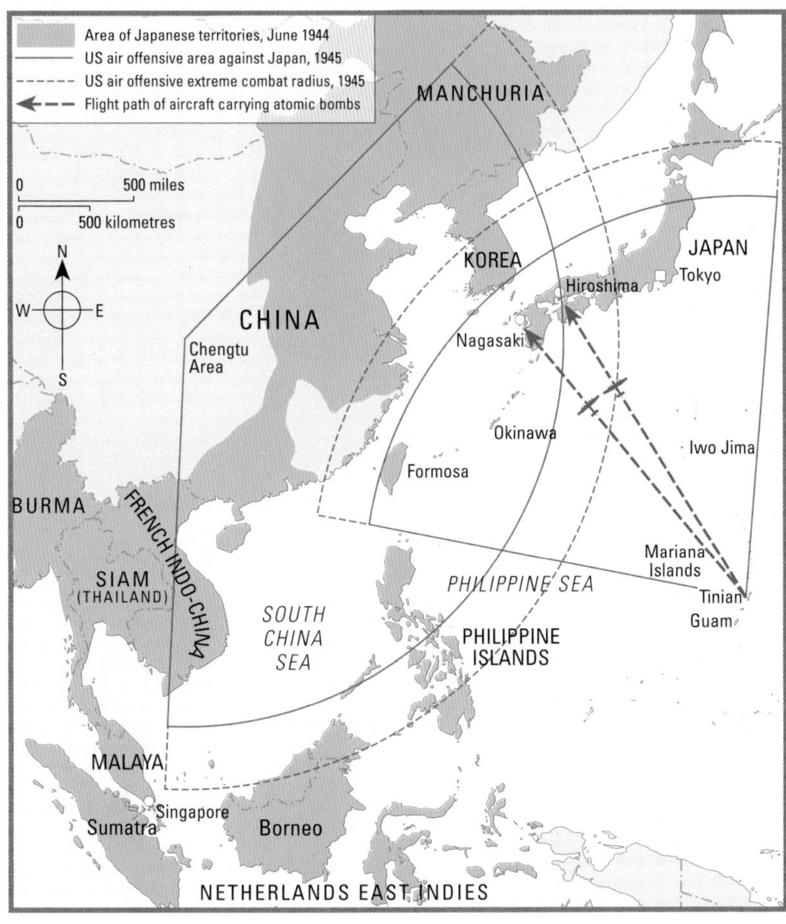

From Tinian, one of the Mariana Islands captured in the course of 1944, B-29 bombers took off to drop atomic bombs on Hiroshima and Nagasaki.

ATOMIC BOMBS: THE FACTS

Date:	6 August 1945
Time:	8.15 am
Target of atomic bomb:	Hiroshima city, population: 350,000
Type of atomic bomb:	Uranium
Bomb's nickname:	'Little Boy'
Length of bomb:	3 metres
People killed:	140,000

Date:	9 August 1945
Time:	11.02 am
Target of atomic bomb:	Nagasaki city, population: 270,000
Type of atomic bomb:	Plutonium
Bomb's nickname:	'Fat Man'
Length of bomb:	3.5 metres
People killed:	73,884

were likely to die in an invasion of Japan. These lives were saved by the use of the bomb. Countless numbers of Japanese would also have died if the war had been prolonged. It has since been argued that lives could have been saved on both sides if surrender terms had been negotiated before using the bomb. Japanese military leaders knew their country was defeated and attempts to negotiate a peace had already begun. What prevented a peace settlement was the fear that the Emperor, who at the time was regarded as a god, would be dethroned if Japan surrendered unconditionally. If it had been agreed that the Emperor could continue to rule, as he was allowed to after 1945, then a negotiated surrender might have taken place. It is also argued that the US knew that a confrontation with the USSR would occur after the war, and the use of the new weapon was intended to demonstrate the United States' superior power.

When the Pacific War was over, a tribunal was set up in Tokyo to punish those found guilty of war crimes. Twenty-five Japanese leaders were put on trial, resulting in executions and long terms of imprisonment. Around 3,000 other individuals were found guilty in other war crimes trials that took place in the Pacific region; 920 were executed. Emperor Hirohito

Officials representing the Japanese government arrive on the battleship USS *Missouri* to sign surrender terms on 2 September 1945; the Pacific War was finally over.

and many members of his family were granted immunity because the United States wanted to avoid the widespread opposition to their occupation of Japan after 1945 that Hirohito's trial would have created. This decision has been criticized, as has the fact that those running the trials all came from countries that had suffered at the hands of Japan in the war. One of the judges (there were no juries) was a survivor of the Bataan death march and could hardly be impartial.

The long-term consequences of the Pacific War were huge. In China, civil war between Chiang Kai-shek's forces and communists under Mao Tse-tung led in 1949 to the creation of the Communist People's Republic of China. In the last week of the war the USSR declared war on Japan, as the Allies had earlier agreed, and invaded northern Korea. This led to an agreed division of the country, with the north under the influence of the USSR and the south under US influence. Within five years of the end of the war, hostilities erupted between north and south, and Korea became a major theatre of war in the Cold War between the USSR and the USA.

Perhaps the most important long-term consequence was the way in which the Pacific War ended the supremacy of European colonial powers in Asia. In Vietnam, nationalist and communist forces opposing the Japanese were not willing to accept the return of their French colonial masters. The French eventually withdrew and the stage was set for American intervention and the Vietnam War. The Dutch too gave up any attempt to retain their colonial possessions and the state of Indonesia emerged. India, Burma, Malaya and Singapore were also to gain their independence from the British. The map of Asia had changed and the US had emerged as the major power in the Pacific.

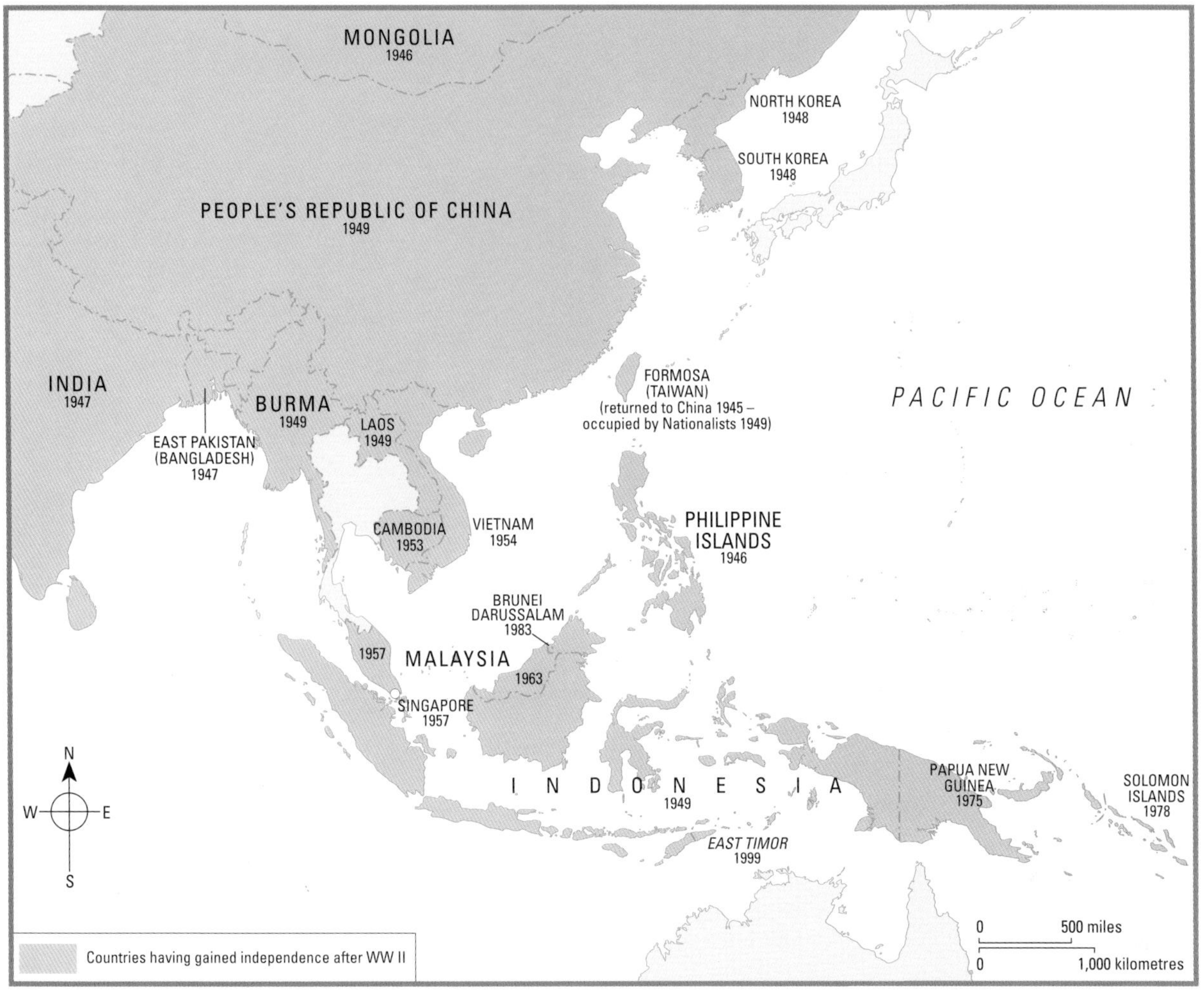

MONGOLIA 1946
NORTH KOREA 1948
SOUTH KOREA 1948
PEOPLE'S REPUBLIC OF CHINA 1949
INDIA 1947
BURMA 1949
LAOS 1949
EAST PAKISTAN (BANGLADESH) 1947
FORMOSA (TAIWAN) (returned to China 1945 – occupied by Nationalists 1949)
PACIFIC OCEAN
CAMBODIA 1953
VIETNAM 1954
PHILIPPINE ISLANDS 1946
BRUNEI DARUSSALAM 1983
1957 MALAYSIA
1963
SINGAPORE 1957
INDONESIA 1949
PAPUA NEW GUINEA 1975
SOLOMON ISLANDS 1978
EAST TIMOR 1999
N E S W
0 500 miles
0 1,000 kilometres
Countries having gained independence after WW II

A map showing countries that gained independence after the war. Comparing this map with the one on page 5 shows some of the great changes brought about by the Pacific War. East Asia changed enormously.

'WAR IS TERRIBLE'

Richard Kennard, a US Marine who fought in the Pacific War, ended a letter home with this thought:

'War is terrible, just awful, awful. You have no idea ... After this is all over, I shall cherish and respect more than anything else all that which is sweet, tender and gentle.'

Much love to you all

(Your son and Lynn's sweetheart)

Dick

[Quoted in *How It Happened: World War II*, edited by Jon E. Lewis]

Food rations being dispensed by servicemen to Japanese civilians at the end of the Pacific War.

PROFILES OF MILITARY AND POLITICAL LEADERS

CHIANG KAI-SHEK (1877-1975)
Leader of Chinese nationalists fighting the Japanese after their invasion of China. He was opposed by Mao Tse-tung, the leader of Communist nationalists who were also fighting the Japanese. Chiang Kai-shek was defeated in the civil war between the two sides that resumed after 1945.

WINSTON SPENCER CHURCHILL (1874-1965)

Prime Minister of Great Britain 1940-45. Churchill had little choice but to accept US leadership in the conduct of the Pacific War, especially after the surrender of British land forces to the Japanese in Singapore. Churchill was a keen supporter of the value of his country's empire. He hoped to restore British influence in south-east Asia after the war and maintain the British empire. In this aim, he was not successful.

ADMIRAL WILLIAM HALSEY (1882-1959)
Early in the Pacific War, Halsey was the commander of an aircraft carrier. His ability and willingness to take the offensive contributed to the success of the Guadalcanal campaign and he was promoted because of this. He was very well liked and admired for his tough approach. His conduct at the battle of Leyte Gulf did, however, lead to criticism of his ability to handle a major campaign.

HIROHITO (1901-1989)
Emperor of Japan from 1926 until his death. There is controversy regarding Hirohito's degree of responsibility for bringing Japan into the war. In 1945, many people regarded him as a war leader who ought to be put on trial and punished. The fact that he was not prosecuted after the war is something that historians still do not agree about. There is evidence, however, that suggests he opposed the military leaders in 1941 but that he could not prevent them from pursuing an aggressive policy that led to the attack on Pearl Harbor. Hirohito played an important role in bringing about the surrender of Japan in 1945.

GENERAL MASAHARU HOMMA (1887-1946)
Japanese army officer who captured the Philippines from the forces of Douglas MacArthur. The campaign, however, took longer than had been planned and Homma was recalled to Japan in August 1942. He remained unemployed for the rest of the war but in 1946 he was put on trial for war crimes committed by his soldiers. Homma claimed that he was unaware of what had happened on the Bataan death march but he was found guilty and executed.

MAJOR-GENERAL CURTIS E. LEMAY (1906-1990)
One of the younger US generals, largely responsible for the air offensive against Japan in 1945. He changed the tactic of high-level precision attacks and adopted a policy of low-level incendiary bombing.

GENERAL DOUGLAS MACARTHUR (1880-1964)
Supreme Allied Commander of the South West Pacific Command during the Pacific War. A controversial leader, MacArthur is regarded by historians as very fortunate to have escaped blame for the defence of the Philippines that resulted in the US defeat. When ordered to escape to Australia in 1942, he famously declared 'I shall return', refusing the suggestion from the US Office of War Information that he should change the phrase to 'We shall return'. MacArthur, very effective in using the 'island-hopping' approach to bypass pockets of strong Japanese resistance, recaptured the Philippines in 1944. If a land invasion of Japan had been necessary, MacArthur would have been the ground commander for the operation. In the Korean War, MacArthur successfully led the US forces but he lost the command when he tried to continue the war against China.

MAO TSE-TUNG (1893-1976)

A founding member of the Chinese Communist Party in 1921, Mao had risen to lead the Party by the time of the Pacific War. He effectively opposed Chiang Kai-shek by dealing with corruption and social issues, and gained support as a nationalist by fighting the Japanese. By 1945, Mao and his troops had gained control over most of the Chinese countryside. Four years later, he declared the independence of the People's Republic of China.

ADMIRAL CHESTER W. NIMITZ (1885-1966)
Commander-in-Chief US Pacific Fleet and Pacific Ocean Areas during the Pacific War. He was overshadowed to some extent by the more flamboyant MacArthur, though he is regarded as possessing far sounder military judgement. Nimitz planned the battle of Midway and chose to act on the information provided by US intelligence deciphering Japanese radio messages. At this early stage in the war, the value of such intelligence reports was not taken for granted. Nimitz commanded the landings on Iwo Jima and Okinawa, and signed the Japanese surrender document on behalf of the United States.

FRANKLIN D. ROOSEVELT (1882-1945)
President of the United States at the time of the attack on Pearl Harbor, Roosevelt died in April 1945 and so did not live to see the surrender of Japan. Roosevelt is credited for his leadership in uniting his country in the war against Nazi Germany and Japan. Historians have recognized Roosevelt's ability to manage two separate wars successfully, one in Europe and one in the Pacific. Roosevelt is also seen to have realized that relations with the USSR would be difficult once the war was finally over.

GENERAL SIR WILLIAM SLIM (1891-1970)
British commander in charge of the defence of Imphal in 1944 and of the campaign that drove the Japanese out of Burma in 1945. He once said 'I must have been the most defeated general in our history', but historians have given him great credit for his tactics and his ability to command troops and win the loyalty of soldiers.

ADMIRAL RAYMOND A. SPRUANCE (1886-1969)
A commander at the battle of Midway, Spruance also took part in the battle of the Philippine Sea and the Okinawa campaign. He also planned the capture of Tarawa and the Marshall islands. The US Navy's official historian praised his 'power of decision and coolness in action'.

GENERAL JOSEPH STILWELL (1883-1946)
A US army commander in the China-Burma-India theatre of war who became well known for his harsh criticisms of Chiang Kai-shek. Stilwell, who spoke Chinese fluently, was very successful as a commander of Chinese troops. He gained admiration and promotion for the way he handled his troops and conducted a difficult campaign. Stilwell was also renowned for his inability to get along with British military commanders.

GENERAL HIDEKI TOJO (1884-1948)
Prime Minister of Japan between 1941 and 1944. Before 1941, Tojo was known for his hard-line attitude towards the US and his willingness to adopt a military solution to political problems. When he became Prime Minister in 1941, many observers sensed that it was only a matter of time before Japan was led into a war. After the war, Tojo was convicted of war crimes and hanged.

HARRY S. TRUMAN (1884-1972)
Vice-President of the United States for 83 days, until the death of Roosevelt in April 1945 made Truman the President. He did not know about the programme to build atomic weapons but, guided by Roosevelt's advisers, he made no major changes in military policy.

ADMIRAL ISOROKU YAMAMOTO (1884-1943)
Commander of the Japanese Combined Fleet 1939-43. Yamamoto had lived in the United States in order to learn English and in the 1930s he was opposed to people like Tojo who favoured war with America. When the prospect of war became certain, Yamamoto became convinced that only a surprise attack on Pearl Harbor would give his country a chance of success. Yamamoto, convincing those who thought his plan was a reckless one, worked out the plan for attacking the US fleet. He also planned the strategy that led to the battle of Midway. Yamamoto was killed by US forces when his aircraft was intercepted and shot down.

GENERAL TOMOYUKI YAMASHITA (1885-1946)
Commander of Japanese forces that conquered Malaya and Singapore, and the commander responsible for the defence of Luzon in the Philippines. After the war, he was put on trial for war crimes committed against civilians in Manila. Yamashita was not responsible for these crimes but he was found guilty and sentenced to death. MacArthur refused to consider his appeal and Yamashita was hanged.

SIGNIFICANT DATES

SEPTEMBER 1931
Japan invades Manchuria.

AUGUST 1937
Japan invades China.

3 SEPTEMBER 1939
Britain, France, Australia and India declare war on Nazi Germany.

15 MAY 1940
Dutch (Netherlands) army surrenders to Nazi Germany.

24 JULY 1941
Japanese troops begin occupying French-controlled Indo-China.

26 JULY 1941
US freezes all Japanese assets.

1 AUGUST 1941
US announces oil embargo against Japan; Britain and Netherlands East Indies soon do the same.

7-8 DECEMBER 1941
Japanese troops land in Malaya and Siam (Thailand). Attack on Pearl Harbor. The Philippines and Singapore bombed.

9 DECEMBER 1941
Australia and New Zealand declare war on Japan.

10 DECEMBER 1941
HMS *Prince of Wales* and *Repulse* sunk off coast of Malaya. Japanese troops land in the Philippines.

14 DECEMBER 1941
Japanese begin invasion of Burma.

17 DECEMBER 1941
Japanese invade North Borneo.

20 DECEMBER 1941
Japanese invade Netherlands East Indies (Indonesia).

25 DECEMBER 1941
Japanese invade and capture Hong Kong.

9 JANUARY 1942
Following the capture of Manila by the Japanese, the siege of Bataan begins.

23 JANUARY 1942
Japanese land on Solomon Islands.

25 JANUARY 1942
Defending forces in Malaya ordered to withdraw to island of Singapore.

15 FEBRUARY 1942
Singapore surrenders.

7 MARCH 1942
Japanese land in New Guinea.

11 MARCH 1942
General MacArthur leaves Philippines for Australia.

7 APRIL 1942
US and Filipino troops surrender on Bataan.

18 APRIL 1942
Doolittle bombing raid on Tokyo and other cities in Japan. Sixteen USAAF B-25 bombers under the command of Colonel James Doolittle launched from the aircraft carrier USS *Hornet* operating off the coast of Japan.

6 MAY 1942
Corregidor island falls to the Japanese.

7-8 MAY 1942
Battle of the Coral Sea.

4-5 JUNE 1942
Battle of Midway.

7-8 AUGUST 1942
First US landings on Guadalcanal. Naval battle of Savo Island.

27 SEPTEMBER 1942
Japanese advance on Port Moresby halted.

12-13 NOVEMBER 1942
Naval battle of Guadalcanal begins.

21 JANUARY 1943
Japanese base at Gona, New Guinea, captured and Sananada Point cleared.

9 FEBRUARY 1943
Last Japanese troops begin to leave Guadalcanal.

20 JUNE 1943
US troops land on New Georgia.

15 AUGUST 1943
US landings on Vella Lavella.

6-7 OCTOBER 1943
Japanese evacuate Vella Lavella.

20 NOVEMBER 1943
US landings on Tarawa and Bougainville.

30 JANUARY 1944
US troops land on Marshall Islands.

17 FEBRUARY 1944
Eniwetok Atoll attacked and secured by US forces.

8 MARCH 1944
Japanese offensive from Burma into India begins.

22 APRIL 1944
MacArthur's forces land in New Guinea.

15 JUNE 1944
Americans land on Saipan. Strategic bombing campaign against Japan begins.

19 JUNE 1944
Battle of the Philippine Sea

9 JULY 1944
Saipan secured.

18 JULY 1944
Japanese defeated at Imphal, India.

21-24 JULY 1944
US landings on Guam and Tinian.

15 SEPTEMBER 1944
US landings on Peleliu.

24 OCTOBER 1944
US landings at Leyte, Philippines. Battle of Leyte Gulf.

9 JANUARY 1945
US forces land on Luzon.

FEBRUARY 1945
Battle for Manila in the Philippines begins.

19 FEBRUARY 1945
US forces land on Iwo Jima.

3 MARCH 1945
Manila captured.

9 MARCH 1945
First fire-bomb attack on Tokyo.

20 MARCH 1945
British-led troops secure Mandalay in Burma.

26 MARCH 1945
Fighting ends on Iwo Jima.

1 APRIL 1945
US troops land on Okinawa.

12 APRIL 1945
Truman becomes US President after the death of Roosevelt.

3 MAY 1945
Allied troops capture Rangoon in Burma.

6 AUGUST 1945
Atomic bomb dropped on Hiroshima.

8 AUGUST 1945
USSR declares war on Japan.

9 AUGUST 1945
Atomic bomb dropped on Nagasaki.

14 AUGUST 1945
Japanese emperor broadcasts to the country, accepting surrender.

2 SEPTEMBER 1945
Formal Japanese surrender signed aboard USS *Missouri* in Tokyo Bay.

3 MAY 1946
Tokyo war crimes tribunal begins.

14-15 AUGUST 1947
India becomes independent.

12 JUNE 1948
Armed struggle against the British in Malaya for independence.

1 OCTOBER 1949
Mao Tse-tung declares Communist People's Republic of China.

31 DECEMBER 1949
Formal surrender of Dutch control over Indonesia.

SEPTEMBER 1951
American-led occupation of Japan ends.

STATISTICS CONCERNING COMBATANT NATIONS

Casualties of the Pacific War

Australia: Over 17,000 deaths; 14,000 wounded.

China: An estimated five million military causalities (killed and wounded); civilian casualties estimated between 10 and 20 million.

India: Over 24,000 deaths in military action; an estimated three million civilian deaths as a result of war-related famine in 1943.

Great Britain: 30,000 deaths; number of wounded unknown.

Japan: 1.8 million deaths in military action; 500,000 civilians killed.

USA: 80,000 deaths; number of wounded unknown.

It is difficult to estimate the number of civilians killed in the course of the war but in total many millions, in the Netherlands East Indies, the Pacific Islands, the Philippines, Burma, Malaya and Korea, died as a result of Japanese occupation and military engagements in their countries.

Principal Combatant Nations

Australia: After Pearl Harbor and the invasion of Malaya, Australia declared war on Japan in December 1941.

China: Invaded by Japanese in 1937, though a region in the north of the country, Manchuria, had been invaded six years earlier. The China Incident, as the Japanese called their fighting there, became part of the Pacific War, and part of World War II as a whole, after the attack on Pearl Harbor in 1941.

Great Britain: Britain and Japan were at war after the Japanese invasion of Malaya in 1941. Britain was already a combatant nation in World War II, having declared war on Nazi Germany in September 1939.

Japan: Japan was at war with China from 1937. After the attack on Pearl Harbor and the invasion of the British colony of Malaya, both occurring at the end of 1941, Japan was at war with the USA and Britain.

USA: After the Japanese attack on Pearl Harbor in December 1941, the USA and Japan were at war.

US Warships Completed or Obtained between July 1940 and September 1945

Battleships	10
Aircraft carriers	27
Escort carriers	111
Cruisers	47
Destroyers	370
Destroyer escorts	504
Submarines	217
Minecraft	975
Patrol ships and craft	1,915
Auxiliary ships	1,612
Landing ships and craft	66,055

Japanese Naval Strength on 7 December 1941

	Existing strength	Under construction
Battleships	10	2
Aircraft carriers	10	4
Cruisers	38	4
Destroyers	112	12
Submarines	65	29
Others	156	88

Comparison of Japanese and US Military Production Figures

	1939	1940	1941	1942	1943	1944	1945
Aircraft USA	5,856	12,804	26,277	47,836	85,898	96,318	49,761
Aircraft Japan	4,467	4,768	5,088	8,861	16,693	28,180	11,066
Tanks USA	–	400	4,052	24,997	29,497	17,565	11,968
Tanks Japan	–	1,023	1,024	1,191	790	401	142
Major naval vessels USA	–	–	544	1,854	2,654	2,247	1,513
Major naval vessels Japan	21	30	49	68	122	248	51

THE KOREAN WAR

CHAPTER 1:
FROM ONE WAR TO THE NEXT

Japanese forces advance into Manchuria in 1931, setting Japan on the path to World War II.

At the start of the twentieth century, Korea was a unified, independent kingdom. It had been ruled by the Yi dynasty for over 500 years. In 1910, however, the country was taken over by its powerful neighbour, Japan. The Japanese ruled Korea as a colony and did their best to wipe out Koreans' sense of national identity. The Japanese language was used for business, government and higher education. Only a minority of Koreans who collaborated with the Japanese benefited from their rule.

In the 1930s Japan set out to expand its empire in Asia. In 1931 the Japanese occupied Manchuria, across Korea's northern border, and then moved further into China, where full-scale war broke out in 1937. Japan's expansion brought it into confrontation with the United States, which backed China's Nationalist leader, Chiang Kai-shek. In December 1941 the Japanese went to war with the United States and Britain, launching World War II in the Pacific. A series of swift military victories allowed Japan to occupy a large area of Asia, including the Philippines, Malaysia and Indonesia. But the tide of war soon turned, and by 1945 Japan was facing total defeat at the hands of the United States and its allies.

AMERICA'S ALLIES One of America's allies in World War II was the Soviet Union, ruled by the communist dictator Joseph Stalin. Between 1939 and 1941 the Soviets had fought a war with Japan on the border between Manchuria and the Soviet Union. But the two countries then agreed a neutrality pact, and from 1941 to 1945 the Soviets were not at war with Japan, even though they were allies of the United States and Britain in their war against Germany. The Soviet Union did eventually declare war on Japan, but not until 8 August 1945 – two days after the Americans dropped the first atom bomb on the Japanese city of Hiroshima. By the time Japan surrendered on 15 August, Soviet troops had invaded Manchuria and had advanced into the far north of Korea.

THE JAPANESE SURRENDER In the final days before the Japanese surrender, the Americans hurried to devise a plan for the occupation of Korea by

SOVIET INTEREST

In March 1946 the head of the Soviet delegation to a joint US-Soviet commission on Korean reunification said:
'The Soviet Union has a keen interest in Korea being a true ... independent country, friendly to the Soviet Union, so that in future it will not become a base for an attack on the Soviet Union.'
[Quoted in *Rethinking the Korean War*, William Stueck]

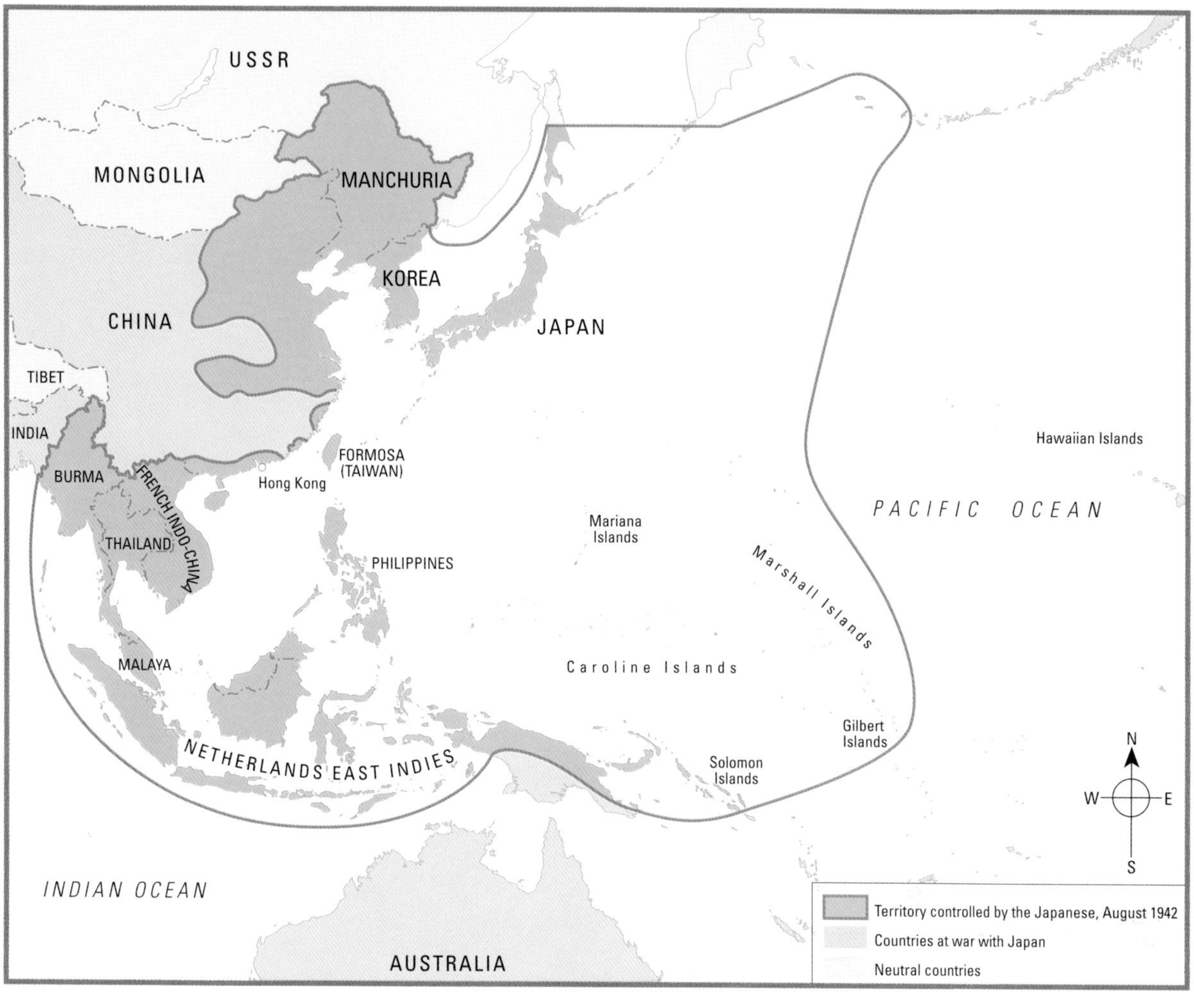

At its greatest extent during World War II, Japan's empire included most of East and South-east Asia. Korea had been Japan's first conquest, formally taken over back in 1910.

the victorious Allies. Military advisers to the US president, Harry S. Truman, drew up a proposal to divide Korea into two zones, with Soviet troops occupying the area north of the 38th parallel and American troops the area south of that line. Stalin accepted the proposal and Soviet troops, commanded by General Ivan Chistiakov, rapidly spread out through their zone. American troops began to arrive in Korea a few weeks later to occupy the south. The American occupation

President Harry S. Truman (centre) holds up the document signed by the Japanese when they surrendered to the Allies in 1945.

Korean students welcome US troops arriving to occupy the south of their country in autumn 1945.

force was commanded by General John R. Hodge.

In brief discussions on Korea during World War II, the Soviets and Americans had broadly agreed that the Koreans would not be ready to rule themselves when the Japanese were removed. The United States proposed that Korea should spend some years under foreign 'trusteeship' before being accorded full independence. Most Koreans, by contrast, expected their country to regain its independence immediately after the Japanese defeat. By the time US troops began to arrive, some political groups in the Korean capital, Seoul, had already declared an independent 'Korean People's Republic'. Throughout the country, Koreans had set up 'people's committees' to run affairs at local level. But neither the Americans nor the Soviets intended to let the Koreans sort out their own future, and both occupation zones came under the military rule of the two foreign powers.

LIVING IN EXILE Many Koreans who actively opposed Japanese rule had been forced to live in exile, some in the Soviet Union, some in China, and

Residents of Seoul, Korea's largest city, make the victory sign to celebrate the defeat of Japan.

NO MODERATION

General Hodge, commander of the US military occupation of South Korea, despaired of finding moderate Korean politicians who would create an American-style democracy. In 1947 he stated:

'It is a very difficult political situation that we run into... How in the dickens are you going to get political-middle-of-the-road out of this mess? I don't know the answer. I wish I did.'

[Quoted in *Korea: The Unknown War*, Jon Halliday and Bruce Cumings]

In 1945 Korea was occupied by Soviet forces north of the 38th parallel and by the Americans south of it. The 38th parallel was just a line on a map – it cut across many roads and railways.

Japanese defeat, these exiles returned to their home country, with different ideas about how it should be run. The Americans and the Soviets each quickly found a former exile to back as Korea's future leader. In October 1945, General Hodge welcomed the return to Korea of Syngman Rhee, a 70-year-old Korean nationalist who had lived in the United States for a quarter of a century. The Soviets, for their part, chose to back Kim Il-sung, a 33-year-old Korean communist who had fought in a guerrilla war against the Japanese in Manchuria in the 1930s and had then spent most of World War II in the Soviet Union.

Neither the Soviets nor the Americans at first intended to divide Korea in two. But each of the two great powers wanted Korea to be united under a government favourable to itself. The chances of agreement being reached in Korea faded as the wider relationship between the Soviet Union and the United States grew worse. In 1947, President Truman declared the 'Truman Doctrine', committing the United States to

Soviet dictator Joseph Stalin wanted to spread communist influence, but without involving his country in a war with the United States.

opposing the spread of communism worldwide. By 1949 the Americans and Soviets were open enemies, confronting one another in the 'Cold War'.

In the absence of agreement on the unification of Korea, each side built up a political system in the area under its military control. North of the 38th parallel, a Soviet-style state was constructed, with power concentrated in the hands of the communist North Korean Workers' Party. Most key positions were held by Koreans who, like Kim Il-sung, had recently returned from the Soviet Union. Soviet forces withdrew from Korea in 1948 and the area north of the 38th parallel became independent as the Democratic People's Republic of Korea (DPRK), with Kim Il-sung as president. Although there were some local revolts against communist rule, the Soviet-installed regime was largely secure in its control of North Korea.

SOUTH OF THE 38TH PARALLEL South of the 38th parallel, events did not go as smoothly. The Americans forcibly suppressed the 'people's committees', which they regarded as hot-beds of communism, and found themselves relying upon administrators and police who had formerly worked for the Japanese. Political life was chaotic, marked by local revolts, violent action by armed political extremist groups, and assassinations.

In 1948 Rhee won elections supervised by the United Nations, and became president of the Republic of Korea (ROK). But Rhee's control of the South was nothing like as secure as Kim's in

YOSU REBELLION

During the guerrilla war in South Korea, government forces had to suppress an uprising in the port of Yosu in October 1948. Official estimates of casualties in this operation were:

South Korean soldiers dead or missing	404
Rebels killed	821
Rebels captured	2,860
Civilians killed	over 1,000

the North. He soon faced a major guerrilla uprising, starting on the island of Cheju-do and then spreading to the Korean mainland. The North Koreans supported the anti-Rhee guerrillas in the South, just as the South Koreans promoted guerrilla activity, on a much smaller scale, in the North. The ROK authorities, with the aid of American advisers, had largely suppressed the guerrilla movement by early 1950, but only through ruthless action that cost tens of thousands of lives.

The ROK and the DPRK both strongly claimed to rule the whole of Korea. From the early summer of 1949 onward there were clashes along the 38th parallel between the forces of the two Koreas, bent on testing one another's defences. By June 1950, it has been estimated that up to 100,000 Koreans had died in guerrilla fighting and border clashes – victims of what has been called a 'Korean Civil War'. Both Kim and Rhee were eager to mount a full-scale invasion across

Kim Il-Sung, leader of North Korea from 1948, had a burning ambition to unite all of Korea under communist rule.

Between 1948 and early 1950, guerrillas backed by North Korea fought against South Korean government forces on the island of Cheju-do and across mountainous areas of the mainland. At the same time, South Korea promoted guerrilla activity inside North Korea.

the 38th parallel, each confident that he would emerge as the ruler of a unified Korea. Until 1950, however, neither could obtain permission for such a move from their powerful backers, the Soviet Union or the United States.

AMERICA'S CAUTION The United States had no desire to support a military adventure that might bring war with the Soviet Union. America's political leaders had an uneasy relationship with Rhee, feeling suspicious of his aggressive nationalism. Stalin was equally unready for a 'hot war' with the United States. The Soviets doubted Kim's ability to conquer the South, and they feared that an invasion would provoke the Americans into sending troops back into Korea.

ON A VOLCANO'S EDGE

Harold J. Noble, first secretary at the US Embassy in South Korea in 1950, claimed that America's failure to foresee a North Korean invasion was the result of living too long 'on the edge of a volcano'. He wrote:

'We knew it would explode some day, but as day after day, month after month, and year after year passed and it did not blow up, we could hardly believe that tomorrow would be any different.'

[Quoted in *Rethinking the Korean War*, William Stueck]

The promise of support from Communist China made it possible for North Korea to invade the South. Here, a Chinese student who has volunteered to fight in Korea is given a rousing send-off.

The communist victory in China left South Korea the only non-communist state in mainland East Asia.

The international situation changed dramatically, however, in October 1949. In that month, in China, the forces of Mao Tse-tung, the leader of the Chinese Communist Party, achieved a decisive victory in their Civil War against the Nationalist forces of Chiang Kai-shek, and a communist People's Republic was proclaimed in Beijing, China's capital. The remaining Nationalist forces took refuge on the island of Formosa (Taiwan), which lay about 200 km to the east of China. Mao signed an alliance with the Soviet Union in February 1950.

The Chinese communist victory inevitably focused American attention on East Asia. Korea, however, was still far from America's main concern. In a speech in January 1950 US Secretary of State Dean Acheson left it out of a list of countries that the United States regarded as within its 'defensive perimeter' in the eastern Pacific zone – a fact carefully noted by the Soviet Union.

Mao's victory seems to have changed Stalin's view of the Korean situation. In January 1950 the Soviet leader agreed to supply Kim Il-sung with the heavy armaments that he had long requested. The following April, the Soviets told Kim that he could attack the South if he got the backing of the Chinese – it was made clear to him that he could not expect the Soviet Union to intervene on his behalf if things went wrong. In May, Mao agreed to support Kim's proposed military action, promising Chinese military support if needed. The way was open for a North Korean invasion of South Korea.

Chiang Kai-shek, leader of the Chinese Nationalists who were defeated by the communists in 1949.

CHAPTER 2:
THE KOREAN WAR ERUPTS

Two days after the start of the war, a newspaper seller in London reports the bad news from Korea.

Soviet T-34 tanks were among the World War II-vintage equipment used by the North Koreans.

The Korean War began at 4.00 am on Sunday, 25 June 1950. After a preparatory artillery barrage, troops of the North Korean People's Army (NKPA) attacked South Korean positions on the Ongjin peninsula, on Korea's west coast. Through the morning the North Korean offensive spread eastward along the 320-km length of the 38th parallel, with thrusts towards Kaesong, Uijongbu, Chunchon, and down the east coast.

An arbitrary line on a map, the 38th parallel was not a defensible border – it followed no natural feature such as a river or mountain range. Also, the invasion achieved almost total surprise. Many South Korean officers and all but one US military adviser were away from frontline units, enjoying a weekend's leave. Kaesong was occupied within hours almost without a fight. There was some stiff South Korean resistance, especially at Chunchon, where the defenders had

US ARMY NUMBERS

Sharply reduced in numbers after World War II, the US Army had to expand rapidly to meet the demands of the war in Korea:

	US Army strength
July 1946	1,891,000 (including Army Air Force)
June 1950	591,000
July 1953	1,530,000

untypically been on the alert for an attack. But in general the North Koreans made rapid progress.

On paper the North Korean and South Korean armed forces were of equal strength, both numbering around 95,000. But the North Korean forces included thousands of battle-hardened troops and experienced officers who had fought on the communist side in the recent civil war in China. Others had served in the Soviet Red Army. They were equipped with good World War II-vintage Soviet equipment, including about 150 T-34 tanks. The South Koreans were in general poorly trained and equipped. They had no tanks and poor anti-tank weapons.

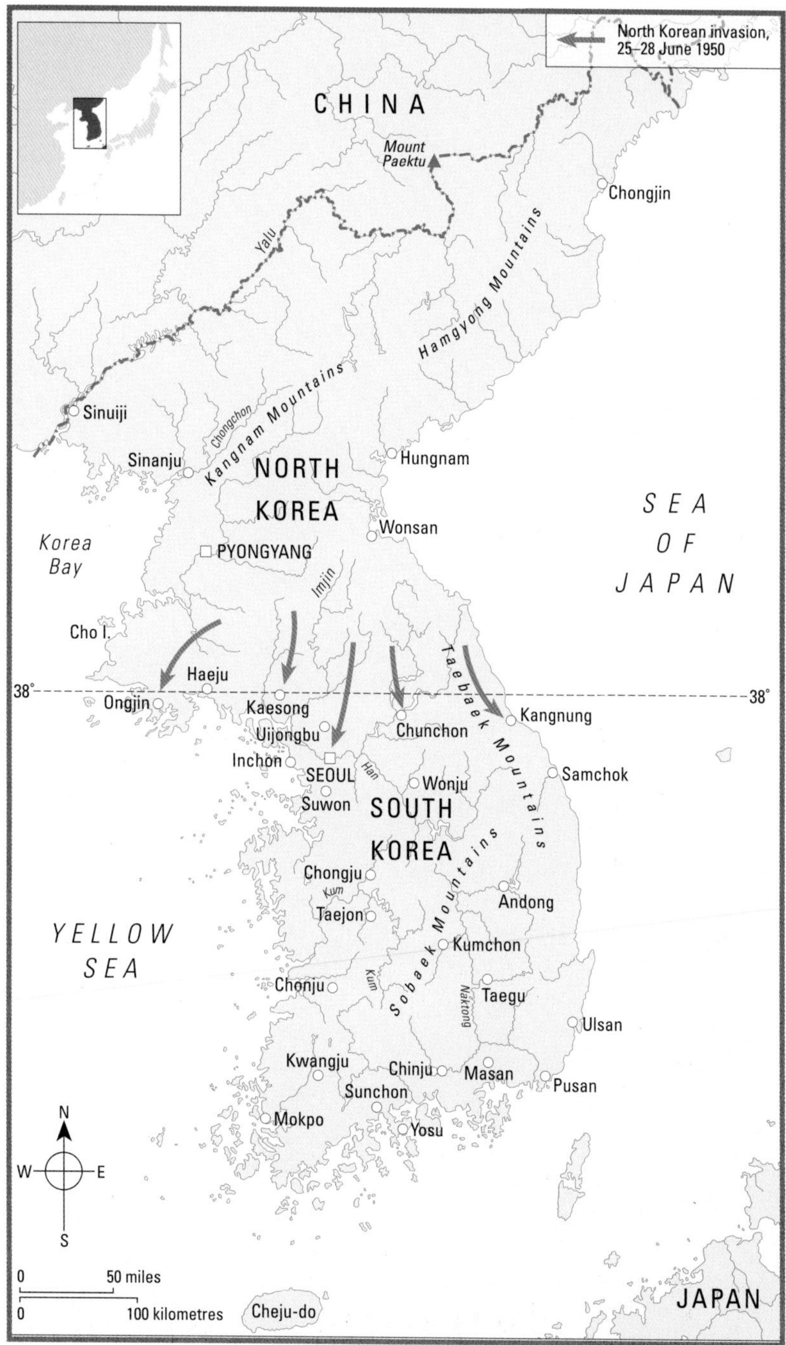

The first North Korean attack on 25 June 1950 was in the west, at Ongjin. Kaesong was soon occupied by the invaders, but they met stiffer resistance in front of Chunchon. The most important thrust was towards Seoul, which fell to the communists on 28 June.

NORTH KOREANS REACH SEOUL

Within three days of the start of the invasion, North Korean troops had reached Seoul, the capital of South Korea. Retreating southward from the city, the South Koreans in panic blew up bridges over the Han River too soon, killing hundreds of civilian refugees and soldiers who were still crossing the river and leaving many of their own troops and essential supplies stranded on the wrong side.

The North Korean government presented its military action as a legitimate response to a 'general attack' by the South Koreans across the 38th parallel. The United States and its allies, by contrast, denounced the North Korean invasion as – in the words of British Prime Minister Clement Attlee – an act of 'naked aggression'. The Americans had no hesitation about intervening militarily in support of the ROK. President Truman authorized air strikes against the North Koreans and the US Navy's Task Force 77 was ordered to sail into position to blockade the Korean coast. There was serious discussion among US political and military leaders about whether they

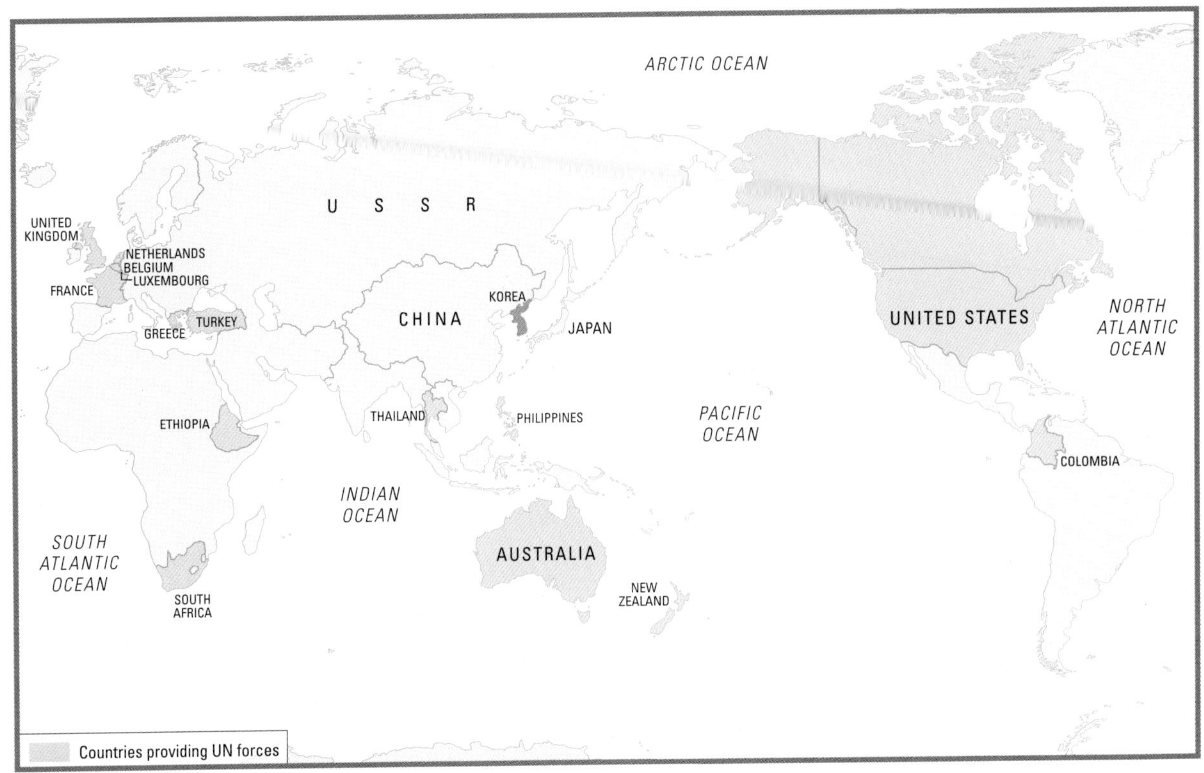

After the United States, Britain made the largest contribution to UN forces. Australia, Canada, New Zealand, Turkey, Colombia, Philippines and Thailand also provided substantial contingents. France, embroiled in a war in Indo-China, sent only a token force.

General Douglas MacArthur (right) is briefed by a staff officer in Korea, September 1950.

should use nuclear weapons to halt the invasion.

The US Commander in the Far East, General Douglas MacArthur, was based in Japan, which was then still under US military occupation. On 29 June, MacArthur flew to Suwon airfield, south of Seoul, to assess the situation for himself. Seeing the disorganized ROK troops in full retreat, MacArthur decided that US ground forces would be needed to turn back the communist advance. On 30 June President Truman authorized the dispatch of US troops to South Korea. The first units arrived there from Japan the following day.

UN DIPLOMATIC ACTIVITY Meanwhile, the outbreak of war in Korea had triggered frantic diplomatic activity. The Americans saw the invasion as part of a worldwide communist strategy directed by the Soviet Union against the 'free world'. The governments of the United States' friends and allies,

UN RESOLUTION

On 27 June 1950 the United Nations Security Council called on UN member states to: '*furnish such assistance to the Republic of Korea as may be necessary to repel the armed attack* [by North Korea] *and to restore international peace and security in the area.*'.

[Quoted by David Floyd in *War in Peace* magazine]

including Britain, did not all fully accept this view, but they did agree that North Korea had been guilty of armed aggression. Under the charter of the United Nations Organization, set up at the end of World War II, any country that carried out an act of aggression was supposed to be resisted by joint action on the part of UN members, who had jointly agreed to uphold world peace.

Immediately after news of the invasion broke, the United States presented a resolution to the United Nations Security Council demanding an immediate North Korean withdrawal to the 38th parallel. The Soviet Union, a permanent member of the Security Council, could have vetoed acceptance of this resolution. But the Soviets were boycotting the Council over the issue of Chinese representation – the Chinese Nationalists continued to represent China at the UN despite their defeat by the communists. In the absence of the Soviet Union, the Security Council backed the resolution. On 27 June, a second resolution was passed calling on UN member states to take collective military action in support of South Korea. Early in July, another resolution determined that forces from UN member states sent to Korea would operate under a Unified Command provided by the United States. MacArthur became commander of UN Forces in Korea.

The involvement of the United Nations gave an international seal of approval to US military intervention in Korea, but its practical effect was

A military band greets an American troopship arriving at the Korean port of Pusan in late July 1950. Holding Pusan was essential for the UN forces if reinforcements and heavy equipment were to be brought in.

British troops from the colony of Hong Kong embark to join the UN forces in Korea, 25 August 1950. US troops had been in Korea since July.

After the fall of Seoul on 28 June the US military headquarters in Korea was moved from Suwon to Taejon. The first US troops to arrive were ordered to block the road south from Suwon, but the North Korean advance swept them aside. By 15 July the North Koreans were on the outskirts of Taejon and threatening Yongdok on the east coast.

limited. US commanders in Korea continued to operate under the US president and US chiefs of staff – there was no question of them taking orders from UN Secretary-General Trygve Lie. And although Britain and some British Commonwealth countries quickly sent naval and/or airforce units to fight in the Korean theatre, initially only American troops joined the ROK forces in the ground war.

The US Army was not well prepared for a ground war. Since the end of World War II it had experienced sharp cuts in funding and troop numbers. As the only country in the world in possession of atom bombs (at least until 1949), the US had felt it could rely on those nuclear weapons for national defence, without spending heavily on conventional weapons or on training men to fight. Nevertheless, US military leaders entered the war with a confident belief that they could easily defeat the North Koreans. MacArthur planned for his men to retake Inchon, the major port nearest to Seoul, within three weeks.

Instead of powering their way to an easy victory, however, the Americans soon found themselves engaged in a desperate struggle to avoid a humiliating defeat. The first US troops hurriedly sent to Korea on 1 July 1950 were known as 'Task Force Smith', after their commander Lieutenant Colonel 'Brad' Smith. Positioned across the road south from Suwon with orders to delay the NKPA advance, they were routed by a North Korean column on 5 July. The same fate befell other US infantry formations brought over from Japan and thrown into the front line. Ill-prepared for combat after peaceful years as an occupation force, they were outfought and outmanoeuvred by the North Koreans who were superior in morale and fighting skill. South Korean guerrilla fighters, who had survived the suppression of their campaign against Rhee in 1948-50, also harassed the Americans and ROK forces. Operating behind the front, the guerrillas cut supply lines and ambushed isolated patrols.

Fighting a series of delaying actions, the Americans fell back on Taejon. There fierce street fighting took place before the city was abandoned on 20 July, with the US divisional commander, General William F. Dean, falling prisoner to the North Koreans. By the end of July, the whole of western South Korea had been lost to the NKPA and the American and ROK forces were withdrawing towards the key port of Pusan. Their hope now was to hold a defensive perimeter around the port until sufficient reinforcements arrived to mount a counterattack. The North Koreans, meanwhile, although severely battered by US air strikes and stiffening US resistance on the ground, continued to press forward, sensing that victory was almost in their grasp.

GRIM REALIZATION

A report by a US infantry unit on their first encounters with the North Koreans in July 1950 described the shock experienced by American soldiers:

'Early overconfidence changed suddenly to surprise, then to dismay, and finally to the grim realization that, of the two armies, the North Korean force was superior in size, equipment, training and fighting ability.'

[Quoted in *The Korean War*, Michael Hickey]

General William F. Dean led the defence of Taejon. Trapped behind enemy lines when the city fell, he was later taken prisoner.

CHAPTER 3: THE TABLES TURNED

General Walton H. Walker commanded Eighth US Army for the first six months of the war. He restored the morale of US and South Korean troops in the defence of the Pusan perimeter.

An American tank defends a position near Masan, on the Pusan perimeter. The arrival of tanks in August 1950 helped halt the North Korean advance.

At the beginning of August 1950, the Americans and ROK were still struggling to stabilize a defensive perimeter around the port of Pusan. A North Korean column was advancing on Masan, near the south coast of Korea, within 50 km of Pusan. Lieutenant General Walton H. Walker, the commander of what was now known as the Eighth US Army in Korea, threw the newly arrived 1st Marine Brigade into the battle to block this advance. More than 6,000 strong, equipped with Pershing tanks that outgunned the Soviet-supplied T-34s, the Marines were a different proposition from the mostly ill-equipped and inexperienced US infantry the North Koreans had previously fought. The attacking column was thrown back with heavy losses.

General Walker made it plain to his men that no further withdrawals were to be permitted. The defensive perimeter he established measured roughly 130 km from north to south and 80 km from east to west. The perimeter was not a continuous barrier but a line of strongpoints. Its defence depended on the swift movement of troops to reinforce areas that came under pressure.

THE PERIMETER HOLDS For six weeks, from the start of August to mid-September, battle raged along the perimeter, switching from sector to sector as the North Korean forces, commanded by General Kim Chaik, sought a decisive breakthrough. There was a critical period at the eastern end of the perimeter in the second week of August when Pohangdon and Yonil airbase fell to the NKPA, and an ROK division had to be evacuated by sea to avoid

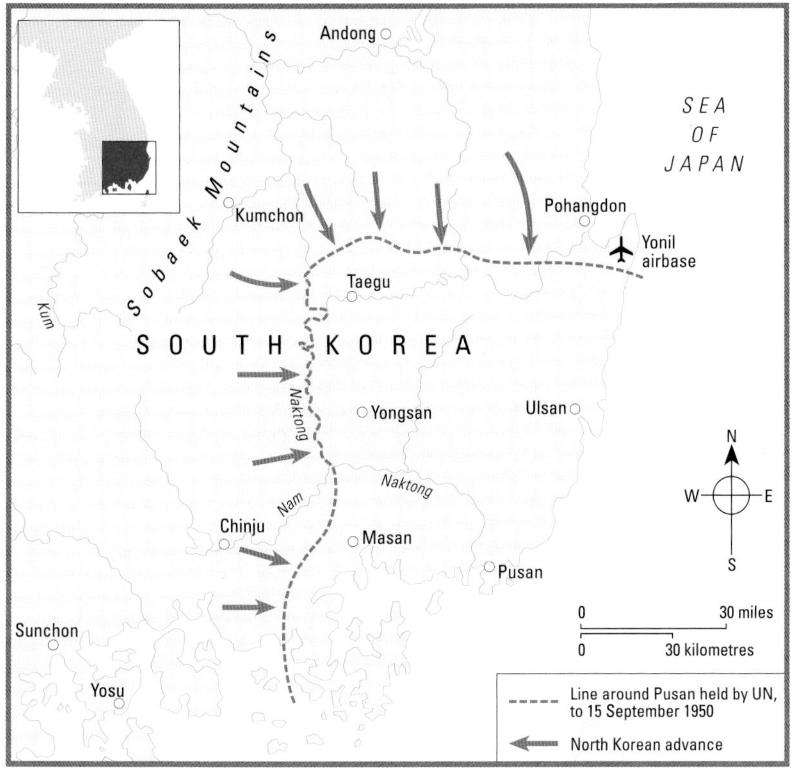

From end July to mid-September 1950 the NKPA made repeated attacks around the Pusan perimeter. UN forces had fortunately cracked enemy codes and so had warning of each new point of attack.

destruction. But an ROK counterattack heavily supported by US air strikes and naval bombardments forced the North Koreans back. Then the focus shifted to the area in front of Taegu, which had become the headquarters for US forces and the seat of the South Korean government. On 18 August the North Koreans came close enough to bring the city under artillery bombardment and the government fled to Pusan. A series of North Korean night attacks in the third week of August, however, failed to break through to Taegu.

KIM IL-SUNG Frustrated at the lack of progress, North Korean leader Kim Il-sung ordered that Pusan was to be captured by 1 September at all costs. But the balance of forces in Korea was shifting in favour of the UN with every week that passed. The North Koreans had suffered heavy losses of both men and equipment. They were now operating far from their home bases, and their long supply lines down the Korean peninsula were under attack from US and Australian aircraft and from UN naval forces patrolling the coast. By contrast, the US ground forces were growing in numbers and improving in quality and equipment. The American

HOLDING THE LINE

On 27 July 1950, General Walton H. Walker, commander of the Eighth US Army in Korea, told his senior officers:

'There will be no more retreating! ... We must fight until the end. Capture by these people is worse than death itself ... If some of us must die, we will die fighting together ... I want everybody to understand that we are going to hold this line. We are going to win ...'

[Quoted in *The Korean War*, Brian Catchpole]

A US tank commander keeps watch from the top of his vehicle outside Taegu in September 1950. Some 4,000 Americans died in the defence of Pusan.

Group which landed at Pusan at the end of August.

On 31 August General Kim Chaik launched a number of simultaneous offensives around the perimeter. As usual, the North Koreans fought with great determination, but each time they managed a temporary breakthrough Walker's forces proved able to hit back effectively. By 8 September the North Korean offensives had been definitively contained. MacArthur was able to assure the US Joint Chiefs of Staff that the Pusan perimeter would hold.

From the outset of the war, MacArthur had planned a seaborne landing at Inchon. This would enable him to retake Seoul and cut the main communication routes between North Korea and its troops in the South. MacArthur believed that the North Korean forces could then be crushed and the war brought rapidly to a successful conclusion. Once the Pusan perimeter was reasonably secure the planned amphibious landings – codenamed Operation Chromite – could go ahead.

COMMAND OF THE SEA

The United States and its allies had total command of the seas around Korea. The Americans also had a wealth of experience of amphibious operations accumulated during World War II. But MacArthur's plan nonetheless appeared hazardous. Inchon could only be

CASUALTIES IN OPERATION CHROMITE

The landings at Inchon and the subsequent retaking of Seoul caused the following military casualties:

	Killed/missing in action	Wounded
US Marines	428	2,031
US Army	163	411
US Navy	8	118
ROK Marines/Army	72	198
NKPA (estimate)	14,000	n.a.

US troops land at Inchon in the course of Operation Chromite. The soldiers had to clamber ashore on to sea walls.

approached along a long narrow seaway known as Flying Fish Channel, which was dotted with rocks, reefs and islands, many of which did not appear on naval charts. Landing ships would only be able to come ashore at Inchon at very high tides, which occurred roughly at monthly intervals. As there were no beaches, the landing craft would have to draw up against sea walls near the port.

A new formation was created to run the operation: X Corps, commanded by MacArthur's chief of staff, General Edward Almond. After several days of intensive air and naval bombardment, which devastated the defences around Inchon, the first US Marines landed on the island of Wolmi-do outside Inchon harbour before dawn on 15 September. Further landings followed later in the day, virtually unopposed, and by the morning of 16 September Inchon was in American hands.

Taking Seoul proved a far tougher proposition. Some 20,000 North Korean troops defended the city fearlessly in the face of massive US firepower. The US Marines reached the outskirts of Seoul on 20 September, but the defenders held out for a further eight days, forcing the Americans to fight their way

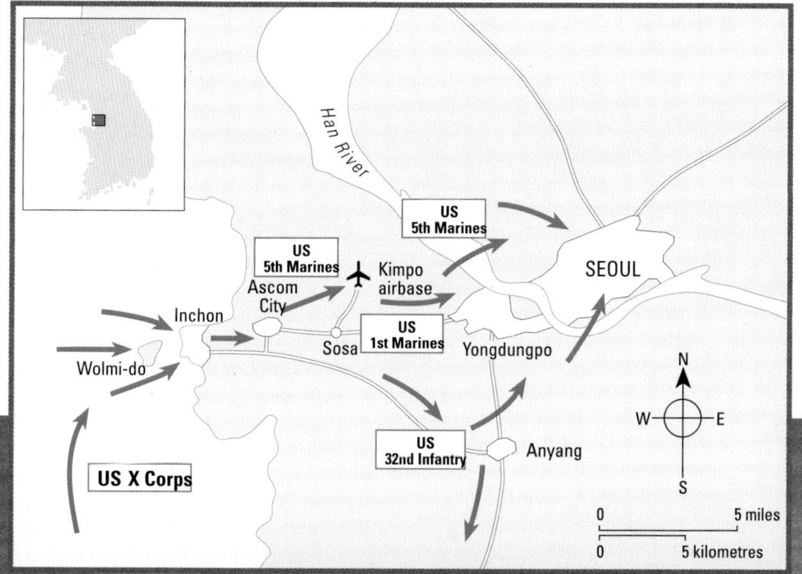

Operation Chromite, launched on 15 September 1950, began with a hazardous amphibious asault on the port of Inchon. Led by US Marines, X Corps then struck inland to seize Seoul.

Landing craft advance towards Inchon. The approaches to the port lay through narrow channels defended by coastal batteries.

American heavy artillery – 155mm howitzers – bombard communist positions in Seoul. The South Korean capital was in ruins by the time UN forces recaptured it in late September 1950.

through the city street by street before it could be secured. By the end of the battle Seoul was an awesome scene of slaughter and destruction.

While the battle for Seoul went on, Walker's Eighth Army went on the attack and broke out of the Pusan perimeter. The breakout had been planned to coincide with the Inchon landings, but North Korean resistance around the perimeter at first remained too strong. On 23 September, however, NKPA troops, fearful of being cut off from the rear by X Corps, began to withdraw northwards. Eighth Army was soon punching holes in the weakening North Korean line. Advanced elements raced north to join up with X Corps near Suwon on 26 September. Three days later MacArthur flew in to Korea in triumph, personally restoring Syngman Rhee to power in Seoul.

MacArthur's sense of triumph was understandable. He had turned the war around, inflicting heavy losses on the NKPA. As well the large numbers killed, tens of thousands of North Koreans had been taken prisoner. Yet many North Korean units successfully withdrew across the 38th parallel, heading further north to regroup. Many thousands of NKPA soldiers melted away into the South Korean countryside, staying to fight alongside the South Korean guerrillas who had already played a significant part in the conflict.

The fighting had been characterized by massacres and acts of savagery on both sides. The North Koreans frequently shot American soldiers whom they had taken prisoner – usually with a single bullet behind the ear. Both the North and South Koreans were guilty of the mass murder of civilians who had fallen into their hands and whom they decided were political enemies. Nervous American troops, thrown into a desperate battle in a country where many of the peasant

CALL FOR SURRENDER

On 1 October 1950 General MacArthur broadcast a message to the commander of the North Korean forces: *'I, as the United Nations Commander in Chief, call upon you and the forces under your command, in whatever part of Korea situated, forthwith to lay down your arms and cease hostilities under such military supervision as I may direct…'* [Quoted in *The Korean War*, Brian Catchpole]

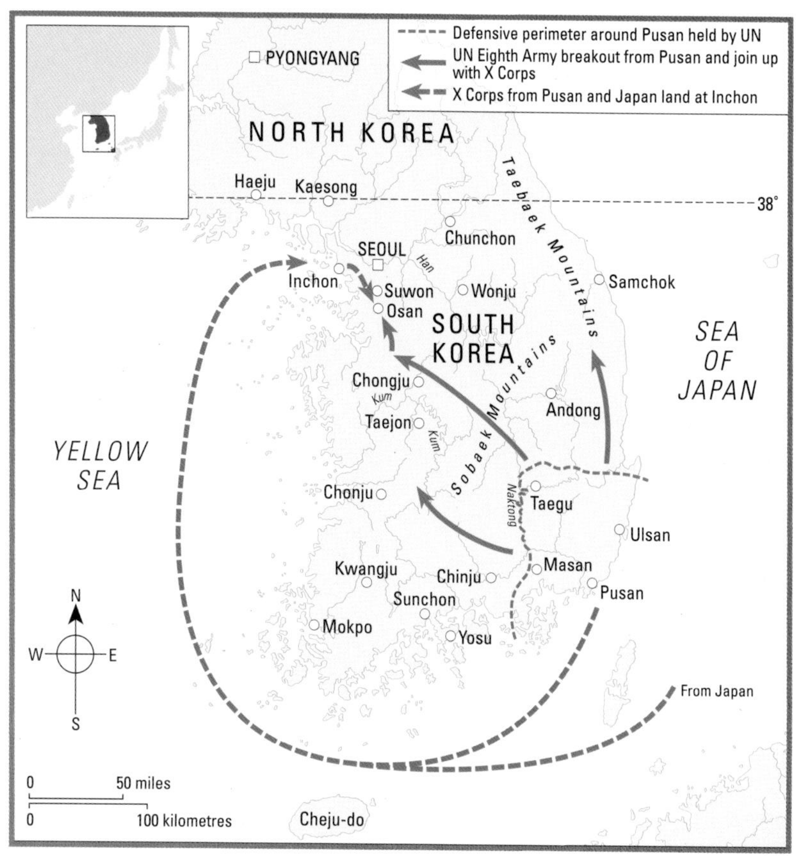

Retreating North Korean troops were trapped between X Corps, holding Seoul and Suwon, and Eighth Army forces advancing north. Large numbers were captured or killed, but some escaped to join South Korean guerrillas in the mountains.

population supported the communist enemy, often took to firing on civilians on the slightest suspicion that they might be involved in guerrilla activity. Quite apart from such violations of the accepted rules of war, the quantity of firepower deployed by the American forces, especially bombs and napalm dropped from the air, inevitably caused widespread devastation.

The war was now set to move into a new, even more destructive phase. On 27 September MacArthur received permission from the US government to continue the war into the North. He was authorized to advance beyond the 38th parallel to complete the destruction of the enemy army.

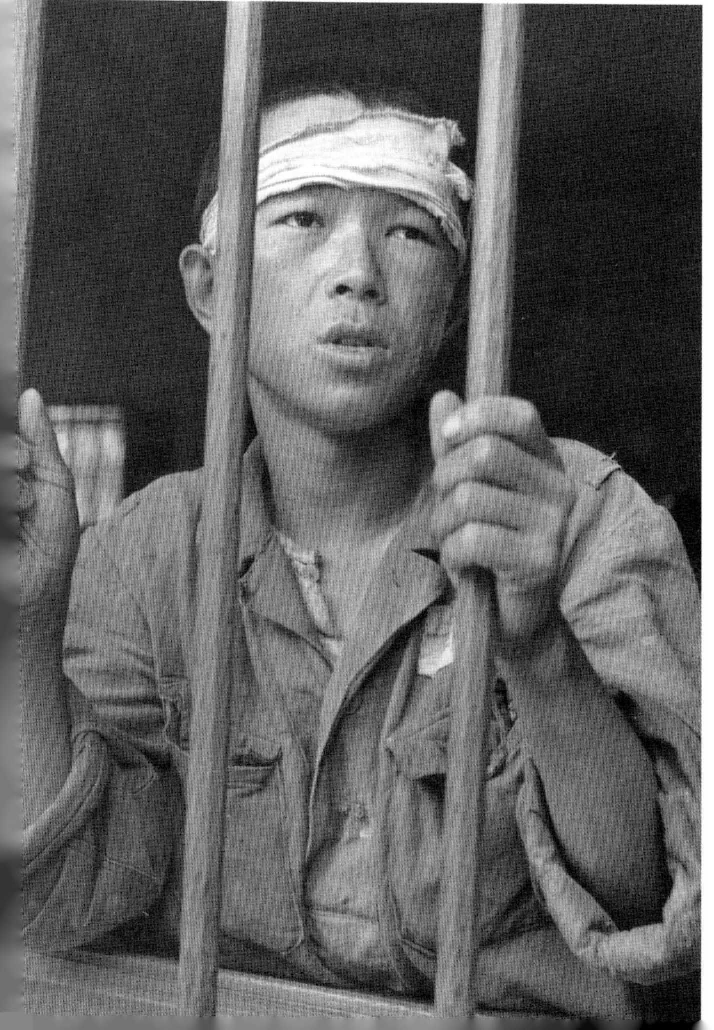

A wounded North Korean soldier is held in a prisoner of war (POW) camp in September 1950. POWs on both sides were often grossly mistreated.

CHAPTER 4: THE CHINESE ENTER THE WAR

American troops advance cautiously near Inchon in 1950. Fighting the Korean War was a particularly grim experience for foot soldiers.

The original US and UN military intervention in Korea had been justified as the defence of South Korea against aggression. By the end of September 1950 this act of aggression had been successfully resisted. The continuation of the war with an offensive across the 38th parallel was proposed by MacArthur with enthusiasm, and accepted with some reservations by the US government. They accepted it because, militarily, it would allow MacArthur to complete the destruction of the North Korean army, preventing it from regrouping and rearming for another attack on the South. Politically, it would open the way for the reunification of Korea under an anti-communist government. America's United Nations allies had more serious doubts about the wisdom of carrying the war into the North but felt bound to go along with the United States.

President Truman remained worried about a direct conflict with Communist China or the Soviet Union. MacArthur was authorized to invade North Korea only on condition that Chinese or Soviet forces did not enter the war in support of Kim Il-sung. MacArthur was expressly banned from carrying out military operations, including air strikes, across the Yalu River, which was the border between North Korea and China. He was also ordered to keep US troops at least 65 km away from the Chinese border.

MACARTHUR'S INVASION PLAN

MacArthur's plan for the invasion of North Korea maintained the division between Eighth Army, under General Walker, and X Corps, under General Almond, which had been created for the Inchon landings. Walker's forces were to advance up the west coast, while Almond's were to make a landing at the North Korean port of Wonsan on the east coast.

The movement of X Corps to Wonsan proved a complicated business. It was only possible to move the

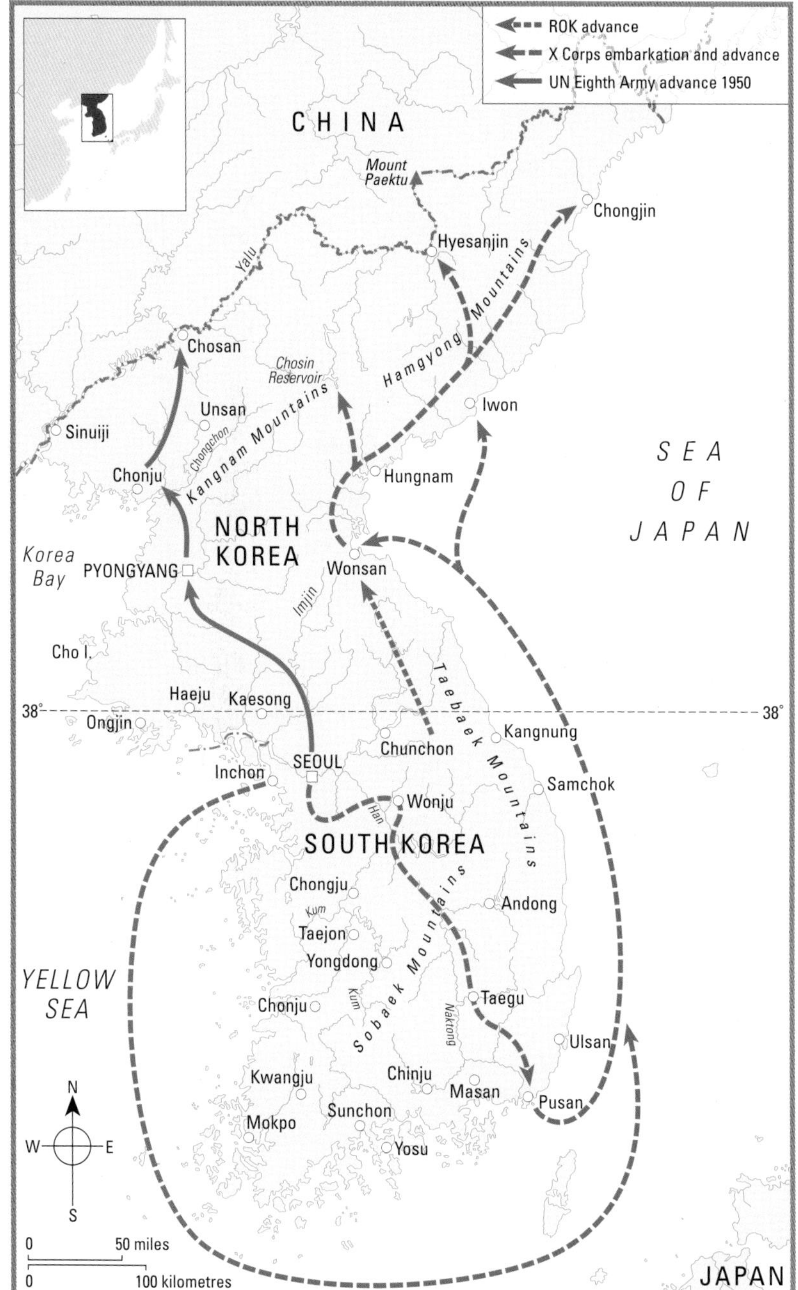

Invading the North, Eighth Army advanced in the west and X Corps with US Marines in the east. ROK units reached the Yalu River at Chosan on 27 October 1950 and X Corps took Hyesanjin on 21 November.

UNIFYING KOREA

On 10 August 1950, Warren Austin, the US Ambassador to the United Nations, spoke in favour of invading the North to unify Korea:

'Shall only part of the country [Korea] be assured freedom? I think not. The United Nations has consistently worked for a unified country, an independent Korea. It will not want to turn from that objective now.'

[Quoted in *Rethinking the Korean War*, William Stueck]

American POWs, taken captive by retreating North Koreans, are paraded in Pyongyang, 1950.

Marines directly by sea from Inchon. The rest of the Corps, some 14,000 men, had to travel across country to Pusan for embarkation. The journey was far from smooth, since guerrillas were operating through much of the area they crossed. By the time X Corps was ready to embark for the planned landings, Wonsan had already been occupied by ROK troops who had advanced overland across the 38th parallel. Since the entrance to Wonsan had been mined, and these mines took time to clear, the Marines were not finally able to land there until 26 October.

By that time the battle for Korea seemed almost over. The Eighth Army had made rapid progress, taking the North Korean capital, Pyongyang, on 12

North Korean civilians inspect their ruined homes after US bombing of Pyongyang in October 1950.

October, and pushing on northward. Syngman Rhee's followers and his police force moved in to Pyongyang and set about establishing his rule there by rounding up and massacring tens of thousands of suspected communists.

MacArthur had originally planned for Eighth Army and X Corps to link up on an east-west line across North Korea roughly at the 40th parallel. But the relative ease of progress made him more confident. He ordered advances northward on both sides of the peninsula, soon authorizing thrusts right up to the Chinese border. By 26 October, advanced units of the ROK 6th Division had reached the Yalu at Chosan. In the east, ROK troops had taken Hungnam and were advancing towards the Chosin Reservoir. At this point, with MacArthur confidently predicting that the Korean War would be over by Christmas, the first reports came in of encounters with Chinese troops.

The Chinese Communist government had begun building up its armed forces along its side of the border with North Korea in July 1950. In early October it gave the United States clear warning that it would take military action if North Korea was invaded. Chinese military commanders were confident that their men could take on and beat the Americans, but China's political leaders were worried about the effect of American airpower. In the second week of October, they obtained from the Soviet Union a promise to supply jet aircraft and to train Chinese pilots to fly them. With this assurance, the order was given for military intervention.

CHINESE PEOPLE'S VOLUNTEERS

Lightly armed troops of the Chinese People's Liberation Army – renamed for service in Korea as the Chinese People's Volunteers (CPV) – began to filter across the Yalu River into North Korea on 19 October. Completely unobserved, they took up positions in the

CHINESE WARNING

On 30 September 1950, Communist Chinese foreign minister Chou En-lai warned the United States in the strongest of terms against invading North Korea, declaring:
'The Chinese people absolutely will not tolerate foreign aggression, nor will they supinely tolerate seeing their neighbours being savagely invaded by imperialists.'
[Quoted in *Rethinking the Korean War*, William Stueck]

Chinese advance to the 38th parallel, December 1950
Area held by UN, end December 1950
Retreat of UN forces to South Korea by sea

CHINA
Mount Paektu
Chongjin
Hyesanjin
Hamgyong Mountains
Yalu
Chosan
Kangnam Mountains
Chongchon
Sinuiji
Sinanju
Hungnam
SEA OF JAPAN
Korea Bay
PYONGYANG
NORTH KOREA
Wonsan
Imjin
Cho I.
Haeju
38°
Ongjin
Kaesong
Taebaek Mountains
Kangnung
Chunchon
SEOUL
Inchon
Han
Samchok
Wonju
Chongju
Kum
Andong
Taejon
YELLOW SEA
SOUTH KOREA
Sobaek Mountains
Chonju
Taegu
Naktong
Ulsan
Kwangju
Chinju
Masan
Pusan
Sunchon
Mokpo
Yosu
N
W
E
S
0 50 miles
0 100 kilometres
Cheju-do
JAPAN

Chinese soldiers first crossed the Yalu into Korea in mid-October 1950. They launched a major offensive in late November, driving UN forces back. By Christmas all UN forces had fallen back to the 38th parallel or been evacuated by sea to Pusan.

Chinese soldiers sent to Korea were mostly battle-hardened veterans of the Chinese Civil War.

mountains south of the Yalu, where the remains of the North Korean army were also concealed. On 25 October the Chinese came into contact with UN forces advancing on the Chosin Reservoir in the east and near Unsan in the west (see map, p.25). There were fierce clashes from then until 6 November, with the Eighth Army suffering heavily enough to be forced to pull back and regroup. But the Chinese then withdrew into the mountains again, disappearing as suddenly as they had appeared.

MacArthur recognized the serious implications of Chinese intervention – on 8 November he told the Joint Chiefs of Staff that the movement of Chinese troops across the Yalu 'threatens the ultimate destruction of the forces under my command'. But once his men had lost contact with the Chinese, he chose to assume that the threat was not real. Britain, whose troops were fighting alongside the Americans in North Korea, at this point proposed negotiations with the Chinese, with the aim of establishing a demilitarized zone between the 40th parallel and the Yalu. The suggestion was brushed aside by the United States. On 24 November MacArthur ordered a final drive to the Yalu River that would, he believed, end the war – casually ignoring the instructions he had been given not to send American forces up to the Chinese border.

WINTER WEATHER The UN commanders on the ground were reluctant to take on this ambitious plan. They faced severe

'AN ENTIRELY NEW WAR...'

On 28 November General MacArthur announced: *'Chinese military forces are committed to North Korea in great and ever increasing strength ... We face an entirely new war.'*

[Quoted in *Rethinking the Korean War*, William Stueck]

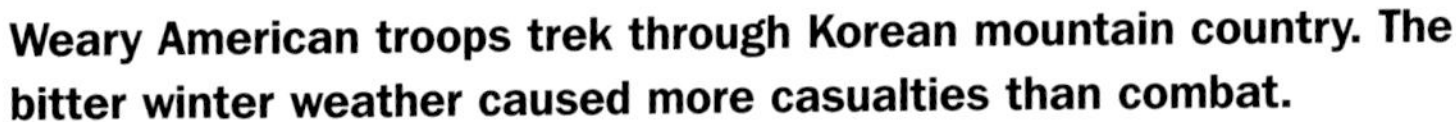

Weary American troops trek through Korean mountain country. The bitter winter weather caused more casualties than combat.

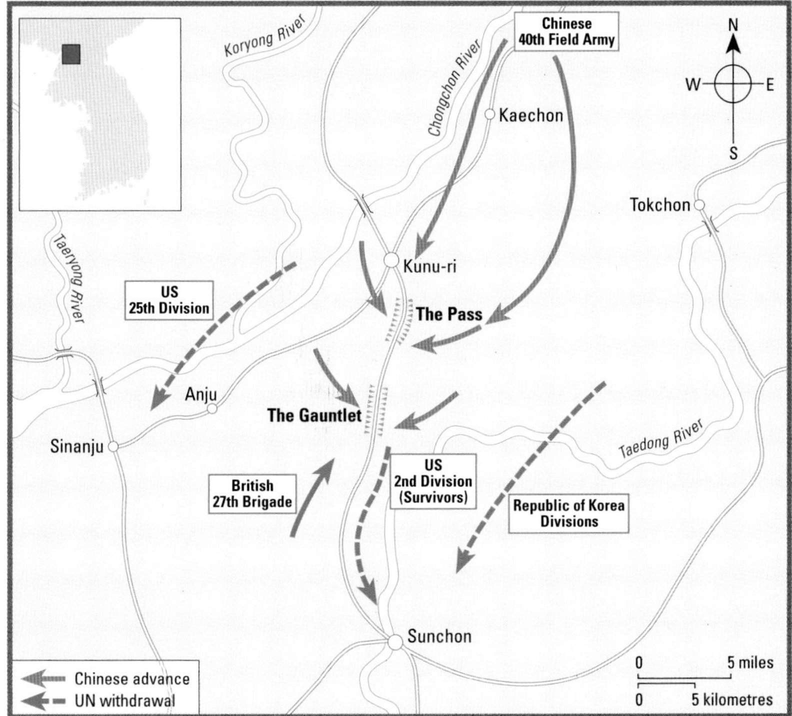

UN forces that had advanced deep into North Korea in November 1950 risked being cut off by fast-moving Chinese infantry operating across country. Ordered to retreat on 28 November, US 2nd Division were ambushed by Chinese forces in passes on the road south to Sunchon and decimated.

winter weather – experienced US Marine commander, General Oliver P. Smith, expressed his belief that 'a winter campaign in the mountains of North Korea is too much to ask of the American soldier or Marine'. They also knew that a Chinese army of unknown strength was somewhere ahead of them. Their worst fears were soon confirmed.

The commander of the Chinese Volunteers, General Peng Dehuai, had at least 200,000 men waiting for this opportunity to launch their own major offensive. Within two days of beginning their advance, the men of Eighth Army – chiefly Americans and South Koreans, with substantial British and Turkish contingents – came under attack by large numbers of Chinese infantry, aided by North Korean troops and guerrillas. The Chinese operated on foot across country, without artillery, tanks or air support. They tore through the right flank of the Eighth Army, sweeping South Korean forces aside in a few hours. On 28 November Eighth Army was ordered to withdraw, but the Chinese had taken up positions on the road behind them, to the south of the Chongchon River. The retreating UN forces had to fight their way through roadblocks and ambushes, suffering heavy losses of men and equipment. The 2nd Division was so badly hit that it ceased to function as a fighting formation.

In the east, part of X Corps had advanced towards the Yalu across the coastal plain while a smaller force, including US Marines and small number of British Royal Marines, headed across the mountains to the Chosin

US Marines carry a wounded comrade to an airstrip for evacuation to hospital during the fighting in North Korea in the winter of 1950.

Reservoir. Once the scale of the Chinese offensive became apparent, General Almond ordered his forces to withdraw toward the port of Hungnam. The Chosin Reservoir, however, was deep within territory occupied by the Chinese and North Korean guerrillas. The approximately 17,000 UN troops around the reservoir had to fight their way back along narrow roads to the sea. Asked by a journalist whether he would describe this action as a retreat, Marine General Smith replied: 'Retreat, Hell. We're just attacking in a new direction.' The communist forces were unable to prevent the UN troops reaching Hungnam by 11 December.

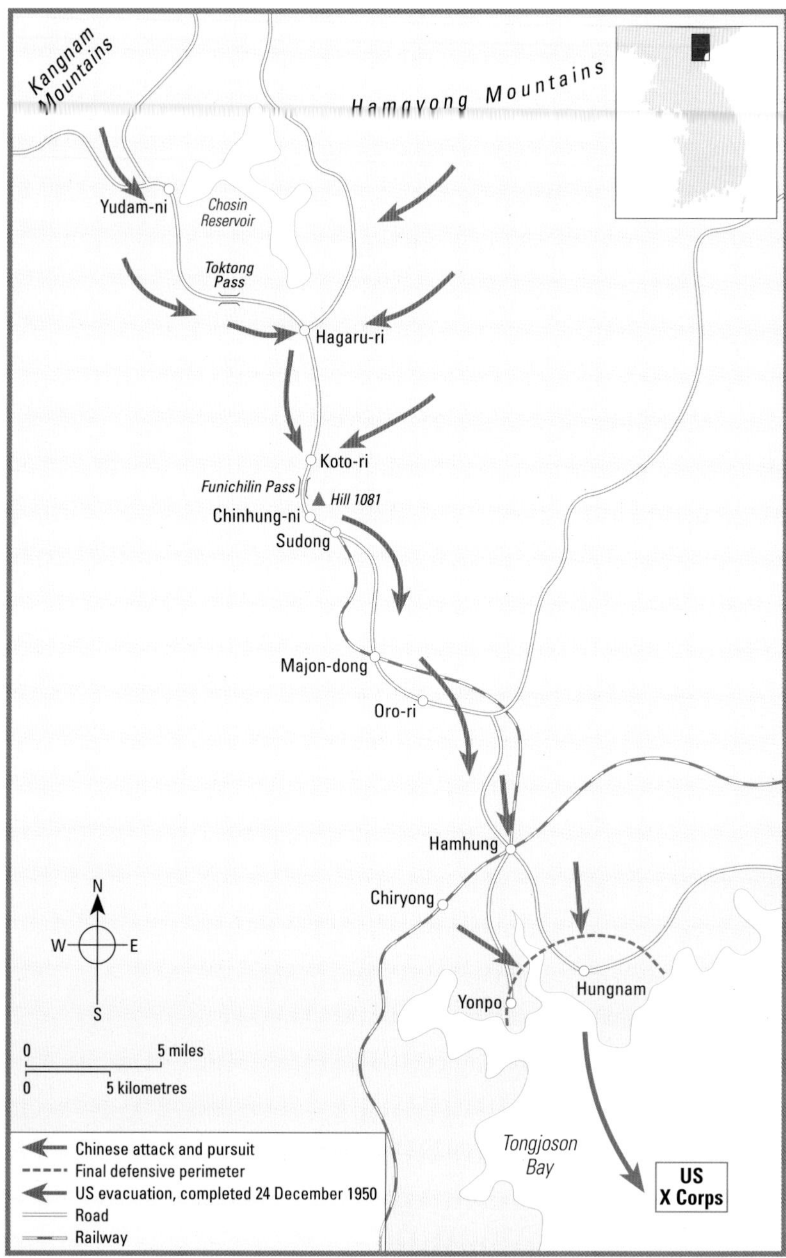

US Marines and other UN troops which had advanced to the Chosin Reservoir were attacked by Chinese forces at the end of November 1950. They held Hagaru-ri in desperate fighting until 6 December. The Marines then fought their way back through the Funichilin Pass and down to the port of Hungnam, which they reached on 11 December.

PYONGYANG WAS ABANDONED By then the Eighth Army had abandoned North Korea. Once in retreat, it proved impossible to turn the men around to make a stand. By 5 December the UN forces had left the Chinese behind them, but still they continued to head southward, with many American units in complete disarray. Although British troops, were prepared to defend it, Pyongyang was abandoned without a fight. It was what the Americans called 'a bug-out'. Only when they reached the 38th parallel was General Walker able to reform his army and establish a defensive line.

X Corps moved back to the South in a far more orderly manner, taking ship from Hungnam and other North Korean ports to Pusan. By 24 December, exactly a month after MacArthur had launched his offensive to end the war, no UN forces remained north of the 38th parallel. Kim Il-sung's communists proceeded to reimpose their rule with great brutality.

The UN armies had suffered a humiliating defeat. The Chinese, however, had also taken a severe battering. At least 40,000 men, many of them among their best troops, had been killed. The Soviet Union had fulfilled its promise to send MiG-15 jet fighters with Soviet pilots to bases on the Chinese side of the

North Korean border, and from early November 1950 they engaged in battles with American aircraft near the Yalu River. But the MiGs did not venture further south and US aircraft remained unchallenged over most of Korea. Using bombs, rockets and napalm, they imposed heavy casualties on Chinese troops. Also, although the Chinese infantry on the whole coped better with the harsh conditions than their enemies, thousands of soldiers suffered from exposure to the extreme cold, contracting frostbite or even in some cases freezing to death. Many units ran desperately short of food – unless they could capture some of the Americans' lavish supplies.

By the end of December 1950, the Chinese and their North Korean allies were sufficiently reorganized and resupplied to resume their offensive, striking across the 38th parallel. After six months of bitter fighting, the ground war was back where it had started.

Turkish troops serving with the UN forces prepare to fight a delaying action against the advancing Chinese in December 1950.

US soldiers take a rest behind the lines in South Korea, January 1951. Even away from the enemy, there was no escaping the weather.

CASUALTIES OF COLD

Among US Marines retreating from the Chosin Reservoir, the extreme cold put more men out of action than the fighting. Marine casualties November-December 1950 were:

Killed in action	718
Missing	192
Wounded in action	3,508
Non-battle casualties	7,313

CHAPTER 5: FIGHTING TO A HALT

The Chinese entry into the war in Korea created an acute sense of crisis in the United States in the winter of 1950-1. There was a real fear that the Korean War might be about to lead to a worldwide 'total war' between the United States and its allies on one side and the Soviet Union and its allies – including Communist China – on the other. President Truman expressed this fear on 9 December 1950, writing: 'It looks like World War III is here...' It was expected that if a world war did occur, nuclear weapons would be used by the United States and also probably by the Soviet Union – the Soviets had exploded their first atom bomb in a test in 1949.

THE THREAT OF A WORLD WAR The threat of a world war, which both the United States and the Soviet Union wanted to avoid, meant that both sides followed self-imposed rules designed to prevent the Korean War escalating. For example, although

President Truman and Prime Minister Attlee (foreground left and right) meet in December 1950. Attlee opposed the use of atom bombs in Korea.

The UN General Assembly – seen here in 1949 – maintained majority support for American policy in Korea throughout the war.

Soviet pilots took part in the air war fought over North Korea, clashing directly with US pilots, the Soviet Union always denied that its aircrew were in the country and limited their operations – they never flew over areas occupied by UN troops. US aircraft did not attack targets inside China, including communist air bases.

Faced with the desperate military situation in Korea at the end of 1950, however, the American government was tempted to break the self-imposed limits set on military action. Two major options were considered. One was to widen the war by attacking the Chinese mainland from the air and sea to destroy China's capacity to wage war. The other was to escalate the war by using atom bombs. Both these options were urged by General MacArthur and strongly opposed by America's major UN allies, including Britain.

At the end of November 1950 a crisis occurred in America's relations with its allies when President Truman hinted publicly that the use of atom bombs in Korea was not ruled out. The leader of the British Labour government, Prime Minister Clement Attlee, had faithfully supported the Americans over Korea, politically and

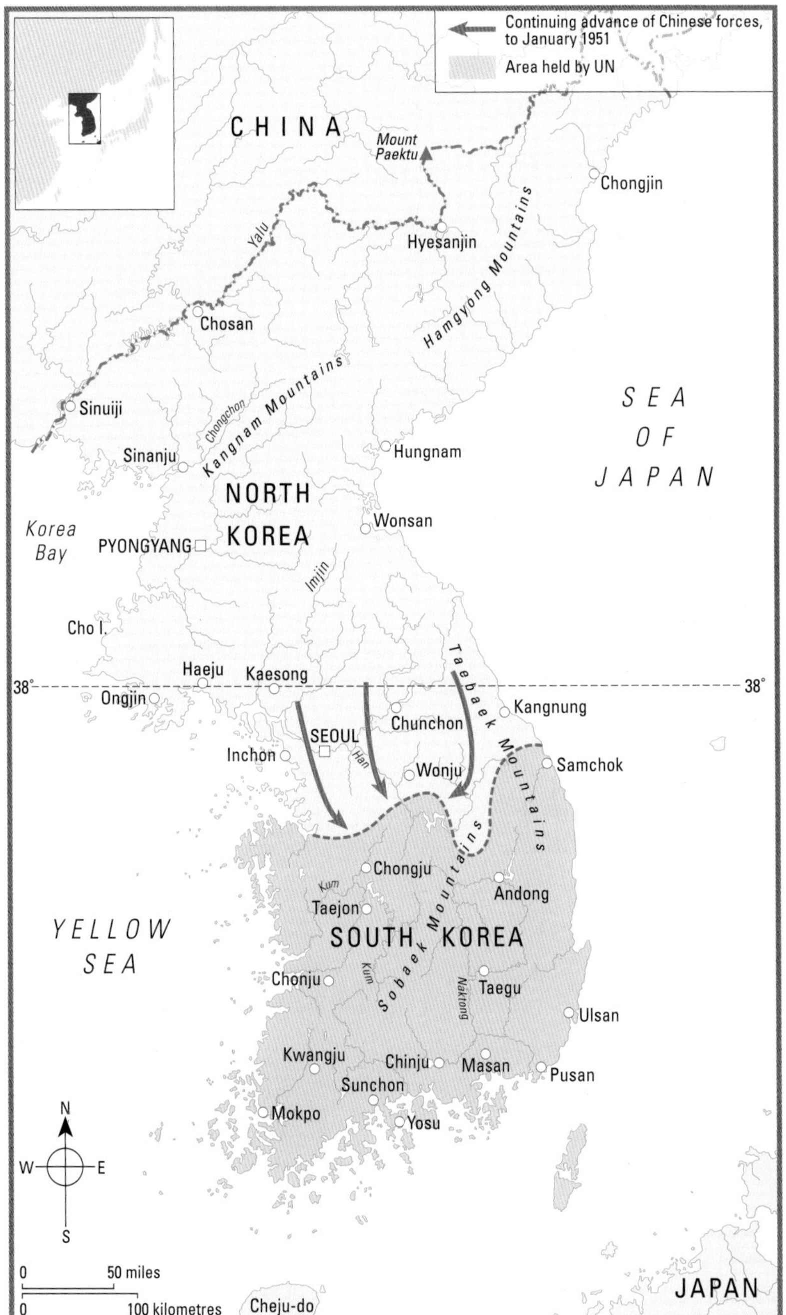

NATIONAL EMERGENCY

On 16 December 1950 US President Truman declared a national state of emergency, telling the American people: *'Our homes, our nation, all the things we believe in are in great danger ... I summon our farmers, our workers in industry and our businessmen to make a mighty production effort to meet the defense requirements of the nation...'*

[Quoted in *Korea: The Unknown War*, Jon Halliday and Bruce Cumings]

The communist forces launched a fresh offensive at New Year 1951, soon recaptured Seoul, and advanced about 80 km south of the city. There UN forces at last formed a defensive line that held its ground.

militarily, despite outspoken criticism of the war by some Labour members of parliament (MPs). The suggestion that the United States might use atom bombs caused uproar in the House of Commons and Attlee asked for an urgent meeting with Truman. In talks in Washington in early December, Attlee extracted from Truman a promise that atom bombs would not be used without Britain first being consulted.

CHINA'S LEGITIMATE GOVERNMENT The United States never, however, finally ruled out the use of atom bombs in Korea and US leaders continued to discuss them as a military option up to the end of the war. Britain also failed to persuade the United States to take a less hostile line on Communist China. The United States had committed itself to the support of Chiang Kai-shek's Chinese Nationalists based on Formosa (Taiwan) and would not recognize the communists as China's legitimate government. After a British-sponsored UN peace initiative was rejected by China in January 1951, Britain reluctantly supported the United States in having Communist China condemned by the UN as an 'aggressor state'.

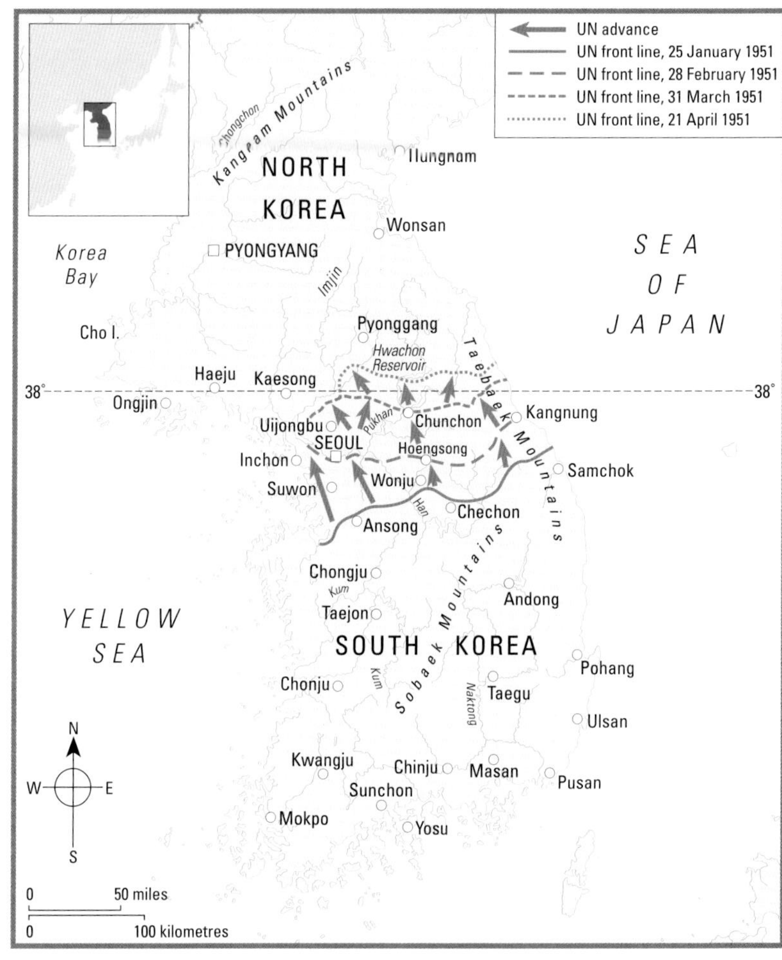

From January to April 1951, under the command of General Ridgway, UN forces steadily pushed the communists back in a series of offensives marked by the heavy use of artillery and air strikes.

Chinese Volunteers who have been taken prisoner are guarded by US Marines in January 1951 – a rare local success for the UN forces at this desperate stage of the war.

Fortunately, a change in the military situation in Korea in the first half of 1951 dampened down the acute crisis. The year started with a renewed communist offensive that once more sent the UN forces reeling into retreat. Chinese troops attacked across the frozen Imjin River before dawn on New Year's Day. Blowing bugles and shouting insults they

DISORDERLY RETREAT

General Matthew B. Ridgway, commander of Eighth Army, described the unruly retreat of South Korean troops in the face of the first Chinese offensive of 1951:

'On New Year's morning I drove out north of Seoul and into a dismaying spectacle. ROK soldiers by truckloads were streaming south, without order, without arms, without leaders, in full retreat. Some came on foot, or in commandeered vehicles of every sort. They had just one aim – to get as far away from the Chinese as possible.'

[Quoted in *The War in Korea*, Matthew B. Ridgway]

bore down upon the South Korean troops on the other bank, most of whom simply turned and fled. The Eighth Army was now under a new commander, General Matthew B. Ridgway, after the death of General Walker in a road accident. Ridgway witnessed with dismay the flight of his troops from the battlefield. The failure of so many of his soldiers to stand and fight left him with no choice but to order a general withdrawal. The decision to abandon Seoul was taken on 3 January. Over the following week UN forces fell back some 70 or 80 km south of the city. American leaders discussed a possible evacuation of all UN ground troops from Korea.

But, reliant on supplies carried mostly on the backs of human porters down the length of the Korean peninsula, the Chinese army was running out of ammunition and food. The Chinese and North Koreans had also suffered heavy casualties and replacement troops were slow to arrive. By mid-January their offensive had run out of steam and they came to a halt. This respite gave Ridgway the chance to organize the first effective UN counter-offensive since the Chinese entered the war.

The UN forces were being rapidly strengthened with fresh troops and equipment. Ridgway had to find a way to make his increased strength effective on the battlefield. The lightly armed Chinese had achieved their successes largely through mobility and surprise, infiltrating and overrunning UN positions in a way that unnerved and demoralized UN troops. Ridgway set out to establish an unbroken line from coast to coast across the peninsula, so that his men could not be outflanked or surrounded. This line was to advance up the peninsula, preceded by an intensive barrage of artillery fire and air attacks which would destroy the enemy without the need for costly assaults by UN infantry. This tactic was chillingly dubbed the 'meatgrinder'.

COUNTER-OFFENSIVE Ridgway launched his counter-offensive on 25 January 1951. The new tactics proved very effective. On the western flank, by 10 February UN forces had recaptured Inchon and

General Matthew B. Ridgway (right) restored the morale of US troops and initiated a war of attrition – the 'meatgrinder' tactics.

Weapons using burning petrol – such as this flamethrower and napalm bombs – were widely employed in Korea. They caused horrific injuries.

reached the Han River. In one five-day period 4,200 Chinese soldiers were reckoned to have been killed for the loss of only 70 UN troops. The Chinese responded by attempting to overcome their enemy's firepower with sheer numbers. They adopted 'human wave' tactics in which thousands of infantry rushed forward in mass frontal attacks on UN positions. These tactics achieved some successes, but at enormous human cost.

Ridgway's offensive ground forward through February and March in a series of operations codenamed, with deliberate ruthlessness, Thunderbolt, Killer, and Ripper. Seoul, by this time the devastated shell of a city, was retaken on 14 March. By 21 April UN forces in the centre and east had once more edged north of the 38th parallel, with the front line in the west running along the Imjin River.

With South Korea back in UN hands, President Truman began to prepare a peace initiative, a course strongly urged by his UN allies. General MacArthur, however, remained totally opposed to the idea of compromise with the Chinese Communists. MacArthur saw the objective of the war as total military victory and was not ready to stop short of controlling Korea up to the Yalu River. He not only argued for strikes against targets inside mainland China, but also wanted Chiang Kai-shek's Chinese Nationalist troops brought in to the war against the Communist Chinese.

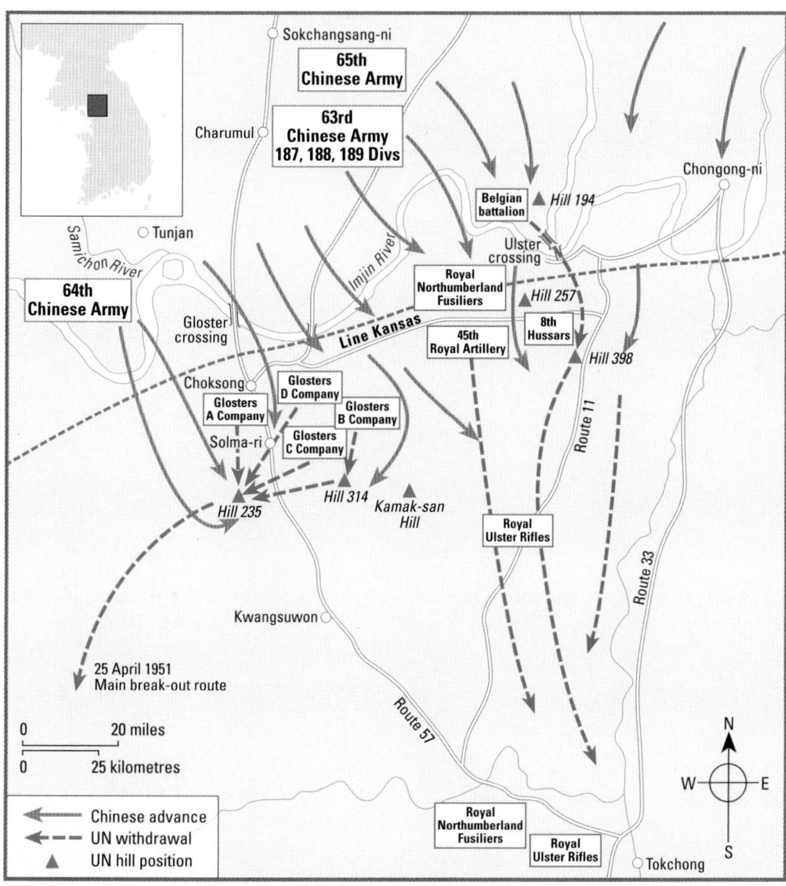

On 22 April 1951 Chinese troops crossed the Imjin River on a sector of the front held by British forces. Surrounded by the enemy, four companies of the Gloucestershire Regiment (the Glosters) held crucial hill positions for three days. Only 39 men eventually escaped.

MACARTHUR'S POLICY

General MacArthur's dismissal followed his public threat, on 24 March 1951, to extend the war to a direct attack on China:

'The enemy [China] *must by now be painfully aware that a decision of the United Nations to depart from its tolerant effort to confine the war to the area of Korea, through an expansion of our military operations to his coastal areas and interior bases, would doom Red China to the risk of imminent military collapse.'*

[Quoted in *The War in Korea*, Matthew B. Ridgway]

MACARTHUR IS DISMISSED

America's UN allies had come to distrust MacArthur deeply – British Foreign Secretary Herbert Morrison described him as 'rash and politically irresponsible'. The American government feared that MacArthur might widen the war by some military action ordered on his own authority. After the general pressed publicly for a more aggressive policy, in direct defiance of instructions from his government, Truman dismissed him from all his commands on 11 April. MacArthur was a powerful and popular figure in the United States, and his dismissal caused a political storm. General Ridgway was promoted to replace MacArthur as UN Commander, while General James Van Fleet took over from Ridgway as army commander on the ground in Korea.

General Van Fleet was faced almost immediately by a fresh military crisis. Despite the heavy losses that they had sustained over the previous months of intense fighting, on 22 April the Chinese once more took the offensive. This time, however, the UN forces were better organized and equipped for defence, and in most instances were prepared to stand and fight – to the death if necessary.

This was nowhere more notable than on the sector of the Imjin River held by the British 29th Brigade. Despite the Brigade's valiant efforts, the Chinese broke through their line. The four companies of the Gloucestershire Regiment ('Glosters') fighting with the 29th Brigade were encircled by the enemy, but still held out for three days. In the end, all but 39 of the Glosters were killed or taken prisoner.

Still regarded as a national hero, General MacArthur is given a tickertape welcome on Broadway, New York, after being sacked as commander of the UN forces in Korea by President Truman in April 1951.

CHINA'S OFFENSIVE IS REPULSED

In the face of such determined resistance, the communist offensive came to a halt at the end of April just short of Seoul. The Chinese and North Koreans are reckoned to have lost some 70,000 men in nine days' fighting, compared with UN losses of about 7,000. A renewed Chinese effort in mid-May achieved little and the exhausted communist forces were soon once more withdrawing northward to the 38th parallel and beyond.

By June 1951, another half year of desperately destructive warfare had again brought the two sides more or less back where the war had started.

RISING NUMBERS

By May 1951, the United States estimated the numbers of troops involved in the fighting as follows:

Chinese	542,000
North Korean	197,000
Total communist	**739,000**
US and UN allies	270,000
South Korean	240,000
Total UN	**510,000**

The Chinese launched an offensive on 22 April that pushed south through the following week. But stiff UN resistance from 1-15 May checked the Chinese advance short of the city of Seoul. A second Chinese effort from 16 May soon ran out of steam, and their forces soon began to withdraw northwards across the 38th parallel.

Chinese front line, 22 April 1951
Chinese front line, 30 April 1951
Chinese front line, 16 May 1951
Chinese front line, 22 May 1951
First advance, 22–30 April 1951
Second advance, 16–22 May 1951

NORTH KOREA
SOUTH KOREA
SEA OF JAPAN
YELLOW SEA
Korea Bay
Kangnam Mountains
Taebaek Mountains
Sobaek Mountains
Hungnam
Wonsan
PYONGYANG
Cho I.
Pyonggang
Hwachon Reservoir
Haeju
Kaesong
Ongjin
38°
Uijongbu
Chunchon
Kangnung
Inchon
SEOUL
Chipyong-ni
Samchok
Suwon
Wonju
Chechon
Ansong
Chongju
Andong
Taejon
Pohang
Chonju
Taegu
Ulsan
Kwangju
Chinju
Masan
Pusan
Sunchon
Mokpo
Yosu
0 50 miles
0 100 kilometres

US Marines watch rocket artillery fire as Chinese positions are heavily bombarded. From 1951 onwards, the war was increasingly a contest of UN firepower pitted against Chinese numbers.

CHAPTER 6: STALEMATE AND NEGOTIATION

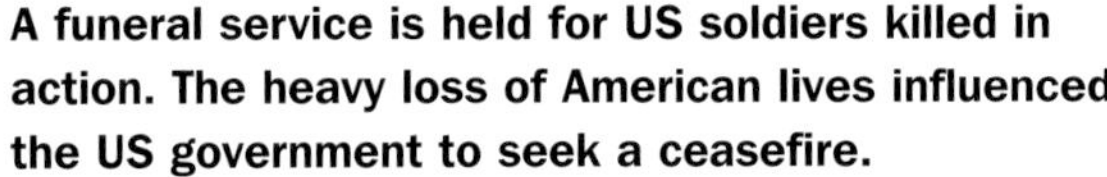
A funeral service is held for US soldiers killed in action. The heavy loss of American lives influenced the US government to seek a ceasefire.

US Marines search a Chinese soldier they have captured. Chinese losses in the fighting – killed and captured – were on a massive scale.

In June 1951 the Chinese Communist government told the Soviet Union that it intended to seek an armistice in Korea. In the same month, the United States privately indicated to the Soviet Ambassador to the UN, Jacob Malik, that a ceasefire at or around the 38th parallel would be acceptable to the United States. With both sides apparently prepared to end the fighting, prospects for rapid agreement looked good. Yet the ceasefire negotiations, which began in July 1951, in fact went on for two years – a period during which many hundreds of thousands of lives were lost.

THE 38TH PARALLEL The failure to make progress in the talks was especially frustrating because the two sides were in rough agreement on the main issue from the outset. They accepted that a ceasefire would, at least for the time being, leave Korea divided at or around the 38th parallel as it had been before the war started. Both Chinese and US leaders had come to the conclusion that the cost of attempting to win the war was too high for any advantage they might stand to gain from a united Korea.

From the summer of 1951 onward, the purpose of the fighting on both sides was not to achieve military victory but to keep up pressure on the enemy while negotiations took place. The UN forces made a last substantial advance in August-October 1951, though

OPPOSING ARMIES

Estimated troops levels of the two armies confronting one another in Korea in the last years of the war were:

	Dec 1951	Dec 1952	July 1953
UN forces	600,000	768,000	932,000
Communist forces	800,000	900,000	1,200,000

they could only push the front line northward by dint of extremely heavy fighting and a corresponding high level of casualties. From November 1951 both sides dug in to what the UN forces called the Main Line of Resistance, entrenched positions across the peninsula where they would remain for the rest of the war.

While the outside powers no longer sought to unify Korea by military victory, their Korean allies, North and South, were far from

The last two years of the war – the time it took to negotiate a ceasefire – saw stalemate on the battlefield. The line finally agreed to separate North and South Korea was not very different from the front line when talks began.

The battleship USS *Missouri* bombards the North Korean coast in May 1951. Shelling by UN warships devastated virtually all of North Korea's port cities, coastal roads and railways.

The UN delegates at the ceasefire talks pose for the cameras in Kaesong, August 1951. Vice-Admiral Turner Joy, the head of the delegation, stands in the middle of the group.

happy with this shift of position. In the North, Kim Il-sung reluctantly accepted that reunification was not on the agenda – he was in a weak position, with his own North Korean forces reduced to a relatively small military role alongside the Chinese and his country under constant attack by American aircraft and warships. In the South, Syngman Rhee was less docile. He protested fiercely against a ceasefire that would leave the communists in control of the North and tried to drum up support in the US Congress for continuing the war until the North was conquered. Rhee had no real influence on the US government, however. The ROK was given only token representation at the ceasefire negotiations, which were conducted by the Americans on one side and the North Koreans and Chinese on the other.

The two sides agreed to open negotiations on 10 July 1951 at Kaesong, in the no man's land between the two armies. Before the talks started, however, communist forces seized the Kaesong area. The head of the UN delegation, Vice-Admiral Turner Joy, thus found himself on the first day of talks meeting the communist negotiators in a building surrounded by North Korean troops. It was eventually agreed to make Kaesong a neutral zone free of military personnel, but the negotiations had got off to a bad start.

LACK OF TRUST There was a total lack of trust and mutual respect between the two sides. General Ridgway referred to the communists as 'treacherous savages' who could not be talked to in the same way as 'enlightened and civilized people'. The chief North Korean negotiator, Nam Il, accused the American representatives of not coming to make peace but 'to look for an excuse for extending the war'. In August the communists accused the UN of an air attack on the conference zone and talks were suspended for over a month before resuming in tents at nearby Panmunjon in October.

At the end of November 1951 the two sides

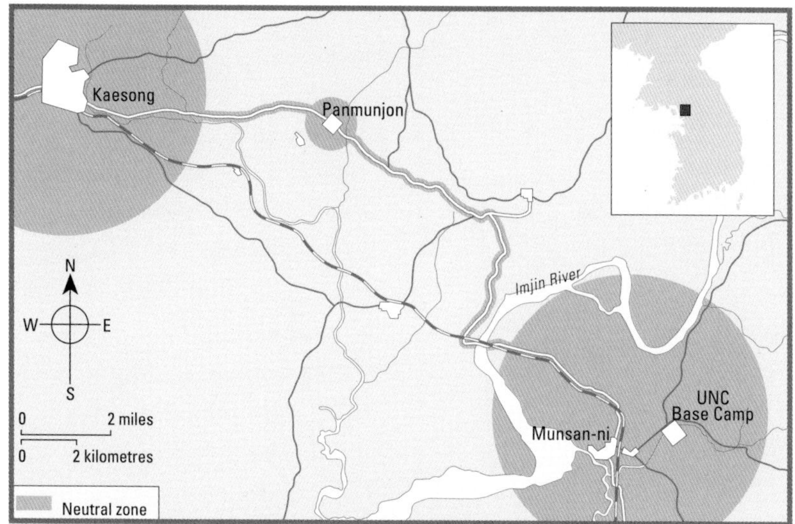

The armistice talks began at Kaesong on the Chinese side of the front line, but from October 1951 the talks shifted to Panmunjon. The area of the talks was declared a neutral zone between the conflicting armies.

tentatively agreed on an armistice line – basically the 'line of contact' between the positions that the two armies had reached at that point in the fighting. The following February there was broad agreement on how a ceasefire would be carried out and supervised. The only major issue then outstanding was the exchange of prisoners of war (POWs). This turned into an absolute block to further progress. There were some 150,000 POWs held by the UN and a substantial but considerably smaller number held in North Korea. The procedure laid down in the Geneva Convention, widely accepted as setting rules for the conduct of war, was for both sides to hand over all their POWs at the end of a conflict. The Americans, however, did not accept an 'all-for-all' exchange. They argued that POWs must have a free choice of whether or not to return to communist North Korea or China. This predictably outraged the communist negotiators.

Attempts to find out whether POWs really wanted to be returned or not were rendered impossible in

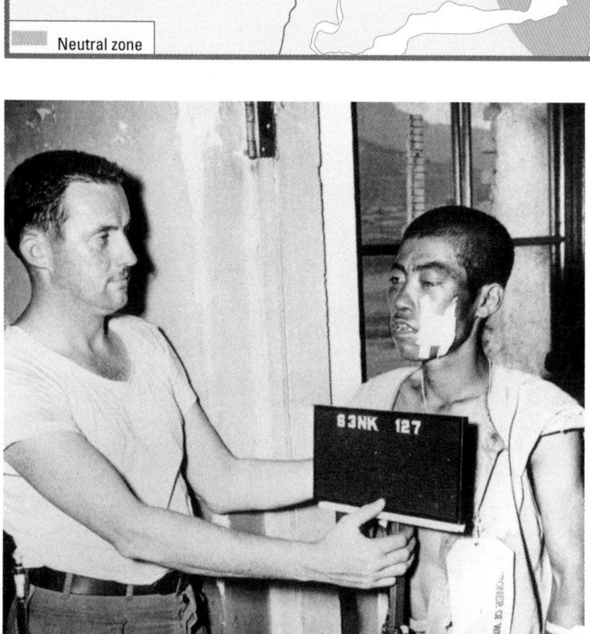

A communist POW has an identification photo taken at a prison camp. The details of exchanging POWs were a stumbling block in the ceasefire talks.

CHINESE PROPAGANDA

The Chinese tried to undermine the morale of UN troops on the Main Line of Resistance with propaganda – for example, distributing Christmas cards with the following message:

'Dear Soldiers, It is Christmas and you are far from home not knowing when you will die. The big shots are home, enjoying themselves, eating good food, drinking good liquor. Why should you be here risking your life for their profits ?...A Merry Christmas and a Happy New Year, From the Chinese People's Volunteers.'

[Quoted in *The Korean War*, Brian Catchpole]

UN forces occupied North Korean coastal islands, from where they raided the mainland. The bombing of dams deprived North Korea of power and ruined irrigation systems. MiG jet bases on the Chinese side of the border were off limits for US bombers.

practice by the brutal and chaotic conditions in POW camps in South Korea. Prisoners were subjected to intimidation both by fellow prisoners and by camp authorities. An uprising by prisoners at the Koje camp in May 1952 had to be crushed by UN military forces with the use of tanks. Meanwhile the treatment of POWs in North Korea also became a subject of concern, with allegations of ill-treatment and 'brainwashing' – psychological pressure and indoctrination – designed to make the UN prisoners convert to communism or denounce the actions of their own side.

As the negotiations dragged on, so did the war. In the winter of 1951-2, much of the UN fighting effort went into establishing full

US Air Force B-29 Superfortresses bomb targets in North Korea. Almost every town and city in the North was devastated by bombing.

A US Navy F-4U Corsair takes off from an aircraft carrier for a ground attack mission against communist forces.

BOMBARDED CITY

In March 1951 Admiral Allan F. Smith described the effect of UN naval bombardment on the North Korean port city of Wonsan: *'In Wonsan you cannot walk in the streets. You cannot sleep anywhere in the 24 hours, unless it is the sleep of death.'*

[Quoted in *Korea: The Unknown War,* Jon Halliday and Bruce Cumings]

control of South Korea. Many areas, especially in the south-west, were still dominated by South Korean left-wing guerrillas and by North Korean soldiers who had been left behind when their original invasion of the South was defeated. ROK General Paek Sun-yop claimed to have largely destroyed the guerrilla movement by the end of January 1952 in an operation codenamed 'Ratkiller'.

NAVAL AND AIR ATTACKS Naval and air attacks on North Korea were the most important way that the UN forces kept up pressure on the communist side during the stalled negotiations. With uncontested control of the sea, the warships of the United States and its allies were able to lay waste North Korean coastal towns with uninterrupted bombardment by their powerful guns. UN forces were also able to seize islands close to the North Korean coast and use them as bases from which to send small groups of special forces across to the mainland on intelligence-gathering and sabotage missions.

Aircraft carriers contributed to the large-scale bombardment of North Korea from the air, which was also carried out by aircraft based in Japan and South Korea. One aim of the air attacks was to cut supply routes from China and the Soviet Union to the communist army in the front line. But bombing was also used as a means of inflicting punishment on the North Koreans, in the hope that this would undermine popular support for Kim Il-sung or persuade the communists to give way in the ceasefire negotiations. Pyongyang and virtually every other town or city of any size in North Korea was devastated by air attacks. On 23 June 1952, in a deliberate escalation of the air war, the huge Supung dam on the Yalu River was

American artillerymen cover their ears as a heavy gun is fired at night, October 1952. Communist troops sheltered deep inside tunnels to find protection against shelling.

destroyed by bombing, along with three other dams, depriving all of North Korea and much of north-east China of their electricity supply.

Meanwhile the ground war on the Main Line of Resistance remained a very costly stalemate. To protect themselves from UN air attacks and artillery, the Chinese and North Koreans dug a network of tunnels about 1,200 km long. In this underground fortress they built up their forces until, by early 1953, there were reckoned to be a million Chinese soldiers committed to the war. They were faced by around 800,000 UN troops. Although neither side was even seeking a military victory, the local and limited offensives they launched, especially in the autumn of 1952, were fiercely fought and left many thousands dead.

CLARK TAKES CHARGE There were changes of leadership on the American side, with General Mark Clark taking over as UN Commander from General Ridgway in May 1952, and Dwight D. Eisenhower, a famous US World War II general, replacing Truman as US president in January 1953. But the crucial change came in the communist camp, when Soviet dictator Joseph Stalin died on 5 March 1953. The new Soviet leadership soon indicated that it saw no reason why an agreement on a ceasefire should be any longer delayed. The talks resumed with a new sense of purpose.

With an armistice agreement at last almost within reach, both sides stepped up the military pressure. In May 1953 the UN air force bombed irrigation dams

TALKING PEACE

In June 1953 US President Eisenhower wrote to Syngman Rhee urging acceptance of an armistice: *'We would not be justified in continuing the war with all the misery that it involves in the hope of achieving, by force, the unification of Korea.'*

[Quoted in *The War in Korea,* Matthew B. Ridgway]

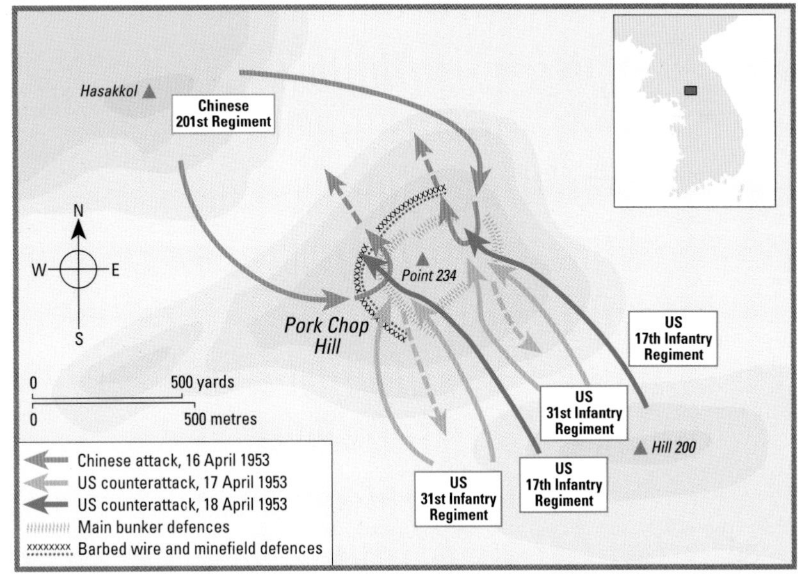

On the static front line, insignificant features were fought over with great ferocity. In April 1953 one such position, Pork Chop Hill, changed hands twice in three days – first seized by the Chinese, then retaken by the Americans.

north of Pyongyang creating widespread flooding and destroying the North Korean rice crop, so the entire population was threatened with starvation. Eisenhower hinted that atom bombs might be used if a ceasefire was not soon agreed. The Chinese maximized pressure along the front line on the ground. Between April and July 1953 large forces fought bitter battles for outposts of no special significance. One such position, Pork Chop Hill, became of such symbolic importance that by July the Americans had five battalions deployed on a hill that had once been defended by 100 men, while the Chinese were prepared to attack it with an entire division. In a single week in July 1953 UN casualties at the front numbered almost 30,000, and casualties on the communist side were probably more than double that figure.

Syngman Rhee made a last desperate attempt to sabotage the ceasefire talks in June by releasing POWs, so they could not be returned to the North. But an agreement on the POW issue was nonetheless hammered out. On 27 July 1953 an armistice was signed at Panmunjon by General William K. Harrison for the UN command and by Nam Il for the communist forces. Three years and 33 days after it had begun, the war was over.

On 27 July 1953 the commander of UN forces, General Mark Clark, signs the armistice agreement at his headquarters, after the initial signing at Panmunjon.

CHAPTER 7: CONSEQUENCES OF THE WAR

The foreign ministers of the United States, Britain, France, the Soviet Union and Communist China met at Geneva in April 1954 to discuss the future of Korea and Indo-China. No agreement was reached on Korea.

Under the terms of the armistice, an international conference was to be held to negotiate a final peace agreement. The Geneva Conference duly assembled in April 1954, but no progress was made on Korea. The UN side proposed reunification after nationwide elections under UN supervision. The communists countered by demanding the withdrawal of all foreign forces from Korea before elections could be held. Negotiations went no further. The United States had already signed a Mutual Defense Treaty with South Korea in August 1953, committing its forces to the defence of the South – they were still there 50 years later. Korea was left divided by a demilitarized zone along the ceasefire line.

SCENE OF DEVASTATION

Devastated by bombing, the condition of North Korean cities at the end of the war was witnessed by Hungarian author Tibor Meray. He said: *'I don't know why houses collapsed and chimneys did not, but I went through a city of 200,000 inhabitants and I saw thousands of chimneys – and that was all.'*

[Quoted in *The Guardian* newspaper, 11 April 2000]

The war had important effects outside Korea. In Asia, it led directly to the economic and political recovery of Japan after the devastation of World War II. Japanese industry expanded rapidly through supplying the needs of the UN war machine. Politically, Japan was transformed from America's most hated enemy of World War II into a valued ally. The war also confirmed the alliance between the United States and the Chinese Nationalists on Taiwan. America's relations with Communist China remained totally hostile until the 1970s – the government in Beijing was finally allowed to represent China at the UN in 1971.

Inevitably, a war that cost almost 34,000 American lives had a considerable impact on the United States. It brought anti-communist sentiment to its highest pitch – between 1950 and 1954, Senator Joe McCarthy was the most prominent figure engaged in a 'witchhunt' that sought to root out communist sympathisers in all areas of American life. Yet for the 1.8 million Americans who had served in Korea it soon came to seem the 'Forgotten War' – there was no memorial to the Korean War veterans in Washington D.C. until 1995.

US political and military leaders were keen to avoid any repetition of the heavy casualties in Korea. The Eisenhower administration regarded having got involved in a 'limited war' as a serious mistake. If such an act of 'communist aggression' occurred again, they planned to respond immediately by using nuclear weapons. But in the 1960s the United States found itself fighting another war on the ground in Asia, in Vietnam, with a similar policy of keeping the war 'limited' – and similar heavy casualties.

For Koreans on both sides of the ceasefire line, the war had been a catastrophe. Probably around one in ten of the Korean population were killed. Most towns and cities were heaps of ruins. Factories, roads, railways and dams were destroyed. The economic hardship experienced in the wake of this destruction was made worse by political oppression. There was no democracy or freedom in the North or the South. Kim Il-sung built North Korea into a regimented single-party

The result of the Korean War, in which millions died, was a minor adjustment of the border between North and South. Fifty years later, the two countries were still divided along the armistice line.

American forces in Vietnam in 1969: the Vietnam War had obvious similarities to the Korean conflict, with a communist North and a pro-American South.

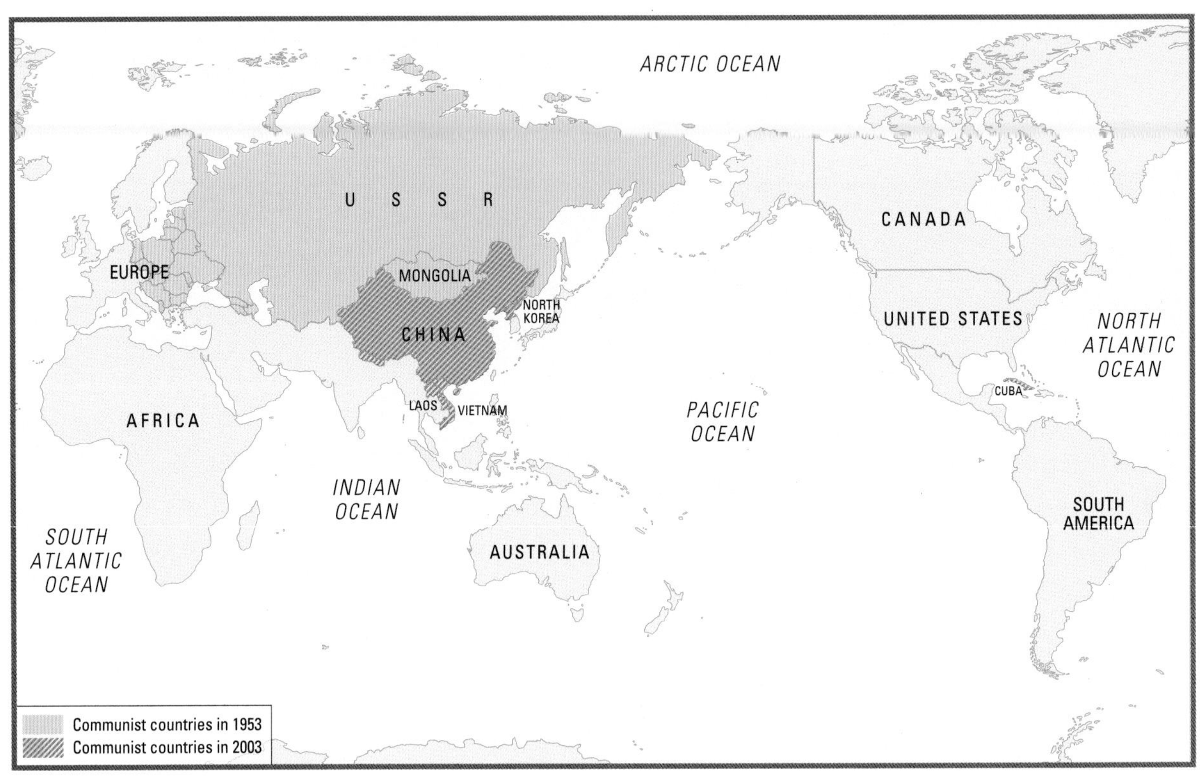

In 1953 North Korea was part of a powerful bloc of communist-ruled states stretching from the Pacific to central Europe. By 2004, the communist world had shrunk significantly.

communist dictatorship which he ruled as the 'Great Leader'. In South Korea, Syngman Rhee ruled as the authoritarian dictator of a police state.

Over time, conditions north and south of the ceasefire line diverged. In the South, Rhee was forced to resign after a student uprising in 1960. There followed a long period of military-dominated government, with opposition politicians frequently arrested or in other ways harassed or suppressed. Genuine multi-party democracy did finally arrive in South Korea, however, in 1988. By then, the South Korean economy had been transformed through state-sponsored capitalism, which produced spectacular growth in shipbuilding, car-making, and other manufacture for export. Most of the population shared in the

The authoritarian South Korean President Syngman Rhee (left) meets South Vietnamese leader Ngo Dinh Diem in 1958. Two years later Rhee was forced to resign, but democracy was slow to follow.

A veteran of the Korean War salutes as he visits the Korean War Veterans Memorial in Washington D.C. Part of the memorial consists of 19 statues created by sculptor Frank Gaylord that represent an American military unit on patrol in Korea.

prosperity this industrial expansion generated, enjoying fast-improving living conditions.

There were no such developments in North Korea. Kim Il-sung ruled until his death in 1994, when he was succeeded by his son, Kim Jong-il. After the collapse of communism in Eastern Europe and the Soviet Union in 1989-91 and the adoption of free-market economic policies by Communist China from the 1980s, North Korea was left as the world's most hardline communist state. The vast majority of its population lived in poverty – in the 1990s there were reports of widespread starvation – and had no personal freedom or human rights.

Over the years relations between North and South have generally been hostile, with occasional minor military clashes or incidents either at sea or across the demilitarized zone. From the 1990s there have been some attempts to create closer relations, with a view to eventual reunification – most notably an official visit by South Korean president Kim Dae-jung to the North in 2000 – but with limited effect.

Fifty years after the end of the Korean War, relations between the United States and North Korea were still antagonistic. In 2002 US President George W. Bush put North Korea on his list of 'rogue states' because of its alleged development of nuclear weapons. There was still a long journey to make before the legacy of the war could finally be overcome.

BUSH CONFRONTS NORTH KOREA

In October 2003, on a visit to Thailand, President George W. Bush told journalists: *'I've said as plainly as I can that we have no intention of invading North Korea [but] we expect North Korea to get rid of her nuclear ambitions. ... She must get rid of her weapons programs ...'*
[Office of the Press Secretary, The White House, 19 October 2003]

PROFILES OF MILITARY AND POLITICAL LEADERS

GENERAL EDWARD ALMOND (1892-1979)
Born in Virginia, Almond was chief of staff to General MacArthur when the Korean War broke out in June 1950. In September MacArthur gave Almond command of X Corps, which was entrusted with the Inchon landings. He remained X Corps commander for the invasion of North Korea and through the subsequent evacuation of the North. Almond left Korea in July 1951, retiring from the Army two years later.

CLEMENT ATTLEE (1883-1967)
British politician Clement Attlee was first elected to parliament as a Labour MP in 1922. He became leader of the Labour Party in 1935 and was a member of Winston Churchill's coalition government during World War II. After Labour's landslide victory in the 1945 general election he became prime minister, a post he held until 1951. Attlee loyally supported the United States in the Korean War, overriding opposition from many Labour MPs. He tried to be a moderating influence on US policy.

CHIANG KAI-SHEK (1887-1975)
Chinese general Chiang Kai-shek became head of the Chinese Nationalist government in 1928. He fought to suppress the Chinese Communists, led by Mao Tse-tung, and from 1937 was also engaged in a war with Japan. An ally of Britain and the United States during World War II, he received large amounts of US aid, but was nonetheless defeated by the Communists in the Chinese Civil War of 1945-9. Chiang and his supporters took refuge on Formosa (Taiwan). His offer of Chinese Nationalist troops to take part in the Korean War was refused by the United States, although General MacArthur had wanted to accept. The confrontation with Communist China brought about by the war ensured that the United States would continue to back his Nationalist government. Chiang still claimed to be the rightful ruler of China at his death in 1975.

GENERAL MARK W. CLARK (1896-1984)
Born in New York, General Clark made his name during World War II first in the fighting in North Africa from 1942 to 1943, and then as Allied commander in Italy. In May 1952 he took over from General Ridgway as UN Commander in Korea. In this capacity he signed the armistice in July 1953, continuing as head of the UN forces until the following October.

DWIGHT D. EISENHOWER (1890-1969)
Born in Texas, Eisenhower rose to fame as a general in World War II. He was supreme commander of Allied forces for the D-Day landings in 1944 and for the subsequent campaign in Europe. When NATO (the North Atlantic Treaty Organization) was formed in 1949, Eisenhower was its first military commander. In 1952 he moved into politics and, as the Republican candidate, won US presidential elections. Expectations that he might take a tougher line on Korea, and even authorize the use of nuclear weapons, helped push the Chinese toward accepting a negotiated settlement in 1953. Eisenhower remained president until 1961.

KIM IL-SUNG (1912-94)
Born when Korea was already under the control of Japan, as a young man Kim Il-sung joined guerrillas fighting against the Japanese in Manchuria. He returned to the Soviet-occupied zone of Korea after the Japanese surrender in 1945 and became leader of the communist Korean Workers' Party. With Soviet backing, he founded the Korean People's Democratic Republic in 1948. He launched the invasion of South Korea in June 1950 in the hope of uniting the country under communist rule. Despite the failure to achieve unification, he remained ruler of North Korea for the rest of his life. He combined hardline communism with a personal dictatorship – he was known as the 'Great Leader' and, when he died, passed on control of North Korea to his son.

ADMIRAL C. TURNER JOY (1895-1956)
Born in Missouri, Charles Turner Joy was commander of US Naval Forces, Far East, when the Korean War broke out in June 1950. He performed ably in establishing total supremacy at sea and deploying his warships in support of land operations. In July 1951 he was chosen to head the UN delegation to the armistice talks. He found the negotiations a frustrating experience and was reassigned at his own request in April 1952.

GENERAL DOUGLAS MACARTHUR (1880-1964)
Born into a military family in Arkansas, MacArthur fought with distinction in World War I. During World War II he was America's senior army commander in the Pacific. By the time Japan surrendered in 1945, MacArthur was a national hero. He effectively ruled Japan during the period of military occupation that followed. Given command of UN forces in Korea in 1950, he was responsible for the landings at Inchon which turned the tide of the war. Overconfidence, however, blinded him to the threat of Chinese intervention after his forces entered North Korea. The military disaster of November-December 1950 weakened his authority. MacArthur was increasingly open in his criticism of the policies of President Truman, advocating direct attacks on Communist China, the use of Chinese nationalist troops, and the use of atom bombs. Truman dismissed him in April 1951.

MAO TSE-TUNG (1893-1976)
A founder member of the Chinese Communist Party in 1921, Mao emerged as the movement's undisputed leader in the 1930s. Developing support among the peasant population of rural China, he fought a guerrilla war against Chiang Kai-shek's Nationalists and, between 1937 and 1945, against the Japanese. He proclaimed the communist People's Republic of China in Beijing in 1949. His decision to send troops into the Korean War enabled North Korea to survive, but at great cost in lives – one of those who died was his own son. Mao remained China's leader until his death.

PAEK SUN-YOP (1921-)
South Korean army officer Paek Sun-yop was a colonel in command of the ROK 1st Infantry Division when the North Koreans invaded in June 1950. He was soon marked out as the most effective of ROK officers, performing well during the defence of the Pusan perimeter. He took part in the ill-fated invasion of the North in October-December 1950 and, in the winter of 1951-2, was in charge of anti-guerrilla operations in South Korea (Operation Ratkiller). He was made ROK army chief of staff in 1952.

GENERAL PENG DEHUAI (1898-1974)
Peng Dehuai was one of Mao Tse-tung's companions on the famous Long March of 1934, in which the Chinese Communists escaped destruction by Chiang Kai-shek's Nationalists. He was a prominent military commander in the guerrilla war against the Japanese in China from 1937 and in the Chinese Civil War, which brought the communists to power in Beijing in 1949. Peng commanded the Chinese Volunteers throughout the Korean War. After the war he was Chinese minister of defence, but in 1959 he expressed criticisms of Mao's policies that put him out of favour. In 1966, during the upheaval known as the Cultural Revolution, he was arrested and tortured. He was still under house arrest at the time of his death.

GENERAL MATTHEW B. RIDGWAY (1895-1993)
Born in Virginia, Ridgway commanded airborne forces in Europe during World War II. Appointed commander of Eighth Army on General Walker's death in December 1950, he rapidly restored morale and adopted the right tactics to exploit the superior firepower of his UN forces. Ridgway was promoted to the post of UN Commander when MacArthur was sacked in April 1951. The following year he succeeded Eisenhower as commander of NATO forces in Europe, and in 1953 he was appointed US Army chief of staff.

JOSEPH STALIN (1879-1953)
Born in Georgia as Iosif Vissarionovich Dzhugashvili, Stalin was one of the Bolshevik communist revolutionaries who seized power in Russia in 1917, founding the Soviet Union in 1923. By 1930 Stalin had made himself Soviet dictator and the recognized leader of the communist movement worldwide. When the Soviet Union was invaded by Germany in 1941, Stalin became an ally of Britain and the United States in World War II. After 1945, he led his country into the Cold War confrontation with the Western allies.

SYNGMAN RHEE (1875-1965)
Korean nationalist Syngman Rhee was 70 years old when Korea was freed from Japanese rule in 1945. He had lived much of his life as an exile in the United States, where he campaigned for Korean independence. Returning to the American occupation zone in Korea, in 1948 he was elected president of the Republic of Korea. Rhee was frequently an embarrassment to the Americans, because of his open contempt for freedom and democracy, and his ruthless methods, including mass killings of suspected communists. Totally dedicated to unifying Korea under his rule, he did his utmost to prevent an armistice agreement in 1953. Rhee ruled South Korea as a police state until 1960, when he was forced to resign in the face of popular protests.

PRESIDENT HARRY S. TRUMAN (1884-1972)
Born in Missouri, Truman was a Democrat senator before being elected US vice-president in 1944. He became president on the death of Franklin D. Roosevelt in April 1945, and was re-elected in 1948. Although Truman committed the United States to oppose the spread of communism worldwide (the 'Truman Doctrine' of 1947), he was attacked by Republicans for allegedly permitting the communist takeover of China in 1949. He did not hesitate to order US military intervention in Korea, but remained determined to limit the scope of the war as far as possible. He did not stand for re-election in 1952.

GENERAL JAMES VAN FLEET (1892-1992)
Born in New Jersey, Van Fleet rose to the rank of major-general during the fighting in Europe in World War II. In 1948-9, as head of the US military mission in Greece, he played a key role in suppressing a communist guerrilla movement. Replacing General Ridgway as commander of Eighth Army in April 1951, he proved an able general, and worked hard to strengthen the South Korean army. He was unhappy, however, with the refusal of his superiors to allow a full-scale offensive to win the war. In February 1953 he gave up his command and became an outspoken critic of American government policy on Korea.

GENERAL WALTON H. WALKER (1889-1950)
Born in Texas, General Walker was in command of US Eighth Army in Japan when the Korean War began. In command of US and South Korean army forces in Korea from July 1950, Walker succeeded in rallying his men and defending the Pusan perimeter. From the Inchon landing onward, Walker commanded Eighth Army but not X Corps. He reluctantly obeyed MacArthur's orders to advance towards the Yalu River in November 1950 and did his best to organize the subsequent withdrawal. He died after a road accident on 23 December 1950.

SIGNIFICANT DATES

1910
Korea is taken over by Japan.

1931
The Japanese occupy Manchuria.

1937
Japan goes to war with China, occupying much of the country.

1939-41
Japan and the Soviet Union fight a border war.

7 DECEMBER 1941
Japanese attack on the US base at Pearl Harbor begins World War II in the Pacific.

6 AUGUST 1945
The United States drops an atom bomb on the Japanese city of Hiroshima.

8 AUGUST 1945
The Soviet Union declares war on Japan and invades Manchuria.

15 AUGUST 1945
Japan surrenders; the United States proposes dividing Korea into two occupation zones, north and south of the 38th parallel.

8 SEPTEMBER 1945
American troops arrive at Inchon to begin the occupation of Korea south of the 38th parallel.

MARCH 1947
President Truman commits the United States to blocking the spread of communism worldwide (the 'Truman doctrine').

AUGUST 1948
The Republic of Korea is proclaimed in South Korea, led by Syngman Rhee.

SEPTEMBER 1948
The Democratic People's Republic of Korea is proclaimed in North Korea, led by Kim Il-sung.

NOVEMBER 1948
A guerrilla uprising against Rhee's rule begins on Cheju-do Island.

DECEMBER 1948
Soviet troops pull out of North Korea.

MAY 1949
Beginning of border clashes between North and South Korean forces.

JUNE 1949
US troops leave South Korea.

25 JUNE 1950
North Korean forces invade South Korea.

27 JUNE 1950
UN resolution calls for collective military action in defence of South Korea.

1 JULY 1950
First US troops arrive in South Korea to fight against the North.

7 JULY 1950
General Douglas MacArthur is appointed UN Commander in Korea.

20 JULY 1950
The key city of Taejon falls to the North Korean army.

AUGUST 1950
The Eighth Army struggles to hold a defensive perimeter around the port of Pusan.

28 AUGUST 1950
First British troops arrive in Korea.

15-28 SEPTEMBER 1950
UN forces carry out landings at Inchon and retake Seoul.

1 OCTOBER 1950
South Korean troops cross the 38th parallel into North Korea.

2 OCTOBER 1950
China warns that it will intervene militarily if US forces enter North Korea.

12 OCTOBER 1950
The Eighth Army occupies the North Korean capital, Pyongyang.

19 OCTOBER 1950
Chinese 'Volunteers' begin to filter into North Korea.

25 OCTOBER 1950
First clashes between UN forces and Chinese soldiers.

26 OCTOBER 1950
US Marines land at the port of Wonsan; South Korean units reach the Yalu River, the border between North Korea and China.

6 NOVEMBER 1950
Chinese Volunteers break off fighting with UN forces.

24 NOVEMBER 1950
MacArthur launches a 'final offensive' to the Yalu River.

28 NOVEMBER 1950
Eighth Army withdraws under heavy attack by Chinese and North Korean troops.

30 NOVEMBER 1950
President Truman indicates publicly that the use of atom bombs in Korea is not ruled out.

DECEMBER 1950
British Prime Minister Clement Attlee begins talks with Truman in Washington, opposing the use of atom bombs.

5 DECEMBER 1950
Pyongyang is abandoned to the communists as UN forces retreat to the 38th parallel.

11 DECEMBER 1950
Marines complete a fighting withdrawal from the Chosin Reservoir to the port of Hungnam.

16 DECEMBER 1950
President Truman declares a state of emergency in the United States.

23 DECEMBER 1950
Death of General Walker, commander of Eighth Army; he is replaced by General Matthew Ridgway.

24 DECEMBER 1950
Last UN forces are evacuated from North Korea by sea.

1-15 JANUARY 1951
A renewed communist offensive drives the UN forces back south of Seoul.

25 JANUARY-21 APRIL 1951
UN counter-offensive (the 'meatgrinder') drives the communist forces back to around the 38th parallel.

11 APRIL 1951
President Truman dismisses General MacArthur from all his commands; General Ridgway is appointed UN Commander.

22 APRIL 1951
New Chinese and North Korean offensive leads to heavy fighting on the Imjin River.

29 APRIL 1951
Communist advance halts on the outskirts of Seoul.

16-21 MAY 1951
Renewed communist offensive fails.

10 JULY 1951
Ceasefire negotiations begin at Kaesong.

23 AUGUST 1951
Negotiations are suspended after communist allegations of UN attacks on the talks zone.

AUGUST-OCTOBER 1951
Heavy fighting as UN forces push the front line northward.

25 OCTOBER 1951
Ceasefire talks begin again at Panmunjon.

27 NOVEMBER 1951
Both sides agree in principle on a ceasefire along the current line separating the two armies.

JANUARY 1952
Operation Ratkiller achieves suppression of most guerrilla activity in South Korea.

17 FEBRUARY 1952
Agreement reached for a peace conference to be held after a ceasefire.

19 APRIL 1952
Ceasefire talks stall over issue of repatriation of prisoners of war.

12 MAY 1952
General Mark Clark replaces Ridgway as UN Commander.

MAY 1952
Communist POWs stage revolt on Koje Island.

23 JUNE 1952
UN air attacks destroy the Supung dam and three other hydroelectric dams in North Korea.

20 JANUARY 1953
Dwight D. Eisenhower is inaugurated as US President.

5 MARCH 1953
Death of Soviet dictator Joseph Stalin.

16 APRIL 1953
Beginning of battle for Pork Chop Hill.

26 APRIL 1953
Ceasefire talks resume in earnest.

13-16 MAY 1953
UN air attacks destroy irrigation dams in North Korea.

18 JUNE 1953
Syngman Rhee releases Korean POWs in effort to sabotage ceasefire talks.

JUNE-JULY 1953
Chinese offensives lead to heavy fighting along the Main Line of Resistance.

27 JULY 1953
Ceasefire agreement is signed.

APRIL-JUNE 1954
Geneva Conference fails to achieve agreement on a peace treaty and reunification of Korea.

1960
Syngman Rhee resigns after popular protests against his rule.

1988
South Korea becomes a multi-party democracy.

1991
South Korea and North Korea admitted to the United Nations.

1994
Death of Kim Il-sung; he is succeeded by his son, Kim Jong-il.

2000
South Korean President Kim Dae-jong visits North Korea.

2003
President George W. Bush lists North Korea among a number of 'rogue states' that he considers a threat to world security, and warns that the US will not permit the country to develop a nuclear capabilty.

STATISTICS CONCERNING COMBATANT NATIONS

Australia
Supplied two infantry battalions, nine naval vessels, a fighter squadron and a transport squadron.

Military personnel	17,164
Casualties:	
Killed or missing in action	411
Wounded	1,216
POWs	21

Belgium
Supplied one infantry battalion.

Military personnel	3,498
Casualties:	
Killed or missing in action	106
Wounded	336
POWs	1

Britain
Supplied two infantry brigades and approximately 50 naval vessels.

Military personnel	60,000
Casualties:	
Killed or missing in action	1,078
Wounded	2,533
POWs	766

Canada
Supplied an infantry brigade, eight naval vessels, and a squadron of transport aircraft.

Military personnel	27,000
Casualties:	
Killed or missing in action	344
Wounded	1,212
POWs	12

China

Casualties:	
Killed or missing in action (estimate)	1,000,000

Colombia
Supplied an infantry battalion and six naval vessels.

Military personnel	6,200
Casualties:	
Killed or missing in action	191
Wounded	448
POWs	29

Ethiopia
Supplied an infantry battalion.

Military personnel	3,518
Casualties:	
Killed in action	121
Wounded	536

France
Supplied an infantry battalion and a naval vessel.

Military personnel	4,000
Casualties:	
Killed or missing in action	281
Wounded	1,008
POWs	11

Greece
Supplied an infantry battalion and transport aircraft.

Military personnel	5,000
Casualties:	
Killed or missing in action	194
Wounded	543
POWs	1

Luxembourg
Supplied a rifle company.

Military personnel	89
Casualties:	
Killed or missing in action	2
Wounded	13

Netherlands
Supplied an infantry battalion and six naval vessels.

Military personnel	5,300
Casualties:	
Killed or missing in action	123
Wounded	645

New Zealand
Supplied an artillery regiment and four naval vessels.

Military personnel	4,500
Casualties:	
Killed in action	34
Wounded	79
POWs	1

North Korea

Military casualties:	
Killed or missing in action	500,000
Civilian deaths (estimate)	2,000,000

Philippines
Supplied a battalion combat team.

Military personnel	7,420
Casualties:	
Killed or missing in action	179
Wounded	299
POWs	40

South Africa
Supplied one fighter aircraft squadron

Military personnel	811
Casualties:	
Killed in action	20
Wounded	16
POWs	6

South Korea

Military casualties:	
Killed or missing in action	415,004
Wounded	1,312,836
POWs	85,000
Civilian deaths	
(estimates)	660,000–1,000,000

Thailand
Supplied an infantry battalion, four naval vessels, and transport aircraft.

Military personnel	6,500
Casualties:	
Killed or missing in action	134
Wounded	1,139

Turkey
Supplied a brigade group.

Military personnel	15,000
Casualties:	
Killed or missing in action	1,148
Wounded	2,068
POWs	219

United States

Total US military personnel	1,789,000
Casualties:	
Combat deaths	33,686
US Army	27,728
US Marines	4,268
US Air Force	1,198
US Navy	492
Wounded	103,284
Unaccounted for	8,176
POWs	7,245

(of whom 2,806 died, included in figure for combat deaths)

*A figure of over 54,000 is sometimes given for US dead in the Korean War, but this higher figure includes all US military deaths worldwide during the Korean War period. There were also 2,830 US non-battle deaths in Korea, making total US deaths in the Korean theatre 36,516.

US air operations in Korea:

US Navy	275,912 sorties
USAF	1,325,000 sorties

Estimated 1,500 enemy aircraft shot down

THE VIETNAM WAR

CHAPTER 1: THE FIRST INDO-CHINA WAR

Japanese troops move into Vietnam in July 1941, beginning their four-year occupation of the country. Vietnam was at that time part of the colony of French Indo-China.

Vietnam is a country in south-east Asia with a population of about 80 million. Its recorded history stretches back more than 2,000 years. In the second half of the nineteenth century, at a time when European countries were extending their rule over much of Asia and Africa, it was conquered by the French. It became part of the colony of French Indo-China, along with its neighbours Cambodia and Laos.

From the start French rule was opposed by Vietnamese nationalists, but all opposition was harshly repressed by the French colonial authorities. In the early decades of the twentieth century, many nationalists took refuge abroad. They included Ho Chi Minh, the son of a Vietnamese official. In 1920, living in France, Ho became a communist. From then on, his life was dedicated to the two goals of achieving national independence for Vietnam and establishing a communist society in which private ownership of industry and land would be abolished.

The French remained firmly in control of Indo-China until the start of World War II (1939-45). Early in that war, in Europe, France was defeated by Germany. As a result, France was in no position to aid its colonists in Indo-China when they came under pressure from the rising power in Asia: Japan. In 1941, the French colonial authorities were forced to allow Japanese troops to occupy Indo-China. Although they left the French officially in control, the Japanese effectively ran the colony.

In the same year, Ho Chi Minh and other Vietnamese nationalists founded a guerrilla organization to fight both the Japanese and the French. They called it the Vietnam Doc Lap Dong Minh Hoi (League for the Independence of Vietnam) –

NATIONALIST OR COMMUNIST?

Tran Ngoc Danh, a colleague of Viet Minh leader Ho Chi Minh, wrote:

'How many times in my life have I been asked: you who know Ho Chi Minh so well, can you say whether he is a nationalist or a communist? The answer is simple: Ho Chi Minh is both. For him, nationalism and communism, the end and the means, complement one another...'

[Quoted in *Historical Atlas of the Vietnam War,* Summers and Karnow]

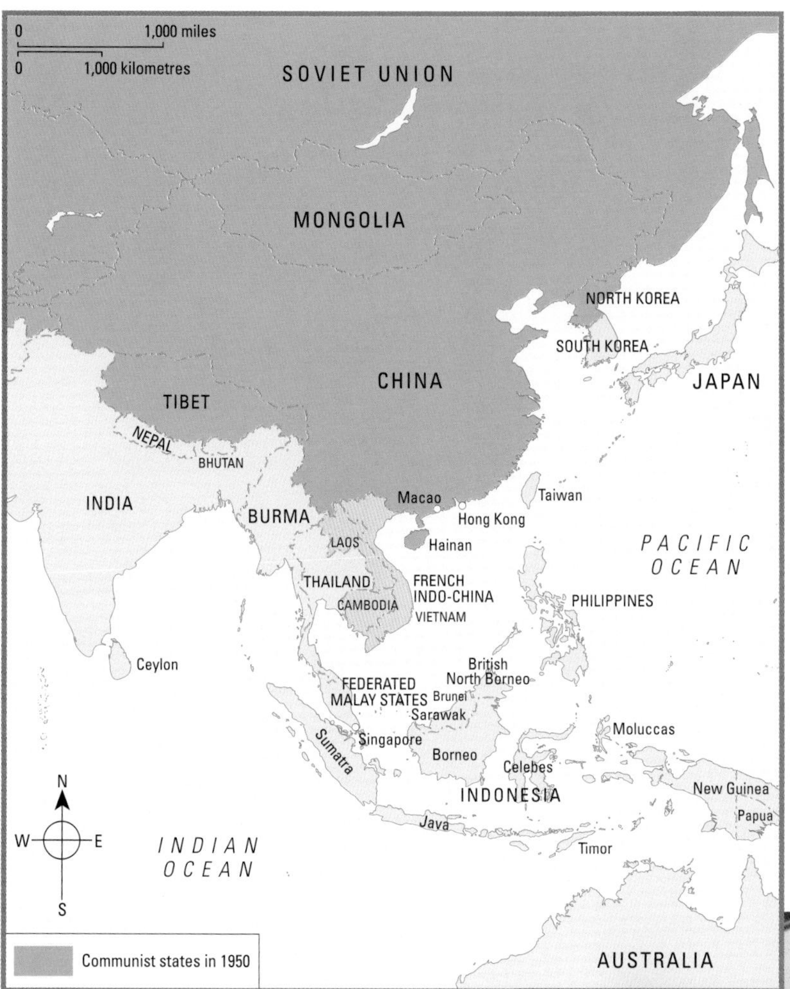

In the early 1950s, French Indo-China was on the edge of the communist-ruled area of Asia. America saw Indo-China as in the front line of its fight to halt the spread of communism.

or Viet Minh for short. The leaders of the Viet Minh were communists, including not only Ho but also the movement's chief military commander, Vo Nguyen Giap. But, as the name of the movement suggests, they appealed above all to the Vietnamese desire for national independence.

During World War II, the Viet Minh received support from the United States, which was itself at war with Japan from December 1941. Ho's guerrillas fought the Japanese with increasing success and won control of large areas of northern Vietnam. In March 1945, the Japanese abolished French rule in Indo-China, but the following August Japan surrendered to the United States and its allies. This left a power vacuum in Vietnam that the Viet Minh were quick to exploit. On 2 September 1945, in the northern city of Hanoi, Ho declared Vietnam independent under a Viet Minh government. In the southern city of Saigon, however, occupied by British troops, the French authorities were reinstalled in control.

At first there was a compromise. In March 1946 the Viet Minh and the French agreed that Vietnam would be a 'Free State' within the French Empire. But the following November

General Vo Nguyen Giap commanded the Viet Minh forces during the First Indo-China War. This picture shows him later, as North Vietnamese Minister of Defence in 1966.

Viet Minh guerrillas cross an improvised bridge during their war against the French in 1953. Operating almost entirely on foot in Vietnam's rough terrain, the Viet Minh were formidable fighters.

fighting broke out between the French and the Viet Minh, first in the northern port city of Haiphong and then in Hanoi. The Viet Minh army withdrew from the cities to the countryside and launched a new guerrilla war against the French.

RED CHINA Until 1949 it seemed that the French would be able to contain the guerrillas. But in that year communists led by Mao Tse-tung won control of Vietnam's massive northern neighbour, China. Supplied with arms and equipment by the Chinese communists, the Viet Minh were able to take the initiative. With much of its territory mountainous and covered in thick jungle, Vietnam was ideal country for guerrillas to operate, hiding from and ambushing more heavily armed conventional troops. The French successfully defended the densely populated area of the Red River Delta in the north when the Viet Minh launched a major offensive in 1951, but isolated French outposts in rural areas were liable to be besieged and overrun.

France lacked the resources to sustain a war in Indo-China over a long period and soon became dependent on the support of the United States. In general, the US favoured independence for countries under European colonial rule. But from 1947 onwards, the United States was also committed to resisting the spread of

'ENDURING MEN...'

Major Marcel Bigeard, a French paratroop officer in Vietnam, expressed his admiration for the Viet Minh guerrillas: '*I can tell you they became the greatest infantry in the world: these enduring men capable of covering 50 kilometres in the night on the strength of a bowl of rice, with running shoes, and then singing their way into battle...*'

[Quoted in *Vietnam: The Ten Thousand Day War*, Michael Maclear]

communism, which was seen as a global threat to US interests. The communist triumph in China in 1949 made the US very worried about any possible further communist expansion in Asia. When communist North Korea invaded South Korea in 1950, American troops were sent in to resist the invasion. At the same time, American aid – money and arms – was provided to help the French fight the communist-led Viet Minh.

By the end of 1953 France's position in Vietnam was becoming desperate. The Viet Minh were not only growing in military strength but also had popular support among a people eager for independence from colonial rule. The French had set up a government under a traditional Vietnamese ruler, Emperor Bao Dai, but it attracted little support.

In an attempt to regain the military initiative, French commanders decided to establish a powerful base at Dien Bien Phu, a

Under French rule, Vietnam was divided into three parts: Tonkin, Annam and Cochin China. In 1954 Viet Minh guerrillas dominated most of Tonkin outside the major cities, part of Annam and much of Cochin China.

A French doctor treats a Vietnamese soldier during the siege of Dien Bien Phu in 1954. Thousands of anti-communist Vietnamese fought alongside the French against the Viet Minh.

French paratroopers are dropped in to Dien Bien Phu. The base was shelled by Viet Minh artillery positioned in the mountains overlooking it.

remote site in northern Vietnam close to the border with Laos. They hoped the base would help block Viet Minh supply lines bringing men and arms into Vietnam, and prevent an expected Viet Minh attack on Laos. The Viet Minh saw an opportunity to inflict a decisive defeat on the colonial power. They assembled powerful infantry forces around Dien Bien Phu, hauling artillery up mountainsides overlooking the French positions, and in March 1954 they launched their attack. The French garrison, which consisted chiefly of elite parachute battalions, resisted fiercely. But they were surrounded and outnumbered, resupplied only by air.

France's only hope of avoiding a humiliating defeat lay in an appeal to the United States. In talks between senior French and American military commanders, a plan was devised for a massive aerial bombardment by US aircraft which would destroy the Viet Minh forces besieging Dien Bien Phu. US President Dwight D. Eisenhower, however, rejected involving American forces directly in support of the French.

Vietnamese communist leader Ho Chi Minh was known as 'Uncle Ho', but he was ruthless in pursuit of his goal of a united, communist Vietnam.

DEFEAT AT DIEN BIEN PHU On 8 May 1954, the final French defences at Dien Bien Phu were overrun. On the same day, a peace conference opened in Geneva, Switzerland, to discuss an end to the war. The following July, a peace agreement, known as the Geneva Accords, gave Vietnam, Laos and Cambodia independence from France. But Vietnam was divided

The Democratic Republic of Vietnam (North Vietnam) was separated from the Republic of Vietnam (South Vietnam) by a demilitarized zone (DMZ) along the 17th parallel.

General Henri Navarre, the French commander in Indo-China at the time of the defeat at Dien Bien Phu, was critical of President Eisenhower's decision not to provide air support: *'There is no doubt that if the American air force had been heavily involved … Dien Bien Phu would certainly have been saved. The US would not have had to become involved later as it was obliged to do.'*

[Quoted in *Vietnam: The Ten Thousand Day War,* Michael Maclear]

in two, with Ho and the Viet Minh taking control north of the 17th parallel and Emperor Bao Dai ruling in the south.

According to the Geneva Accords, this division was supposed to be temporary. Vietnam was to be reunited in two years' time, after democratic elections to choose a government for the whole country. But no such elections were ever held. In the north, Ho established the Democratic Republic of Vietnam (usually referred to as North Vietnam), a state ruled by the communist Vietnamese Workers' Party. North Vietnam became a hardline communist state very much like those that then existed in the Soviet Union, China, North Korea, and Eastern Europe. In the south, Emperor Bao Dai was soon replaced as ruler of the Republic of Vietnam (South Vietnam) by Ngo Dinh Diem, a tough leader who had the backing of the United States.

After the Geneva Accords, about 900,000 Vietnamese, feeling there was no place for them in a communist state, chose to move from North Vietnam to the South. At the same time, some 100,000 Viet Minh fighters withdrew from South Vietnam to the North. The division of Vietnam was destined to last for more than twenty years.

CHAPTER 2: THE US IS SUCKED IN

By 1962, US Army officers were 'advising' South Vietnamese soldiers fighting communist-led guerrillas and US helicopter pilots were flying them into battle.

The United States regarded the French defeat in Indo-China and the establishment of a communist state in North Vietnam as a serious setback in its efforts to resist the spread of communism worldwide. The Americans were determined to prevent any further expansion of communist rule in South-east Asia. To this end, from 1954 onwards they undertook to support the state of South Vietnam, aiming to turn it into a stable country capable of defending itself against an attack from North Vietnam or internal subversion. In 1956 the United States set up a Military Assistance Advisory Group in the Southern capital, Saigon (it later became the Military Assistance Command Vietnam – MACV). US money, arms and military advisers were provided to build up an Army of the Republic of South Vietnam (ARVN).

The United States was well aware that the future of South Vietnam also depended on good government. Here problems quickly mounted. Ngo Dinh Diem belonged to the Catholic minority in Vietnam, and soon aroused the hostility of Vietnamese Buddhists.

South Vietnamese President Ngo Dinh Diem visits New York in May 1957. At this time he enjoyed the full support of the United States, but the Americans later came to see him as a liability.

His regime was neither liberal nor democratic – opposition newspapers were closed down and the secret police, the Can Lao, was much feared. In rural South Vietnam, Diem failed to carry through a land reform which might have won over the peasants to his side. Instead, he raised taxes and replaced locally elected village leaders with his own appointed officials. Soon discontent was rife in the countryside. In 1957-8, isolated terrorist attacks began to occur, including the assassination of government officials.

In May 1959, the government of North Vietnam decided that the time was ripe to promote a guerrilla war in South Vietnam, with the aim of overthrowing Diem and reuniting Vietnam under communist rule. Thousands of experienced Viet Minh cadres (officers) were sent back from the North into South Vietnam with orders to begin building up a guerrilla movement in the countryside. Work began on organizing a supply route from the North to the South through Laos and Cambodia – a complex pattern of roads and tracks that became known as the Ho Chi Minh Trail. Arms and men were also carried into the South by sea, mainly by small boats sailing down to the Mekong Delta south of Saigon.

The southern guerrilla movement called itself the National Liberation Front (NLF), although to the US the guerrillas were always

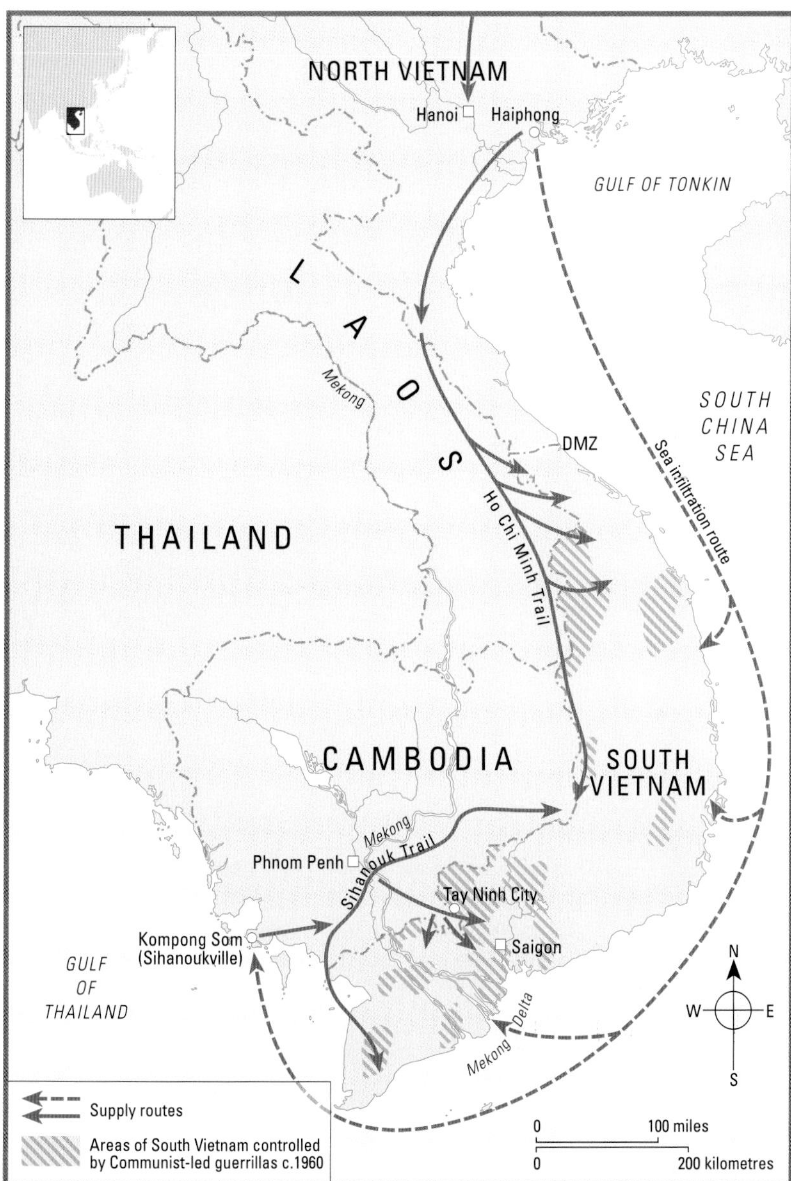

Supplies from North Vietnam were carried to guerrillas in the South along jungle trails in Laos or Cambodia and by small boats along the coast. Much of the equipment originated in China.

DOMINO THEORY

One of the major justifications for America's support for South Vietnam lay in the 'domino theory' – the belief that if South Vietnam fell to communism many other countries in Asia would also fall like a line of dominoes. Senator (later President) John F. Kennedy stated in 1956: '*Burma, Thailand, India, Japan, the Philippines and obviously Laos and Cambodia are among those whose security would be threatened if the red tide of communism overflowed into Vietnam.*'

[Quoted in *America in Vietnam*, Guenter Lewy]

the Viet Cong (VC). The NLF was officially founded in 1960. It took care to appeal to Vietnamese nationalism, describing the guerrilla war as a continuation of the struggle previously fought against the French, with the Americans now as the 'imperialist' power.

The NLF swiftly built up a strong position in rural South Vietnam. Young men were recruited from the villages – sometimes voluntarily, sometimes not – and taken to remote areas for training as full-time members of the guerrilla army. They created the Viet Cong 'mainforce', capable of taking on the ARVN and, later, the Americans, in major operations. At the same time, many peasants who stayed in the villages constituted a 'part-time' aid to the guerrillas, not only providing intelligence and

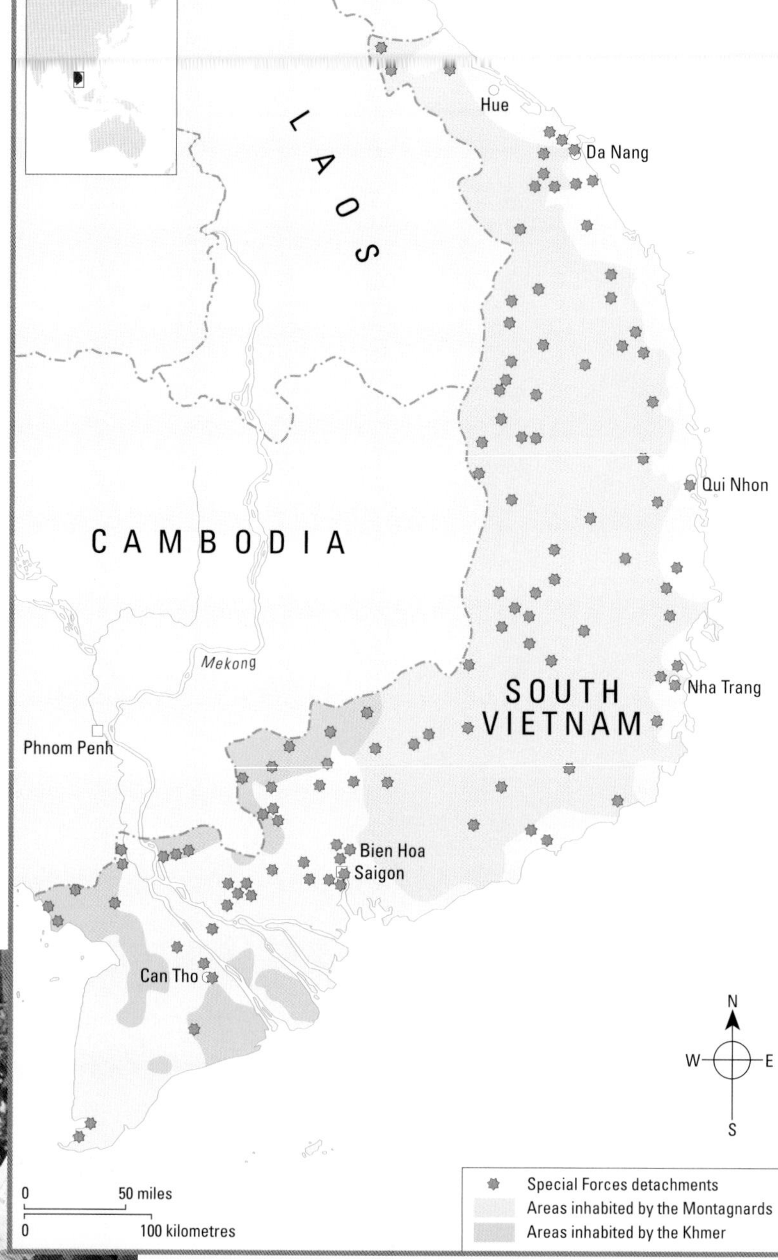

A US military adviser (second from left) looks on as an ARVN officer examines captured papers.

Jungle and mountain areas of South Vietnam were inhabited by people who were not ethnic Vietnamese. US Special Forces were able to organize many of them for anti-communist activity.

US TROOPS IN SOUTH VIETNAM

The US military commitment to South Vietnam rose steeply between 1960 and 1964.

	1960	1961	1962	1963	1964
US military personnel	875	3,164	11,326	16,263	23,310
US deaths in action	0	1	31	77	137

food supplies, but also planting booby-trap bombs or taking part in ambushes of military patrols.

The first US casualties in Vietnam were military advisers wounded in a Viet Cong raid at Bien Hoa in July 1959. The following January an ARVN force was defeated by guerrillas north-east of Saigon. The US responded by increasing its force of military advisers in South Vietnam, from around 1,000 in 1960 to over 11,000, by the end of 1962, including 300 helicopter pilots who went into battle alongside the ARVN.

SPECIAL FORCES Strategies for counter-insurgency – that is, for defeating guerrilla movements – were a hot topic at this time. America's new president in 1961, John F. Kennedy, was convinced that wars against communist-led 'national liberation movements' were going to be crucial in the future. Kennedy was a keen advocate of the Green Berets, US Special Force troops who were trained in unconventional warfare techniques. From 1962, the Green Berets were sent in to organize resistance to the Viet Cong guerrillas among the Montagnard tribespeople – non-Vietnamese who lived in remote mountainous areas of Vietnam. The Montagnard Civilian Irregular Defense Groups (CIDGs) led and armed by the Green Berets operated with some success within Viet Cong-dominated areas. But their effect on the war was in the end only marginal.

Potentially a more effective form of counter-insurgency was the Strategic Hamlets programme, which also got under way in 1962. This involved shifting South Vietnamese peasants from their villages into large fortified settlements, where they could be defended from coercion by the guerrillas and, in theory, won over to the government side. In practice, however, nothing was done to win the 'hearts and minds' of the rural population. The Strategic Hamlets were little better than concentration camps and being herded into them only made the peasants more hostile to the South Vietnamese government.

Another programme begun at this time was the spraying of chemical defoliants from the air to destroy crops being grown to feed the Viet Cong and to clear areas of vegetation that might be used by the guerrillas

US Air Force planes loaded with chemical defoliants fly on a mission to spray an area of South Vietnamese forest where guerrillas were active.

A Buddhist monk burns himself to death in the street in protest at the policies of President Diem. The majority of South Vietnamese were Buddhists, but Diem was a Catholic.

as cover. Defoliant spraying was to expand into a large-scale – and highly controversial – operation, but it had little immediate effect in restricting guerrilla activity.

By 1963 the Viet Cong were in effective control of a large and expanding area of the South Vietnamese countryside. At the same time, Diem's position as the country's leader was collapsing. His rule had grown increasingly dictatorial and incompetent. Vietnamese Buddhists were in open conflict with the Diem regime. The American public was shocked by images of Buddhist monks burning themselves to death in the streets as a protest against Diem's rule.

In the autumn of 1963, the US government secretly gave the go-ahead to a group of South Vietnamese generals, led by General Duong Van Minh, who were plotting a military coup. On 1 November Diem was arrested and shot dead, along with his brother Nhu. Within three weeks of Diem's death, John F. Kennedy was shot and killed in Dallas, Texas, and replaced as US president by Lyndon B. Johnson. The new president confirmed the policy of supporting South Vietnam against what the United States termed 'communist aggression'.

General Minh and his colleagues proved even less capable than Diem of creating a stable government in Saigon that might win the war against the guerrillas. They soon

GULF OF TONKIN RESOLUTION

The resolution passed by the US Congress on 7 August 1964, in the wake of the Gulf of Tonkin incident, denounced the alleged attacks on US warships as *'part of a deliberate and systematic campaign of aggression that the Communist regime in North Vietnam has been waging …'* and declared *'… that the Congress approve and support the determination of the President, as Commander in Chief, to take all necessary measures to repel any armed attack against the forces of the United States and to prevent further aggression.'*

President Lyndon B. Johnson (seated) calls on the US Congress to support military action in Vietnam after the Gulf of Tonkin incident.

squabbled bitterly among themselves and coup followed coup. In March 1964 US Secretary of Defense Robert McNamara visited Saigon to assess the situation. He concluded that South Vietnam was on the verge of total collapse. The US either had to admit defeat and allow Saigon to fall to the communists or increase its military involvement in the war.
The number of US military advisers in South Vietnam was consequently increased to 23,000 and General William C. Westmoreland was sent to head the MACV. But McNamara believed the war against the guerrillas in the South could only be a holding operation – buying time. The only way to save South Vietnam would be to persuade, or force, the North Vietnamese government to call a halt to the fighting.

NO INVASION The United States believed an invasion of North Vietnam was out of the question, as it would have led the Chinese to send in troops – as they had when North Korea was invaded by US-led forces in 1950. But US covert operations in North Vietnam and Laos had been taking place since 1961, and in January 1964 President Johnson secretly authorized hit-and-run raids by gunboats along the North Vietnamese coast.

US warships were sometimes sent to patrol the Gulf of Tonkin, off the coast of North Vietnam, in support of these secret raids. On 2 August 1964, the American destroyer USS *Maddox* was sailing about 16 km off the North Vietnamese coast when it was attacked by North Vietnamese torpedo boats. The boats were driven off with the aid of aircraft from the carrier USS *Ticonderoga*. President Johnson announced that any further 'unprovoked military action' by North Vietnam would lead to 'grave consequences'.

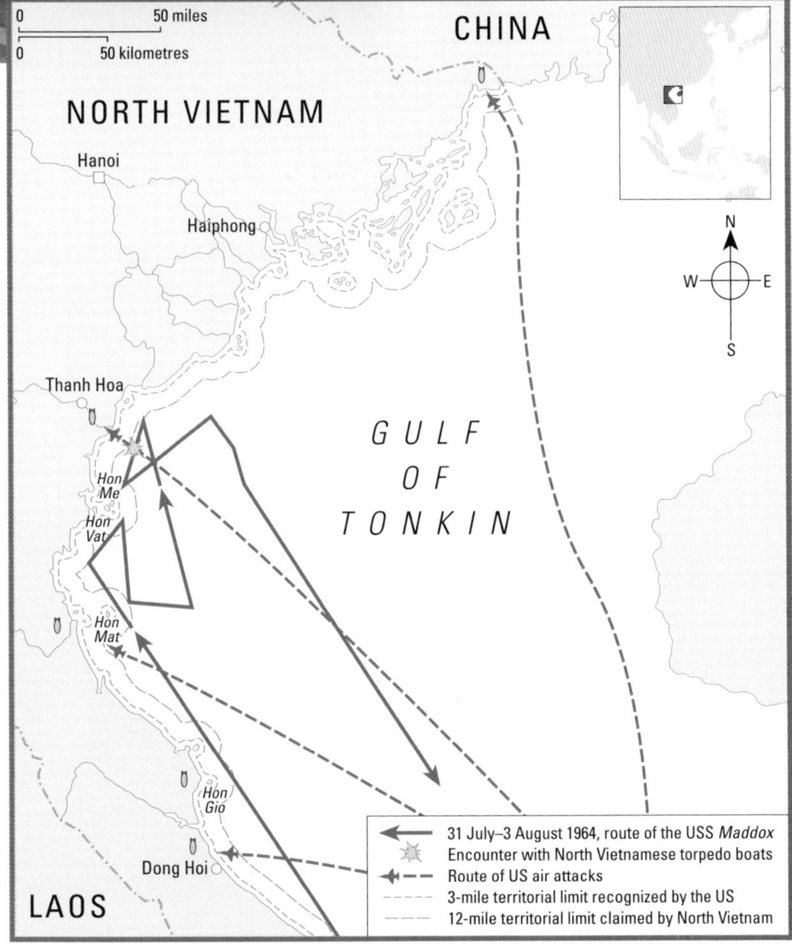

The attack or (disputedly) attacks on the USS *Maddox* by North Vietnamese torpedo boats led to retaliatory air strikes launched from US aircraft carriers.

Two days later, on the night of 4-5 August, *Maddox* and another destroyer reported that they had once again been attacked by enemy vessels. It has been widely questioned whether this second attack actually took place. However, President Johnson ordered immediate air strikes in retaliation, and aircraft from the carriers *Ticonderoga* and *Constellation* bombarded North Vietnamese ports. On 7 August, the US Congress passed what is known as the Gulf of Tonkin Resolution, which in effect gave the US government a free hand to escalate US involvement in Vietnam in any way it saw fit.

ROLLING THUNDER The next US bombing raids on North Vietnam followed in February 1965, in retaliation for guerrilla attacks on US bases in South Vietnam. Then, on 2 March 1965, the United States initiated a sustained bombing campaign against the North. Known as Operation Rolling Thunder, this campaign continued, with a number of interruptions, until October 1968.

ROLLING THUNDER STATISTICS

The Rolling Thunder bombing campaign against North Vietnam in 1965-8 was on a massive scale:

Sorties flown by US Navy and Air Force fighter bombers	304,000
Sorties by B-52 bombers over North Vietnam	2,380
Bombs dropped (tons)	537,000
US aircraft lost in combat	922

The aim of Rolling Thunder was to persuade North Vietnam to call off the fight in the South. The bombing raids were carefully graded, with attacks periodically stepped up or reduced as a way of bullying or coaxing the North Vietnamese into stopping the war. Many targets were permanently off-limits – mostly to avoid provoking North Vietnam's powerful supporters, China and the Soviet Union. Although the rules of engagement changed from time to time, for

A low-flying US fighter aircraft casts a shadow near a bomb-shattered road bridge in North Vietnam during the Rolling Thunder bombing campaign.

North Vietnamese women operate a Soviet-supplied anti-aircraft gun. North Vietnam's effective air defences took a heavy toll of US aircraft.

much of the period no attacks were made on Haiphong port, the main entry point for Soviet supplies to North Vietnam.

The bombing cost the United States heavy losses, because the North Vietnamese had Soviet-supplied anti-aircraft guns and missiles, as well as MiG fighter aircraft. The American fliers were forced to observe many limits that restricted them in combat – for example, at first they were not allowed to attack missile sites because they might injure or kill Soviet technicians and thus risk widening the war.

Rolling Thunder is now generally recognized to have been a failure. It inflicted a great deal of damage on North Vietnam's industries, military installations and transport system. It is also reckoned to have killed more than 50,000 civilians. But the bombing had no decisive military effect, while psychologically if anything it stiffened North Vietnamese resistance. It also provided fuel for the anti-war protest movements that arose in the U.S. and internationally in response to the war in Vietnam.

The Rolling Thunder bombing campaign was carried out mostly by US jets flying from South Vietnam and from aircraft carriers, with B-52s also taking part. For fear of bringing China into the war, air strikes were banned close to the Chinese border.

CHAPTER 3: SEARCH AND DESTROY – 1965-1967

By 1965 the South Vietnamese government had lost control of most of rural South Vietnam. Around 70 per cent of South Vietnam's villages were in the hands of the communists. The South Vietnamese army – the ARVN – was demoralized and poorly led. It was no match for the communist forces, which now consisted not only of Viet Cong guerrillas but also of soldiers of the North Vietnamese Army (NVA), who had been sent into the South down the Ho Chi Minh Trail. Guerrillas were firmly in control of territory just 30 km from Saigon.

US Marines come ashore from landing craft on a beach in South Vietnam in August 1965. Originally deployed to defend US bases, Marines soon took on an offensive role in Vietnam.

Communist guerrillas dominated large areas of the South Vietnamese countryside in 1965-7. American forces at times penetrated deep inside these hostile areas in the effort to seek out and destroy the enemy.

B-52 bombers, based in Thailand or on the distant islands of Guam or Okinawa, flew many thousands of missions during the war, hitting targets in Vietnam, Cambodia and Laos.

The US government had hoped that if the ARVN troops were given arms and training, they would do the fighting and dying. But now it was clear that only a large-scale commitment of US combat troops could prevent a communist victory. On 8 March 1965, the first combat force of US Marines landed in South Vietnam at Da Nang. By the end of the year there were over 180,000 US military personnel in South Vietnam, supported by an awesome supply operation across the Pacific.

The United States was not the only country to send in troops to defend the South Vietnamese government. Soldiers from Australia, New Zealand, South Korea, Thailand and the Philippines – all members of the South-east Asia Treaty Organization (SEATO) – fought alongside the Americans. But from 1965 until 1969, it was overwhelmingly the United States' war, with these allies and the ARVN itself playing only a relatively marginal part in the fighting. European allies, including Britain, kept out of the Vietnam War.

In theory, the struggle between the forces of the world's greatest military power and lightly armed Viet Cong and NVA infantry appeared one-sided. In reality the US forces, led by General Westmoreland, faced a difficult task. Westmoreland was not allowed to invade North Vietnam, for fear of widening the war, and nor he was not allowed to use nuclear weapons. The US government also refused him permission to send major forces into Laos or Cambodia to block the communist supply routes down South Vietnam's long land border. The Ho Chi Minh Trail was subjected to massive attack by B-52 bombers, but this did not stop the movement of men and supplies. The Viet Cong and NVA were able to replace losses in South Vietnam with fresh arrivals from the North.

With their aircraft, warships and artillery, the Americans deployed a truly amazing quantity and variety of firepower in South Vietnam. In line with traditional US military thinking, Westmoreland believed that the way to win the war was to engage the enemy in combat and use this firepower to destroy the

FULL-SCALE COMMITMENT

Between 1965 and 1968 the US military commitment in Vietnam was at its height, both in terms of numbers of troops and casualties:

	1965	1966	1967	1968
US military personnel	184,300	385,300	485,600	536,100
US deaths in action	1,369	5,008	9,378	14,592

Viet Cong guerrillas move along the waterways of the Mekong Delta, south of Saigon, in 1966. Many villages in the Delta were guerrilla strongholds.

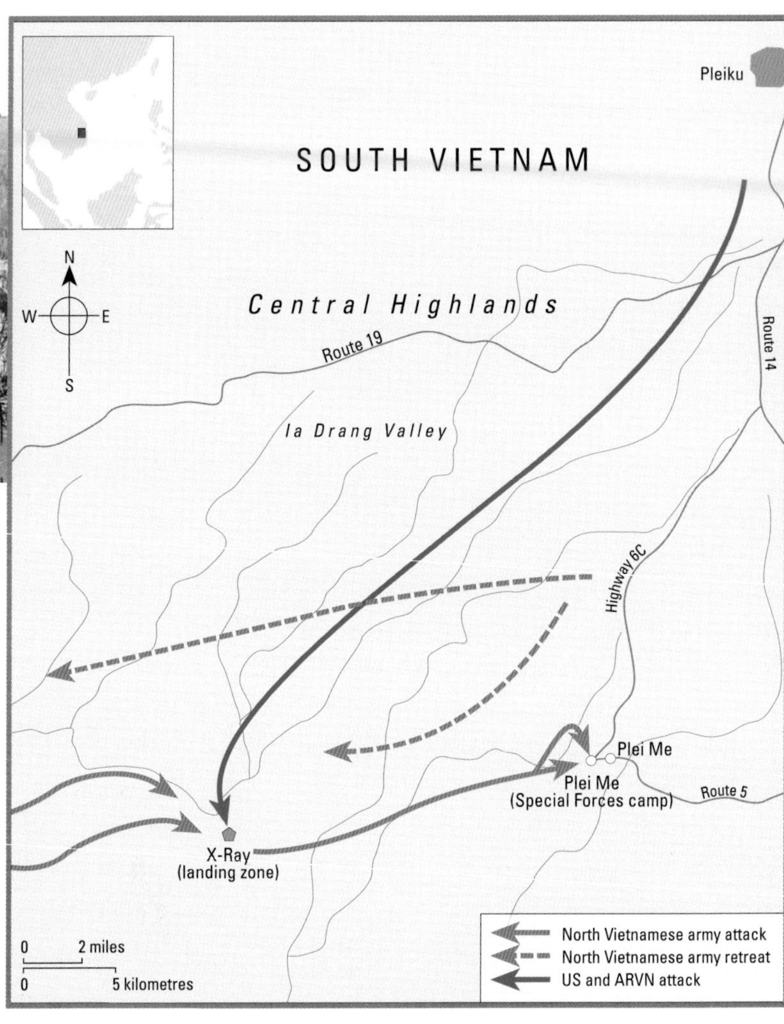

The battle of the Ia Drang Valley began with an NVA attack on a US camp at Plei Me. US troops flew in by helicopter to landing zone X-Ray. After two days' fighting, the NVA withdrew.

enemy forces. But, unlike in a conventional war, there was no front line where the enemy would stand and fight. Vietnam was a country well suited to guerrilla warfare, whether in the mountainous jungle of the Central Highlands, the waterways of the Mekong Delta, or the densely populated ricefields where guerrillas could hide among the villagers.

Both the Viet Cong and the NVA infantry were elusive, skilled in evading combat until a moment of their own choosing. So Westmoreland developed a strategy of 'search and destroy' – first seek out the enemy, and then call in the firepower.

AIR MOBILITY For mobility, the Americans decided to rely primarily on fleets of helicopters – tanks were regarded as of limited use because, travelling on roads, they were considered too easy to ambush. Helicopters could carry troops rapidly to the point of battle, ferry supplies to firebases deep inside hostile territory, provide a kind of airborne artillery (helicopter gunships), and evacuate the wounded.

The first major test of US forces in South Vietnam came at the battle of the Ia Drang Valley in November 1965. This took place in the remote Central Highlands, where the North Vietnamese were building up a substantial body of NVA troops, sent down the Ho Chi Minh Trail. The US command was concerned that the NVA might push down from the Central Highlands to the sea, effectively cutting South Vietnam in half.

The newly formed US 1st Cavalry Division was based in the area, at Ankhe, near Pleiku. With about 400 helicopters, the 1st Cavalry was the US Army's first division created specifically to fight airmobile warfare. A battalion of the 1st Cavalry flew in to relieve a Special Forces base at Plei Me, near the Cambodian border, which had come under NVA attack. A fierce battle was joined between the NVA and the air cavalry. US artillery and aircraft – including B-52 bombers flying in from Guam in the Pacific – subjected the NVA to heavy bombardment. In two days' fighting, the NVA were estimated to have suffered 2,000 casualties, before disappearing back into the jungle.

The US Army rated the Ia Drang Valley a considerable success. It certainly showed that the introduction of US forces was going to prevent any swift communist victory in South Vietnam. But the battle also revealed what a tough fight the Americans had on their hands. At one helicopter Landing Zone (LZ), a force of 400 US airborne troops, encircled by the NVA, suffered 279 casualties in a day's fighting.

At first the United States fought a primarily defensive campaign, while building up troop strength and logistical support. By the end of 1966, however, with more than 385,000 US soldiers in South Vietnam, Westmoreland was ready to take the offensive with search and destroy operations on a large scale. The aim was to seize control of areas of the country that were currently controlled by the guerrillas, and to inflict heavy losses on the enemy.

One solidly guerrilla-dominated area was between Saigon and the Cambodian border,

POLITICAL WARFARE

Criticizing American policy at this stage of the war, Henry Kissinger, US Secretary of State from 1969 to 1975, wrote:
'We fought a military war; our opponents fought a political one … We lost sight of one of the cardinal [main] maxims of guerrilla war: the guerrilla wins if he does not lose; the conventional army loses if it does not win.'
[Quoted in *America in Vietnam*, Guenter Lewy]

The US Air Cavalry rides into action during an operation in 1967. Before the Vietnam War, helicopters had never been used in mass formation.

including the so-called 'Iron Triangle', a mere 50 km from the South Vietnamese capital. Here the Viet Cong had constructed elaborate systems of tunnels with concealed entrances, making underground fortresses from which their mainforce units could launch attacks on their enemy. The guerrillas could also count on the support of the local villagers, many of whom operated as part-time members of the Viet Cong.

In January 1967 Operation Cedar Falls was launched against the Iron Triangle. It was to be a 'hammer and anvil' operation. US and ARVN troops took up blocking positions on the south-western side of the Triangle, forming the 'anvil'. Helicopter and ground attacks from the north and west would provide the hammer. The Viet Cong were meant to be trapped and crushed between the two.

The operation, lasting nineteen days, went much as planned. The US and ARVN forces occupied the Triangle. Volunteers sent in to explore the networks of

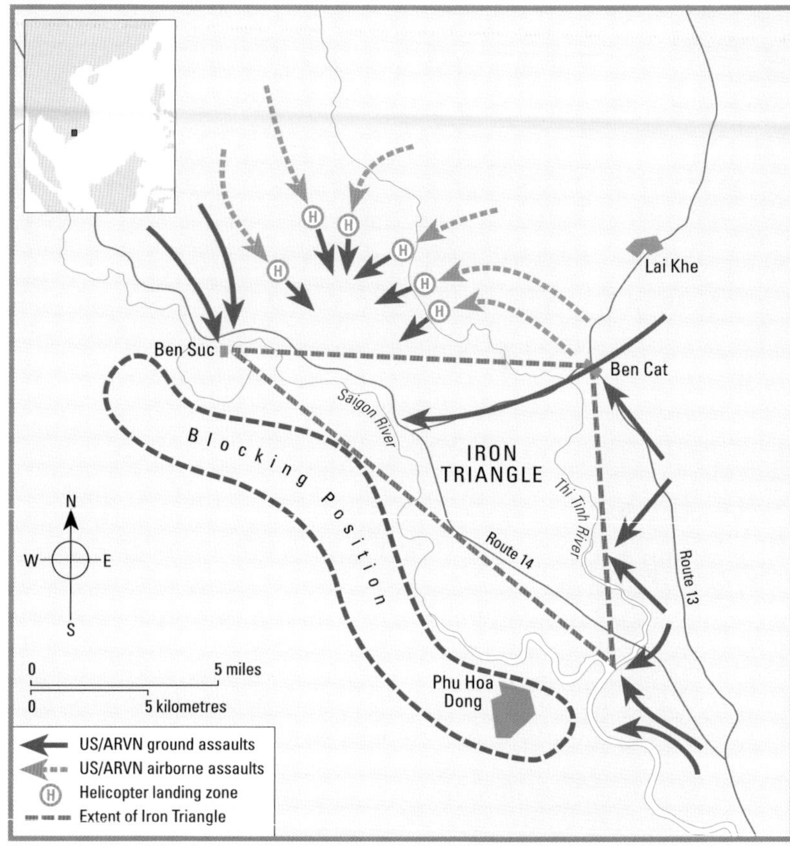

In Operation Cedar Falls in January 1967, US and ARVN troops swept through the Iron Triangle, a Viet Cong stronghold near Saigon. (Below) Men of US 25th Infantry Division leap from a helicopter near Cu Chi during Operation Cedar Falls.

A distressed US soldier is given water after searching one of the tunnels dug by Viet Cong guerrillas in the Iron Triangle near Saigon. The tunnels were subsequently sealed and blown up.

FREE-FIRE ZONE

Villages in South Vietnam were sometimes cleared of their peasant population to create 'free-fire zones'. A US official described this process in 1967:

'The inhabitants are allowed time to pack their belongings and collect their livestock and then are moved to one of the 65 refugee camps in the province. Shortly thereafter the hamlet is destroyed … friendly forces continue to receive fire from such hamlets and encounter mines, but they are no longer inhibited from returning fire and calling in artillery and air strikes.'

[Quoted in *Guerrilla Warfare*, Robin Corbett]

tunnels – known as 'Tunnel Rats' – unearthed large quantities of supplies and stacks of documents giving details of Viet Cong and NVA military plans. The tunnels were destroyed and areas of forest cleared by bulldozer. Yet the fighting was relatively light, because most of the Viet Cong mainforce managed to disappear into the jungle. Only days after Cedar Falls ended, guerrillas were once more operating in the area.

One of the first American actions in Operation Cedar Falls was the destruction of the village of Ben Suc on the edge of the Triangle. Airborne troops descended on the village, interrogated the population, and arrested suspected Viet Cong members. The villagers were then carried off to a refugee camp and Ben Suc was burned to the ground. Witnessed by journalists, the destruction of the village aroused controversy in the United States, where a vocal anti-war movement was gathering strength.

The fate of Ben Suc was not a one-off event. When the United States took on guerrillas in populated countryside, deploying their massive firepower, the local population inevitably suffered terribly. US forces operated under rules that forbade the unnecessary destruction of civilian lives or property. But often it was unclear who was a civilian and who a guerrilla. If US Army patrols suffered a steady stream of casualties

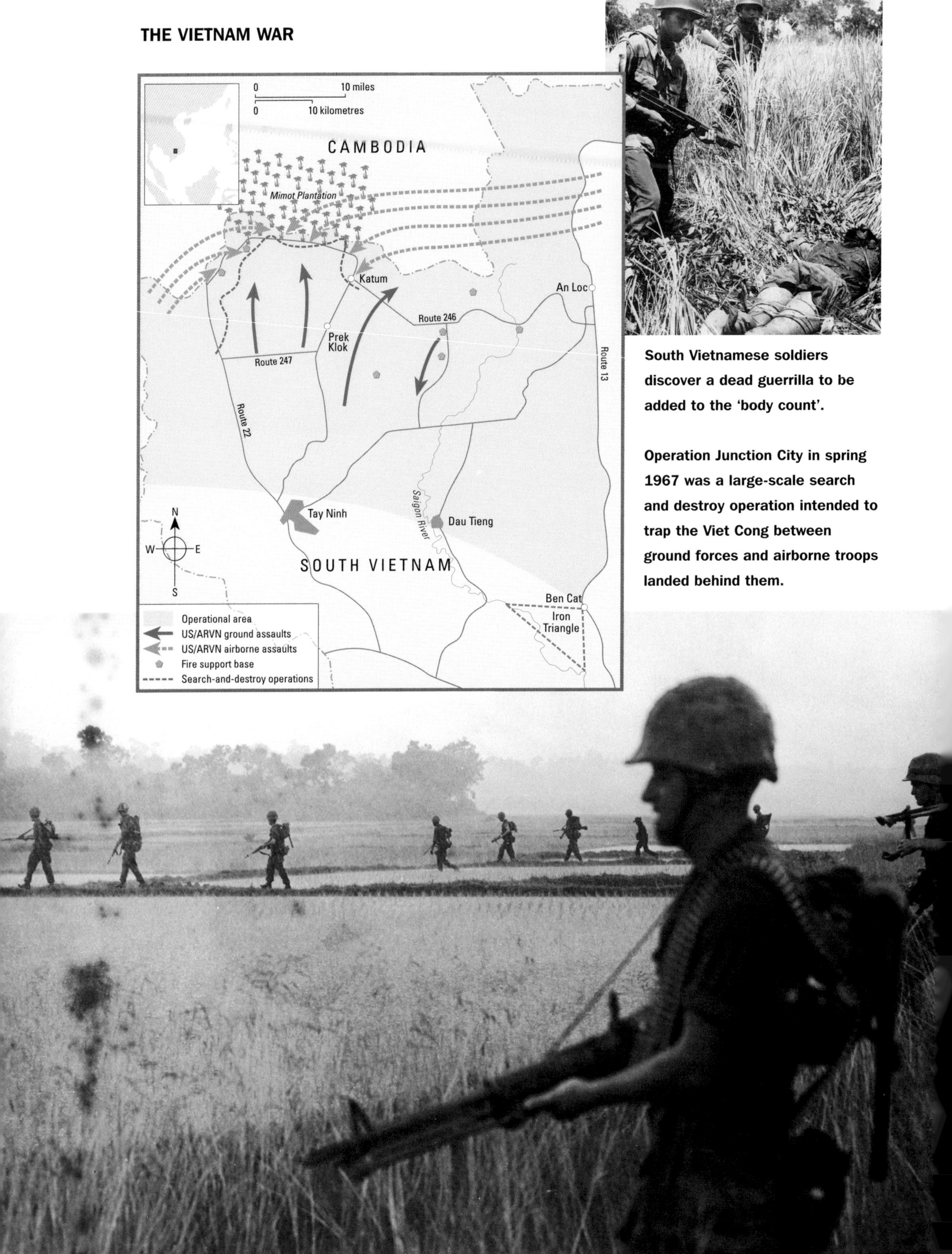

South Vietnamese soldiers discover a dead guerrilla to be added to the 'body count'.

Operation Junction City in spring 1967 was a large-scale search and destroy operation intended to trap the Viet Cong between ground forces and airborne troops landed behind them.

from sniper fire or booby trap bombs in a particular area, the response was often to order the local people to collect their belongings and leave. This created what was called a Free Fire Zone. Anyone who remained behind could be regarded as Viet Cong and treated accordingly. Even when not deliberately driven out, many peasants fled their homes in what had become a battlefield. As a result of the countryside clearance, some 1.5 million South Vietnamese were thought to be living in refugee camps by the end of 1967.

COUNTRYWIDE CONFLICT By that time the number of US military personnel committed to South Vietnam was approaching a half a million. They were fighting from the Mekong Delta in the south – where the US Army and Navy combined in aggressive pushes up rivers in guerrilla territory – to near the border with North Vietnam, where US military outposts came under attack from the NVA. Whenever US forces succeeded in engaging their enemy, they won the fight. But they could never achieve a victory that was in any sense decisive.

Operation Junction City, in February-April 1967, showed clearly what could and could not be achieved. The operation involved more than 25,000 US and ARVN troops in an attempt to destroy NVA and Viet Cong bases near the Cambodian border. They duly overran the bases and killed around 2,800 enemy – about ten times the casualties they themselves suffered. But they were unable to occupy the area permanently and enemy operations were only briefly disrupted.

Looking for solid evidence of progress in the war, the US government had settled for the 'body count' – regularly updated figures of the number of guerrillas killed in action. Although these figures were undoubtedly exagerrated, they did show the damage that the US forces were able to inflict on the Viet Cong and NVA. But the communists' will to fight on was undaunted. The body count that mattered more to the future of the war was that of US lives lost. By the end of 1967 some 16,000 US servicemen had been killed in Vietnam. The question inevitably was how long Americans would go on accepting these sort of losses. The answer came in 1968.

US Marines advance through a paddyfield during a search and destroy operation in 1967. Soldiers in rural Vietnam had to be constantly on the watch for snipers or for mines that could kill or maim.

DISILLUSION WITH WAR

By 1967 US Defense Secretary Robert McNamara had become disillusioned with the war. Before he resigned his post in the autumn of that year, McNamara stated:

'The picture of the world's greatest superpower killing or seriously injuring 1,000 non-combatants a week, while trying to pound a tiny backward nation into submission … is not a pretty one.'

[Quoted in *The Ten Thousand Day War*, Michael Maclear]

US troops rush a wounded colleague to a waiting helicopter. Thousands of lives were saved by the speed with which helicopters evacuated casualties.

CHAPTER 4:
THE DECISIVE YEAR – 1968

US airborne troops prepare to board a helicopter at a landing zone near Khe Sanh in April 1968.

From January to April 1968 the US Marine base at Khe Sanh was besieged by about 40,000 NVA troops.

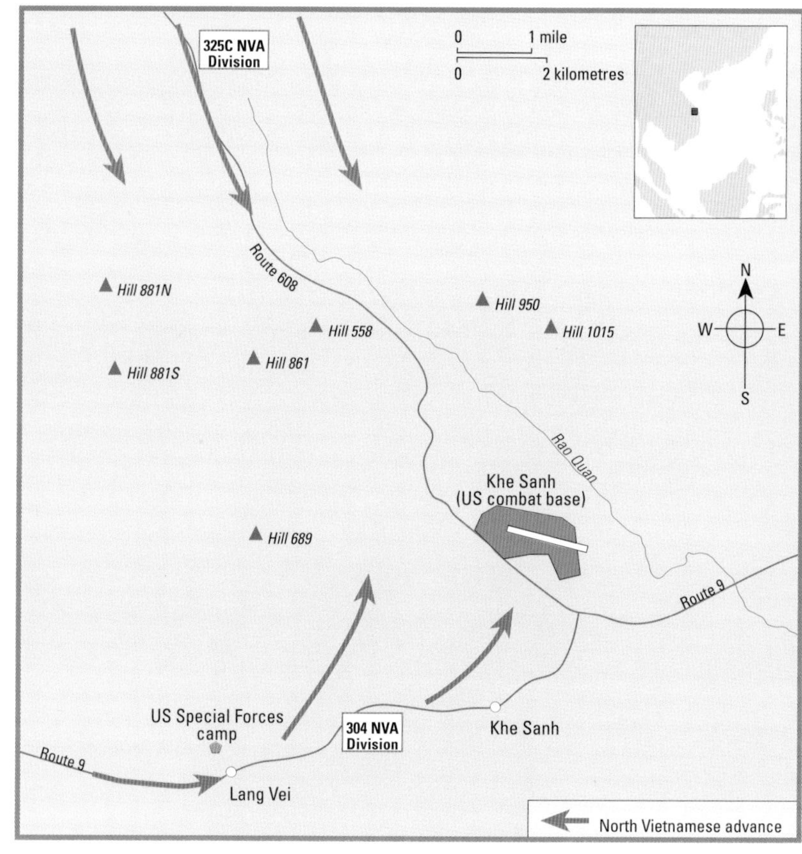

By the start of 1968, the North Vietnamese leadership had decided that the time was ripe for a final push to drive the Americans out of South Vietnam. The Viet Cong and NVA guerrillas were ordered to prepare to take over South Vietnam's towns and cities in a coordinated offensive throughout the country. Ho and his colleagues expected that the guerrillas would be welcomed by Vietnamese in the urban areas as liberators and that mass desertions would lead to the collapse of the South Vietnamese army (ARVN).

As a prelude to this offensive, on 21 January 1968 two NVA divisions, numbering around 40,000 troops, laid siege to 5,000 US Marines in a base at Khe Sanh,

DEVASTATING FIREPOWER

Writing of the part played by airpower in the defence of the base at Khe Sanh, General Westmoreland wrote:
'Without question the amount of firepower put on that piece of real estate exceeded anything that has been seen before in history.'
[Quoted in *Historical Atlas of the Vietnam War,* Harry Summers Jr. and Stanley Karnow]

American soldiers hurry to board a helicopter during the operation to break the siege of Khe Sanh in April 1968.

in the far north of South Vietnam. A repeat of the French defeat at Dien Bien Phu looked possible. The Americans were, however, able to keep the besieged base supplied by air. Round-the-clock air attacks, including heavy bombing by B-52s, battered the NVA troops dug in around the base. The US Marines also took a pounding from NVA rocket and artillery fire, but held firm during 77 days of fighting. On 8 April, an American relief column broke through to Khe Sanh, lifting the siege.

By then the major communist offensive had come and gone. The operation was timed to begin on 30-31 January. This was the start of the Vietnamese Tet national holiday, when the ARVN would be least prepared to fight, with many military personnel on leave. After some preliminary attacks on the 30th, the Tet offensive began in earnest on the night of the 31st. More than a 100 cities and towns in South Vietnam were attacked. The number of communist fighters committed to the offensive numbered around 85,000, mainly Viet Cong guerrillas except in the north of the country, where NVA troops took the leading role.

The offensive took the US Army and ARVN by surprise and initially achieved many of its objectives.

Two South Vietnamese soldiers take part in the fighting against communist guerrillas in Saigon during the Tet offensive, January 1968.

Viet Cong guerrillas, captured by South Vietnamese troops, kneel blindfolded in a Saigon street, February 1968.

A MILITARY PARADOX

During the Tet offensive, one US major involved in retaking the Mekong Delta town of Ben Tre from the Viet Cong allegedly told an interviewer:
'We had to destroy the town in order to save it.'
[Quoted in *Guerrilla Warfare,* Robin Corbett]

In Saigon a platoon of guerrillas broke into the US Embassy compound and larger forces attacked other key military and political installations. Vietnam's former imperial capital, Hue, was occupied by the NVA. But there was no uprising of local people in support of the communists. Counterattacks mounted by the US Army and the ARVN soon recaptured most urban areas – far from collapsing, the ARVN performed far better than expected. Saigon was largely clear of communist fighters within a week. Only Hue was held by the communists for a prolonged period.

Militarily, Tet was a disaster for the Viet Cong and, to a lesser degree, the NVA. The communists probably lost around 30,000 men in the first two weeks of February 1968, compared with around 3,000 of the US Army, ARVN and their allies killed. The fighting of the first half of 1968 as a whole more or less destroyed the Viet Cong guerrilla movement, leaving the war to be carried on largely by the NVA.

The political impact of the Tet offensive was, however, disastrous

Khe Sanh (firebase)
Quang Tri
Hue
LAOS
Phu Bai
Phu Loc
Da Nang
Hoi An
Tam Ky
Chu Lai
Quang Ngai
Bong Son
Kontum
Pleiku
Ankhe
Hau Bon
Qui Nhon
CAMBODIA
Tuy Hoa
Ban Me Thuot
SOUTH VIETNAM
Mekong
Nha Trang
Dalat
Phnom Penh
Phan Rang
Tay Ninh
Phu Cuong
Duc Hoa
Bien Hoa
Phan Thiet
Gia Dinh
Saigon
Chau Phu
Moc Hoa
Phuoc Le
Sa Dec
My Tho
Vinh Long
Ben Tre
Rach Gia
Can Tho
Phu Vinh
Soc Tran
Bac Lieu
Ca Mau
N
W
E
S
0 50 miles
0 100 kilometres
Area of prolonged confrontation
30 January, first wave of attacks
31 January, second wave of attacks

In the Tet offensive at the end of January 1968, communist forces attacked towns and cities across South Vietnam.

Folk singer Joan Baez, one of the most prominent celebrity anti-war campaigners, takes part in a protest rally in New York.

for the US government. There had been an anti-war movement in the United States since the very start of the Vietnam War. It drew the support of many students and of some prominent individuals, including Civil Rights leader Martin Luther King. They believed America was fighting against a popular liberation movement and doing so in a particularly brutal way. Protests had ranged from large-scale demonstrations to individual refusal to be drafted into the army or the burning of draft cards – the cards sent to people so that they could be called up into the armed forces if required. Among famous people prosecuted for refusing the draft was world boxing champion Muhammad Ali.

But until the Tet offensive the majority of US citizens had continued to support the war effort, if with mounting doubts. Then, after almost three years of large-scale commitment of US forces, the American public saw on their televisions fighting taking place in the streets of South Vietnam's cities and even outside the US embassy. Inevitably, public confidence in the chances of success in the war was severely shaken.

Unknown to the public, the US government had also lost confidence in winning the war. After Tet, with the siege of Khe Sanh and the battle for Hue still

US Marines in action during the street fighting in Hue in spring 1968. About 1,000 Marines were killed or wounded in the battle to retake the city from the NVA.

raging, General Westmoreland requested commitment of another 200,000 US troops to Vietnam. With these extra men – and permission to invade Cambodia and Laos to cut communist supply lines – Westmoreland said that he could win the war. But a report by US Defense Secretary Clark Clifford concluded that: 'All that can be said is that additional troops would enable us to kill more of the enemy …'

ELECTION YEAR 1968 was a presidential election year in the United States. On 31 March 1968 President Johnson announced that he would not stand for re-election. At the same time, the Rolling Thunder bombing raids on North Vietnam were scaled down and the United States sought to open peace negotiations. From that point onwards, the United States was no longer seeking victory, but looking for a way out of Vietnam.

The destruction wrought upon South Vietnam during 1968, graphically reported by the media in America and across the world, made an awesome spectacle. In Hue, for example, US Marines and Army soldiers aided by the ARVN fought for more than three weeks to retake the city from the NVA. The house-to-house fighting, plus shelling by US warships, reduced large parts of the city to rubble. The non-combatant dead in Hue included at least 2,800 South Vietnamese government officials, military officers and others rounded up and massacred by the communists.

In the course of 1968 almost 15,000 US servicemen were killed in action in Vietnam – nearly 300 a week. The death toll on the communist side almost certainly exceeded 100,000. The number of Vietnamese civilians killed has never been accurately calculated. It is in this context of war at its most brutal

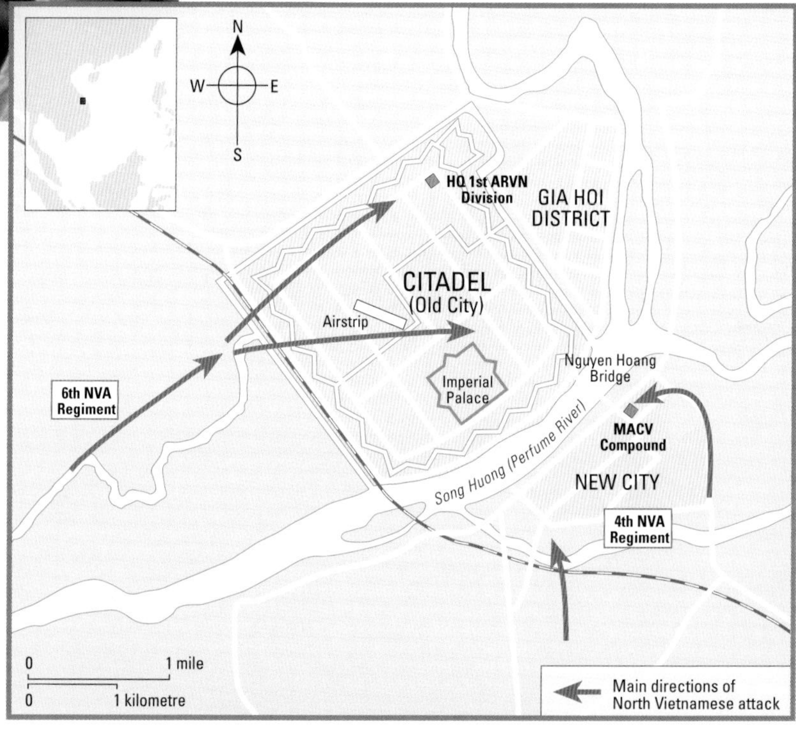

On 31 January 1968 NVA troops attacked the city of Hue. They occupied the old Citadel, apart from the ARVN headquarters, and threatened the MACV Compound, the US headquarters. It took 24 days to retake the Citadel from the NVA.

hat the most notorious atrocity of the conflict took place. On 16 March more than 300 South Vietnamese civilians, including women and children, were massacred in cold blood by American soldiers at the hamlet of My Lai. A number of US officers and NCOs were later prosecuted for their part in the killings, and one, Lieutenant William Calley, was convicted.

The 1968 US presidential election was dominated by the issue of the war. There were violent clashes between anti-war demonstrators and police at the Democrat party convention in Chicago in August. The election was won in November by Republican Richard M. Nixon, who had promised both to 'get tough with the communists' and 'bring our boys back home'.

By then the first steps towards an American withdrawal from Vietnam had already been taken. Refused the extra troops he believed necessary, Westmoreland was replaced as US commander in Vietnam by General Creighton W. Abrams in June 1968. At the end of October, the bombing of North Vietnam was halted. Peace talks were scheduled to begin at the start of 1969. A new phase of the war had begun.

GETTING OUT OF VIETNAM

American author William Broyles Jr., who served as a Marine in Vietnam, wrote:
'There was no single goal in Vietnam; there were 2.8 million goals, one for every American who served there. And in the end the nation's goal became what each soldier's had been all along: to get out of Vietnam.'

[From *Brothers in Arms*, William Broyles]

A man killed in a bombing raid in Hue. Scenes of war such as this, shown on television every evening (for this was the first televised war) helped to stir up anti-war sentiment in the USA.

CHAPTER 5: VIETNAMIZATION 1969-1971

ATTACKING SPIRIT

General Melvin Zais, commander of the US 101st Airborne Division, vigorously defended the decision to fight for Hamburger Hill:

'That hill was in my area of operations, that was where the enemy was, that's where I attacked him … If I find him on any other hill in the A Shau, I assure you I'll attack him again.'

[Quoted in *America in Vietnam*, Guenter Lewy]

American soldiers cross a river in the A Shau Valley, rugged country ideal for guerrilla operations.

Despite the shocks of Khe Sanh and the Tet offensive, through the second half of 1968 and into 1969 the war went on much as before. US troops continued to carry out major offensive operations to seek out and destroy the enemy. Such operations only came to an end after the battle of the A Shau Valley in May 1969.

The battle began on 10 May when the US 101st Airborne Division flew in by helicopter to take on North Vietnamese troops dug in on the slopes of a hill in the valley, which was close to the border with Laos. A fierce battle was joined as the Airborne Division, soon backed up by other US and ARVN troops, assaulted the NVA positions. The hill was soon nicknamed Hamburger Hill, because of the number of men chewed up on its slopes.

On 20 May the NVA positions were overrun by the US and South Vietnamese – a clear military victory. But the battle for Hamburger Hill caused an outcry in the United States. The US casualties had been 46 dead and some 400 wounded. Earlier in the war, the American public had considered such losses acceptable. In May 1969 they were widely regarded as unacceptably high. US soldiers had also begun to lose their will to fight. From this time onward, morale in many units of the US Army in Vietnam went into sharp decline. Many soldiers had no desire to risk their lives for what was widely regarded as a lost cause.

After Hamburger Hill, the US government, with President Nixon now in charge, ordered General Abrams to avoid any further large-scale battles. In June 1969, Nixon announced the first US troop withdrawals from Vietnam. He declared it a priority that the South Vietnamese Army (ARVN) should take over the prime combat role in the war. This policy was known as 'Vietnamization'.

Richard M. Nixon, US President from 1969 to 1974.

In a sense, there was nothing new about this policy. From the start of its involvement in Vietnam, the official aim of the United States had been to make South Vietnam into a self-sustaining independent country, capable of defending itself. When US troops poured in to the country from 1965 onward, this goal had been for a time largely overlooked as the United States concentrated on direct military confrontation. But back in mid-1967, General Abrams had been tasked with turning the ARVN into an efficient fighting force. When Abrams took over from Westmoreland as head of US forces in Vietnam in mid-1968, measures were already afoot for rapidly expanding ARVN troop numbers and improving their equipment.

At the same time, anti-communist South Vietnamese had found a man who could give them some real leadership. General Nguyen Van Thieu had emerged as the most capable of the South Vietnamese generals who vied for power in the mid-1960s. In September 1967 Thieu was confirmed in power by presidential elections which were, by South Vietnamese standards, reasonably free and fair. Although labelled a 'puppet' of the

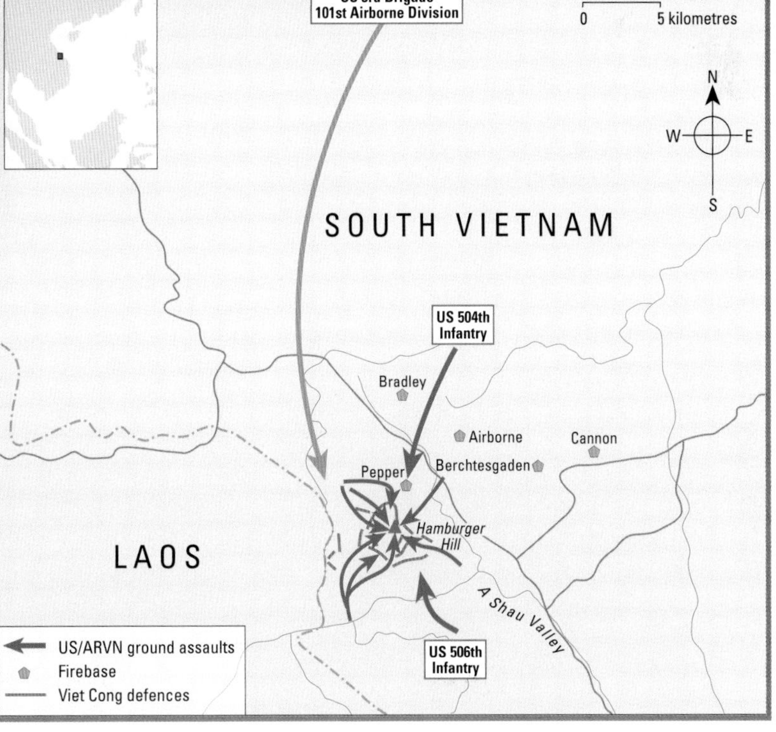

In May 1969 troops of the US 101st Airborne were flown into the A Shau Valley, where they engaged the NVA on Hamburger Hill. After reinforcements were brought in, the hill was captured on 20 May.

Pictures like this – of a US soldier holding a gun to the head of a Vietnamese peasant woman – helped persuade many people that the war was wrong.

SCALING BACK

Between 1969 and 1971 the number of US military personnel in Vietnam fell sharply, but combat deaths fell even more steeply:

	1969	1970	1971
US military personnel	475,200	334,600	156,800
US deaths in action	9,414	4,221	1,380

United States by the communists and the anti-war movement, Thieu proved a leader of independent spirit who pursued what he regarded as South Vietnam's best interests.

Along with trying to build up the ARVN, the Americans and the South Vietnamese government made progress with the 'pacification' of the South Vietnamese countryside. 'Pacification' meant getting rid of the communist organization in rural South Vietnam and making the country secure under government control. The principal organization behind this effort was CORDS (Civil Operations and Revolutionary Development Support), in which the Central Intelligence Agency (CIA) played a leading role. From the summer of 1968, the pacification campaign had increasing success. In many areas refugees were resettled on the land and local pro-government militias took responsibility for keeping their villages secure. A land reform programme, distributing land to peasants, helped win their 'hearts and minds'. At the same time, through the ruthless 'Phoenix programme', from 1968 to 1971 thousands of communist activists in South Vietnam were identified and either arrested or killed.

Ironically, by the second half of 1969, when support for the war among the American public was evaporating, the security situation in South Vietnam

By 1971 most densely populated parts of South Vietnam had been brought firmly under government control ('pacified') and fighting with communist forces took place largely in border areas.

US Marines cross the Vu Gia river in pursuit of communist forces in June 1969. By that time, such offensive operations were being phased out as they cost too many American lives.

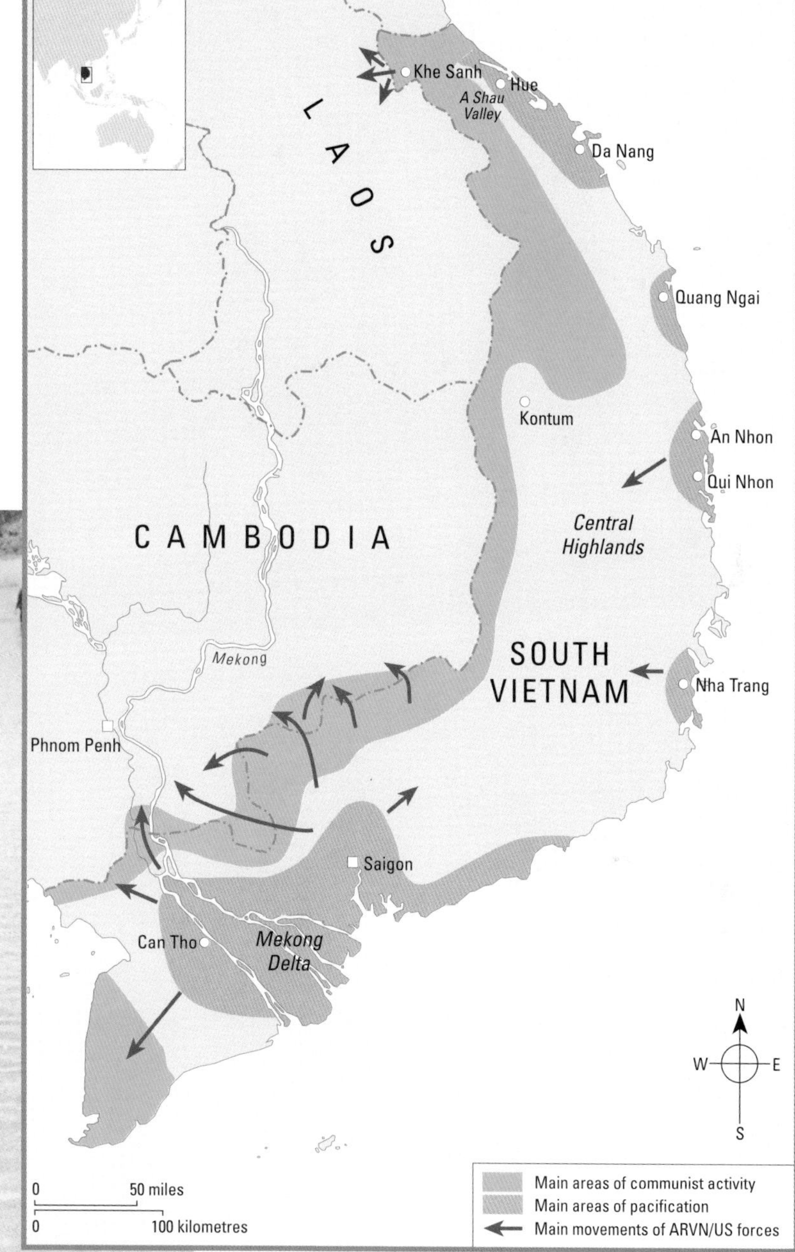

had vastly improved. Fighting went on mostly in areas close to the border with Cambodia and Laos, away from major centres of population. Heavy losses among South Vietnamese communists, especially in the Tet offensive and the Phoenix programme, had mostly ended the insurgency in South Vietnam. Large areas of the countryside were securely in the government's hands. In North Vietnam, the death of Ho Chi Minh in September 1969 deprived the communists of a national leader of great stature.

Between the second half of 1969 and spring 1972

Young North Vietnamese soldiers who were captured during the incursion into Cambodia in 1970.

BUYING TIME

The main aim of the US/South Vietnamese incursion into Cambodia in 1970 was to postpone a major NVA offensive until the ARVN was in a fit condition to defend South Vietnam. President Nixon declared:

'We have bought time for the South Vietnamese to strengthen themselves against the enemy.'

[Quoted in *Historical Atlas of the Vietnam War*, Harry Summers Jr. and Stanley Karnow]

the general level of combat in Vietnam was much lower than in the previous four years. American troop levels fell steadily as Nixon fulfilled the promise to 'bring the boys home'. But the troop withdrawals did not mean that the president was prepared to accept a communist victory in Vietnam. While scaling down the troop numbers, Nixon simultaneously widened the war. In March 1969 he secretly authorized the bombing of communist bases in Cambodia by B-52s.

CAMBODIA Since gaining independence from the French, Cambodia had been ruled by Prince Norodom Sihanouk. He had tried to keep his country free of involvement in the war in Vietnam, a policy which had meant turning a blind eye to the presence of Vietnamese communist bases and supply lines in Cambodia. The Nixon administration put pressure on Sihanouk to crack down on the communist presence. Then, in March 1970, Sihanouk was overthrown in a coup led by the pro-American General Lon Nol.

The bombing and the political instability in Cambodia created a dangerous situation. There were fears that the NVA might attack the Cambodian capital, Phnom Penh. Cambodia also had its own communist guerrilla movement, the Khmer Rouge, which was a growing threat to the government. At the end of April 1970 Nixon authorized a US/South Vietnamese attack across the border from South Vietnam into Cambodia. Aimed at communist bases, the 'incursion' was intended to relieve communist pressure on Phnom Penh and to disrupt NVA preparations for a major attack against South Vietnam. The main targets were two salients known as Parrot's Beak and Fish Hook. Around 25,000 ARVN and US troops, with powerful air support, pushed 30 km inside Cambodia, overrunning communist bases and seizing large quantities of arms and ammunition.

The incursion into Cambodia provoked a wave of anti-war demonstrations across the United States. On 4 May, at Kent State University, Ohio, National Guardsmen shot four student demonstrators dead and wounded 11 others. There was also a hostile reaction in the US Congress, where the Gulf of Tonkin Resolution (see page 14) was repealed and the president was ordered to withdraw US troops from Cambodia by the end of June. In December 1970 Congress banned any further use of US ground troops beyond the borders of South Vietnam. When an incursion into Laos was carried out in January to March 1971 to attack NVA bases and the Ho Chi Minh Trail, only ARVN troops took part, with the support of US aircraft and long-range artillery. The 'Vietnamization' of the war had in effect taken place.

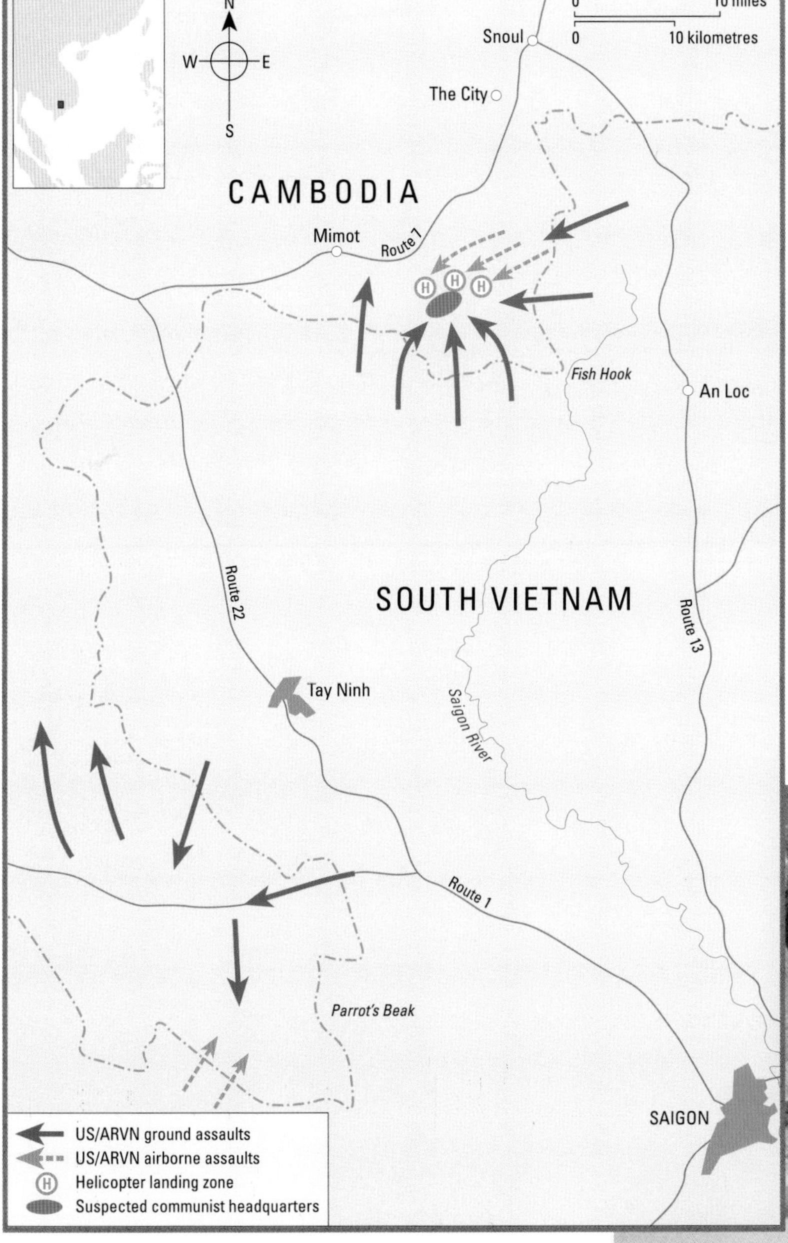

In April-May 1970, US and ARVN forces crossed from South Vietnam into Cambodia to attack communist bases. The incursions targeted the Parrot's Beak and Fish Hook salients.

One of the student anti-war protesters shot dead at Kent State University in May 1970.

CHAPTER 6:

EASTER OFFENSIVE TO CHRISTMAS BOMBING

President Nixon (foreground right) visits Beijing in February 1972. By normalizing America's relations with Communist China, Nixon threatened North Vietnam with potentially losing Chinese support.

Cheerful US Marines embark on the journey home from South Vietnam in March 1971. About 150,000 US soldiers were left in Vietnam by that year's end.

By the start of 1972, peace talks between the warring sides in Vietnam had been under way for three years. The official negotiations, held in Paris, involved representatives of the United States, the South Vietnamese government, the North Vietnamese government and the communist Provisional Revolutionary Government of South Vietnam (PRG). There were also secret meetings between US National Security Adviser Henry Kissinger and the head of the North Vietnamese delegation at the talks, Le Duc Tho. But neither public nor secret negotiations brought any progress towards ending the fighting.

There was, however, diplomatic progress on the wider world stage.

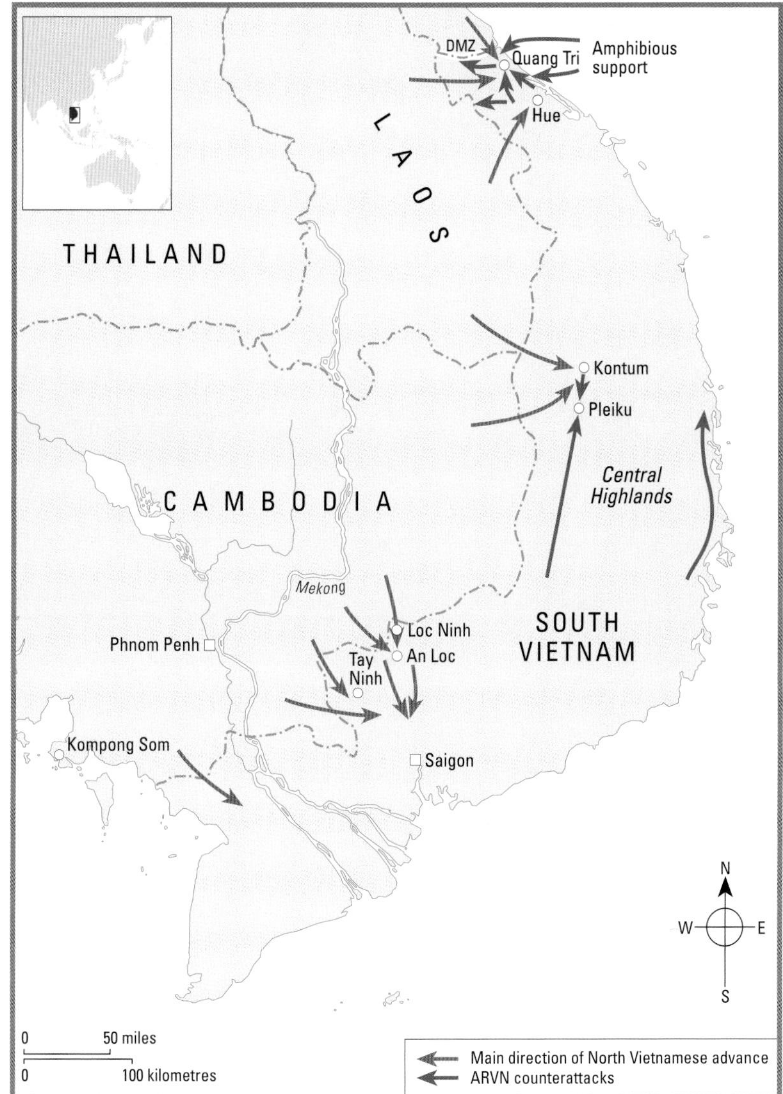

In the NVA's 1972 Easter offensive, the fighting raged around Quang Tri in the north, Kontum in the Central Highlands, and An Loc on the road to Saigon.

FLIGHT FROM QUANG TRI

A German journalist witnessed the disorganized retreat of South Vietnamese soldiers after the fall of Quang Tri City in May 1972: *'Around noon the first bunch of fleeing soldiers started arriving at the May Chanh bridge … Some were drunk and kept firing wildly into the air. The line of lorries and army vehicles roared on south as if the devil himself were at their heels.'*

[Quoted in *Death in the Ricefields*, Peter Scholl-Latour]

President Nixon had undertaken a bold initiative to improve relations between the United States and the two major communist powers, China and the Soviet Union. In February 1972 Nixon became the first US president to visit communist China. North Vietnam was dependent on the major communist powers for arms supplies and diplomatic support. If they grew more friendly with the United States, North Vietnam risked being isolated. This probably influenced the North Vietnamese decision to take a military gamble.

General Vo Nguyen Giap, the North Vietnamese minister of defence, had long been known as a master of guerrilla warfare. But by 1972 he believed the time was ripe to try a new military strategy. With less than 100,000 US military personnel left in South Vietnam and further withdrawals planned, there was no possibility that US ground forces would be committed again to major fighting. This left the defence of South Vietnam – on the ground at least – in the hands of the ARVN, an army that the North Vietnamese believed they could beat. Giap planned a full-scale invasion of the South by the NVA, using tanks and heavy artillery in support of large troop formations.

The NVA offensive began on Good Friday, 30 March 1972 – for this reason it is often known as the Easter, or Eastertide, offensive. Giap distributed his 130,000 troops on three lines of attack. The offensive opened with a push into Quang Tri Province, immediately south of the DMZ; in early April the NVA struck towards An Loc north of Saigon; and later that

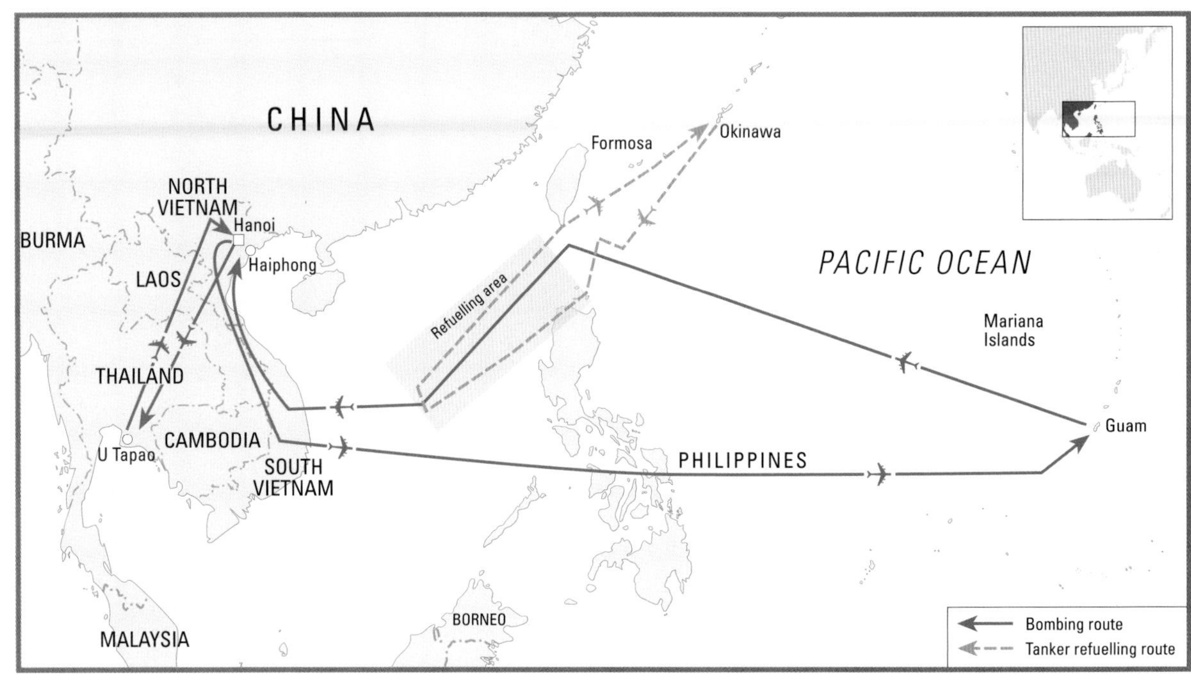

Between 18 and 29 December 1972, American B-52 bombers carried out intensive raids chiefly against targets in the North Vietnamese cities of Hanoi and Haiphong, dropping about 20,000 tonnes of bombs in total. The B-52s based on Guam required in-flight refuelling to achieve the round trip. Other bombers flew from the U Tapao base in Thailand.

month another front was opened in the Central Highlands with a thrust towards Kontum.

The Americans and South Vietnamese had expected a major North Vietnamese attack since the previous year. They had observed the build-up of troops and supplies. But they had been unable to predict the exact timing of the offensive and were largely caught off guard. In places the NVA's use of tanks and long-range artillery caused the South Vietnamese defenders to retreat in near-panic. On each of the three fronts the NVA made gains. By 13 April the North Vietnamese had put An Loc under siege and were advancing towards Saigon, eventually coming within 65 km of the capital. On the northern front, Quang Tri City (see page 39) fell to the NVA on 1 May.

South Vietnamese soldiers inspect the bodies of two of their enemies killed north of Quang Tri in April 1972. Communist losses in the Easter offensive were heavy.

> **HEAVY BOMBING**
>
> On ordering the Linebacker bombing campaign against North Vietnam, President Nixon forthrightly told his advisers:
> *'The bastards have never been bombed like they're going to be bombed this time.'*
>
> [Quoted by Michael Orr in *War in Peace* magazine, 1984]

By then Kontum was also under threat, raising the prospect of the North Vietnamese advancing down to the coast and cutting South Vietnam in two. The sight of South Vietnamese soldiers and civilian refugees fleeing south from Quang Tri City seemed about to herald the collapse of South Vietnam.

LINEBACKER RAIDS

The United States responded to the offensive by resuming its bombing campaign against the North. The new air campaign was codenamed Linebacker. Having switched from guerrilla to conventional warfare, the NVA now required far more supplies – for example, of fuel and ammunition – to keep the war in the South going. The Linebacker raids struck at the entire North Vietnamese supply chain, including not only roads, bridges and railways, but also fuel depots, ammunition dumps and warehouses in North Vietnam's cities. Most controversially, the entrances to North Vietnamese ports were mined in May to prevent supplies arriving by sea from the Soviet Union. Linebacker was more effective than Rolling Thunder had been, partly because the US air forces now benefited from the introduction of the first laser-guided bombs ('Smart' weapons) and partly because the air operations were less inhibited by politically imposed restrictions on targeting.

People search for survivors in the rubble of a Hanoi hospital, destroyed by a bomb from a B-52 during the Linebacker 2 raids, December 1972. The bomb had been aimed at a nearby barracks.

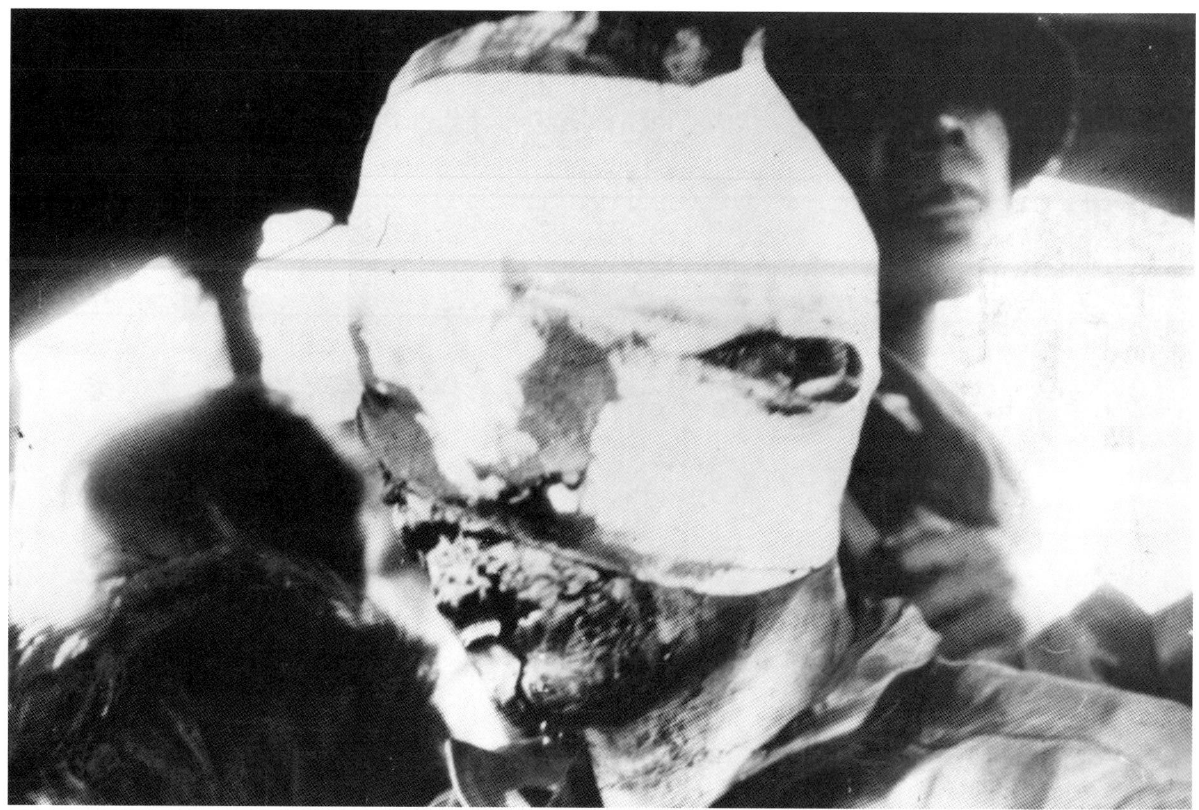

A wounded ARVN soldier: many South Vietnamese who had fought hard felt betrayed by the 1973 peace agreement that allowed the Americans to pull out of the war.

The impact of the Linebacker raids was one factor that contributed to a turn of the tide in the war during May 1972. The performance of the ARVN improved after President Thieu replaced some incompetent generals with better commanders and sent better motivated units to hold key positions. US and South Vietnamese airpower played a decisive role in support of the ground forces, with a variety of strike aircraft, gunships, attack helicopters and bombers hammering the North Vietnamese troops. At An Loc in the second week of May, for example, flights of B-52 bombers struck NVA positions every 55 minutes for almost 30 hours. Along the coast around Quang Tri, firepower from the air was supplemented by the guns of US warships stationed offshore.

The NVA's progress slowed and then halted. An NVA assault on Kontum was driven back at the end of May and by mid-June the siege of An Loc had been lifted. An ARVN counter-offensive retook Quang Tri City in mid-September. Typically, the soldiers on the communist side fought with remarkable determination under the awesome barrage of bombs, shells and napalm to which they were subjected. But their losses of men and equipment were severe. According to some estimates, around 100,000 NVA troops were killed between March and October 1972 – more than double the losses on the South Vietnamese side. Yet the offensive still left the NVA in possession of significant areas of South Vietnamese territory.

US BOMBING OF NORTH VIETNAM 1972

Linebacker 1 (April-October 1972)

Bombs dropped	156,000 tonnes
US aircraft lost	44

Linebacker 2 (December 1972)

Bombs dropped	20,000 tonnes
US aircraft lost	26 (including 15 B-52s)

The 1973 peace deal allowed the NVA to stay in occupation of areas of South Vietnam that they had seized in the Easter offensive.

PEACE TREATY On 22 October 1972 the Linebacker raids were halted and shortly afterwards it was announced that the US and North Vietnam had reached an agreement in principle on a peace deal. The United States would pull out of Vietnam, but North Vietnamese forces would be allowed to stay where they were inside South Vietnam. In return, the North Vietnamese accepted that President Thieu would, for the time being, remain in power in Saigon.

Progress to a signed peace agreement proved far from easy, however. In mid-December, with talks once more stalled, Nixon ordered renewed bombing of North Vietnam on an unprecedented scale. Between 18 and 30 December, a series of raids by B-52s – more than 100 bombers at a time – destroyed almost every target of any military value in Hanoi and Haiphong. Codenamed Linebacker 2, the bombings killed around 1,600 civilians.

In January 1973, peace talks resumed. Agreement was soon reached on terms almost identical to those on the table before the Christmas bombing. A peace deal was formally signed on 27 January. For the United States, the war in Vietnam was over.

Henry Kissinger (facing camera) signs the Paris peace agreement on behalf of the United States, 27 January 1973.

CHAPTER 7: COMMUNISM TRIUMPHANT

South Vietnamese President Nguyen Van Thieu – photographed here with his wife – knew that his country's independence depended on continuing American support, both financial and military.

US National Security Adviser Henry Kissinger and North Vietnamese negotiator Le Duc Tho were jointly awarded the Nobel Peace Prize for their part in achieving the 1973 peace agreement. Le Duc Tho, however, declined to accept the award, on the grounds that there was no peace. The agreement, in reality, merely opened a new phase of the war. ARVN and NVA forces were fighting small-scale local battles in the week that the agreement was signed.

President Thieu had been very reluctant to sign the peace accord. He felt that an agreement that left 150,000 North Vietnamese troops within his country's borders amounted to a sell-out. Thieu obtained a written assurance from President Nixon that the United States would intervene militarily in support of South Vietnam if the North Vietnamese broke the peace agreement by resuming major offensive action. So, although the last US troops pulled out of Vietnam in March 1973, South Vietnam remained dependent for its survival on American financial aid and on the promise of US military intervention.

TESTING RESOLVE

Gerald Ford, who succeeded Richard Nixon as US President in August 1974, was regarded by the North Vietnamese as a weak leader. A North Vietnamese journalist wrote:

'We tested Ford's resolve by attacking Phuoc Long in January 1975. When Ford kept American B-52s in their hangars, our leadership decided on a big offensive against South Vietnam.'

[Quoted in *Historical Atlas of the Vietnam War*, Harry Summers Jr. and Stanley Karnow]

American prisoners of war are freed by their North Vietnamese captors at Gia Lam airport, Hanoi, in 1973, in accordance with the terms of the Paris peace accords.

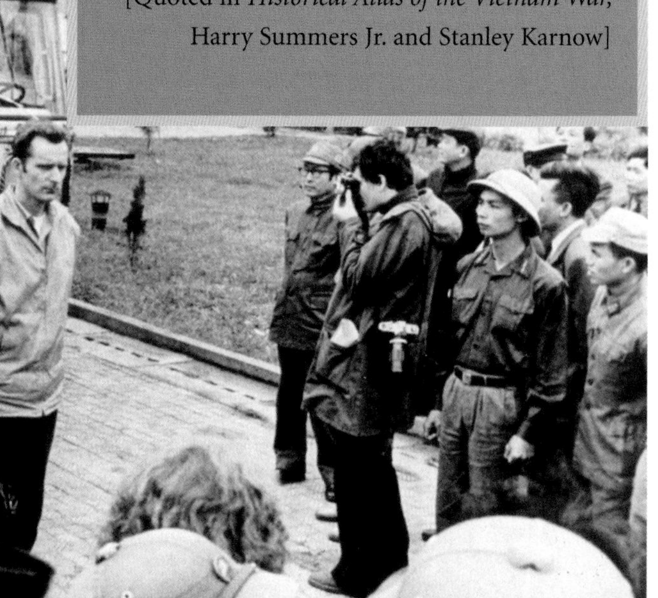

The NVA's victorious offensive in March-April 1975 began with a breakthrough in the Central Highlands, followed by the seizure of the north and a final drive on Saigon.

Nixon was embroiled in the Watergate affair, a political scandal involving illegal entry into the Democratic headquarters during the 1972 presidential election campaign which eventually led to the president's enforced resignation in August 1974.

Meanwhile the balance of power in Vietnam gradually shifted. For most of 1973, the ARVN had the upper hand. US arms rushed in during the period before the peace agreement meant that the South Vietnamese were substantially better equipped than their enemy. The North Vietnamese, for their part, took time to recover both from their losses in the fighting of 1972 and from the damage caused by the US Linebacker bombing campaigns.

But from the end of 1973, the balance began to move decisively in favour of North Vietnam. While the Soviet Union increased its aid to North Vietnam, the US Congress cut back aid to the South. The United States had built up the ARVN into an American-style army, reliant on sophisticated armaments and 'gas-guzzling' vehicles. As money ran short, the South Vietnamese could not afford the spare parts, ammunition and fuel to keep their war machine running.

During 1974 the fighting, although still localized, grew in scale. The ARVN lost some 31,000 troops killed in action in the course of the year. Meanwhile, the North Vietnamese transformed the jungle tracks of

It soon became clear that the United States could not be relied upon to fulfil its promises to its South Vietnamese ally. The US Congress, reflecting the mood of the American people, was hostile to any continued military involvement in South-east Asia. In August 1973 a Congressional vote halted the bombing of Cambodia, which had continued after the pull-out from Vietnam. The following November, a War Powers Resolution banned the president from sending US forces into action without the prior approval of Congress. By then,

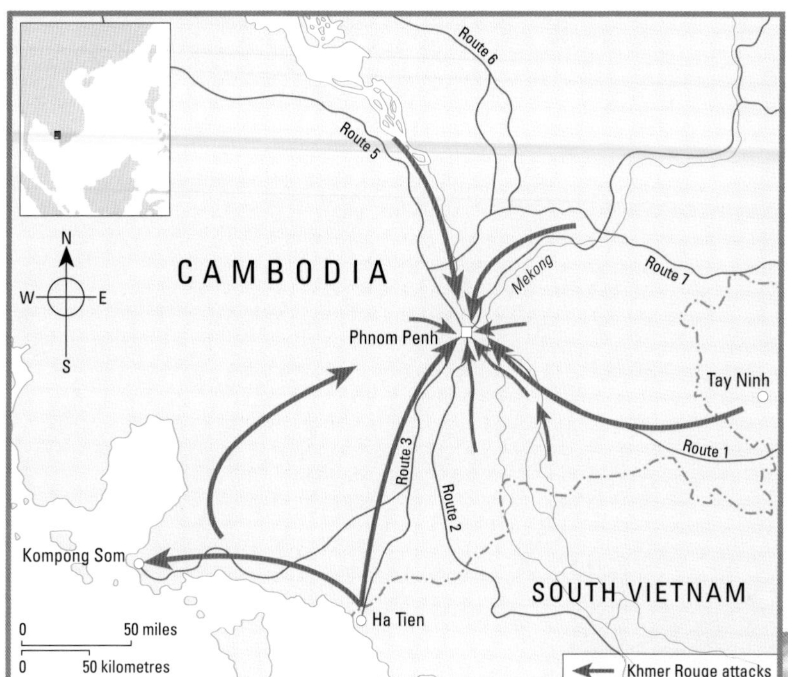

In Cambodia, Khmer Rouge guerrillas advanced from all sides to besiege the capital, Phnom Penh, which fell to the communists on 17 April 1975.

South Vietnamese civilians, desperate to escape the fighting near Xuan Loc in April 1975, struggle to board an ARVN Chinook helicopter as it takes off.

the Ho Chi Minh Trail into a paved road, down which men and supplies poured into their zones of South Vietnam. They even built an oil pipeline into the South to keep their vehicles supplied with fuel.

PUSH FOR VICTORY In December 1974 the North Vietnamese government took the decision to go for military victory. The only thing that might have deterred them would have been renewed American intervention – the Easter offensive had taught them that they could not take over South Vietnam in the face of US airpower. But in January 1975, when the NVA seized a South Vietnamese provincial capital, Phuoc Binh, the United States did nothing. The North Vietnamese leadership concluded that they could safely go ahead with the conquest of South Vietnam.

Commanded by General Van Tien Dung, who had taken over from General Giap, the NVA began the final offensive at the start of March 1975. The main thrust of the attack was through the Central Highlands towards the coast. Poorly led and demoralized, the ARVN forces rapidly disintegrated. By the first week of April, the northern half of South Vietnam was under NVA

NVA soldiers on the balcony of the presidential palace in Saigon look down on North Vietnamese tanks parked in the palace grounds after the communist victory, 30 April 1975.

control. Major cities such as Quang Tri and Hue were abandoned by the ARVN with hardly a fight. Pushing south towards Saigon, the NVA met stiffer resistance. It took them two weeks to overcome ARVN troops at Xuan Loc, north of the capital. But the ultimate outcome of the war was no longer in doubt.

On 21 April President Thieu resigned, denouncing the United States as a country that had 'not honoured its promises'. An evacuation of Americans and selected South Vietnamese from Saigon turned into a race against time as the NVA closed on the city. The last people to leave were lifted by helicopter from the roof of the US Embassy early on the morning of 30 April. A few hours later, an NVA tank crashed through the gates of the South Vietnamese presidential palace.

In parallel with the collapse of South Vietnam, Cambodia had fallen to communist forces. The Khmer Rouge guerrillas had been within artillery range of the Cambodian capital, Phnom Penh, since early 1974. From the start of 1975, the besieged city was dependent on a US airlift for essential supplies. The defensive perimeter eventually crumbled after months of sustained pressure, and on 17 April the Khmer Rouge marched into Phnom Penh as victors. By the end of 1975, when the communist Pathet Lao took power in Laos, the whole of former French Indo-China was under communist government.

'A WAR THAT IS FINISHED ...'

In April 1975, as the NVA closed in on Saigon, President Ford spoke of America's decision not to intervene. He said:

'Today, Americans can regain a sense of pride that existed before Vietnam. But it cannot be achieved by refighting a war that is finished as far as America is concerned.'

[Quoted in *Historical Atlas of the Vietnam War,* Harry Summers Jr. and Stanley Karnow]

CHAPTER 8:
AFTERMATH

Spraying large areas of Vietnam with defoliants left a desolate landscape. It may also have caused long-term damage to local people's health.

These are the skulls of Cambodian people killed by the Khmer Rouge. They were found by the Vietnamese after they invaded Cambodia in 1979.

Many well-meaning anti-war campaigners in the United States and elsewhere had hoped that the communists in Indo-China would behave reasonably after victory. These hopes had been encouraged during the war by the North Vietnamese leadership, who had talked of installing a coalition government in South Vietnam, in which communists would share power with other Vietnamese nationalists. But in fact the two halves of the country were swiftly united as the Socialist Republic of Vietnam under the same communist regime that had ruled North Vietnam. In a significant symbolic gesture, Saigon was renamed Ho Chi Minh City.

More than 200,000 former South Vietnamese officials and army officers were arrested after the communist victory and sent to 're-education camps'. Their treatment was mild, however, compared with that meted out to its former enemies by the Khmer Rouge in Cambodia – now renamed Kampuchea. There, many thousands of supporters of the previous regime were killed. Almost the entire population of Phnom Penh was forcibly relocated to the countryside, where huge numbers died of disease, malnutrition,

ECOLOGICAL DAMAGE

The long-term damage caused to Vietnam by the spraying of defoliants has been a highly controversial issue. According to official US figures:

Total area of Vietnam defoliated 1962-70	5,229,000 acres
Percentage of South Vietnamese forests sprayed 1965-71	46.4 per cent
Percentage of South Vietnamese cultivated land sprayed 1965-71	3.2 per cent

brutal ill-treatment or execution in the 'Killing Fields'.

In former South Vietnam people were also relocated from the cities to the countryside, although with less brutality than witnessed in Kampuchea. Inevitably, life in rural areas was harsh. Anti-personnel mines were scattered around the land and millions of acres had been sprayed with the chemical defoliant Agent Orange, which allegedly caused major long-term health problems (not only for the Vietnamese but also for American Vietnam veterans). In the southern cities, the departure of the Americans brought poverty to thousands who had depended on them for their income. But communist economic policies made matters worse by cracking down on private businesses. In the spring of 1978 thousands of Vietnamese began to flee the country by sea. Many of these 'boat people' were ethnic Chinese, a group who found themselves especially at odds with the communist regime.

If the aftermath of the war was a shock to many Western anti-war campaigners, it also proved a surprise to those, in the United States and elsewhere, who had supported the war as a way of stopping the expansion of the

In winter 1978-9, Vietnam invaded and occupied Kampuchea (Cambodia). China responded by invading Vietnam in February 1979, although the Chinese troops withdrew in March of that year.

Chinese troops direct artillery fire during China's border war with Vietnam in 1979.

'communist bloc'. Instead of communist China and Indo-China forming a united front, perhaps dedicated to expanding communism further across Asia, the communist countries turned to fighting one another.

The Vietnamese had a long history of resistance to Chinese domination. There was also a tradition of hostility between the Khmers – the dominant ethnic group in Kampuchea – and the Vietnamese. Generally submerged during the war against the US and its allies, these tensions resurfaced after the Americans had gone. From 1977, the Khmer Rouge began staging raids into Vietnam in places where the border was disputed. Low-level conflict rumbled on until Christmas 1978, when the Vietnamese mounted a full-scale invasion of Kampuchea. They captured Phnom Penh on 7 January 1979, installing a new government in power. Driven out of the cities, the Khmer Rouge returned to guerrilla warfare, harassing the Vietnamese from bases along the border with Thailand. Vietnamese forces stayed in the country until 1989, when they withdrew to clear the way for a negotiated agreement on the country's future.

WAR WITH CHINA The main backer of the Khmer Rouge regime in Kampuchea had been China. On 17 February 1979, Chinese troops invaded Vietnam. China's intention was not to conquer Vietnam, but to inflict a military defeat to teach the Vietnamese a lesson. In the event, the Chinese army found it hard to make any progress against stiff resistance and withdrew from Vietnam on 6 March.

These events left Vietnam solely reliant on the Soviet Union as a source of foreign aid. The collapse of communism in Eastern Europe in 1989, followed by the break-up of the Soviet Union in 1991, was a huge shock to Vietnam's leaders. Yet the 1990s brought improvement at last in the lives of many of the Vietnamese people. New economic policies, encouraging free enterprise, revitalized Vietnam's cities. In 1995, relations with the United States were at last restored. Vietnam entered the new millennium still under the rule of the communist party, and still extremely poor, especially in rural areas, but with increasing hope for the future.

By then the United States had long emerged from the shadow cast by the Vietnam War. In the 1970s, it seemed that American self-confidence might have been permanently dented by the experience of a conflict from which, for the first time in its history, the United States had not emerged victorious. But with the passage of time, the hostility of the American people to the engagement of US troops in wars abroad weakened. US forces fought in the Gulf War in 1991, and later in Afghanistan and Iraq – although it seemed unlikely that the American people would ever again accept anything like the level of casualties seen in Vietnam.

By the 30th anniversary of the end of America's war in Vietnam, the conflict had become history for a younger generation. To older people, it was part of the living past, still vividly recalled. A major source of income for Vietnam at the start of the twenty-first century was the spending of US tourists, many of them former soldiers revisiting the battlefields where they had fought in their youth.

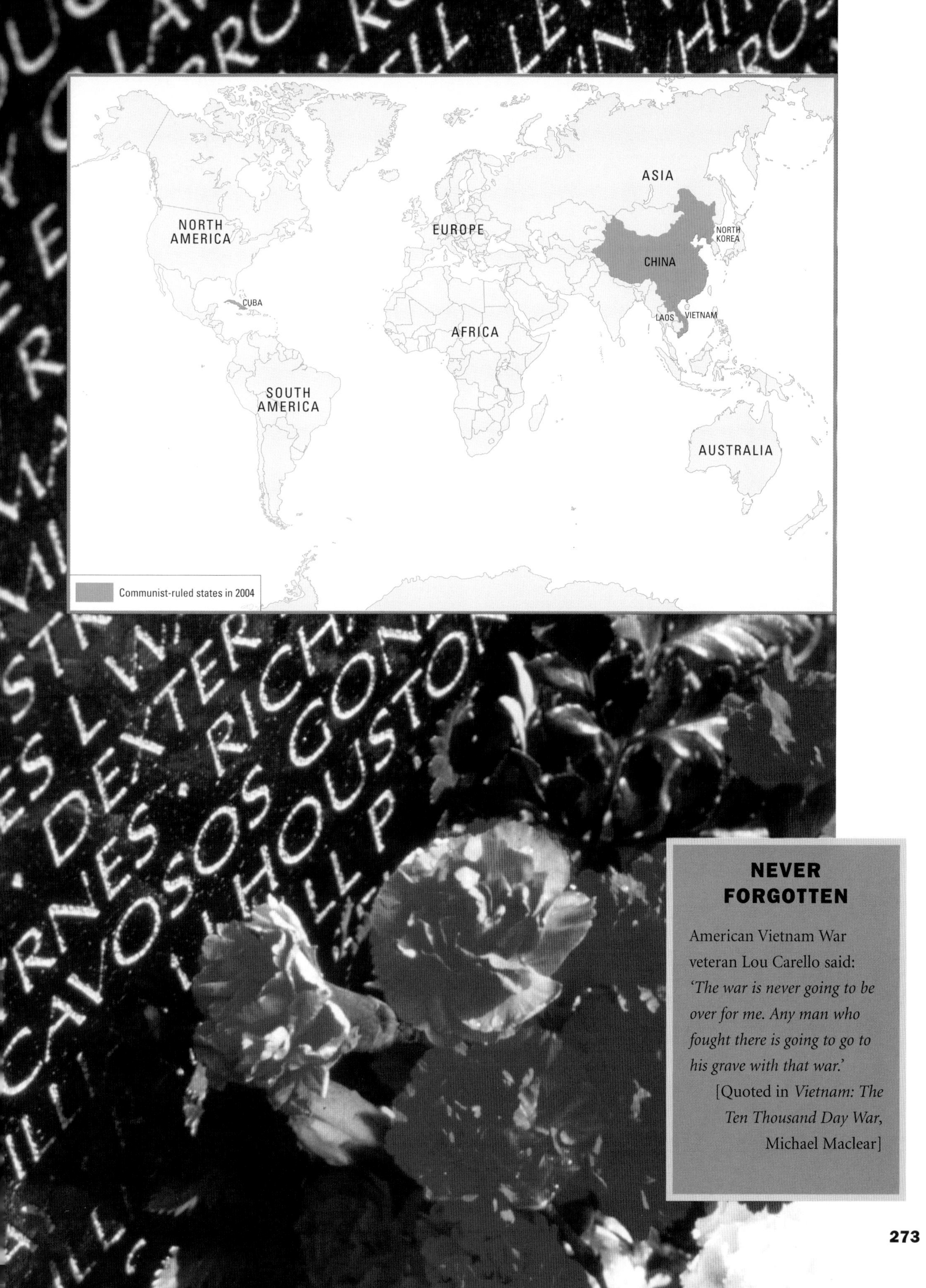

NEVER FORGOTTEN

American Vietnam War veteran Lou Carello said: *'The war is never going to be over for me. Any man who fought there is going to go to his grave with that war.'*

[Quoted in *Vietnam: The Ten Thousand Day War*, Michael Maclear]

PROFILES OF MILITARY AND POLITICAL LEADERS

GENERAL CREIGHTON W. ABRAMS (1914-1974)
Born in Massachusetts in 1914, Abrams had been a US Army officer for thirty years by the time he was appointed deputy commander of MACV in 1967. He took over from General Westmoreland as head of MACV in the summer of 1968 and was in charge during the period of Vietnamization of the war and the withdrawal of US troops. Abrams was appointed US Army chief of staff in 1972, a post he held until his death in 1974.

LIEUTENANT WILLIAM L. CALLEY (1944-)
Aged 23, William Calley dropped out of college in 1966 and enlisted in the US Army. He was sent to Vietnam in November 1967. Calley was a platoon commander at My Lai hamlet in March 1968, when several hundred Vietnamese civilians were massacred. In 1971 Calley was found guilty of the murder of twenty-two civilians, although other officers involved in the incident were cleared. Initially given a life sentence, Calley was only briefly imprisoned. Paroled by President Nixon, he was freed and went on to run his father's jewellery store.

WILLIAM COLBY (1920-1996)
Born in Minnesota in 1920, William Colby devoted most of his life to espionage and undercover activity. He was head of the CIA office in Saigon from 1959 to 1962 and returned to Vietnam in 1968 to head the CORDS pacification programme and the controversial Operation Phoenix. He was subsequently head of the CIA from 1973 to 1975. Colby died, under somewhat mysterious circumstances, in 1996.

EMPEROR BAO DAI (1913-1997)
Born in Hue in 1913, Bao Dai succeeded his father as Emperor of Vietnam – a powerless ceremonial position – in 1925. He abdicated the throne in 1945, but was installed as Vietnamese head of state by the French in 1949. After the peace agreement of 1954, Bao Dai was briefly leader of South Vietnam, but the following year he was replaced by his prime minister, Ngo Dinh Diem. Bao Dai died in exile in France in 1997.

PRESIDENT NGO DINH DIEM (1901-1963)
Born in 1901, Diem belonged to Vietnam's Catholic minority. In 1954 he emerged as the United States' preferred choice of leader for South Vietnam and in October 1955 displaced the former emperor, Bao Dai. Diem's rule was marred by corruption and by favouritism towards Catholics, which brought him into conflict with Vietnam's Buddhist majority. In November 1963 he was overthrown in a military coup approved by the United States. Diem was killed in the course of the coup, along with his brother, Ngo Dinh Nhu.

GENERAL VAN TIEN DUNG (1917-2002)
Born in 1917, Dung joined the Indo-Chinese Communist party in 1937. He played a senior role in the wars against the French and against South Vietnam and the US. In 1974 he was appointed commander-in-chief for the 'Ho Chi Minh' campaign which, the following year, brought about the fall of Saigon. In 1980 he was appointed Vietnam's Minister of Defence. He died in 2002.

PRESIDENT GERALD FORD (1913-)
Born in Nebraska in 1913, Ford was leader of the Republican minority in Congress before becoming US vice-president in 1973 and president in August 1974, on President Richard Nixon's resignation. Hamstrung by the Democrat majority in Congress, in 1975 he was unable to provide extra aid to the South Vietnamese government, let alone authorize a resumption of US military intervention. Ford was defeated in the 1976 presidential election by Jimmy Carter.

GENERAL VO NGUYEN GIAP (1912-)
Giap was born in Quang Binh province in 1912. After joining the Vietnamese Communist Party, he was arrested by the French colonial authorities in 1930 but soon released. In 1939 Giap was ordered by the Party to flee to China to avoid arrest. He joined Ho Chi Minh there. However, his sister-in-law was executed by the French and his wife and child both died in a French prison. From 1942 to 1945 Giap took part in guerrilla warfare against the Japanese in Vietnam, and from 1946 to 1954 he masterminded the Viet Minh campaign against the French, including the victory at Dien Bien Phu. As defence minister in North Vietnam, he directed the guerrilla war against the South Vietnamese government and US forces up to 1972. His decision to resort to conventional warfare in the 1972 Easter offensive, however, led to heavy losses. Although officially still in his post, he was sidelined during the final takeover of the South in 1975.

HO CHI MINH (1892-1969)
Born Nguyen That Thanh in 1892 (although on occasion he also claimed a birth date of 1890), Ho left Vietnam for Europe in 1911 and there, in 1920, became a founding member of the French Communist Party. In 1925 Ho moved to China, where he became the leader of Vietnamese exiles dedicated to freeing their country from French rule. He went back to Vietnam in 1941, founding the Viet Minh guerrilla movement. In 1945 he declared Vietnam independent with himself as president. He led the Viet Minh in the subsequent guerrilla war against France and became president of North Vietnam when the French departed in 1954. He remained the country's leader until his death in 1969.

PRESIDENT LYNDON B. JOHNSON (1908-1973)
Born in Texas in 1908, 'LBJ' was a leading figure in the Democrat Party and became US vice-president under John F. Kennedy in 1961. He assumed the presidency when Kennedy was assassinated in November 1963 and was confirmed in office in presidential elections the following year. Johnson wanted to be a social reformer, transforming the United States into a fairer 'Great Society'. But the Vietnam War diverted money and energy from the reform programme and brought Johnson under increasingly harsh criticism. In March 1968 he announced that he would not stand for re-election. He died in 1973.

PRESIDENT JOHN F. KENNEDY (1917-1963)
Born into a wealthy Catholic family in 1917, Kennedy was decorated for bravery in World War II and subsequently entered politics as a Democrat. In 1960 he narrowly defeated Richard Nixon in presidential elections, becoming his country's youngest ever president. He was responsible for building up the number of US military advisers in South Vietnam from 1961 and approved the overthrow of Diem in November 1963. Kennedy was assassinated three weeks after Diem's downfall. It has been claimed that Kennedy was on the brink of pulling the US out of military involvement in Vietnam when he died, but there is no solid evidence for this.

HENRY KISSINGER (1923-)
Born in Germany in 1923, Henry Kissinger settled in the United States in 1938. He was a leading academic when, in 1969, he was selected by President Nixon to be his adviser on national security. He dominated US foreign policy under Nixon, becoming US Secretary of State in 1973, a post he continued to hold under President Ford until 1977. Kissinger was awarded the Nobel peace prize, jointly with Le Duc Tho, for his part in negotiating the January 1973 Vietnam peace accord.

ROBERT S. MCNAMARA (1916-)
Born in 1916 in San Francisco, McNamara was president of the Ford Motor Company when, in 1961, he was invited to become secretary of defence in the Kennedy administration. In this post, which he also held under

President Lyndon Johnson, McNamara was one of the main architects of the Vietnam War. By 1967, however, he had come to think that the war was a disastrous mistake. He resigned in March 1968 and went on to become president of the World Bank, a position he held until 1981.

GENERAL DUONG VAN MINH (1916-2001)
Known as 'Big Minh', South Vietnamese General Doung Van Minh was one of the leaders of the coup that overthrew President Diem in 1963. After the coup, Minh was South Vietnamese head of government for three months before in his turn being thrown out of power in a coup. In subsequent years Minh was a leading opponent of President Thieu, and an advocate of compromise with the communists. Just before the NVA took Saigon in April 1975, Minh became South Vietnamese president, and it was he who formally surrendered the country to the North Vietnamese.

PRESIDENT RICHARD M. NIXON (1913-1994)
Born in California in 1913, Nixon became US vice-president in 1952, but lost the 1960 presidential election to the Democrat John F. Kennedy. In a remarkable comeback, Nixon was again chosen as Republican presidential candidate in 1968 and won. Nixon was a tough anti-communist and made forceful use of air power in South-east Asia, but he fulfilled a promise to get US troops out of Vietnam. His diplomatic initiatives also created a new relationship between the USA and communist China and the Soviet Union. After his re-election in 1972, however, he became involved in the Watergate scandal and was forced to resign the presidency to avoid impeachment [being put on trial] in 1974.

GENERAL LON NOL (1913-1985)
Born in 1913, Cambodian General Lon Nol was a leading figure in his country's government from independence in 1955. Under Prince Sihanouk he served as defence minister, army chief of staff and, later, prime minister. In 1970 Lon Nol overthrew Sihanouk in a coup and seized power, but his efforts to crack down on the Khmer Rouge guerrillas were disastrous. He fled Cambodia in 1975, just before the Khmer Rouge victory. Lon Nol died in 1985.

DEAN RUSK (1909-1994)
Born in Georgia in 1909, he held government posts under President Harry Truman after World War II. Rusk was appointed Secretary of State by President Kennedy in 1961 and continued in the same post under President Johnson. He was a crucial decision-maker during the period when the United States was drawn in to full-scale military involvement in Vietnam. Rusk remained secretary of state until President Nixon took office in 1969. He subsequently became a law professor at the University of Georgia.

NORODOM SIHANOUK (1922-)
Born in 1922, Sihanouk was elected king of Cambodia in 1941. When Cambodia gained independence from France in 1955, he abdicated from the throne, but continued to run the country, first as prime minister and then as head of state. In 1970 he was overthrown in a coup and formed a government-in-exile in China. He became an unlikely ally of the communist Khmer Rouge, who made him official head of state again in 1975. After another period in exile from 1979, in 1991 Sihanouk returned to Cambodia once more as head of state – this time opposing the Khmer Rouge – and in 1993 became king again, when the monarchy was restored.

PRESIDENT NGUYEN VAN THIEU (1923-2001)
Born in 1923, Thieu joined the Viet Minh after World War II but soon

left because of his opposition to its communist leadership. He then fought for the French in the South Vietnamese Army which, after 1954, became the ARVN. He was one of the leaders of the 1963 coup that overthrew President Diem and took part in the military governments in South Vietnam over the following four years. In 1967 he was elected president as head of a civilian government. Re-elected unopposed in 1971, he only reluctantly agreed to the 1973 peace accords. In 1975 he fled South Vietnam shortly before the fall of Saigon. Thieu died in 2001.

LE DUC THO (1911-1990)
Born in 1911, Le Duc Tho was a founder member of the Indo-Chinese Communist Party in 1930. He played a leading role in the Viet Minh guerrilla campaign against the French and in organizing the guerrilla war in South Vietnam in the 1960s. He acted as a special adviser to the North Vietnamese delegation at the Paris Peace talks, but declined to accept the Nobel peace prize that he was awarded jointly with Henry Kissinger in 1973. He remained a member of Vietnam's ruling politburo until 1986, dying in 1990.

GENERAL WILLIAM C. WESTMORELAND (1914-)
William Westmoreland was born in South Carolina in 1914. By the age of 42 he was a major-general in the US Army. In 1964 he was appointed to command the US forces in Vietnam. Westmoreland followed an aggressive strategy, using large formations of troops to seek out and destroy the enemy. US political leaders, however, became increasingly sceptical of his claims to be winning the war, and the Tet offensive fatally undermined his credibility. In the summer of 1968 Westmoreland was brought back to the United States, where he held the post of army chief of staff until his retirement in 1972.

SIGNIFICANT DATES

1858
France begins conquest of Vietnam.

1930
The Indo-Chinese Communist Party is founded by Ho Chi Minh and others.

1941
The Viet Minh movement is founded to fight for Vietnamese independence.

SEPTEMBER 1945
Ho Chi Minh declares Vietnam independent, with himself as president.

NOVEMBER 1946
French forces drive the Viet Minh out of Hanoi and Haiphong.

1949
Communists under Mao Tse-tung take power in China.

1950-3
Armed by China, the Viet Minh fight against the French.

MARCH-MAY 1954
The French are defeated by the Viet Minh at Dien Bien Phu.

JULY 1954
Geneva peace accords end the First Indo-China War. Ho Chi Minh and his colleagues take power in North Vietnam.

OCTOBER 1955
In South Vietnam, Ngo Dinh Diem defeats former emperor Bao Dai in a referendum and declares himself president of the Republic of Vietnam.

1959
Guerrilla war begins in the South, backed by North Vietnam.

1960
Communists found the National Liberation Front (NLF) to coordinate the guerrilla struggle.

1961
President Kennedy sends first US Army helicopter pilots to South Vietnam.

1962
US Special Forces – the Green Berets – are deployed in South Vietnam.

MAY 1963
Serious clashes between Vietnamese Buddhists and the Diem regime.

2 NOVEMBER 1963
Diem is killed in the course of a military coup.

22 NOVEMBER 1963
President Kennedy is assassinated in Dallas, Texas; Lyndon B. Johnson becomes President of the United States.

MAY 1964
General Westmoreland is appointed commander of US forces in Vietnam.

AUGUST 1964
Reports of attacks by the North Vietnamese on US warships in the Gulf of Tonkin lead to a resolution in US Congress authorizing military action in Vietnam.

FEBRUARY 1965
US launches air strikes on North Vietnam in retaliation for guerrilla attacks on US bases in South Vietnam.

MARCH 1965
First US Marines land in South Vietnam, officially to defend US bases; Rolling Thunder bombing campaign against the North begins.

NOVEMBER 1965
Battle of Ia Drang Valley, first major encounter between the US Army and the NVA.

1966
US troop levels in Vietnam rise to 385,000; US death toll for the year tops 5,000.

JANUARY 1967
Operation Cedar Falls attacks the guerrilla-dominated Iron Triangle.

FEBRUARY-MAY 1967
Operation Junction City targets communist bases near the Cambodian border.

MAY 1967
Civil Operations and Rural Development Support (CORDS) is established, an organization dedicated to the 'pacification' of rural South Vietnam.

SEPTEMBER 1967
Nguyen Van Thieu wins presidential election in South Vietnam.

OCTOBER 1967
Thousands of US anti-war protesters gather around the Pentagon in Washington DC to condemn the war.

JANUARY-APRIL 1968
Siege of the US Marine base at Khe Sanh.

JANUARY-FEBRUARY 1968
Viet Cong and NVA attack South Vietnamese towns and cities in the Tet offensive.

MARCH 1968
Robert McNamara resigns as US Defense Secretary; President Johnson announces that he will not stand for re-election as president.

JULY 1968
General Abrams replaces General Westmoreland as commander of US forces in Vietnam; the Phoenix programme is instigated, targeting communist activists in South Vietnam.

AUGUST 1968
Anti-war protesters battle with US police in Chicago during the Democratic convention.

OCTOBER 1968
Bombing of North Vietnam is halted.

NOVEMBER 1968
Richard Nixon wins US presidential election.

JANUARY 1969
Peace talks begin in Paris.

MARCH 1969
Nixon authorizes the secret bombing of Cambodia.

APRIL 1969
US troop levels in Vietnam peak at 543,482.

MAY 1969
Battle of Hamburger Hill in the A Shau Valley.

JUNE 1969
Nixon announces the first US troop withdrawals and that priority is to be given to 'Vietnamization'.

SEPTEMBER 1969
The president of North Vietnam Ho Chi Minh dies.

MARCH 1970
In Cambodia, General Lon Nol takes power in a coup that deposes Norodom Sihanouk.

APRIL-JUNE 1970
US and ARVN forces carry out an 'incursion' into Cambodia.

4 MAY 1970
Four young anti-war demonstrators are shot dead by the US National Guard at Kent State University, Ohio.

JUNE 1970
US Congress repeals the Gulf of Tonkin Resolution.

JANUARY-APRIL 1971
ARVN forces carry out incursion into Laos.

MARCH 1971
Lt. William Calley is found guilty of killings of Vietnamese civilians at My Lai in March 1968.

AUGUST 1971
Australia and New Zealand announce withdrawal of troops from Vietnam.

FEBRUARY 1972
President Nixon visits China and holds talks with Chairman Mao.

30 MARCH 1972
North Vietnam opens its Easter Offensive against the South.

APRIL-OCTOBER 1972
US Linebacker 1 air bombing campaign against North Vietnam.

APRIL-JULY 1972
NVA siege of An Loc resisted by ARVN with support of US airpower.

1 MAY 1972
Quang Tri City falls to the NVA.

16 SEPTEMBER 1972
Quang Tri City recaptured by ARVN.

OCTOBER 1972
Breakthrough announced in Paris peace talks.

18-30 DECEMBER 1972
B-52 bombers batter North Vietnamese cities in Operation Linebacker 2.

27 JANUARY 1973
Peace agreement signed in Paris.

29 MARCH 1973
Last US troops leave Vietnam.

AUGUST 1973
US Congress forces a halt to the bombing of Cambodia.

AUGUST 1974
President Nixon resigns because of the Watergate scandal; Gerald Ford becomes president.

SEPTEMBER 1974
President Ford announces a partial amnesty for Vietnam War deserters and draft evaders.

JANUARY 1975
The NVA seizes a South Vietnamese provincial capital, Phuoc Binh. The North Vietnamese leadership approves a plan for the final defeat of South Vietnam.

MARCH 1975
The ARVN crumbles in the face of an NVA offensive; the northern half of South Vietnam is abandoned to the NVA.

17 APRIL 1975
The Cambodian capital Phnom Penh falls to the Khmer Rouge.

21 APRIL 1975
President Thieu resigns as NVA forces approach Saigon.

30 APRIL 1975
The NVA enters Saigon as the last US personnel flee; South Vietnam surrenders.

DECEMBER 1975
Laos becomes a communist People's Democratic Republic.

1976
The Socialist Republic of Vietnam is founded; Saigon becomes Ho Chi Minh City.

JANUARY 1977
President Jimmy Carter pardons most Vietnam War draft evaders.

DECEMBER 1978
Vietnam invades Kampuchea (Cambodia), ousting the Khmer Rouge regime the following month.

FEBRUARY-MARCH 1979
Border war between China and Vietnam.

1989
Vietnamese forces withdraw from Cambodia.

1995
Relations between Vietnam and the United States are normalized.

STATISTICS CONCERNING COMBATANT NATIONS

The figures given below for numbers of armed forces show (where figures are available) firstly the maximum number of personnel from a country that were operating in Vietnam at any one time, and then the total number of people from that country who served in Vietnam from the beginning to the end of the war. Below that are listed the known casualty figures for both troops and civilians (again where available).

AUSTRALIA

Personnel in South Vietnam (max.)	c.8,000
Total Australians who served in South Vietnam (1965-71)	59,520
Casualties	
Combat deaths	394
Total deaths	501
Wounded	2,069

REPUBLIC OF KOREA (SOUTH KOREA)

Troops in Vietnam (max.)	47,872
Combat deaths	4,407

NEW ZEALAND

Personnel in South Vietnam (max.)	517
Combat deaths	39

THAILAND

Troops in Vietnam (max.)	c.10,000
Combat deaths	351

UNITED STATES

Personnel (max., 30 April 1969)	543,482
Total US military personnel served in South Vietnam (1964-73)	2,594,000
US Casualties	
Combat deaths	47,539
Deaths from other causes	10,797
Total dead	58,336*
Wounded	303,704
Of which severely disabled	75,000

*61 per cent of the Americans killed in Vietnam were 21 years old or younger.

US AIR WAR

Total bombs dropped on South-east Asia	6.7 million tons

(for comparison: total bombs dropped on Germany in World War II 2.7 million tons)

DEMOCRATIC REPUBLIC OF VIETNAM (NORTH VIETNAM)

Armed forces numbers	(1972)
Army	480,000
Air Force	9,000
Navy	3,000
Total combat deaths (including Viet Cong)	440,000
North Vietnamese civilian deaths (est.)	65,000

REPUBLIC OF VIETNAM (SOUTH VIETNAM)

Armed forces numbers (1971)

Regular forces	
Army	410,000
Air Force	50,000
Navy	42,000
Marines	14,000
Total regular	516,000
Territorial forces	
Regional forces	284,000
Popular forces	248,000
Total territorial	532,000
Grand total	1,048,000
Casualties, South Vietnam	
Military deaths (to 1974)	220,357
Military wounded	499,000
Civilian deaths (estimate)	522,000

THE ARAB-ISRAELI CONFLICT

CHAPTER 1: THE FOUNDING OF ISRAEL

Jewish immigrants arriving in New York City, around 1920. During the early decades of the twentieth century, many thousands of Jews fled persecution in Europe to seek a new life in the USA.

The conflict between Palestinian Arabs and Jews began in the late nineteenth century, and intensified after the setting up of the Jewish state of Israel in 1948. The conflict is essentially about land and who controls it. The land in question is a small area on the eastern coast of the Mediterranean Sea, measuring about 26,000 square kilometres. The Jews have claimed that this land was promised to them by God, as stated in the Bible. It was also the historical site of the Jewish kingdoms of Israel and Judah during the first millennium BC. The Palestinian Arabs' claim to the land is based on the fact that they have lived there continuously for hundreds of years.

During the nineteenth century, there was a rise in anti-semitism (hatred of Jews) in many parts of eastern Europe and Russia, rooted in religious antagonisms and the perceived wealth and economic power of the Jews. From the 1880s, Jewish communities came under severe attack, and by 1914, some five million Jews had fled to new homes in the USA, Britain, Canada, Australia and South Africa.

Some Jews were worried that their people would never be safe from anti-semitism as long as they remained a minority in the countries where they lived. They believed that the Jews needed a homeland of their own. To that end, in the 1890s, a movement known as Zionism came into being. Zion was one of the hills of Jerusalem, the capital of the historical land of Israel. The Zionists wished to establish a new Jewish nation on the site of ancient Israel.

At that time, the land they wished to reclaim was known as Palestine and was governed by the Ottoman Empire, a Turkish empire that extended throughout the Middle East. In the 1880s, there were around 462,000 people living in Palestine, including 447,000 Arabs and 15,000 Jews. The Zionist movement led to a large rise in Jewish immigration to Palestine, and by 1914, there were around 60,000 Jews living there – about 10 per cent of the population. The Palestinian Arabs were unhappy about these new arrivals, and at times they clashed with the Jewish settlers.

In the late nineteenth century, Arabs throughout the Middle East began to develop an awareness of themselves as a separate nation, and there was a

The bodies of Jewish men killed in a campaign of anti-semitic persecution in the Ukraine in 1900.

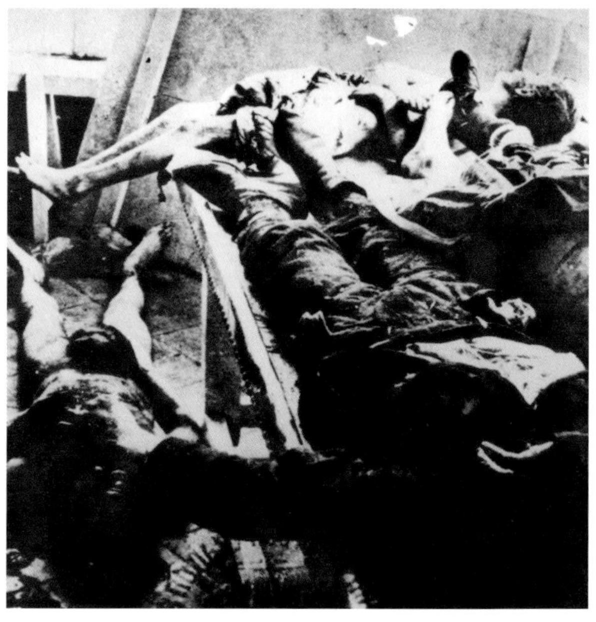

HOMELAND

'Palestine is our unforgettable historic homeland.... The Jews who will it shall achieve their State. We shall live at last as free men on our own soil, and in our own homes peacefully die. The world will be liberated by our freedom, enriched by our wealth, magnified by our greatness. And whatever we attempt there for our own benefit will redound mightily and beneficially to the good of all mankind.'

[From *Der Judenstaat*, Theodor Herzl]

Palestine under Ottoman rule was divided into sanjaks, or sub-provinces. (A wilayat is a province.) Between 1900 and 1918, Zionist colonies rose in number from 19 to 47. The Palestinians lobbied their Turkish leaders to end Jewish immigration and land purchases by Zionists.

Jewish immigrants from Russia work on a kibbutz in Palestine in 1912. Between 1880 and 1914, over 60,000 former Russian or eastern European Jews settled on land in Palestine or worked as hired labourers.

growing movement to overthrow their Turkish rulers. By this time the Ottoman Empire was in decline, and the great powers of Europe – Britain, France and Germany – were looking for ways to extend their influence in the area.

The British government secretly made contact with Arab nationalist leaders in 1915-16, persuading them to rise against the Ottoman Empire, which was then an ally of Germany. In return, Britain promised to support the establishment of an independent Arab state in the Arab territories of the Ottoman Empire, including Palestine.

In 1917, the British government also announced its support for the establishment of a Jewish homeland in Palestine. The Balfour Declaration as it was known (after the British Foreign Minister, Arthur Balfour) contradicted Britain's earlier promise to the Arabs.

After the fall of the Ottoman Empire in 1921, the status of its former territories was discussed at a meeting of the League of Nations (an organization of countries established in 1919 to promote international peace and security). It was agreed that Palestine would be placed under British control. This was known as the British Mandate. Arabs were angry that Britain did not fulfil its promise to create an independent Arab state. They were also worried by the increasing numbers of Jews arriving from Europe. Clashes between the Arabs and Zionist Jews grew increasingly violent during the 1920s and 1930s. Jewish immigration to Palestine continued to rise, particularly after the anti-semitic Nazi Party came to power in Germany in 1933.

THE BALFOUR DECLARATION

'His Majesty's Government view with favour the establishment in Palestine of a national home for the Jewish people, and will use their best endeavours to facilitate the achievement of this object, it being clearly understood that nothing shall be done which may prejudice the civil and religious rights of existing non-Jewish communities in Palestine, or the rights and political status enjoyed by Jews in any other country.'

[From the *Balfour Declaration*, 2 November 1917]

T.E. Lawrence, better known as Lawrence of Arabia, a British army officer and champion of Arab nationalism who helped to organize an Arab revolt against the Turks during World War I.

THE UNITED NATIONS PARTITION

After the Holocaust – the systematic extermination of nearly six million European Jews by the Nazis during World War II – Jewish demands for an independent homeland in Palestine grew much harder to ignore. The British authorities, faced with growing Arab-Jewish violence, and terrorist attacks against government buildings by Zionist militias, wished to end their mandate. In 1947, they requested help from

British soldiers keep watch at Nablus, Palestine, in 1936. Between 1936 and 1939, British and Jewish targets came under attack during an Arab revolt.

The United Nations partition plan of 1947. The Arab leadership claimed that it violated the rights of the non-Jewish majority in Palestine.

United Nations (UN), an organization of countries formed in 1945 to replace the League of Nations

It was clear to all that the only way to resolve the Arab-Jewish conflict would be to divide Palestine in two. A UN-appointed committee proposed partitioning Palestine into two states, one Jewish, the other Arab. The division would ensure that each state would contain a majority of its own population. The Jewish state would control 55 per cent of Palestine. Under the plan, the disputed area containing Jerusalem and Bethlehem would become an international zone.

THE 1947-9 WAR Zionist leaders agreed to the plan, although they were unhappy not to be offered Jerusalem, a sacred city to the Jews. The Arabs rejected the plan. They believed the UN had acted under Zionist pressure to grant statehood to the Jewish settlers. On 29 November 1947, the UN General Assembly voted to accept the plan. Within days, military conflict erupted between Palestinian Arabs and Jews. The first phase of the fighting, which lasted until 1 April 1948, took the form of a low-level guerrilla conflict between small Arab and Jewish forces. There were no major battles, but numerous gunfights. Little territory was gained by either side. The British administration's authority had declined to such an extent that they were powerless to keep order, and simply let the two sides fight between themselves.

On 1 April 1948, Zionist forces took the initiative, and within weeks they had captured most of the territory allotted to them under the plan. On 15 May 1948, the British departed from Palestine, and Zionist leaders declared the founding of the state of Israel. Neighbouring Arab states – Egypt, Syria, Transjordan, Lebanon, and Saudi Arabia and Iraq which lay to the east of Transjordan – immediately invaded the new state. They did this, they said, to save Palestine from the Zionists. However, they also had ambitions to control parts of Palestine themselves.

The Israeli forces were fewer in number than their Arab opponents, but they were better trained and

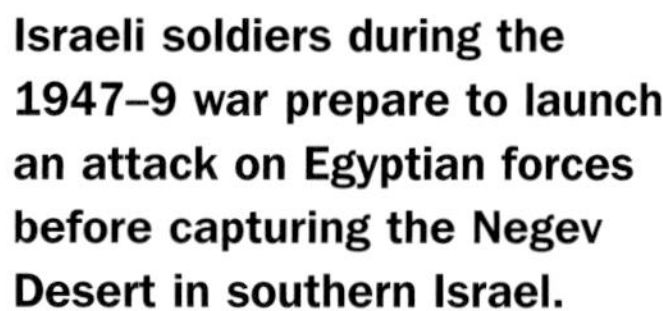

Israeli soldiers during the 1947–9 war prepare to launch an attack on Egyptian forces before capturing the Negev Desert in southern Israel.

The Arab invasion of May 1948, following Israel's declaration of nationhood. Jordanian forces launched an assault on Jerusalem, as Iraqi troops took up positions in various West Bank towns. Meanwhile, an Egyptian attack in the south wiped out a number of Israeli kibbutzim, and Syrian and Lebanese forces penetrated parts of northern Israel.

organized. The battle was evenly balanced during the first two months of fighting, but when secret arms shipments began reaching Israel from Europe, the war swung in Israel's favour, and its forces began capturing territories beyond those granted by the UN partition.

The war ended when the UN arranged a series of ceasefires between the Arabs and Jews in late 1948. Armistice agreements were signed by Israel and the Arab states between February and July 1949. Under these agreements, former Palestine was divided into three parts: Israel controlled over 77 per cent of the territory (22 per cent more than it had been allotted by the UN); Transjordan took over East Jerusalem and the area known as the West Bank (this being the west bank of the River Jordan). Egypt occupied the coastal plain around the city of Gaza, known as the Gaza Strip. The Palestinian Arab state proposed by the UN partition plan was never established.

David Ben-Gurion, Israel's first prime minister, reads out the declaration of the founding of the State of Israel, in Tel Aviv, on 15 May 1948.

THE 1947-9 WAR

Start date:	29 November 1947
End date:	24 February 1949
Days	453
Total death toll	c.12,373
Combatants	**Losses**
Israel	6,373
Egypt	c.3,000
Syria	c.2,000
Jordan	c.1,000

CHAPTER 2: THE SUEZ CRISIS AND THE SIX-DAY WAR

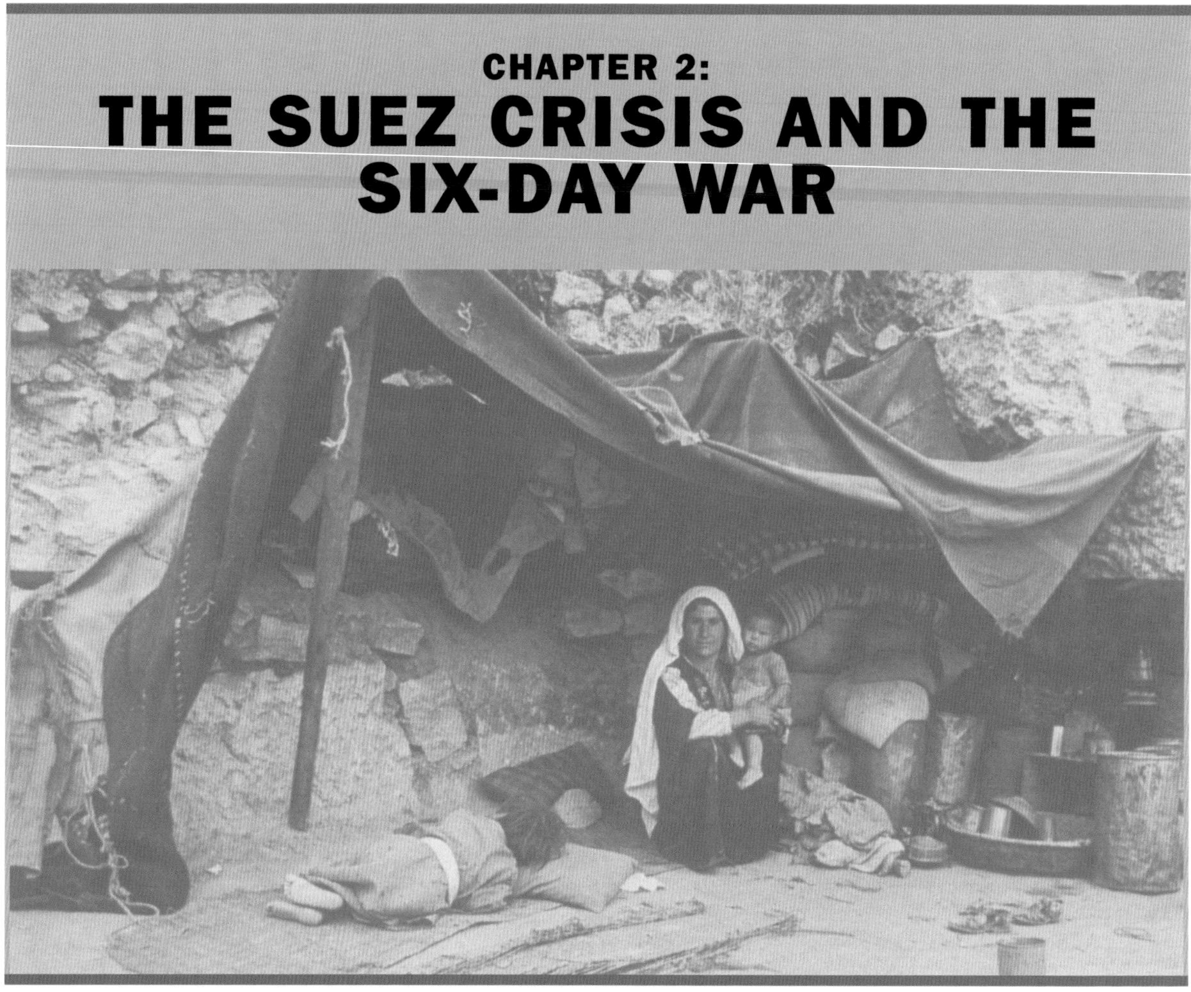

A Palestinian refugee family camp out in Amman, Transjordan, in June 1949. Despite a UN resolution recognizing the Palestinians' right to return to their homes, Israel barred refugees from re-entering Israel after the war.

According to UN estimates, the fighting in the 1947-9 war caused 726,000 Palestinian Arabs to flee Israel and become refugees. 470,000 moved to the West Bank (controlled by Transjordan, which in 1950 was renamed Jordan) and Gaza Strip (controlled by Egypt). 256,000 went to live in neighboring Arab states. Some 150,000 Palestinian Arabs remained in Israel, or returned to their homes during 1949. The reasons for the Palestinian exodus are disputed. Many Palestinian Arabs claim they were deliberately driven out by the Israelis. Israel says they were encouraged to leave by Arab government leaders.

An uneasy peace existed between Israel and the Arab states after 1949. Despite the signing of the armistice agreements, none of the Arab states recognized Israel's new borders, or even its right to exist. Both sides began building up their military forces. The Soviet Union, originally a supporter of Israel, aligned itself with the Arab states, and began supplying them with military aid. The USA remained a supporter of Israel, although it did not begin supplying military aid until the 1960s. Israel acquired most of its weaponry from Britain and France.

THE SUEZ WAR The Suez Canal in Egypt was built in 1869 by a French company, Universal Company of the Suez Ship Canal, and the canal was jointly owned by the Egyptian and French governments. The canal, which ran through Egyptian territory, linked the Mediterranean and the Red Sea,

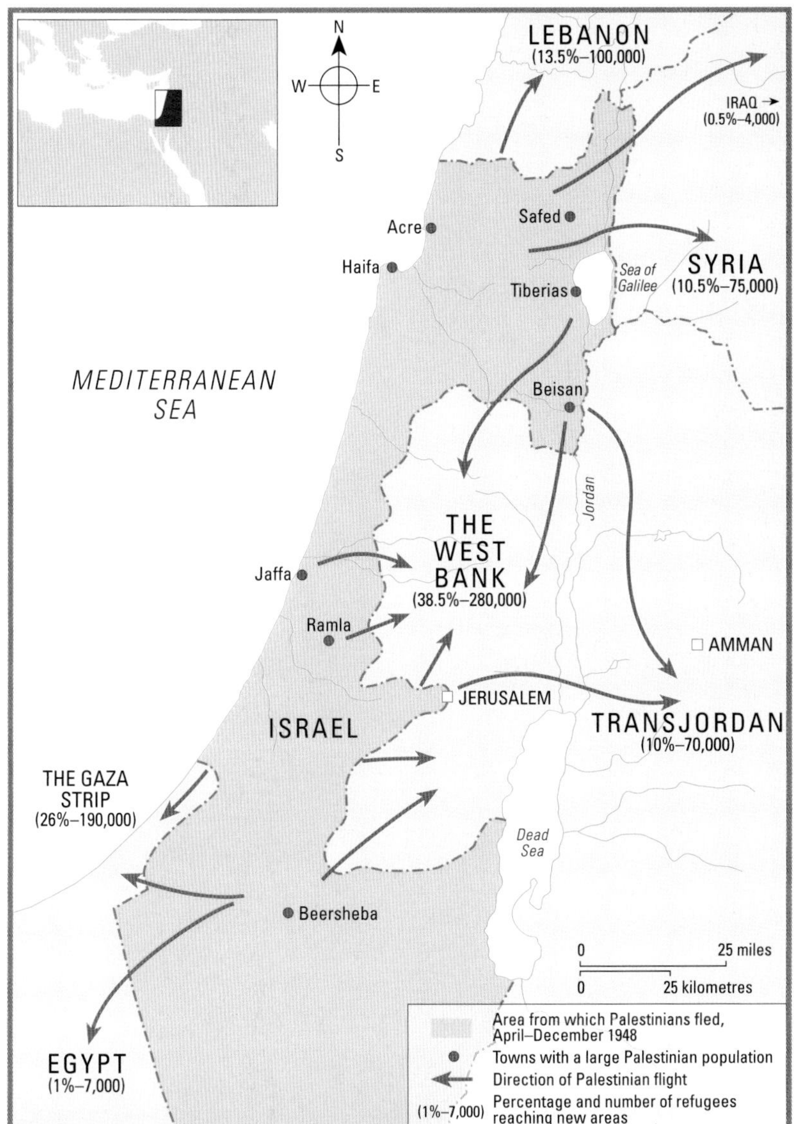

The map shows where the Palestinian refugees fled, and roughly how many settled in each area. The UN set up an agency to care for the refugees. Today, more than 3.7 million Palestinians are registered with it.

and was a vital trade route to the east. In 1882, debts forced Egypt to sell its share in the canal to Britain.

The canal continued to be jointly controlled by Britain and France until 1956. Early in that year, tensions between Egypt and Israel increased as Egyptians and Palestinians launched a series of border raids against the Jewish state, from Gaza. Israel responded with attacks of its own. In July, Egyptian leader Gamal Abdel Nasser nationalized (brought under national control) the Suez Canal. Nasser, who was a supporter of Arab nationalism, did not like the fact that European countries had power over a part of Egyptian territory. The tolls he could charge ships passing through the canal

Nasser arrives in the Egyptian capital, Cairo, in August 1956 following his announcement that he had nationalized the Suez Canal.

LIQUIDATION

'It is well-known and understood that the Arabs, in demanding the return of the refugees to Palestine, mean their return as masters of the Homeland and not as slaves. With a greater clarity, they mean the liquidation of the State of Israel.'

[Egyptian Foreign Minister Muhammad Salah al-Din quoted in *Al-Misri*]

British paratroopers board an aircraft bound for Suez during the 1956 crisis. Britain and France began bombing Egyptian airfields on 30 October, then sent in troops on 5 November.

THE 1956 SINAI CAMPAIGN

Start date:	29 October 1956
End date:	6 November 1956
Days	8
Total death toll	2,763
Combatants	**Losses**
Israel	231
Egypt	2,500
Britain	22
France	10

would also be a valuable source of revenue for Egypt.

By closing the Suez Canal to Israeli shipping and blockading the Straits of Tiran – another key trading route for Israel – Nasser strained relations between Egypt and Israel still further. He had also made enemies of Britain and France who had major economic and trading interests in the canal. A secret meeting took place between Israel, Britain and France, near Paris. It was agreed that Israel should invade Egypt, and that Britain and France would intervene and ask the Israeli and Egyptian armies to withdraw from the canal zone. An Anglo-French force would then take control of the canal.

On 29 October, Israel invaded the Gaza Strip and the Sinai Peninsula, and advanced rapidly towards the canal zone. Britain and France, as previously agreed, offered to reoccupy the canal and separate the two armies. Nasser refused this request, so Britain and France launched a joint attack. However, before the invading forces could reach the canal, the USA put pressure on Britain and France to withdraw their troops. The US government was concerned about the damage their action might do to relations with the Arab states. It also feared the possible escalation of the conflict after the Soviet Union threatened to intervene on Egypt's side. The Anglo-French troops were pulled out on 22 December 1956.

French soldiers at Port Said, Egypt. After capturing this city, Anglo-French forces advanced to within 40 km of Suez City before the British agreed to a ceasefire.

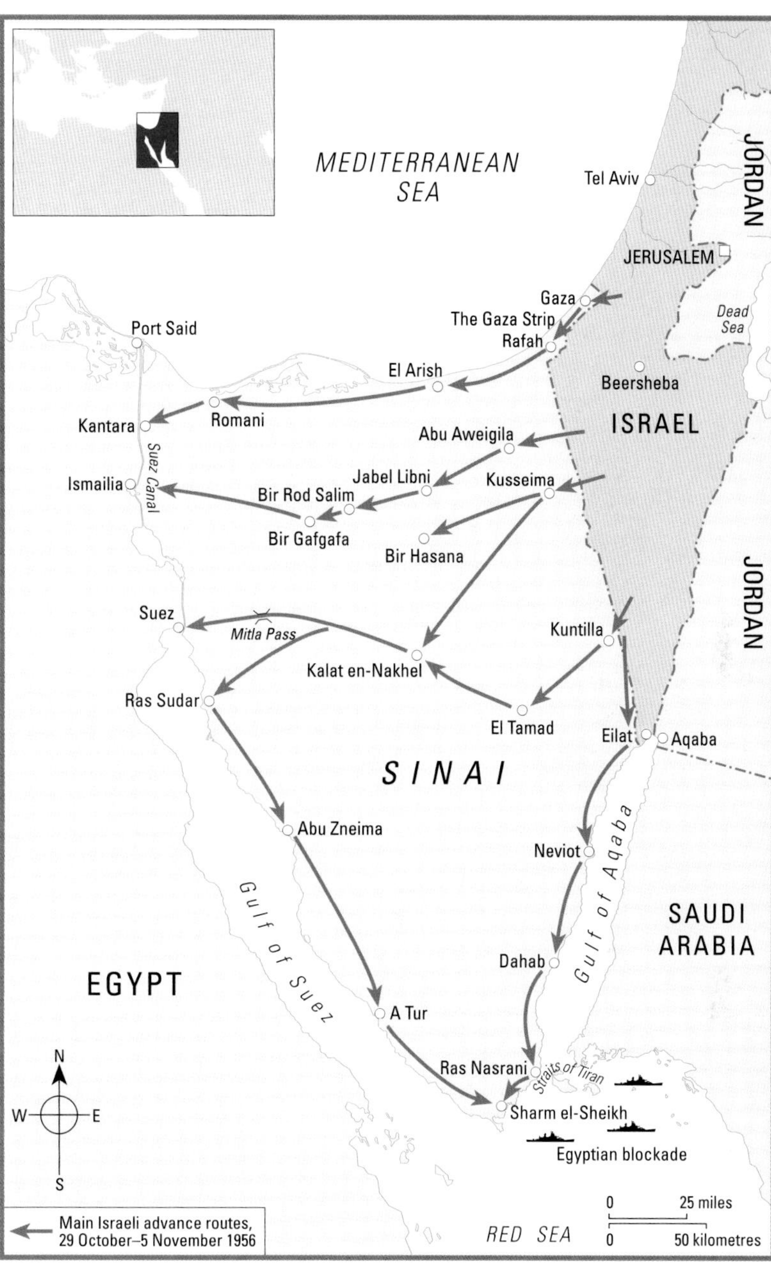

The main routes followed by Israeli forces during their 1956 invasion of Gaza and Sinai. Israeli armoured divisions captured almost the entire territory by 5 November. The operation took just 100 hours.

During the conflict, Israel captured both the Sinai Peninsula and the Gaza Strip, but in March 1957 it was forced by the UN to return to its previous borders. Israel failed to win back its shipping rights in the Suez Canal, but regained the freedom to use the Straits of Tiran. A demilitarized zone, policed by UN forces, was set up in the eastern and southern areas of Sinai, extending from Gaza to Sharm el-Sheikh, to act as a buffer between Israel and Egypt.

In August 1963, Israel began putting into effect its National Water Carrier Plan (NWCP), pumping water from the Sea of Galilee to irrigate south and central Israel. Syria, angered by this, readied its troops for attack. Israel did likewise. The UN persuaded both sides to pull back from conflict.

During 1964, the Arab leaders met at a series of conferences to agree joint strategies on how to deal with Israel. Several decisions were reached: they agreed to form the Palestine Liberation Organization (PLO) to represent the cause of Palestinian nationalism and help to unite Palestinians wherever they lived; they restated their intention to destroy Israel; and they

Levi Eshkol with his wife, Miriam. Israeli prime minister from 1963 until his death in 1969, the most significant moment of Eshkol's premiership was the 1967 Six-Day War.

The frontiers of Israel between 1949 and 1967. None of Israel's Arab neighbours recognized Israel's borders, or even its right to exist, at this time. From the mid-1960s, Syrian, Egyptian and Palestinian border attacks on Israel became more frequent.

decided to divert the Banias stream – one of the sources of the River Jordan, that feeds the Sea of Galilee – to prevent Israel from carrying out its NWCP.

Syria and Lebanon began work on the diversions in early 1967. Israel tried to block progress by firing on the tractors and earth-moving equipment carrying out the work on the Syrian side of the border. The Syrians responded by shelling Israeli towns in the north. Both sides began carrying out air strikes against targets across the border. As tensions escalated, the Soviet Union informed Syria that Israel was massing troops on the Syrian border in preparation for an invasion. The claim was untrue, but Syria did not know this, and called upon Egypt for help.

'THE ARAB PEOPLE WANT TO FIGHT' On 15 May 1967, Nasser sent Egyptian troops into the Sinai. Three days later, he asked UN forces to withdraw from the demilitarized zone. The UN Secretary-General U Thant immediately complied with this request, and Egyptian troops were sent into Sharm el-Sheikh. On 21 May, Nasser closed the Gulf of Aqaba and the Straits of Tiran to Israeli shipping. Israeli prime minister Levi Eshkol interpreted this as an act of aggression against Israel.

Nasser's popularity rose in the Arab world; as in 1956, many were pleased to see him standing up for Palestinian interests by confronting the Israelis. On 27 May, Nasser announced, 'Our basic objective will be the destruction of Israel. The Arab people want to fight.' PLO Chairman Ahmed Shukhairy echoed these sentiments, saying it would be the PLO's privilege to strike the first blow; they would expel all the Zionists from Palestine who had arrived after 1917, and eliminate the state of Israel. Other Arab states were persuaded to join Egypt and Syria in committing themselves to war. On 30 May, Jordan signed a defence pact with Egypt, and on 4 June, Iraq did the same. Iraqi president Rahman Aref declared, 'Our goal is to wipe Israel off the map.'

The Israeli cabinet was divided on what to do about these threatening moves. Former prime minister David Ben-Gurion preferred to wait, while Moshe Dayan, a veteran soldier of the 1947-9 war, favoured an immediate attack on Egypt. The USA placed pressure

'...WITH ALL OUR MIGHT'

'We are engaged in defensive fighting on the Egyptian sector, and we shall not engage ourselves in any action against Jordan, unless Jordan attacks us. Should Jordan attack Israel, we shall go against her with all our might.'

[A message sent by Prime Minister Eshkol to King Hussein of Jordan on the morning of 5 June 1967. That afternoon, under pressure from Egypt, Jordan launched its attack against Israel.]

King Hussein of Jordan on a visit to a Royal Air Force base in the UK in 1966. Jordan signed a mutual defence pact with Egypt in May 1967, and took part in the 1967 conflict with Israel, losing control of the West Bank and Jerusalem in the process.

A map showing the Israeli advance on three fronts during the Six-Day War. An important element in Israel's success was its virtual destruction of the enemies' air forces, giving it air superiority throughout the war.

on Israel not to attack, but the mood in the cabinet gradually tilted towards aggressive action. Dayan was appointed Minister of Defence on 31 May. Menachem Begin, another supporter of war, was also invited to join the government. On 3 June, the cabinet was informed that the USA would not intervene if Israel went to war. The decision to attack was made on 4 June 1967.

THE SIX-DAY WAR Israel began its offensive at 7.45 am on 5 June 1967 with a surprise attack on the Egyptian air force. Egypt had the best-equipped and most modern of all the Arab air forces, but its airfields were poorly defended, with few anti-aircraft guns or armoured bunkers. The Israeli jets bombed and strafed the Egyptian planes and runways. In less than three hours they had destroyed virtually the entire air force

As well as destroying many Egyptian aircraft on the ground, the Israelis used tarmac-shredding penetration bombs on the runways, so that even undamaged planes could not take off.

ELEMENT OF SURPRISE

'We pulled up to 6000 feet. I looked down and saw the Egyptian MiGs shining – sparkling on the sides of the runways – with the pilots sitting inside the cockpits. I looked to my right and saw fire and smoke coming up from all the other bases near Inshas [an airfield east of Cairo]. *It was then that I realized that we had managed to surprise them.'*

[Ran Ronen, Israeli Squadron Commander, recalling an attack on an Egyptian airbase on 5 June 1967]

on the ground, giving Israel air superiority for the remainder of the war.

Part of the Israeli Defence Force (IDF), consisting of three divisions, began to advance through the Gaza Strip and the Sinai Peninsula, encircling then defeating a powerful Egyptian force at Abu Aweigila. When Egyptian Minister of Defence, Abdel Amer heard that Abu Aweigila had fallen, he panicked and ordered all units in the Sinai to retreat. By 8 June, the Israelis had completed their conquest of the Sinai.

Nasser, desperate for help from Jordan, sent a message to its ruler King Hussein on 5 June in which he pretended that the Egyptians were winning their battle with the Israelis. Hussein gave the order to attack, and the Jordanian army began firing on Israeli positions in Jerusalem. Israeli forces counterattacked, destroying the tiny Jordanian air force and encircling eastern (Arab-controlled) Jerusalem. On 6 June, an Israeli armoured brigade captured the West Bank towns of Ramallah and Jenin, and the following day they took control of Jerusalem's Old City and the West Bank town of Nablus. By 8 June, all of Jerusalem and the West Bank had fallen to Israeli forces.

From the start of the conflict, Syrian artillery had been shelling civilian targets in northern Israel from the Golan Heights, a 1,000-metre-high plateau on Syria's south-western frontier with Israel. On the evening of 5 June, Israeli jets destroyed two thirds of the Syrian air force, and forced the remaining third to

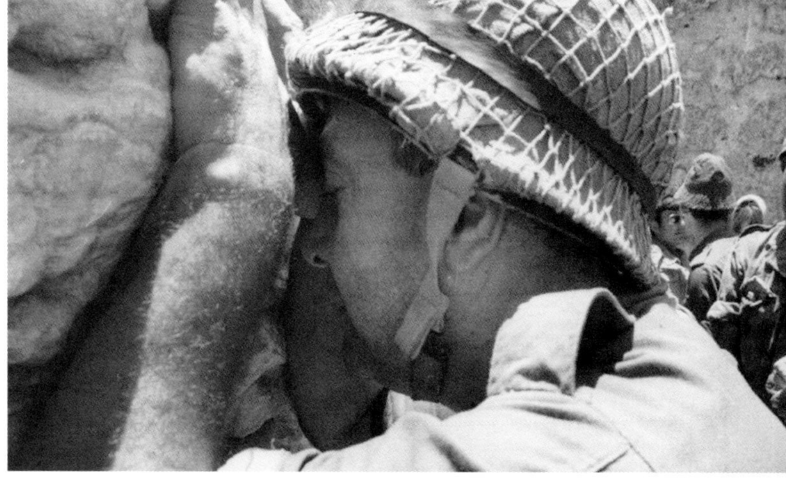

Israeli soldiers at Jerusalem's Wailing Wall – a holy place for Jews – following their capture of the Old City in 1967.

retreat to distant bases. The Israeli government was divided on whether or not to attempt to take the mountainous Golan Heights, a far more difficult operation than fighting on the flat desert of the Sinai. Levi Eshkol was in favour of an attack, but Moshe Dayan was against, concerned about fighting a war on several fronts. However, as good news poured in from the Sinai and the West Bank, Dayan warmed to the idea, and authorized the operation.

Early on the morning of 9 June, Israeli jets began bombing Syrian positions on the Golan Heights, and four Israeli brigades secured a base on the plateau from where they could be reinforced. On 10 June, the Syrian forces began retreating under heavy bombardment. By the afternoon, the IDF controlled the Golan Heights, and was poised to advance on the Syrian capital, Damascus.

At this stage the Soviet Union, a firm ally of Syria, became alarmed. The Soviet premier, Alexei Kosygin sent a telegram to US president Lyndon Johnson,

THE SIX-DAY WAR

Start date:	5 June 1967
End date:	10 June 1967
Days	6
Total death toll	c.19,200

Combatants	Forces (approx)	Losses
Israel	150,000 troops	776
	1,000 tanks	n/a
	200 aircraft	46
Egypt	100,000 troops	c. 10,000
	900 tanks	n/a
	385 aircraft	300
Jordan	60,000 troops	c 6,000
	300 tanks	n/a
	24 aircraft	20
Syria	50,000 troops	c. 2,500
	200 tanks	n/a
	97 aircraft	50

Israeli units advance into Syria on 10 June 1967. During the assault on the Golan Heights, Israel lost 115 soldiers.

By the end of the 1967 war, Israel had expanded its territory from 21,000 to 67,000 square kilometres. It would retain these new frontiers until October 1973.

12 June 1967: Israeli troops salute their country's flag, now flying over the former Syrian territory of the Golan Heights.

threatening military action against Israel unless they ceased fighting in the next few hours. Both the US government and the UN urged the Israelis to stop their advance, concerned that this might develop into a far more serious confrontation. At 6.30 pm on 10 June, Israeli commanders ordered a ceasefire.

In the aftermath of the conflict, it was immediately clear that Israel had won a stunning victory. In just six days, Israeli forces had conquered the Gaza Strip, the Sinai, the Golan Heights and the West Bank, more than trebling its territory. Israel had inflicted a damaging defeat on its enemies, and established itself as the dominant military power in the region.

Israel had triumphed despite facing a combined Arab force that was greater in numbers and had more up-to-date weapons and equipment. Israel benefited from better leadership on the battlefield, superior training, and using tactics of surprise, speed and air superiority. The Israelis (many of whom had lost family members in the Holocaust of World War II) were also arguably better motivated, as most of them believed they were fighting for their very survival as a nation.

CHAPTER 3: THE OCCUPIED TERRITORIES AND THE RISE OF THE PLO

An Israeli soldier stands guard at the new border with Jordan in June 1967.

Israel's conquests brought their own problems. After the Six-Day War, the Jewish state found itself ruling over more than 750,000 Palestinian Arabs, most of whom were hostile to their new government. Far from bringing Israel a greater sense of security, the 1967 victory only served to increase anti-Israeli sentiment among Palestinians and other Arabs. In November 1967, the UN gave its own verdict on the war, when the Security Council adopted Resolution 242, calling upon Israel to withdraw from territories it seized by force, and calling upon all the states to live in peace and recognize each other's (pre-June 1967) boundaries.

LAND FOR PEACE The Israeli government initially offered to return all of its new territories, except Jerusalem, in return for peace treaties with its Arab neighbours. The 'land-for-peace' offer was rejected by Egypt on 18 July 1967, and the following day it was withdrawn. Any further peace initiatives along these lines by the Israelis would be strongly opposed by elements within their own population. Religious Zionists had noted that the conquest of the West Bank, Gaza and the Golan Heights had brought Israel's borders roughly into line with those of the Biblical land of Israel. They were determined that these territories become a permanent part of Israel, and they lobbied the government to annex them and allow Jewish settlements to be built there.

In 1977, settlement expansion became official government policy, and increasing numbers of Jewish settlers made their homes in these areas. By 2003, 220,000 Jews had settled in the West Bank and Gaza, and an additional 200,000 had moved into areas of Jerusalem conquered in 1967. Some 15,000 Jews have settled in the Golan Heights, which was formally

RESOLUTION 242

In its Resolution 242, the UN Security Council called for: '*(i) Withdrawal of Israeli armed forces from territories occupied in the recent conflict; (ii) Termination of all claims or states of belligerency* [being at war] *and respect for and acknowledgement of the sovereignty, territorial integrity and political independence of every State in the area and their right to live in peace within secure and recognized boundaries free from threats or acts of force...*'

The West Bank and Gaza Strip.

Refugees cross between Jordan and Israel in 1967. Today, over half the three million Palestinians living in the West Bank and Gaza are refugees.

annexed from Syria by Israel in 1981. These settlements are in breach of UN Resolution 242, and have been a source of great anger and resentment for the Palestinian Arabs living in the occupied territories. Israel insists it has not broken international law with regard to the West Bank and Gaza Strip because they were not part of the sovereign territory of any state when Israel took them over. The territories (formerly part of the British Mandate) had been annexed by Egypt (in the case of Gaza) and Jordan (the West Bank) as part of the armistice agreement at the end of the 1947–9 War. However, they had never been internationally recognized as permanent parts of those countries. Therefore, Israel argues that it is not a foreign occupier, but a legal administrator of territory whose precise status remains to be determined.

From June 1967, Israel established a military administration to govern the Palestinians living in the West Bank and the Gaza Strip, which became known collectively as the occupied territories. Although Israel granted Palestinians living in the West Bank freedom of worship, in order to enforce security and counter terrorism there, Israeli authorities placed restrictions on the freedom of movement and freedom of the press for Palestinian residents of the occupied territories. Curfews were imposed, and roads, schools and community institutions were closed. Houses of suspected terrorists were demolished, and hundreds of Palestinians, accused of terrorist offences, were deported to Jordan or Lebanon, or imprisoned.

JERUSALEM Jerusalem has always had a special status because of its importance as a holy place to Jews, Muslims and Christians. The UN partition plan of 1947 advised that Jerusalem become an international city. The armistice agreed between Israel and Jordan after the 1947–9 war split the city in two: Israel took control of West Jerusalem while Jordan occupied East Jerusalem. East Jerusalem included the old walled city which contained religious sites important to Jews, Muslims and Christians. The city remained divided until 1967, when Israel captured East Jerusalem from Jordan, and then annexed it soon afterwards.

Unlike the military administrations of Gaza and the West Bank, Arab East Jerusalem was governed under Israeli civil law. The Israeli authorities redrew Jerusalem's boundaries, extending them northwards and southwards. Large Israeli settlements were established around the northern, eastern and southern boundaries of the city, creating a physical barrier between the Palestinian Arabs in East Jerusalem, and their countrymen living elsewhere in the

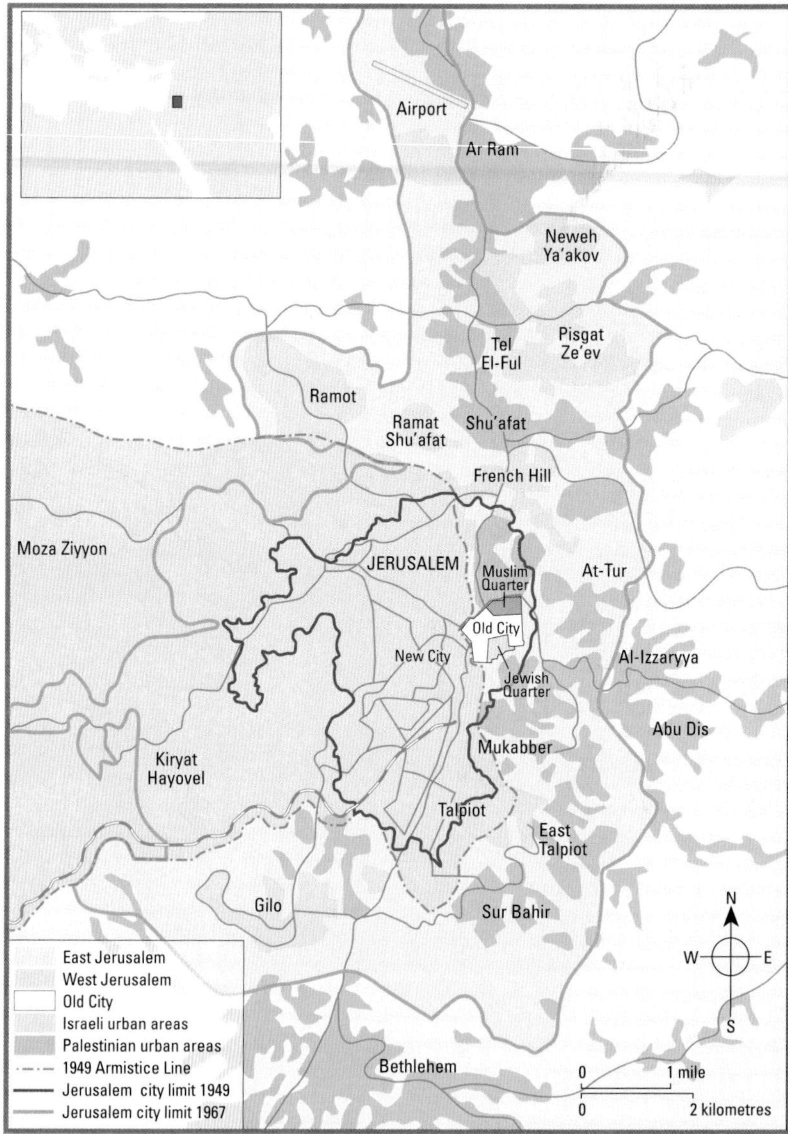

A map of Jerusalem since the Israeli conquest of 1967. Israel annexed 10 square km of Jordanian Jerusalem and 103 square km of the nearby West Bank, renaming the entire area East Jerusalem.

Jews praying at the Wailing Wall in Jerusalem in 1973. Also known as the Western Wall, this is all that remains of the Jerusalem Temple, destroyed by the Romans in the first century AD, and regarded by Jews as the holiest place on earth.

West Bank. In 1980, the Israeli parliament passed a law making its annexation of Jerusalem official.

Jerusalem remains one of the most problematic issues in the Arab-Israeli conflict. Neither Israel nor the Palestinians agree with the UN plan to make Jerusalem an international city. Israel sees Jerusalem – the capital city of ancient Israel – as its 'eternal capital', and it is unlikely that an Israeli government would ever voluntarily give it up. Arabs regard East Jerusalem as part of the occupied West Bank, and want it to be the capital of a future Palestinian state.

THE CHANGING BALANCE OF POPULATION IN JERUSALEM

	Jews	Arabs
1948	100,000	65,000
1967	195,700	65,763
1984	346,700	126,100
1993	401,000	155,000
2000	454,600	215,400

THE PALESTINE LIBERATION ORGANIZATION The Palestine Liberation Organization (PLO) was founded in Egypt in 1964 to represent the large numbers of Palestinian Arabs living as refugees in Syria, Jordan and Egypt. In its early years the organization was controlled by the Arab nations who hoped to use it to advance their interests in the region. However, after the Six-Day War, many Palestinian Arabs lost faith in the Arab regimes, and began to build their own nationalist movements. One of these groups, called Fatah and led by a young Palestinian named Yasser Arafat, took over the PLO in 1967.

The PLO, now independent of the Arab regimes, became an umbrella organization for about eight different nationalist groups, each with their own views of how to achieve the ultimate goal of a Palestinian state. Arafat, as leader of the largest group, Fatah, became chairman of the PLO in 1969. The other major factions included the Popular Front for the Liberation of Palestine (PFLP), the Democratic Front for the Liberation of Palestine (DFLP) and the Palestine People's

An Arab Muslim passes two orthodox Jews in a Jerusalem street. On 27 June 1967, the Israeli parliament voted to give free access to Jerusalem's holy sites to people of all religions.

Party (PPP). Despite their differences, most members of these groups – and the majority of Palestinians – regarded the PLO as their representative.

After the Six-Day War, some 400,000 Palestinians fled from the West Bank to Jordan. Here the PLO regrouped and decided to adopt terrorist tactics. From 1968, they embarked on a campaign of hijackings, and border raids into Israel from Jordan and Syria. On one occasion, in March 1968, a Jordanian-PLO force managed to inflict a rare defeat on Israeli troops at the town of Karameh in Jordan. The Israeli assault was launched after a terrorist attack left two Jewish schoolchildren dead. They were driven back by Palestinian guerrillas supported by Jordanian troops and artillery. The victory at Karameh won Arafat worldwide fame, and enabled him to recruit many more Palestinians to his cause.

One of the airliners blown up by the PFLP at Dawson's Field, Jordan, in 1970. This action led to the expulsion of the PLO from Jordan.

Jordanian premier Abdel Min'em Rifa'i with PLO leader Yasser Arafat (left) in 1969.

In 1970, the PFLP blew up three passenger planes at Dawson's Field, a military airport in Jordan. By this time, the increasingly violent activities of the PLO were putting pressure on King Hussein, who felt that he was losing control of his own country. In 1970–71, the PLO were driven out by the Jordanian army, and forced into southern Lebanon. From this new base, the PLO continued to raid and shell northern Israel.

During the 1970s, the PLO began to alter its strategy. Worried by its terrorist image, it began to seek international legitimacy as a government-in-exile. At the Arab League conference in Morocco in 1974, the PLO was officially recognized by the Arab peoples as the representative organization of the Palestinians, and in November of that year, Arafat was invited to address the UN General Assembly. The UN then granted the PLO observer status (entitling it to participate as an observer in all the sessions and debates of the General Assembly). To Israel's discomfort, Arafat had changed the image of the PLO from a group of ruthless terrorists to an internationally respected movement.

'SOMETHING HAD TO BE DONE...'

'The humiliation of having aircraft flown into Jordan and innocent passengers being whisked away to various parts of the country, and being unable to do anything about it, and having aircraft blown up, was something that questioned whether Jordan really existed. Well, that was the limit. As far as I was concerned, something had to be done – and done quickly.'

[King Hussein of Jordan on his decision to expel the PLO]

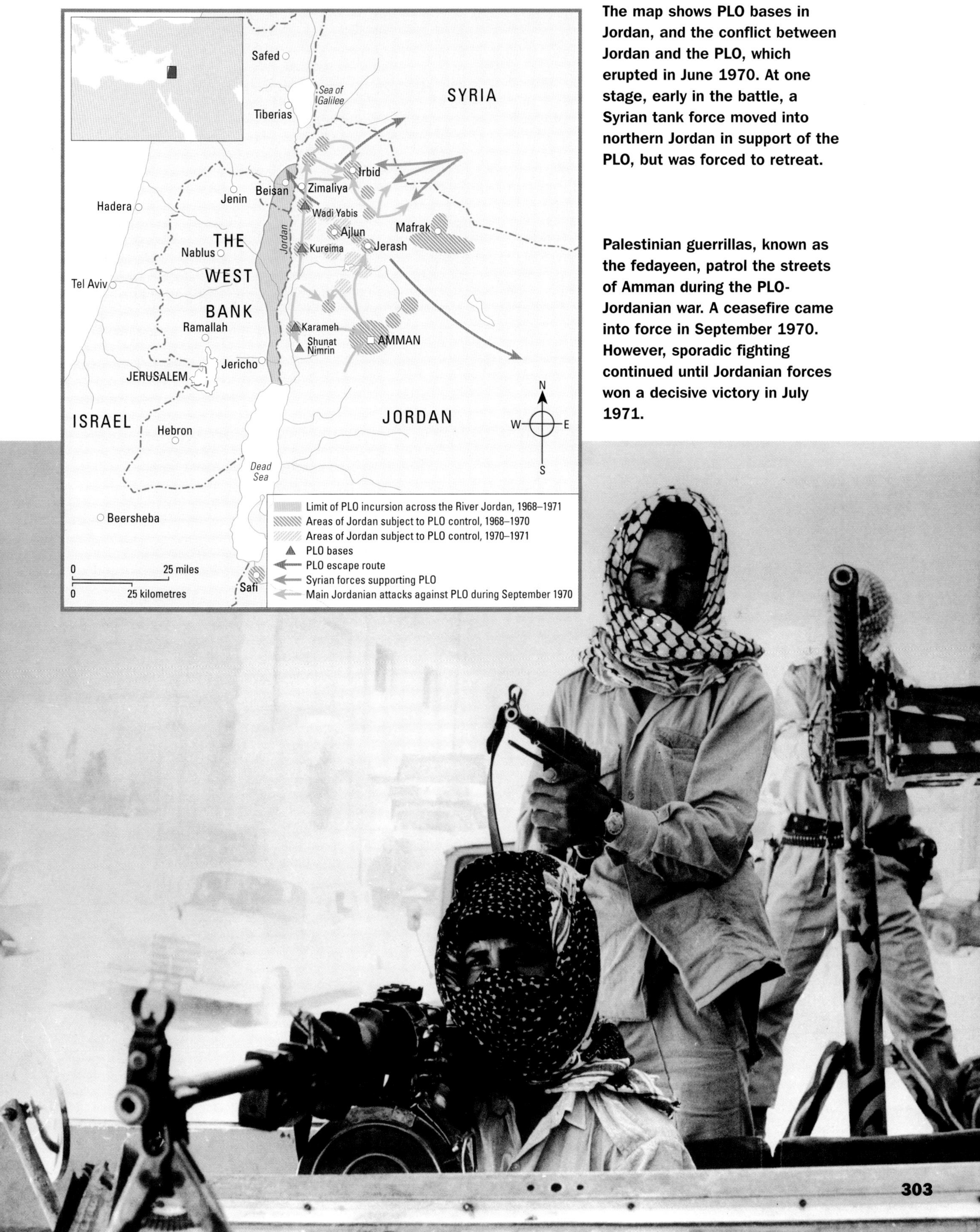

The map shows PLO bases in Jordan, and the conflict between Jordan and the PLO, which erupted in June 1970. At one stage, early in the battle, a Syrian tank force moved into northern Jordan in support of the PLO, but was forced to retreat.

Palestinian guerrillas, known as the fedayeen, patrol the streets of Amman during the PLO-Jordanian war. A ceasefire came into force in September 1970. However, sporadic fighting continued until Jordanian forces won a decisive victory in July 1971.

CHAPTER 4: THE YOM KIPPUR WAR AND CAMP DAVID

Artillery fire against Israel during the Yom Kippur War. The Egyptian-Syrian attack was well-supported, both militarily and financially, by other Arab states.

Soviet premier Leonid Brezhnev greets Anwar Sadat in Moscow in 1971. Sadat was seeking military support for Egypt from the Soviet Union.

From 1968, Egypt engaged in a series of low-level but persistent attacks against Israel in the Sinai Peninsula, aimed at wearing Israeli forces down. The cross-border confrontations grew increasingly intense until, under pressure from the US, both sides signed a ceasefire in August 1970, and declared their acceptance of UN Resolution 242. Shortly after this, Nasser died, and was replaced by a new leader, Anwar Sadat.

Unlike his predecessor, Sadat was genuinely interested in making peace with Israel. In February 1971 he announced that if Israel partially withdrew its forces from the Sinai, Egypt would reopen the Suez Canal and sign a peace agreement with Israel. By this time, Israel had a new prime minister, Golda Meir, who refused the Egyptian offer, despite pressure from the USA to accept. Over the next two years, further offers of peace were also turned down. Israel, now receiving US military aid, felt itself to be in a strong position in relation to Egypt, whose forces had yet to recover to their pre-1967 strength.

Israeli plans to build a Mediterranean port near Rafah in Sinai, and its talk of creating settlements there, worried Sadat. He thought that the only way to

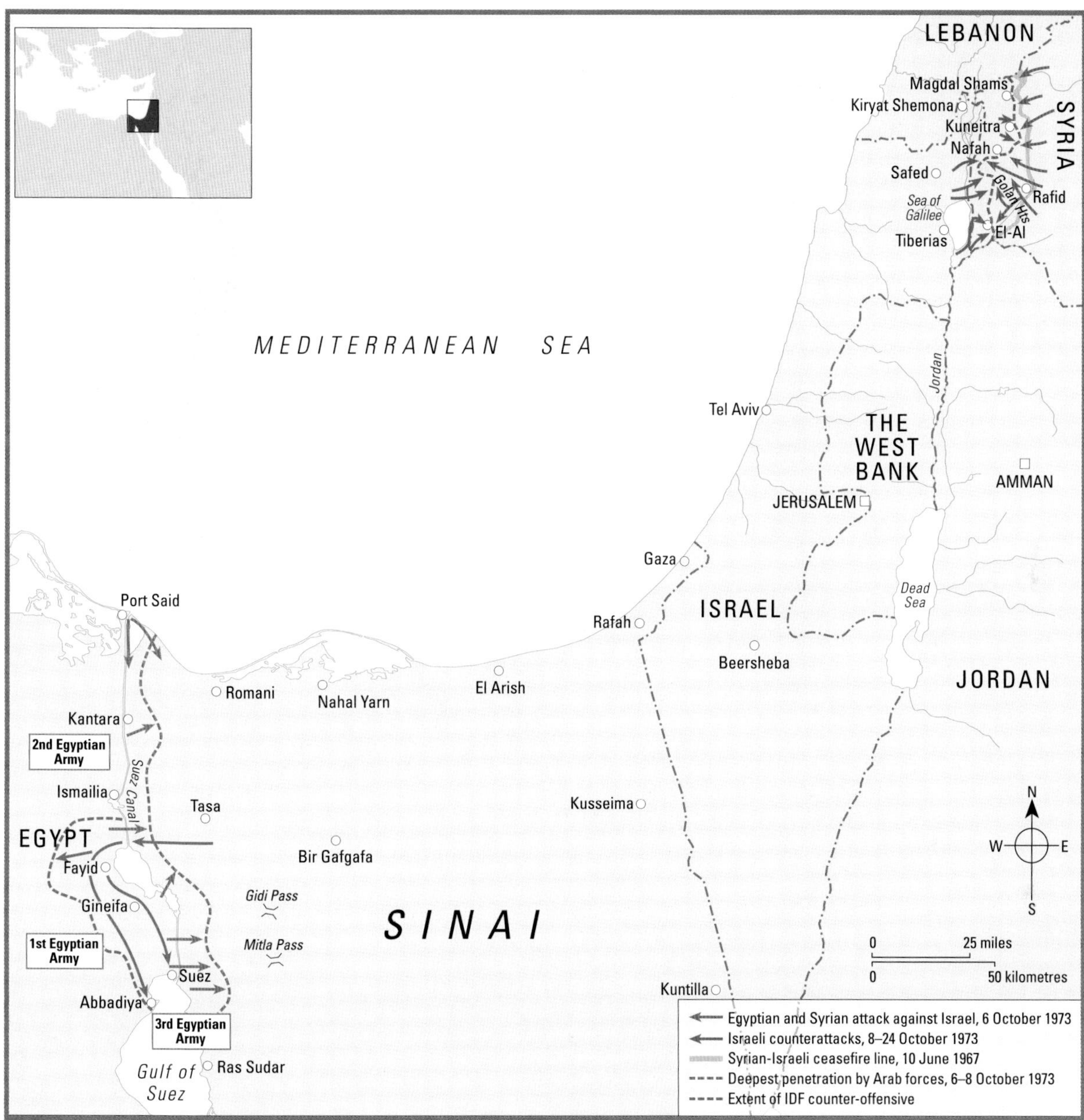

A map showing the lines of attack and counterattack during the Yom Kippur War. For the first four days of the conflict, Egypt and Syria made strong headway against surprised Israeli defences. However, after three weeks of fighting, the IDF was able to push the attacking forces back beyond their original lines.

recover this territory, and to lift Egypt's standing in the Arab world, would be to stage an attack on Israel.

THE OCTOBER WAR On the afternoon of 6 October 1973, Egypt and Syria launched a joint invasion of Israel, code-named Operation Badr. They chose the day deliberately: it was Yom Kippur or the Day of Atonement, the holiest day in the Jewish calendar, and the Israelis were caught completely by

AIR ATTACK

'It was one o'clock in the afternoon, and I was driving my jeep to meet my commander. Suddenly I saw planes. I was very surprised. The Israeli air force flying on Yom Kippur! … [then] I understood we were in a war.'

[General Amram Mitzna, Armored Corps, IDF]

surprise. Golda Meir and Defence Minister Moshe Dayan had believed that their forces in the Sinai were sufficient to deter any attack, and they dismissed intelligence reports that enemy soldiers were massing on their borders preparing to invade.

Huge numbers of Egyptian troops poured virtually unopposed across the Suez Canal and established a beachhead. A tiny force of Israelis manning the outposts along the canal were destroyed after offering limited resistance. Within days, Egypt had successfully reconquered the entire western bank of the Sinai peninsula. Israel's counterattacks on land and in the air were successfully repelled by Egypt's new Soviet-made anti-tank and anti-aircraft missiles. These missiles were neutralized only after Egyptian radar stations (which directed their strikes) were destroyed.

Meanwhile, to the north, Israeli defences, including just 170 tanks, were overrun by far greater Syrian forces (including 1,500 tanks and 1,000 artillery pieces) which penetrated deep into the Golan Heights and came within sight of the Sea of Galilee in northern Israel. During three days of desperate fighting, Israel's 7th Brigade managed to hold a line of rocky hills defending the northern side of their headquarters in Nafah (see page 27). However, the Syrians came very close to capturing Nafah from the south after destroying the Israeli 'Barak' armoured brigade. Israeli reserve forces arrived in time to prevent this, and swiftly counterattacked. By 11 October they had

THE OCTOBER WAR

Start date:	6 October 1973
End date:	22 October 1973
Days	16
Deaths per day	781
Total death toll	c.14,188
Combatants	**Losses**
Israel	2,688
Egypt	8,500 (approx)
Syria	3,000 (approx)

An Israeli armoured column advances into Syria on 17 October 1973. On that day, the Arab nations declared an oil embargo against the West for its support of Israel, which led to big petrol price rises.

reversed the Syrian gains, advancing to within artillery range of the Syrian capital, Damascus, just 40 kilometres away.

On the night of 16/17 October, General Ariel Sharon, commanding an Israeli division in the Sinai, disobeyed orders from his more cautious superiors, and crossed to the Egyptian side of the canal where he established a bridgehead between the Egyptian second and third armies. The IDF was able to cut off supplies to the Egyptian third army fighting in the peninsula, and Israeli forces came to within 100 kilometres of Cairo, Egypt's capital city. Israeli attempts to capture Suez City ended in failure. Under pressure from the USA and USSR, both sides agreed to a ceasefire on 20 October. A ceasefire was agreed with Syria on 22 October 1973, based on a return to pre-war borders.

After being caught so badly off guard, Israeli forces had managed a rapid recovery, and recaptured nearly all the territory they had won in 1967. Nevertheless, the war was a great shock to the Israelis, and losses had been heavy. They had underestimated the strength of their enemies, and had come very close to defeat. The Israeli government's lack of preparedness led to the resignation of Golda Meir and Moshe Dayan.

Occasional clashes continued across the ceasefire lines in the Sinai and Golan. The tension was only eased on 5 March 1974, when Israeli forces withdrew from the west bank of the canal, and Egypt

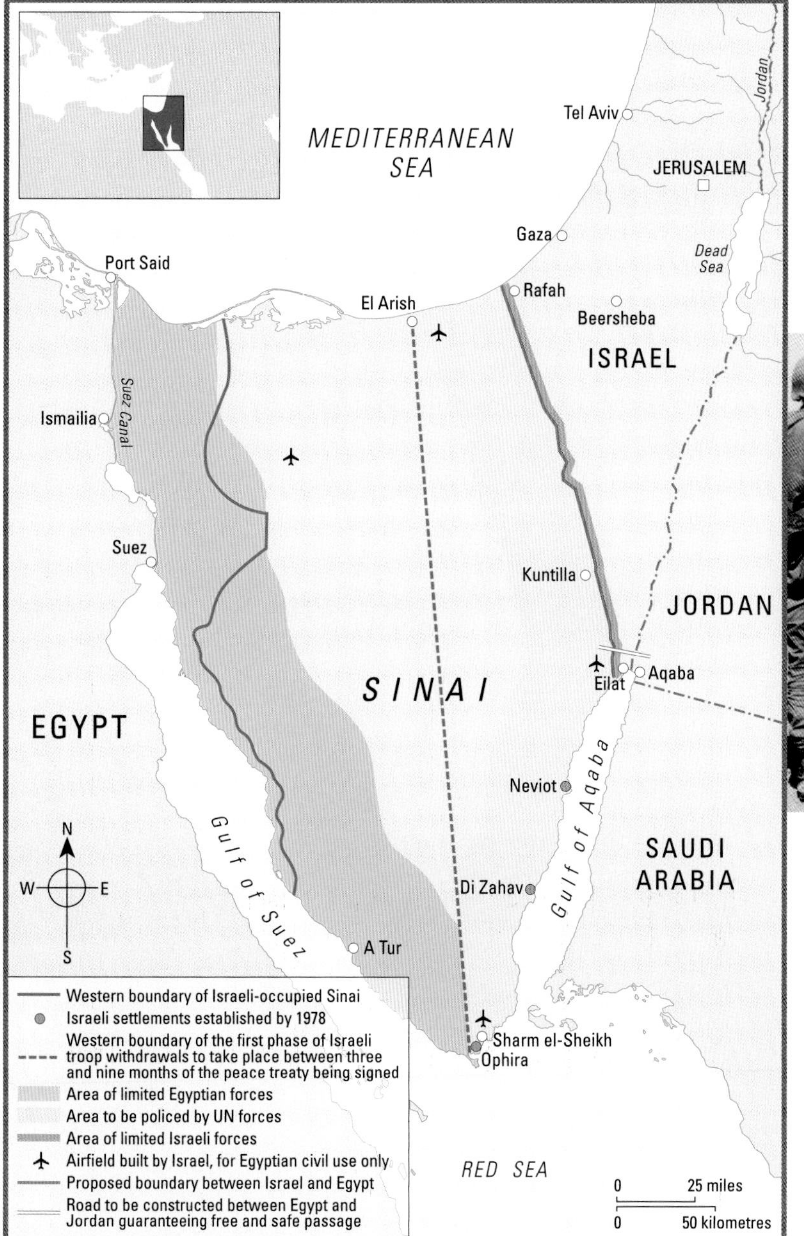

Following the end of the conflict, blindfolded Egyptian prisoners of war are led back to the western side of the Suez Canal, so they can return home.

The Sinai boundary changes agreed at Camp David (see p.30) in September 1978. Under the agreement, the Sinai would be returned to Egypt, but part of the territory would be policed by the UN as a security measure.

Begin (left), Carter (centre) and Sadat meet at Camp David in September 1978. The US president formed a relationship of friendship and mutual trust with Sadat, but found it harder to work with Begin.

took back control. On 31 May, Syria and Israel signed a disengagement agreement, and a UN peacekeeping force was established in the Golan Heights. Following the war, US Secretary of State Henry Kissinger tried in vain to negotiate an Arab-Israeli peace settlement by encouraging Israel to withdraw partly from the Sinai Peninsula and the Golan Heights. However, the US was successful in achieving a limited agreement between Egypt and Israel in September 1975 in which Israel withdrew most of its forces from the Sinai, and a UN-policed buffer zone was introduced between Egyptian and Israeli forces.

In November 1977, Sadat visited Jerusalem in an effort to secure peace between Egypt and Israel. He offered the Israelis permanent peace, and recognition of Israeli sovereignty, if Israel would withdraw from the occupied territories, including Arab Jerusalem, and agree to the establishment of a Palestinian state. Israeli prime minister Menachem Begin could not accept this, but did offer limited self-rule for the Palestinians in the West Bank and Gaza.

CAMP DAVID In September 1978 US President Jimmy Carter invited Sadat and Begin to the presidential holiday retreat at Camp David in Maryland. Following twelve days of secret and often ill-tempered discussions, two agreements were signed. The first dealt with Egypt-Israel relations: both countries recognized each other, and the Sinai was returned to Egypt. This led to the Egypt-Israel Peace Treaty – the first between Israel and an Arab state – signed in March 1979. Israel completed its withdrawal from the Sinai Peninsula in 1982.

The second agreement tried to solve the Palestinian problem. It proposed giving Palestinians in

TOUGH TALKING

'I want you to understand that my right eye will fall out, my right hand will fall off, before I sign a single scrap of paper permitting the dismantling of a single Jewish settlement.'

[Menachem Begin speaking to US National Security Adviser Zbigniew Brzezinski about the Sinai settlements at Camp David]

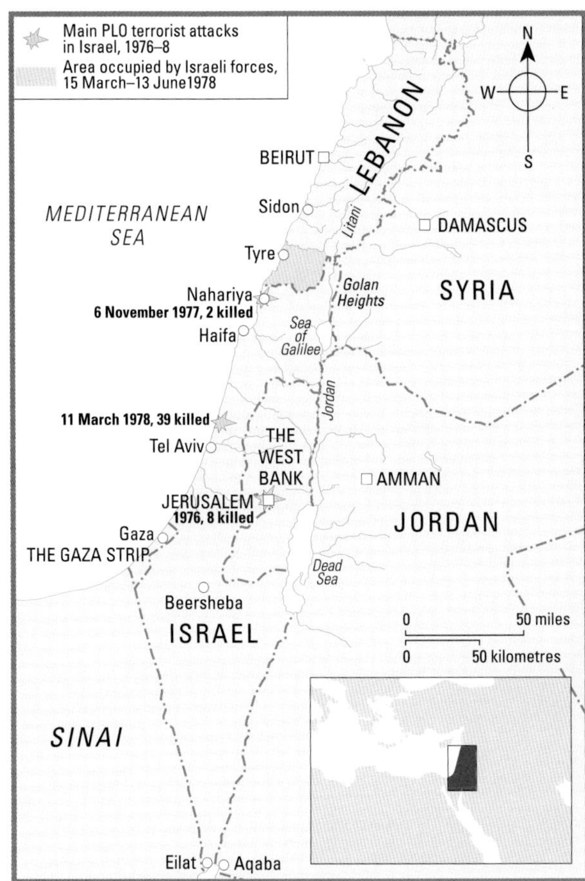

This map reveals PLO attacks on Israel (1976-1978), and Operation Litani, Israel's occupation of southern Lebanon (March-June 1978) which was undertaken in an attempt to strike back at the PLO.

the occupied territories autonomy (self-rule) for a five-year period, after which time the final status of the occupied territories would be decided. This was rejected by the PLO and other Arab states because it did not guarantee full Israeli withdrawal from the occupied territories or the establishment of an independent Palestinian state. Israel also made the agreement more difficult to achieve by continuing to build new settlements in these areas.

OPERATION LITANI Another reason for the failure to achieve an Israeli-Palestinian peace agreement in 1978 was the growing conflict on Israel's northern border with Lebanon. The arrival of the PLO in Lebanon in 1971, after their expulsion from Jordan, had caused tensions within the different ethnic communities of Lebanon – Muslim, Christian and Druze. Each sect had its own private army, and there were frequent clashes between PLO fighters and Christian militias in the capital city, Beirut. This led to a full-scale civil war beginning in 1975.

From 1976, PLO forces based in southern Lebanon engaged in a number of terrorist attacks on Israeli forces both in the occupied territories and in Israel itself. Following a PLO attack on a bus north of Tel Aviv, causing heavy casualties, Israel decided to attack PLO bases in Lebanon.

The invasion of southern Lebanon, known as Operation Litani, took place in March 1978. Israeli forces occupied most of the area south of the Litani River, which had been used as a base for anti-Israeli attacks. The UN Security Council responded by passing Resolution 425 calling for the immediate withdrawal of Israeli forces, and a UN peacekeeping force was set up in Lebanon. Israeli forces withdrew in June 1978, handing over positions along the border to a pro-Israeli force, a group of Lebanese Christian militiamen known as the South Lebanon Army. Israel was thus able to maintain a 20-km wide security zone to protect itself from cross-border attacks.

A street battle in Beirut during the civil war in Lebanon. Palestinian forces joined Lebanese Muslim factions in a fight against Christian militias based in east Beirut.

CHAPTER 5: THE WAR IN LEBANON AND THE INTIFADA

Ariel Sharon, a key planner behind Operation Peace for Galilee, went beyond the original idea to attack PLO strongholds in southern Lebanon, and launched a full-scale assault on Beirut.

Despite Operation Litani and the establishment of a security zone, towns in Galilee in northern Israel continued to suffer attacks from PLO forces in southern Lebanon. To add to Israel's anxiety, Syria had become involved in Lebanon. In 1976 Syrian forces had moved in at the request of one of the parties fighting the civil war, a Christian sect called the Maronites, and Syria had used this as an opportunity to take over part of Lebanon for itself.

Tensions between Syria and Israel escalated further in April 1982 when Syria began positioning anti-aircraft missile batteries in Lebanon's Bekaa Valley. Israel saw this as a threat to its air reconnaissance activities over Lebanon. The Israeli government decided that another invasion of Lebanon was necessary to destroy both the PLO bases, and the Syrian missiles. Israel also wished to form a partnership with the Maronite Christians; a Maronite government in Lebanon would – the Israelis hoped – be able to rid Lebanon of its Palestinian and Syrian elements. By mid-1977 the Maronites began to fear the growing dominance of their former allies, the Syrians, who were behaving increasingly like an army of occupation. The Maronite leaders were happy to form a new allegiance with Israel, the only force in the region powerful enough to confront Syria.

OPERATION PEACE FOR GALILEE

On 3 June 1982, an attempt was made to assassinate the Israeli ambassador in London. The Palestine National Liberation Movement was responsible, a rival organization to the PLO. Nevertheless, for the Israelis this was the excuse they were looking for to begin their invasion of Lebanon, which they named Operation Peace for Galilee. The invasion, planned by Defence Minister Ariel Sharon and Chief of Staff Rafael Eitan, began on 6 June. The Israeli army advanced into Lebanon, quickly overrunning PLO positions in the south, and reaching the outskirts of Beirut, Lebanon's capital and the headquarters of the PLO, by 8 June.

On 9 and 10 June, the Israeli Air Force (IAF) attacked and destroyed the nineteen Syrian missile batteries and their radar sites in the Bekaa Valley. The Syrian Air Force counterattacked, and a massive air battle took place, involving around 200 planes. The IAF inflicted a heavy defeat on the Syrians – who suffered from the lack of ground support – destroying

THE ISRAELI INVASION OF LEBANON

Start date:	6 June 1982
End date:	21 August 1982
Days	77
Total death toll	4,428
Combatants	**Losses**
Israel	368
PLO forces	3,000
Syria	600

Source: Martin Gilbert

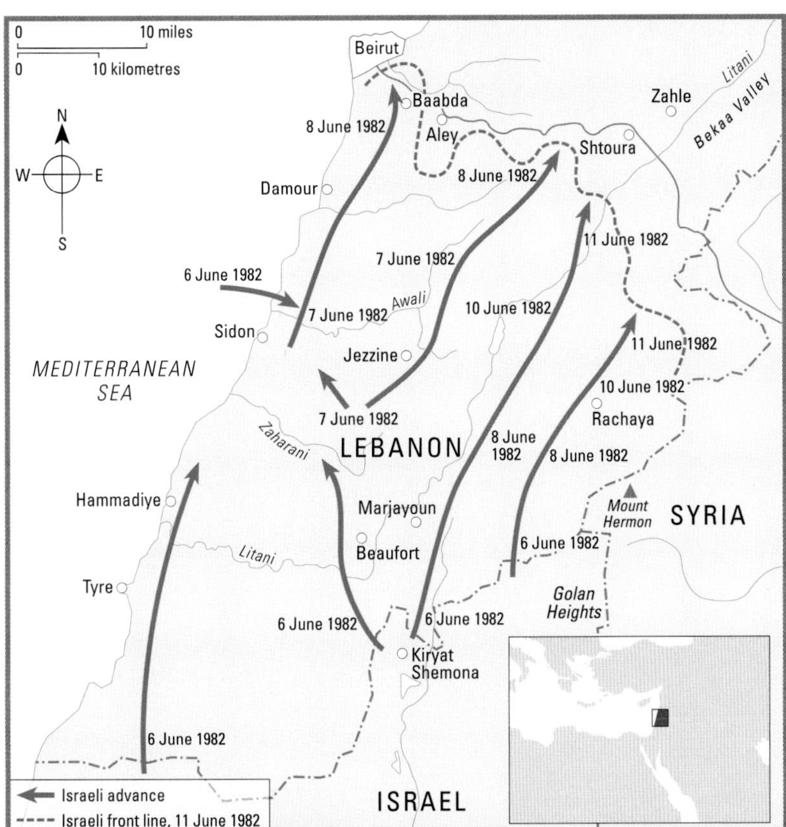

at least 87 of their aircraft, for the loss of around five Israeli planes. Under US pressure, Syria and Israel agreed a ceasefire on 11 June.

However, neither the USA nor the UN could persuade Israel to withdraw its forces from Lebanon. For two months, from 13 June to 12 August, the Israeli army besieged Beirut. The almost-continuous bombardment left 18,000 dead and 30,000 wounded,

During Operation Peace For Galilee, the Israeli forces advanced rapidly into Lebanon, overrunning PLO bases in towns like Sidon and Damour, before reaching Beirut just two days after crossing the border.

An Israeli tank on the streets of Beirut during the 1982 war. The IDF would sometimes strike at civilian targets if their intelligence informed them that PLO arms and munitions were hidden there.

A military convoy moves south across the Lebanese border as part of the Israeli withdrawal from Lebanon in 1985.

most of the casualties being civilians. Israel insisted that it would only end the siege when the 9,000-strong PLO force surrendered or left Lebanon, together with the Syrian forces stationed in Beirut. In August, US mediators succeeded in agreeing a ceasefire and the evacuation of PLO fighters from Lebanon. The evacuation began on 21 August. The PLO members moved to a number of different Arab countries, and the PLO leadership eventually settled into a new base in Tunisia.

Israel had succeeded in removing the PLO from Beirut, but had failed to neutralize the threat from

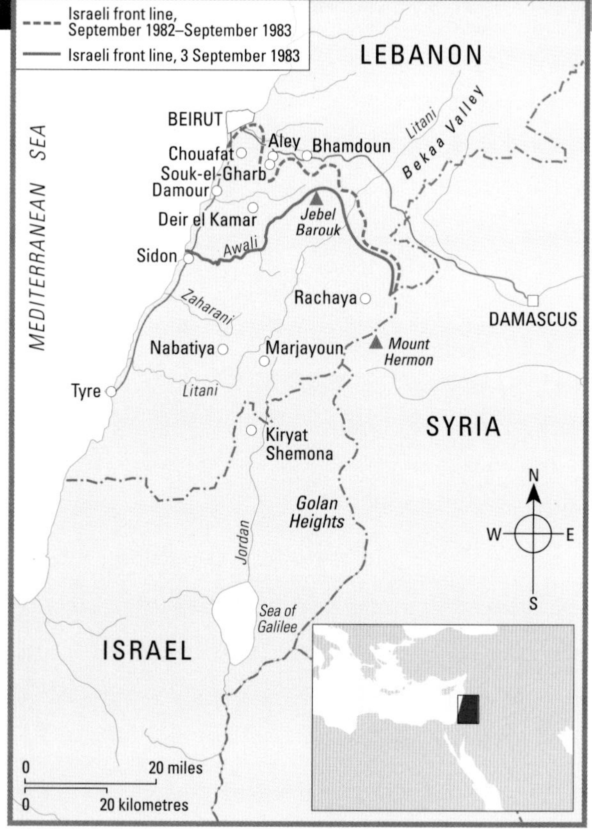

This map shows the Israeli troops in Lebanon pulling back to the Awali River on 3 September 1983. This was part of a staged withdrawal of Israel's military presence in Lebanon.

RESPONSIBILITY

'It was only my allies, the Lebanese, who pushed me into leaving Beirut. Only when they told me, "Please, Arafat, this is enough ... what are you waiting for, Abu Ammar? Look, we are facing death from shelling and bombing from the sea, the land, the air ..." that I began to feel responsible for killing their children.'

[Yasser Arafat]

Syria, which continued to control 35 per cent of Lebanon. The Maronite Lebanese government – although sympathetic to Israel – was too weak to prevent Syrian-backed Lebanese and Palestinian factions from continuing to attack Israel. A peace treaty between Lebanon and Israel that called for Syrian troop withdrawals was signed in May 1983, but was cancelled by the Lebanese in March 1984, under pressure from Syria.

Many in Israel began to see the Lebanese invasion as a costly mistake. Over 300 Israelis had died in the operation, and hostile elements had not been defeated. Furthermore, Israel's international standing had been damaged by the invasion, which many saw as an unjustifiable act of aggression. There were anti-war demonstrations in Israel demanding withdrawal. In September 1983, the Israeli Army withdrew as far as the Awali River. In June 1985, Israel withdrew from most of Lebanon, but maintained an eight-km-wide security zone along the border, policed by Israeli troops

An Israeli soldier in Sidon, southern Lebanon. By 1984, heavy casualty rates and a lack of clear goals led many Israelis to question the wisdom of the invasion.

Palestinians throw rocks at Israeli tanks and soldiers in Ramallah on the West Bank in May 1988. The PLO later claimed to have organized the intifada, but it is more likely to have been a spontaneous uprising.

and members of the Maronite South Lebanon Army. Israeli forces finally withdrew completely from Lebanon in May 2000.

THE INTIFADA By the mid-1980s, the plight of the Palestinians had aroused a great deal of sympathy around the world, but their situation had remained largely unchanged since 1967: Israel's occupation of the West Bank and Gaza Strip looked set to continue indefinitely, new Israeli settlements continued to be built, and PLO leaders – now based in Tunisia – seemed powerless to prevent this. The anger felt by many Palestinians at their apparently hopeless situation was ready to boil over.

On the afternoon of 8 December 1987, an Israeli vehicle crashed into a car filled with Arabs queuing at a road block in Gaza. Four of the Arabs were killed, and by nightfall a rumour had spread through Jabalya – the largest refugee camp in Gaza – that this 'accident' had been a revenge attack for a previous killing. This was the spark that set off a mass uprising which came to be known as the *intifada* (meaning 'shaking off' in

THE INTIFADA

Year	Palestinians killed by Israeli security forces	Palestinians killed by Israeli civilians	Israeli civilians killed by Palestinians	Israeli security forces personnel killed by Palestinians
9-31 Dec 1987	22	0	0	0
1988	290	20	8	4
1989	286	19	20	11
1990	126	19	17	5
1991	96	8	14	5
1992	136	2	19	15
1993 (to 13 Sep)	131	7	22	20
TOTAL	**1,087**	**75**	**100**	**60**

[Source: http://www.btselem.org/English/Statistics/Total_Casualties.asp]

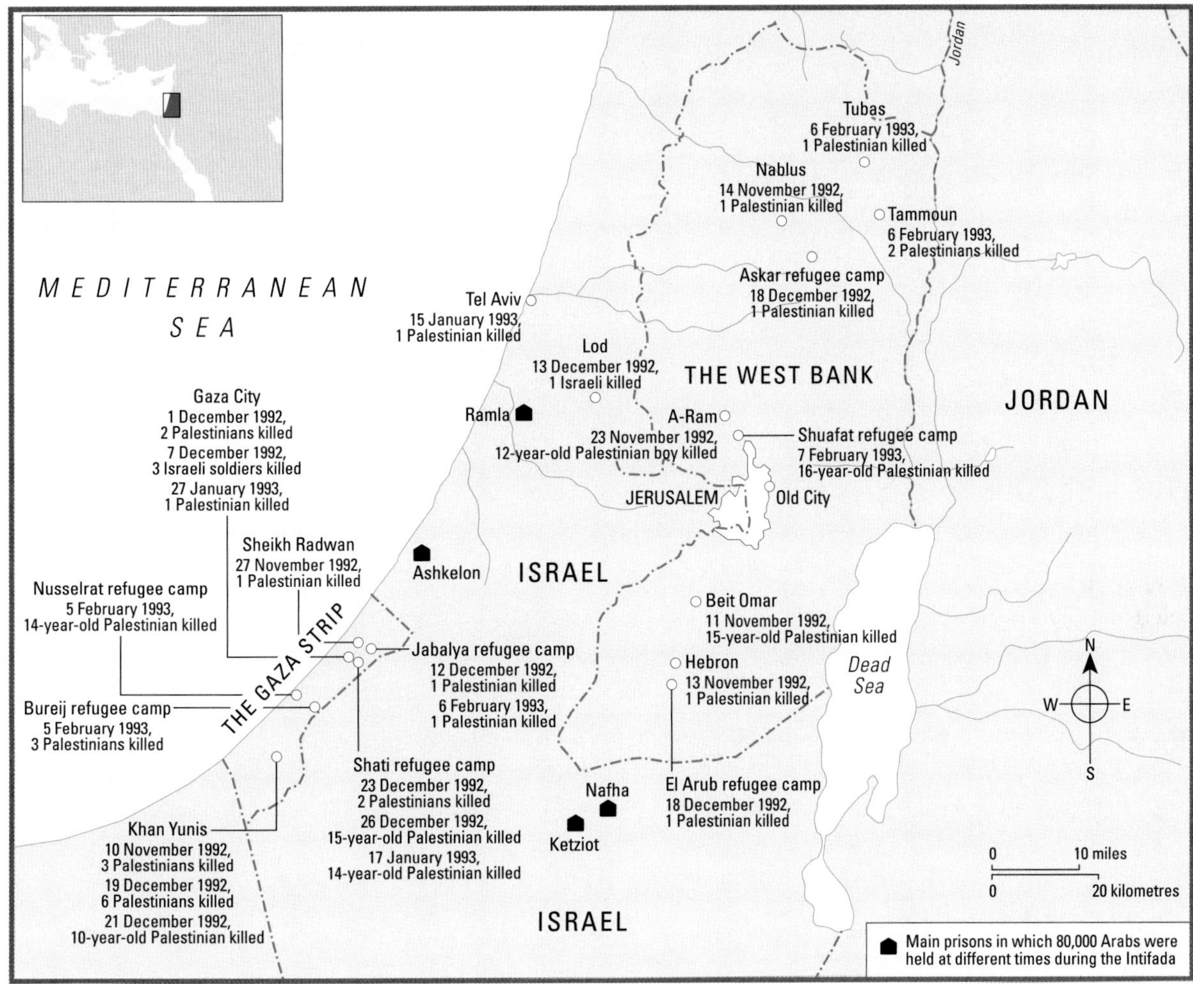

The locations of intifada-related killings reported between November 1992 and February 1993, when the violence intensified. As the intifada progressed, the weapons of the Palestinians changed from rocks to petrol bombs, grenades, guns and explosives.

Arabic). Riots in Jabalya soon spread to Gaza City, and Nablus on the West Bank, and even into Jerusalem.

Unlike previous riots, the Palestinians were not deterred by the arrival of Israeli troops and armoured personnel carriers, but continued demonstrating and throwing bottles and stones. Gaza City streets were barricaded with stones and burning tyres, fiercely defended by Palestinian youths. Israeli forces hit back, killing 22 Palestinians and injuring hundreds more by the end of December. By that time some order had been restored with the introduction of road blocks, body searches and identity cards, but it was clear that the uprising had not been defeated.

While this first phase of the intifada was spontaneous, the next phase was planned. It was organized by different PLO groups – Fatah, the PFLP, the DFLP and the PPP – under the overall control of the United National Leadership of the Uprising (UNLU). Thousands of Palestinians were involved, including many who had no previous experience of resistance, such as women and children. The intifada involved different forms of resistance, including both violence and civil disobedience. As well as stone-throwing and the buiding of barricades, there were demonstrations, strikes, boycotts of Israeli products, and mass refusal to pay taxes.

Israel tried to smash the intifada with brute force. Between 1987 and 1991, Israeli forces killed 820 Palestinians and imprisoned some ten thousand others. By 1990, most UNLU leaders had been either killed or arrested, and the intifada had begun to run out of momentum, although it continued until September 1993.

The intifada failed in its main aim of bringing the Israeli occupation to an end. However, it succeeded in refocusing international attention on the Palestinian liberation struggle. It also shifted political power away from the PLO leadership in Tunisia (who had not started the uprising, nor played a significant part in running it) towards Palestinian groups based in the occupied territories.

THE GULF WAR On 2 August 1990, Iraq invaded Kuwait, a small oil-rich country on its southern border. This act of aggression was widely condemned worldwide. A coalition of countries, led by the USA, was formed, threatening to take military action against Iraq unless it withdrew. The coalition included a number of Arab countries, including Saudi Arabia and Egypt. A large US military force began gathering in the Persian Gulf.

Iraq's leader, Saddam Hussein, cunningly attempted to split the coalition by linking Iraq's action to Israel's occupation of the West Bank and Gaza. He declared that he would only withdraw from Kuwait after Israel withdrew from the territories it had seized. In these circumstances, the PLO leadership felt they had no choice but to support Iraq. Arafat and Hussein released a joint statement saying they were united in their struggle against Israeli occupation and American intervention in the Gulf. Despite this provocation, the Arab states stood firm with the coalition, and Saudi Arabia and other Gulf states threw out a number of Palestinian activists. The PLO lost some international support for its stance. Palestinians, however, were inspired by Saddam Hussein's boast, and many saw him as a possible liberator of their people.

On 16 January 1991, the UN-imposed deadline for Iraqi withdrawal from Kuwait expired, and the coalition forces unleashed Operation Desert Storm – the removal of Iraqi forces from Kuwait by force. The occupation of Kuwait lasted just seven months before the coalition drove the invaders out. During the fighting, Israeli citizens were issued with gas masks because of the danger from Iraqi chemical weapons.

The remains of an Iraqi Scud, shot down by a Patriot missile near Riyadh, Saudi Arabia. A total of 46 Scuds were fired at Saudi Arabia during the Gulf War, while 39 of these missiles were fired at Israel.

US fighter jets flying over burning Kuwait oilfields during the Gulf War. Iraqi soldiers set fire to many of the oil wells in late February 1991.

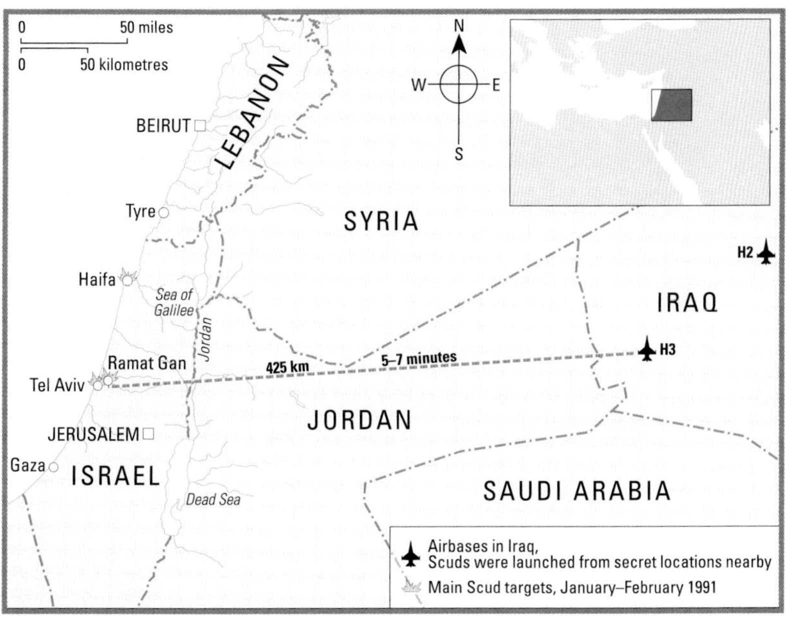

The map shows the main Israeli targets of Iraq's Scud missile campaign in January and February 1991 and the launch sites in western Iraq. Many Scuds were shot down by US-supplied Patriot missiles.

POPULAR RIOT

'It was clear that this uprising [the 1987-1993 intifada] *was on a new scale, and that these people were not "terrorists", but the population itself. There was a real threat that they might overwhelm the Israeli soldiers who were there in very small numbers. If they did, this would leave the soldiers with only two possibilities: to run away, or to shoot. … We were not technically prepared to deal with a violent popular riot on this scale.'*

[Ehud Barak, Israeli Deputy Chief of Staff]

Parts of the occupied territories were placed under curfew in case the war sparked unrest in the Palestinian community.

On 17 January, Iraq launched eight Scud missiles into Israel, hitting parts of Tel Aviv and Haifa. Saddam Hussein's tactic was to try to draw Israel into the conflict, knowing that Arab countries would find it hard – if not impossible – to fight alongside Israel against another Arab state. The US government gave Israel Patriot surface-to-air missiles to counter the Scuds, and urged Israel not to respond to the attack. The Scud attacks increased popular Palestinian support for Saddam, the first Arab leader to match words with deeds, and attack Israel's heartland. Israel suffered further Scud strikes, but did not hit back, and it won a lot of international sympathy for its restraint.

CHAPTER 6: THE PEACE PROCESS

When he became prime minister in 1988, Yitzhak Shamir had a reputation as a hardliner, having opposed the 1979 peace treaty with Egypt. Yet he was prepared to let the Israeli government take part in the 1991 Madrid peace talks.

By November 1988, the intifada was almost a year old, yet the Palestinians seemed no further along the road towards independence. Palestinian activists in the occupied territories asked the PLO leadership in Tunisia to give a clearer political framework to their struggle. In response to this, the PLO made a number of key decisions: it agreed to recognize the state of Israel; it declared an independent Palestinian state in the West Bank and the Gaza Strip; and it renounced terrorism.

Israel failed to respond to this gesture. To Israel, the PLO remained a terrorist organization with which it refused to negotiate. However, two events in 1991 served to help the cause of peace. Firstly, with the collapse of the Soviet Union, Arab states such as Syria and Egypt lost a key supporter, and so they had to be more accommodating in their dealings with Israel's most powerful ally, the USA. Secondly, following the Gulf War, the USA felt grateful for the support of the Arab states, and in return was willing to promote a settlement to the Arab-Israeli conflict, if necessary by putting pressure on Israel.

THE MADRID CONFERENCE In October 1991, the USA organized a peace conference in Madrid, Spain, with the aim of resolving the long-running conflict. Israel, Syria, Lebanon, Jordan and the Palestinians were invited. It was the first time Israel had entered into direct negotiations with any of these states. Israeli prime minister Yitzhak Shamir insisted that the PLO must be left out of the talks, and the Palestinians were represented by a delegation from the occupied territories. However, the delegation was guided by PLO leaders staying in nearby hotels.

The talks consisted of both bilateral negotiations between Israel and each Arab state, and multilateral negotiations dealing with issues concerning the whole Middle East, such as water, arms control, economic development and refugees. The discussions which began in Madrid continued over the next three years in different places around the world. The Israel-Jordan talks resulted in the signing of a peace treaty between the two states in October 1994.

Despite numerous meetings between the Israeli and Palestinian delegations at Madrid, little progress was made. Further talks were held in Washington in mid-1992 following the election of a new Israeli government headed by Yitzhak Rabin. However, by

ENOUGH

'We who have come from a land where parents bury their children, we who have fought against you, the Palestinians, say to you today in a loud and clear voice, enough of bloodshed and tears. Enough.'

[Yitzhak Rabin, Israeli PM, before the signing of the Oslo Accords, 13 September 1993]

The agreed boundary between Israel and Jordan following the 1994 peace treaty. The treaty confirmed that each country could obtain their fair share of water from the Jordan River.

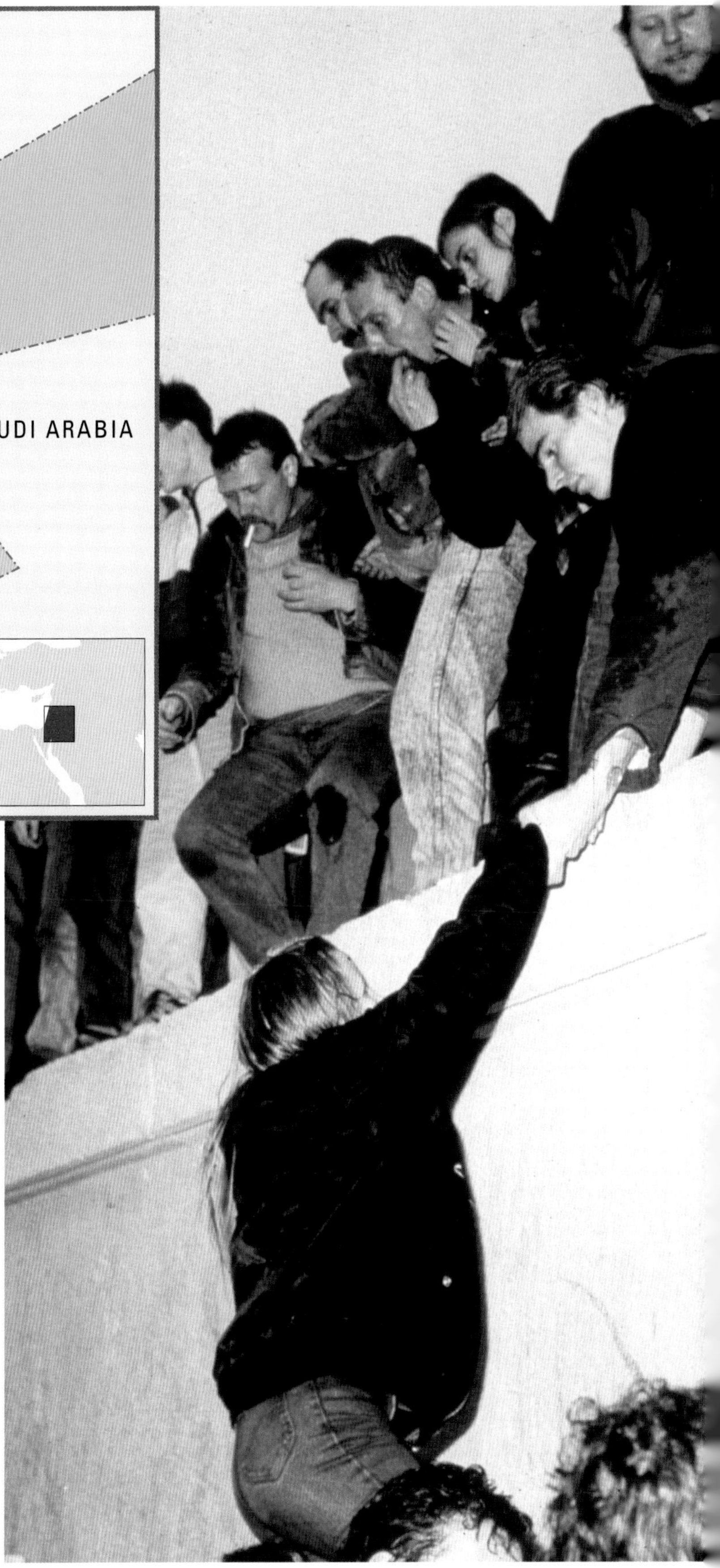

The fall of the Berlin Wall on 9 November 1989 (pictured here) and the end of the Cold War marked the beginning of a new drive towards peace in the Middle East as former Cold War rivals, Russia and the USA, placed pressure on Israel and the Arab nations to negotiate.

December these talks had also become bogged down. The slow pace of negotiations made people in the occupied territories impatient, and this led to renewed violence. Chiefly responsible for this new wave of terrorism were Islamist (strict Islamic) groups such as Hamas and Islamic Jihad, who had started to offer Palestinians a popular and radical alternative to the secular (non-religious) PLO.

THE OSLO ACCORDS In mid-1992, a series of secret, informal talks began in Oslo, Norway,

Yitzhak Rabin (left) shakes hands with Yasser Arafat at the signing ceremony in September 1993 of the Oslo Accords at the White House, Washington DC. President Bill Clinton looks on.

PALESTINIANS AND ISRAELIS KILLED IN ISRAEL AND THE OCCUPIED TERRITORIES (14 SEPTEMBER 1993–28 SEPTEMBER 2000)

Year	Palestinians killed by Israeli security forces	Palestinians killed by Israeli civilians	Israeli civilians killed by Palestinians	Israeli security forces personnel killed by Palestinians
1993	165	15	36	25
1994	113	39	58	16
1995	42	3	16	30
1996	69	5	41	34
1997	18	3	29	0
1998	21	7	9	3
1999	9	0	2	2
2000	14	0	2	1
TOTAL	**451**	**72**	**193**	**111**

[Source: B'tselem, the Israeli Information Center for Human Rights in the Occupied Territories]

The new distribution of territory as agreed in the Oslo Accords. Under this interim agreement, the West Bank was divided into three areas: Area A was placed under full Palestinian control; Area B was placed under joint Palestinian-Israeli control; and Area C remained under full Israeli control.

between two Israeli academics and a PLO delegation. The talks had no official status, although they were conducted with the knowledge and approval of Yossi Beilin, Israel's deputy prime minister. During these talks, the PLO delegation adopted a surprisingly flexible position, in contrast to their attitude at the official talks in Washington. This attitude, plus Rabin's realization that the real terrorist threat was now coming from the Islamist groups and not the PLO, persuaded him to reverse Israel's refusal to negotiate with the PLO. Soon the Israeli delegation was upgraded to include senior government officials.

Together they worked out a 'Declaration of Principles', which has become the foundation of peace negotiations between Israel and the Palestinians ever since. The Declaration of Principles stated that Israel and the PLO recognized each other's legitimacy, and that Israel would start to withdraw from the occupied territories over a five-year period, beginning with the Gaza Strip and Jericho. A Palestinian Authority (PA) was formed from the PLO with limited powers of self-rule in the occupied territories.

The document that resulted from these talks, known as the Oslo Accords, was signed at a Washington ceremony hosted by US president Bill Clinton on 13 September 1993. During the ceremony, Yasser Arafat, leader of the PLO, and Yitzhak Rabin, Israeli prime minister, shook hands.

In May 1994, Israel and the PLO signed the Gaza-Jericho agreement in Cairo, which led to the establishment of the PA. That month, Israeli forces withdrew from Jericho and most of the Gaza Strip. In November, Rabin handed new powers to the PA, including responsibility for taxation, health, transport and social services. The following October, Israeli

Following the signing of the Gaza-Jericho agreement in May 1994, Israeli troops hand over control of their Gaza City base to the Palestinian Authority.

The funeral of Yitzhak Rabin. The Israeli prime minister was a joint winner of the 1994 Nobel Peace Prize for his efforts at promoting peace with the Palestinians. But he was also hated by right-wing Israelis who blamed him for giving away too much.

forces began a phased withdrawal from most of the West Bank. In January 1996, Yasser Arafat was elected president of the PA.

THE PEACE PROCESS STALLS

Despite these positive developments, not everyone welcomed the peace process. Militant groups like Hamas were not prepared to recognize Israel under any circumstances, and many ordinary Palestinians were worried that the Oslo Accords did not guarantee the ultimate setting-up of a Palestinian state. On the Israeli side, many were concerned that the lands they had fought for would be returned to the Palestinians with no real promise of security in return.

The carrying out of the Oslo Accords took place against a background of increasing terrorist violence against Israel from Hamas, Islamic Jihad, and a Lebanese-based Shi'ite group called Hezbollah. As more Israelis were killed, popular opinion shifted towards a more hardline approach. Yitzhak Rabin was assassinated in November 1995 by an Israeli extremist opposed to the peace process. In May 1996, a conservative government came to power in Israel, headed by Benjamin Netanyahu, an opponent of the Oslo Accords. Although Netanyahu claimed to support the peace process, his government agreed to expansion of Israeli settlements in the occupied territories, which went against the spirit of the agreement.

The USA put pressure on the Israelis to put a stop to settlement building, and to continue with the troop withdrawals. In October 1998, Netanyahu and Arafat signed a new agreement in Washington, known as the Wye Memorandum. Israel agreed to withdraw from an additional 13 per cent of the West Bank in return for a pledge from the Palestinians to crack down on terrorism.

CAMP DAVID II In July 2000, President Clinton invited the new Israeli prime minister Ehud Barak and Yasser Arafat to Camp David to negotiate the final status of the occupied territories and Jerusalem. By this time, Israeli withdrawals had left 40 per cent of the West Bank and 65 per cent of the Gaza Strip under the full or partial control of the PA. Barak insisted that East Jerusalem plus 80 per cent of the land containing the Jewish settlements on the West Bank would remain part of Israel; the rest could be

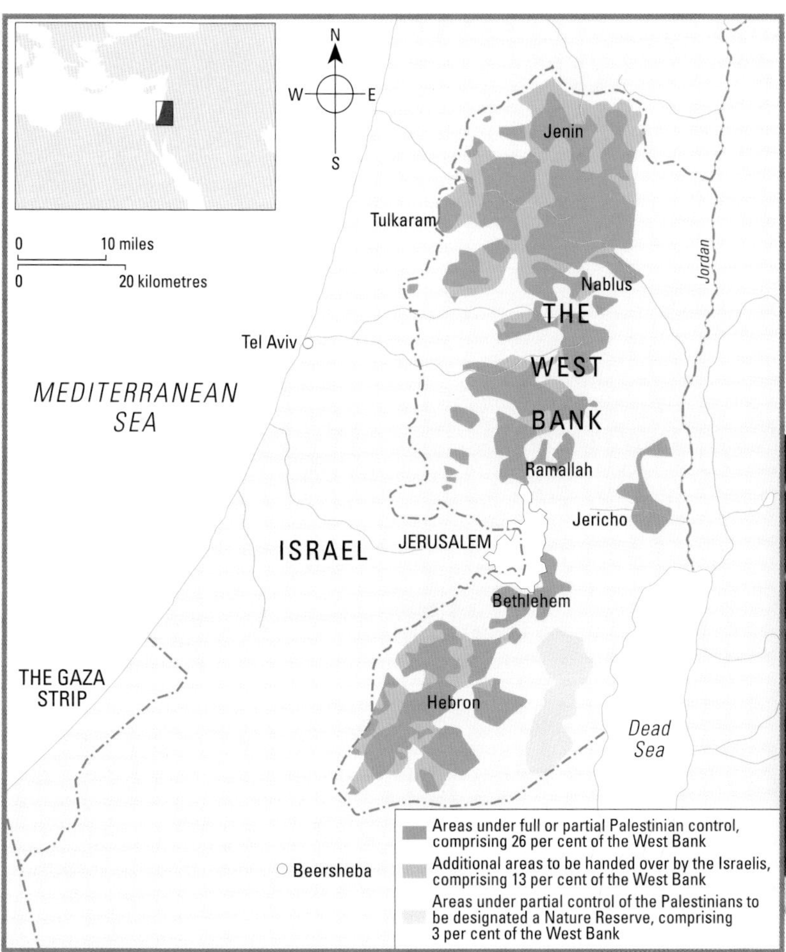

A map showing the agreed reallocations of territory under the Wye Memorandum of November 1998. An additional 12 per cent of the West Bank would be transferred from Area C to Area B, and 1 per cent would move from Area C to Area A.

handed over to the PA. This was more than any Israeli leader had previously offered. Arafat, however, insisted on Israeli withdrawal from the vast majority of the occupied territories, including East Jerusalem. No agreement could be reached, yet Barak was nevertheless criticized in Israel for having offered too much.

Benjamin Netanyahu (left) and Yasser Arafat meet with President Clinton at the White House on 15 October 1998. The Wye Memorandum was signed eight days later.

ISRAELI SETTLER POPULATION GROWTH IN THE WEST BANK AND GAZA STRIP: 1972-2001

Year	West Bank (not including East Jerusalem)	Gaza Strip	Total
1972	800	700	**1,500**
1983	22,800	900	**23,700**
1989	69,800	3,000	**72,800**
1992	101,100	4,300	**105,400**
1995	133,200	5,300	**138,500**
1998	161,300	6,100	**167,400**
2001	201,800	6,500	**208,300**

[Source: Foundation for Middle East Peace]

CHAPTER 7: THE SECOND INTIFADA AND THE ROAD MAP

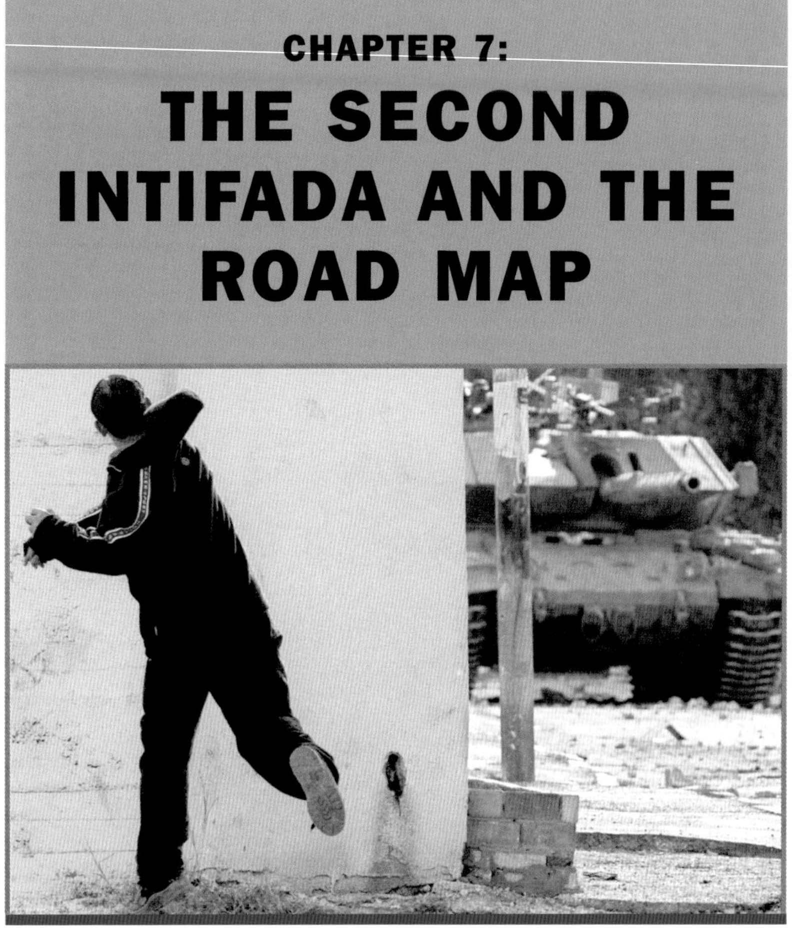

A Palestinian rioter hurls stones at a tank in a West Bank town during the second popular rising, or intifada.

The frustration felt by many Palestinians at the slow progress of the peace process, combined with continuing social and economic hardship, led to renewed violence in the occupied territories in late 2000. The spark for this second intifada came on 28 September when Ariel Sharon, leader of Likud, Israel's most powerful right-wing party, visited Temple Mount, the site of not only the al-Aqsa mosque, a holy Muslim shrine in Jerusalem, but also the Biblical First and Second Temples, sacred to Jews and important to Christians. Sharon was accompanied by around one thousand armed riot police, and some party colleagues. His visit caused widespread protests among Palestinians in Jerusalem, and during these demonstrations Israeli police shot dead six unarmed protestors. Outrage at these killings led to over a month of rioting in the West Bank and Gaza Strip.

The second intifada was led by Islamists and local leaders of Fatah, the largest and most radical faction of the PLO. They demanded total Israeli withdrawal from the occupied territories, removal of all Jewish settlements, the establishment of a sovereign state of Palestine with its capital in Jerusalem, and the right of return of all Palestinian refugees. They were critical of PLO leader Yasser Arafat for offering the Israelis too much in peace negotiations; they also criticized the PA for providing weak leadership and poor services.

Another feature of the second intifada was a rise in suicide bombings and other terrorist attacks inside Israel. These had caused over 160 civilian deaths by April 2002. The organizations which carried out these attacks – Hamas, Islamic Jihad and the al-Aqsa Martyrs Brigade, a militant wing of Fatah – had a more extreme aim: the complete destruction of Israel.

Israel called upon the PA to crack down on the rioters and terrorists of the second uprising, and the PA security forces did occasionally carry out mass arrests of Islamists and members of terrorist organizations. However, the violence continued, and so Israel decided to send its own armed forces into the occupied territories in 2001 to attack the rioters and terrorist bases directly.

In December 2001, Yasser Arafat himself became a target of Israeli anger for his failure to crack down on, and – the Israeli government claimed – his unspoken support for, the terrorists. For the next five months, the PLO leader became a virtual prisoner as Israeli tanks surrounded his presidential compound in the West Bank town

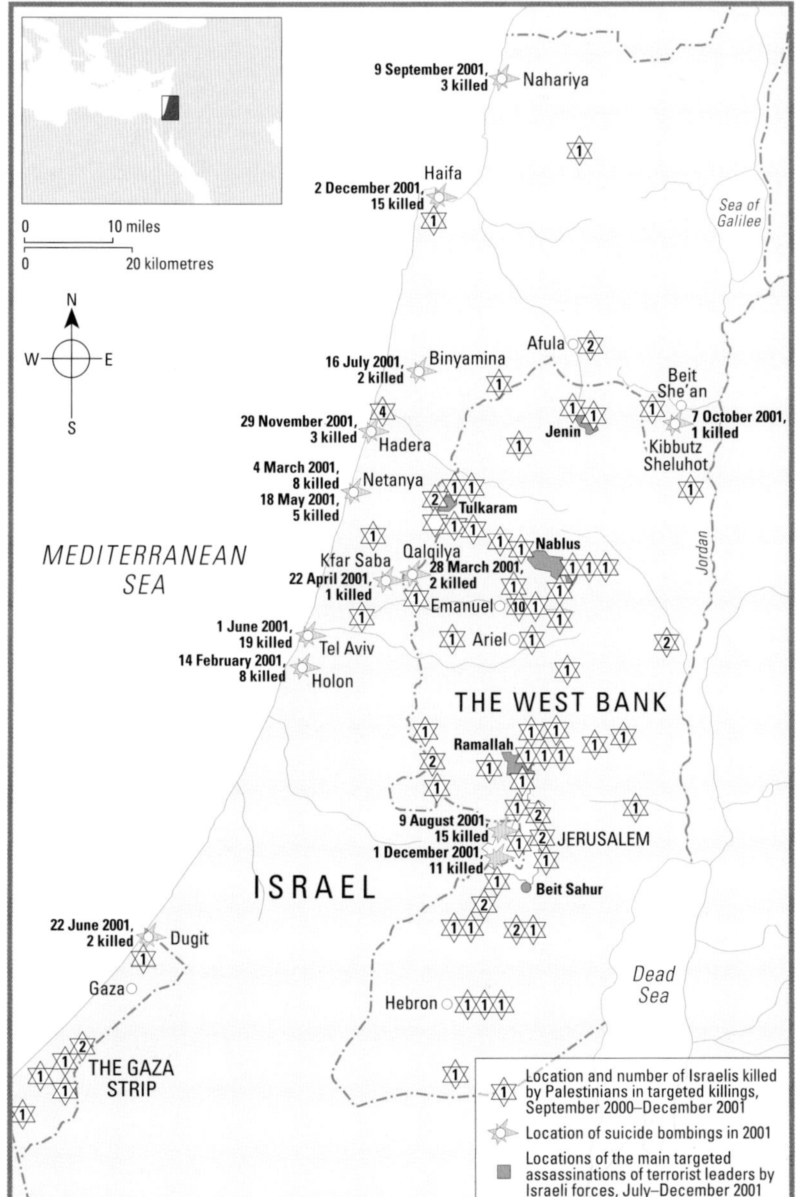

Three bombs carried by two suicide bombers explode in Jerusalem on 1 December 2001, killing at least eight people.

The map shows the locations of terrorist attacks on Israelis, and assassinations of terrorist leaders by Israel, during 2000 and 2001. As attacks on troops and civilians mounted, the Israelis began to target people who were directing the violence.

THE SECOND INTIFADA

(figures apply to the period 29 September 2000–1 June 2003)

Year	Palestinians killed by Israeli security forces	Palestinians killed by Israeli civilians	Israeli civilians killed by Palestinians	Israeli security forces personnel killed by Palestinians
2000	272	6	18	19
2001	454	7	65	21
2002	990	13	88	101
to 1 June 2003	305	6	16	18
TOTAL	**2,021**	**32**	**187**	**159**

[Source: B'tselem, the Israeli Information Center for Human Rights in the Occupied Territories]

of Ramallah. This had the effect of increasing support for Arafat among Palestinian militants.

Between April and June 2002, in response to a wave of suicide bombings, Israeli forces invaded and reoccupied the West Bank towns of Ramallah, Bethlehem, Jenin, Tulkaram, Qalqilya, Nablus and Hebron. PA buildings and suspected terrorist bases were shelled, weapons were confiscated, house-to-house searches were conducted, arrests were made and strict curfews were imposed. The Palestinians claimed the Israelis massacred civilians in Jenin. Israel insisted it had merely responded to organized armed resistance. The UN Security Council demanded that Israel withdraw from the reoccupied West Bank towns without delay.

THE ROAD MAP TO PEACE In April 2003, a new peace plan, known as the 'road map to peace', was published. Drawn up by the UN, USA,

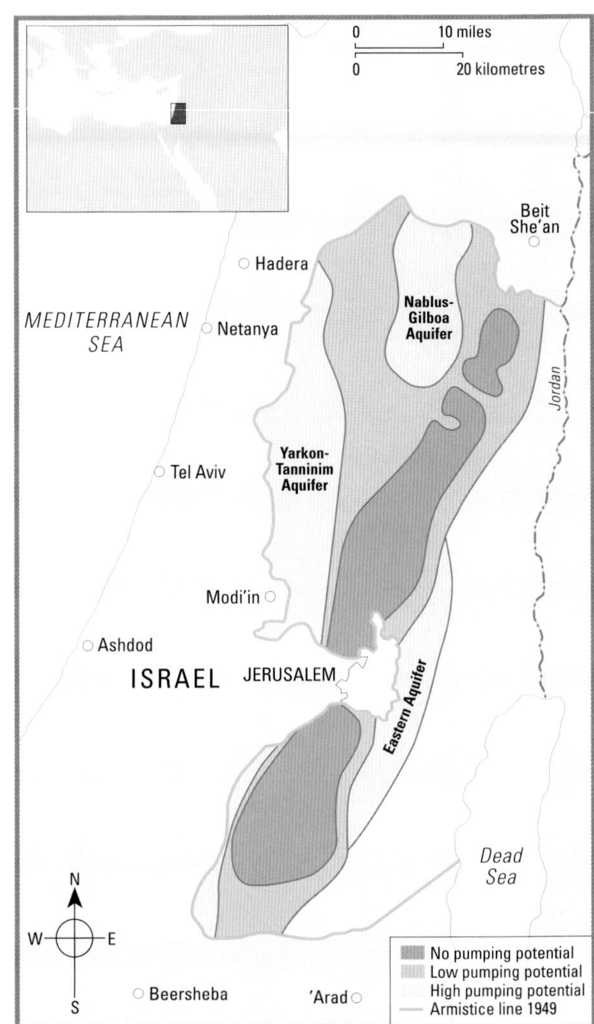

Water resources on the West Bank. Access to water supplies for Palestinians and Israelis remains an important issue which will need to be resolved before a lasting peace can be achieved.

An Israeli tank, looking for Palestinian militants, blocks access to a refugee camp in Jenin, June 2002.

PEACE

'My vision is two states, living side by side in peace and security.... I call on the Palestinian people to elect new leaders, leaders not compromised by terror. I call upon them to build a practicing democracy, based on tolerance and liberty. If the Palestinian people actively pursue these goals, America and the world will actively support their efforts.'

[Speech by President George W. Bush, June 2002]

An Israeli soldier passes a sign protesting at the building of the security fence through a Palestinian village on the West Bank.

European Union and Russia, with Israeli and Palestinian consultation, the plan sought a two-state solution to the conflict: setting up an independent Palestinian state in the occupied territories, alongside Israel. The plan set out to achieve this in three stages by 2005.

The first stage required the following: the end of Palestinian violence; the reform of Palestinian political institutions (which had been accused of corruption, and tacit support of terrorism); the dismantling of all Israeli settlements in the occupied territories constructed since March 2001; progressive Israeli withdrawal from designated areas of the occupied territories. Stage two would involve the creation of an independent Palestinian state. There would also be discussions at this stage on crucial issues such as the sharing of water resources and economic development. At stage three, the parties would reach agreement on final borders, the status of Jerusalem, the return of Palestinian refugees, and Israeli settlements – leading to a permanent end to the conflict.

Before the plan's publication, Yasser Arafat came under increasing pressure to step down as leader of the PA. His failure to clamp down on terrorism had discredited him in the eyes of many in the international community – although he remained popular with Palestinians. In March 2003, Yasser Arafat appointed a prime minister of the PA. He was Mahmoud Abbas, a strong believer in the peace process, to whom Arafat surrendered many of his powers.

There was progress on the plan in June 2003, when a ceasefire was declared by the terrorist groups, and Israel began to withdraw its forces from the occupied territories and release some Palestinian prisoners. However, any optimism quickly receded when terrorist attacks recommenced in August, and Israeli troops halted their withdrawals and began a campaign of assassinations of top terrorist leaders. On 6 September,

Thirteen kilometres of the security fence will be in the form of a concrete wall (shown here being built) around the town of Qalqilya, and also separating parts of Jerusalem from adjacent Palestinian areas.

Mahmoud Abbas resigned after emerging the loser in a power struggle with Arafat, and having failed to control Palestinian violence. Arafat appointed Ahmed Qureia as his replacement. As suicide bombings continued, Israel vowed to exile – or possibly assassinate – Yasser Arafat.

THE FUTURE While the international community continues to try to promote peace in the region, recent developments on the ground are making the road map, or any similar effort at achieving a two-state solution to the conflict, more and more unlikely. Since April 2003, Israel has begun constructing a 'security fence' around the Palestinian-controlled territories as a means of protecting itself and ending terrorist attacks. There are fears that the six-metre high fence, topped with barbed wire and lined with guard towers, will make any new Palestinian state little more than a reservation, without access to the resources it needs to form a viable, independent nation.

On the Israeli side of the fence, new houses are being built for Jewish settlements in the West Bank. New roads, telecommunications, electricity and water supplies are binding the settlements ever more closely to the state of Israel. The Israeli people increasingly see these settlements as permanent parts of their country, which cannot be given away during peace talks. Seeing this, increasing numbers of Palestinians despair of ever achieving an independent state of Palestine. They are starting to believe that their only choice is to accept Israel's control of their land and to demand equal rights.

New homes are built at the Jewish West Bank settlement of Ariel in June 2003, despite international pressure on Israel to stop expanding its settlements.

This one-state solution might not be welcomed by Jewish Israelis, because within a few years, such a state would lose its Jewish majority. There are currently 5.4 million Jews and 4.93 million Arabs in Israel and the occupied territories. It is estimated that by 2020 – due to the higher birth rate of Arabs compared to Jews – there will be 6.69 million Jews and 8.49 million Arabs. With Arabs demanding equal rights and 'one citizen one vote', there may well be pressure on Israel to abandon its Jewish identity. Israel's Jewish community would of course stubbornly resist any such move.

The current state of the Arab-Israeli conflict is marked by periodic moves towards peace followed by sudden outbreaks of

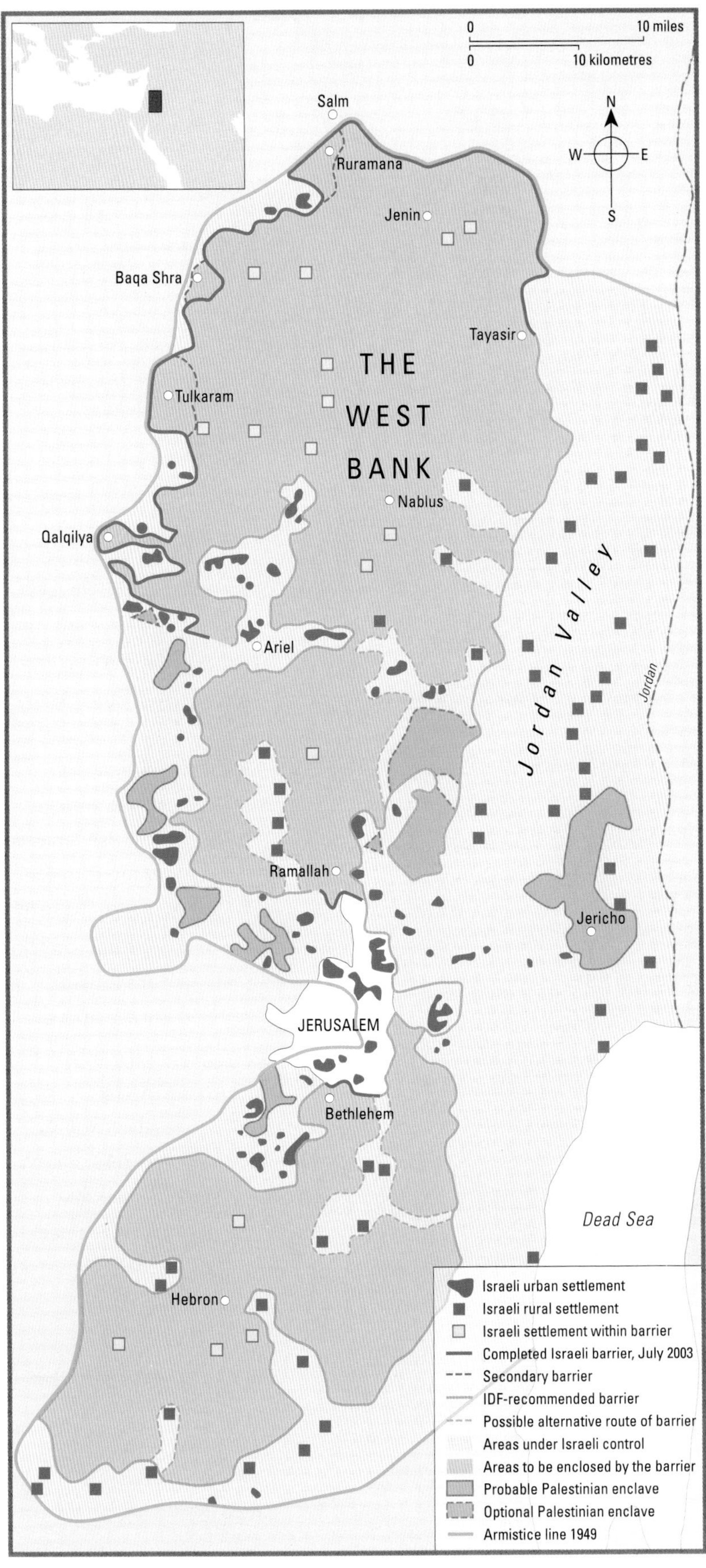

FEAR OF WAR

'As one who participated in all the wars of the state of Israel, I saw the horror of wars. I saw the fear of wars. I saw my best friends being killed in battles. I was seriously injured twice … I believe I understand the importance of peace, not more but not less than many of the politicians who speak about peace, but never had this experience.'

[Israeli prime minister Ariel Sharon, July 2003]

A map showing the projected route of the security fence in the West Bank. In October 2003, the UN passed a resolution saying the barrier was 'in contradiction to international law'. Despite this, Israeli public opinion is strongly in favour of the fence.

renewed violence, and there seems little prospect of an immediate resolution. However, the region has provided some surprising examples of progress towards peace, such as the treaties between Israel and Egypt in 1979 and Israel and Jordan in 1994. There is always a chance – through international pressure and enlightened leadership – that the parties currently locked in battle might discover a way of sharing the land and resources they are now fighting over, and bring the conflict which began over a century ago to an end.

PROFILES OF MILITARY AND POLITICAL LEADERS

ABBAS, MAHMOUD (1935-)
Also known as Abu Mazen, Abbas was born in Safad, Palestine. He was a founding member of Fatah and a member of the PLO Executive Committee since 1968. He has headed the PLO Department for National and International Relations since 1980. Abbas is considered a moderate, and is strongly in favour of a peaceful settlement with Israel. He coordinated negotiations during the Madrid conference and the Oslo Accords. Although popular in the international community, Abbas lacks support among ordinary Palestinians. He was prime minister of the PA for just four months in 2003, before being replaced.

ALLON, YIGAL (1918-1980)
An Israeli military commander and politician, Allon was born in Galilee. He was a co-founder in 1941 of the Palmah, a highly trained Zionist commando unit, becoming its commander in 1945. During the 1947-9 War, he commanded the southern front, driving invading Arab armies from Israel. In 1954 he was elected to the Knesset, and from 1961 to 1968 served as Minister of Labour. He became deputy prime minister in 1968, and then Minister of Education and Culture. From 1974 to 1977, he was Foreign Minister.

ARAFAT, YASSER (1929-)
The future leader of the PLO was born in Gaza. In 1958, he met fellow Palestinian activist Abu Jihad. He then moved to Jerusalem where he founded Fatah in 1959. Arafat was elected chairman of the PLO in 1969. After the PLO's clash with Jordan in 1971, he moved to Lebanon and remained there until besieged by the Israeli army in 1982, after which he moved to Tunisia. During the 1970s and 1980s, Arafat gradually changed the PLO from a terrorist group into an organization resembling a government-in-exile, committed to seeking a peaceful settlement with Israel. In 1993 he signed the Oslo Accords with Israel, returning to the occupied territories in 1994, and in 1996 he was elected president of the PA. Since then he has increasingly been seen by Israel and the USA as an obstacle to peace because of his refusal to condemn Palestinian militants. He was placed under house arrest between December 2001 and April 2002, and in 2003 the Israeli government threatened him with permanent exile. Yet he remains a popular figure among Palestinians.

ASAD, HAFIZ (1930-2000)
Asad was born at Qardaha in Syria. In 1964 he entered the Syrian government, and rose to become leader of a faction of the ruling Ba'ath Party. That faction siezed power in 1970, and Asad became President of Syria, a post he held until his death.

ASHWARI, HANAN (1946-)
A Palestinian academic and politician who became official spokeswoman for the Palestinian delegation during the peace conferences of 1991 to 1993. She promoted a moderate and reasonable image of the Palestinian cause to the West. Ashwari was elected as an independent to the Palestinian Legislative Council in 1996.

BAKER, JAMES (1930-)
As US Secretary of State from 1989 to 1992, Baker worked hard at promoting a peaceful settlement to the conflict. In March 1991, he became the first American Secretary of State to meet with a Palestinian delegation. His attempts at setting up a general Middle East peace conference were impeded by Israel's insistence that it would only conduct bilateral talks with individual Arab states.

BALFOUR, ARTHUR JAMES (1848-1930)
As British foreign secretary from 1916 to 1919, Balfour proclaimed British support for the setting up of a Jewish state in Palestine in the famous Balfour Declaration of 1917. Balfour had previously served as prime minister from 1902 to 1905.

BARAK, EHUD (1942-)
Born in Kibbutz Mishmar Hasharon, Barak joined the IDF in 1959 and served in various positions of command in the 1967, 1973 and 1982 wars. In April 1991 he was appointed Chief of the General Staff and was promoted to Lieutenant General, the highest rank in the Israeli military. Barak oversaw the IDF's redeployment in Gaza and Jericho following the May 1994 agreement, and he played a major role in the peace treaty with Jordan. Elected as a member of the Labor Party to the Knesset in 1996, he served as prime minister and minister of defence from May 1999 to February 2001.

BEGIN, MENACHEM (1913-1992)
A passionate Zionist from an early age, Begin was born in Brest-Litovsk (in present-day Belarus). In the 1930s he lived in eastern Europe, fighting on behalf of Jews, and arranging for their immigration to Palestine. In the

1940s he joined the Jewish terrorist organization Irgun, organizing various attacks on the British. From 1948, Begin was a right-wing opposition party leader in the Knesset, and in 1977 he was elected prime minister. He helped initiate the peace process with Egypt which led to the 1979 Israel-Egypt Peace Treaty. Begin's government launched Operation Peace for Galilee, Israel's invastion of Lebanon, in 1982.

BEN-GURION, DAVID (1886-1973)
Israel's first prime minister, Ben-Gurion was born in Plonsk, Poland, and was a leader of a Zionist youth group in his teens. He moved to Palestine in 1906 and helped set up the first kibbutz (an agricultural workers' commune). In 1935 he was elected chairman of the World Zionist Organization, and was a prominent leader in the struggle to establish the state of Israel. In May 1948 he became prime minister and defence minister of the new state, and oversaw the establishment of Israel's institutions, the development of new towns, and the settlement of outlying areas. He also led Israel during the 1956 Suez War, finally resigning as prime minister in 1963.

BUSH, GEORGE HERBERT WALKER (1924-)
As president of the USA from 1989 to 1993, George Bush organized a coalition of Western and Arab states which combined to defeat Saddam Hussein's Iraq in the 1991 Gulf War. Out of gratitude for Arab support in the Gulf War, Bush placed pressure on Israel to participate in a general Middle East peace conference.

BUSH, GEORGE WALKER (1946-)
The 43rd president of the USA was elected in 2000. Following the 11 September terrorist attacks on the USA, Bush declared war on terrorism. Islamist terror groups such as Al Qaeda, Hezbollah and Hamas – and the countries which supported them – became targets in this new kind of war. In April 2003, Bush threw his weight behind a new attempt to end the Arab-Israeli conflict, authorizing the publication of the 'road map to peace'.

CARTER, JIMMY (1924-)
As president of the USA from 1977 to 1981, Carter was instrumental in mediating the Egypt-Israel Peace Treaty of 1979. Although a committed supporter of Israel, Carter believed that the Palestinians should have a homeland and be compensated for the losses they had suffered. He invited Begin and Sadat to the presidential lodge at Camp David for a conference which lasted from 4 to 17 September 1978, a meeting which led to the peace treaty, signed the following year.

CLINTON, BILL (1946-)
As US president from 1993 to 2001, Bill Clinton worked tirelessly to promote peace in the Middle East. In 1993 he hosted the signing of the Declaration of Principles on the White House lawn in Washington. The Clinton administration encouraged bilateral talks between Israel and Jordan that led to the signing of the July 1994 Washington Declaration. A new diplomatic push for peace was led by Clinton in 1998, leading to the Wye Memorandum, signed by Arafat and Netanyahu in October. In July 2000, Clinton hosted a Camp David Peace Summit between Barak and Arafat, which ended without agreement.

DAYAN, MOSHE (1915-1981)
Born in Galilee, Dayan was just fourteen when he joined the Haganah, a Jewish underground organization that defended Jewish settlements from Arab attacks. In 1941, he joined the British army in the Middle East, and lost his left eye during a battle in Lebanon. During the 1947-9 War, Dayan led the defence of Jewish settlements in the Jordan Valley and helped to defeat Egyptian forces in the south. In the 1950s, he organized raids on Arab positions in Gaza and elsewhere, and led Israel's Suez campaign in 1956. In 1959 he entered the Knesset and served as Minister of Agriculture from 1959 to 1964, and then as Minister of Defence from 1967 to 1974. It was Dayan who persuaded the Israeli government to launch the pre-emptive strike that began the Six-Day War. He was also blamed for Egypt's surprise attack in 1973, leading to his resignation. As foreign minister between 1977 and 1979, Dayan was instrumental in negotiating the Camp David Accords with Egypt.

EBAN, ABBA (1915-2002)
An Israeli diplomat and politician. As foreign minister, Eban worked to maintain Israel's good relations with the USA and establish its assocation with the European Community. During the 1960s, Eban fought for Israel's cause at the United Nations.

ESHKOL, LEVI (1895-1969)
Born in Oratovo in the Ukraine, Eshkol joined a Zionist group as a youth and came to Palestine at 19. In 1940, he joined the Haganah and in 1947 he helped to establish the IDF. He served as ministers of agriculture and finance, obtaining funds to develop the country and equip the army, before becoming prime minister in 1963. He died in office. He is widely credited with having provided the IDF with the funding and equipment necessary to win the 1967 war.

HERZL, THEODOR (1860-1904)
The founder of the Zionist movement was born in Budapest,

Hungary. As a student in Vienna, and later as a journalist in Paris, he was appalled by the anti-semitism he encountered. Herzl believed that anti-semitism would always be a factor in society, and the only solution for Jews was their mass emigration to a land they could call their own. In 1896, he published *The Jewish State* in which he expanded on this idea. Herzl formed the Zionist Organization and collected funds from Jews around the world to help realize his dream. In 1897, the First Zionist Congress was held at Basle, Switzerland. By the time of his death Zionism had become a mass movement. His remains were brought to Israel in 1949 and reinterred on Mount Herzl in Jerusalem.

HUSSEIN, KING OF JORDAN (1935-1999)
Born in Amman, King Hussein bin Talal assumed the throne of Jordan in 1952. Throughout his 47-year-reign he struggled to promote peace in the Middle East. After the 1967 war, he helped draft UN Resolution 242 calling on Israel to withdraw from the occupied territories in exchange for peace. In 1991, he played an important role in bringing about the Madrid Peace Conference, providing the means for Palestinians to negotiate their future, and also negotiating Jordan's own peace treaty with Israel.

HUSSEIN, SADDAM (1937-)
The ruthless dictator of Iraq came to power in 1979 with ambitions to make Iraq the regional superpower. In 1980 he invaded Iran, beginning an eight-year war that ended in stalemate, and in 1990 he invaded Kuwait. A US-led coalition defeated Iraq and forced its retreat from Kuwait in the 1991 Gulf War. His regime was overthrown by coalition forces in the second Gulf War in 2003, and Hussein fled to an unknown destination. In December 2003 he was captured by US Special Forces and held in custody pending his future trial.

JIHAD, ABU (1935-1988)
Co-founder with Arafat of Fatah in 1959, Jihad became the military chief of Fatah in the 1960s. He established PLO relations with Jordan, Syria and Saudi Arabia, and organized the Palestinian resistance in the occupied territories. A close ally of Arafat and appointed his official deputy in 1980, Jihad was assassinated by Israeli agents in 1988.

KISSINGER, HENRY (1923-)
As Secretary of State under US presidents Nixon and Ford, Kissinger guided US foreign policy from 1969 to 1975. He played an important role in negotiating a ceasefire in the Middle East after the 1973 war, and was awarded the 1973 Nobel Peace Prize.

MEIR, GOLDA (1898-1978)
Born in Russia and educated in the USA, Meir emigrated to Palestine in 1921. She was active in the struggle against the British and served in various government ministries after 1948. In 1965 she helped to form the Israel Labour Party, and became prime minister in 1969. She accepted blame for Israel's lack of preparation in the 1973 war, and resigned in 1974.

MUBARAK, MUHAMMAD HOSNI (1928-)
The president of Egypt since 1981 began his career in the Air Force. In 1975 he was appointed vice president, and assumed the presidency after Sadat's assassination. Mubarak oversaw the handing back of the last third of Sinai in April 1982, and has sought to maintain peaceful relations with Israel. He aligned Egypt with the coalition forces in the 1991 Gulf War, and has dealt harshly with Islamist opposition groups in Egypt, leading to an attempt on his life in 1995.

NASSER, GAMAL ABDEL (1918-1970)
The future Egyptian president came to power as leader of a revolutionary group from within the Egyptian army called the Free Officers, who overthrew the king in 1952. Nasser was officially elected president in 1956. Nasser hoped to modernize Egypt by building the Aswan Dam which would allow more of Egypt's land to be brought under cultivation, as well as generate more electricity for the country, and allow water to be stored for times of drought; but after the USA cancelled the loan, he nationalized the Suez Canal, hoping to raise funds that way. The Suez War of 1956 made Nasser a hero in the Arab world. He formed the United Arab Republic with Syria in 1958, but the union was dissolved in 1961 after a coup in Syria. After defeat in the 1967 war, Nasser resigned, but the people took to the streets, demanding his return to government.

NETANYAHU, BENJAMIN (1949-)
Born in Tel Aviv and educated in the USA, Netanyahu returned to Israel in 1967 and enlisted in the IDF, serving in an elite anti-terror unit and achieving the rank of captain. Since 1979 he has organized conferences and written books on countering international terrorism. He served as Israeli ambassador to the UN during the 1980s. In 1988, Netanyahu was elected to the Knesset as a Likud member and was appointed deputy foreign minister. In 1993 he became Likud Party Chairman and served as prime minister from 1996 to 1999, during which time he was accused of hindering the peace process by allowing Jewish settlement building to continue.

PERES, SHIMON (1923-)
Born in Poland, Peres moved to Palestine in 1934, where he joined the Haganah in 1947. From 1953 to 1959 he served as Director General of the Defence Ministry, developing Israel's aircraft industry and nuclear program. In 1959 he was elected to the Knesset, and has remained a member ever since, serving in various ministries, including prime minister from 1984 to 1986 and from 1995 to 1996. During the 1990s, Peres worked hard to maintain the momentum of the peace process and shared the Nobel Peace Prize in 1994.

RABIN, YITZHAK (1922-1995)
Rabin was born in Jerusalem, and served in the Palmach (Jewish commando unit) and then the IDF for 27 years. After his retirement from the military in 1968 he was appointed Israeli ambassador to the USA. In 1973 he was elected to the Knesset and served as prime minister from 1974 to 1977. He focused on improving the economy and strengthening the IDF, and in 1975 he concluded the interim peace agreement with Egypt. Rabin was elected prime minister again in 1992, and made the decision to negotiate directly with the PLO. In 1993 he and Arafat signed the Declaration of Principles in Washington; the following year he signed the Gaza-Jericho Agreement and the Israel-Jordan peace treaty, and shared the Nobel Peace Prize. On 4 November 1995, Rabin was assassinated by a Jewish extremist in Tel Aviv.

REAGAN, RONALD (1911-)
As US president from 1981 to 1989, Reagan was a strong supporter of Israel, and believed in maintaining Israeli military superiority in the Middle East. Under his presidency, the USA initiated various Middle East peace plans, including the Reagan Plan and the Schultz Plan (named after US Secretary of State George Schultz).

SADAT, ANWAR (1918-1981)
Sadat served as Nasser's public relations minister and trusted deputy from 1952. Yet he was fairly unknown when he became president of Egypt in 1970. He quickly proved a bold and decisive leader, offering Israel a peace treaty in return for the Sinai lands, and expelling Soviet advisers when the USSR proved an unreliable ally. Meanwhile he secretly planned a surprise attack on Israel to retake the Sinai after his peace initiatives were rebuffed, which was carried out in October 1973. Egyptian forces were soon repelled, but Sadat's move had created a new momentum for a peace settlement, which he accelerated with a visit to Israel in 1977. This led to the Camp David Accords and the eventual peace treaty with Israel in 1979. Sadat won the Nobel Peace Prize for his efforts, but his recognition of Israel aroused popular anger among Islamists at home, and he was assassinated by Muslim fundamentalists in 1981.

SHAMIR, YITZHAK (1915-)
Born in Poland, Shamir came to Palestine in 1935, and joined the Jewish terrorist organization, Irgun, directed against the British occupation, and later the Stern Gang, a militant faction of Irgun. After independence, Shamir joined Mossad, the Israeli intelligence service, and was elected to the Knesset in 1973 as a member for Likud. He became foreign minister in 1980 before becoming prime minister from 1983 to 1984. Shamir was a hardliner, who opposed Israel's peace treaty with Egypt and the withdrawal from Lebanon. He softened his stance when he returned to office in 1990, agreeing not to respond to Iraq's Scud missile strikes, and taking part in the Madrid peace talks. He stepped down from the Likud leadership in 1993.

SHARON, ARIEL (1928-)
Sharon, born in Kfar Malal, joined the Haganah aged 14, and commanded an infantry company in the 1947-9 war. In 1953 he led the '101' special commando unit that carried out border raids, and commanded a paratroop corps in the 1956 war. In the 1967 and 1973 wars he was commander of an armoured division, and in the latter conflict he led the crossing of the Suez Canal which brought victory. He was elected to the Knesset in 1973 and again in 1977, serving as agriculture and defence minister in the Begin administration. He organized the 1982 invasion of Lebanon, and resigned when he was found indirectly responsible for the massacre at Sabra and Shatila refugee camps in west Beirut. He continued in government, serving in various ministries, before becoming Likud party leader in 1999. He became prime minister in 2001, and was reelected in 2003.

WEIZMANN, CHAIM (1874-1952)
Born in Russia, Weizmann became active in the Zionist movement whilst studying in Europe. His scientific assistance to the Allies during World War I brought him into close contact with British leaders, giving him crucial influence over British policy towards Palestine, and the issuing of the Balfour Declaration in 1917 is partly attributed to Weizmann. In 1920 he became president of the World Zionist Organization, and played a key role in the adoption of the partition plan by the UN in 1947 and in the recognition of Israel by the USA. Weizmann served as the first President of Israel from 1948 until his death four years later.

SIGNIFICANT DATES

1890s
Beginning of Zionist movement.

1900s
Clashes between Palestinians and Jewish settlers.

1917
Balfour Declaration.

1921
Start of British Mandate.

29 NOVEMBER 1947
UN General Assembly votes to accept partition plan.

DECEMBER 1947
War between Palestinian Arabs and Jews begins.

1 APRIL 1948
Zionist offensive begins.

15 MAY 1948
British Mandate ends. Zionist leaders declare the founding of the state of Israel.

16-17 MAY 1948
Neighbouring Arab states invade.

11 JUNE-8 JULY 1948
UN-negotiated ceasefire.

8-18 JULY 1948
Israeli offensives capture many new towns, enlarging Israeli territory.

18 JULY-15 OCTOBER 1948
UN-negotiated ceasefire. Israel establishes itself in newly conquered territory.

1948-9
726,000 Palestinian Arabs become refugees.

FEBRUARY-JULY 1949
Armistice agreements signed by Israel and the Arab states.

JULY 1956
Nasser nationalizes the Suez Canal.

29 OCTOBER 1956
Israel invades Gaza Strip and Sinai Peninsula.

31 OCTOBER 1956
Britain and France launch joint attack on Egypt.

6 NOVEMBER 1956
British and French agree to ceasefire under pressure from USA.

22 DECEMBER 1956
Anglo-French troops evacuated.

MARCH 1957
Israel withdraws from Sinai and Gaza.

AUGUST 1963
Israel begins implementing its National Water Carrier Plan, leading to a near-conflict with Syria.

1964
Formation of PLO.

APRIL-MAY 1967
Border clashes between Israel and Syria.

18 MAY 1967
Nasser demands the evacuation of UN peacekeeping forces, and remilitarizes Sinai.

21 MAY 1967
Nasser closes the Straits of Tiran.

30 MAY 1967
Egypt and Jordan sign a mutual defence treaty.

5 JUNE 1967
Israel launches an aerial attack on Egypt's airfields, virtually destroying the Egyptian Air Force on the ground, followed by a ground invasion of Gaza and Sinai. Jordanian and Syrian armies begin shelling Israeli positions. Israel destroys the Jordanian and most of the Syrian Air Forces.

6 JUNE 1967
Israel captures Ramallah and Jenin.

7 JUNE 1967
Israel captures East Jerusalem and Nablus.

8 JUNE 1967
Israel completes its reconquest of Gaza, Sinai and the West Bank.

9 JUNE 1967
Israel launches invasion of Golan Heights.

10 JUNE 1967
Israel completes conquest of Golan Heights. Ceasefire agreed.

NOVEMBER 1967
UN Security Council adopts Resolution 242 calling on Israel to withdraw from territories seized in June.

1970-1
PLO driven from Jordan and forced into southern Lebanon.

FEBRUARY 1971
Sadat offers peace with Israel in return for Israeli withdrawal from Sinai.

6 OCTOBER 1973
Egypt and Syria launch joint invasion of Israel.

11 OCTOBER 1973
Syrian forces pushed back to their own frontier.

16/17 OCTOBER 1973
Israeli forces cross Suez Canal,

cutting off supplies to Egyptian armies in Sinai.

20 OCTOBER 1973
Ceasefire agreed between Egypt and Israel.

22 OCTOBER 1973
Ceasefire agreed between Syria and Israel.

5 MARCH 1974
Israeli forces withdraw from west bank of Suez Canal.

31 MAY 1974
UN peacekeeping force established on Golan Heights.

SEPTEMBER 1975
Israel withdraws most of its troops from Sinai and a UN-policed buffer zone is placed between Egyptian and Israeli forces.

NOVEMBER 1977
Sadat visits Israel in efforts to secure peace.

MARCH 1978
Operation Litani launched: Israel invades southern Lebanon to attack PLO bases there.

JUNE 1978
Israeli forces withdraw from southern Lebanon.

SEPTEMBER 1978
Israel-Egypt discussions take place at Camp David, USA.

6 JUNE 1982
Operation Peace for Galilee launched: Israel launches full-scale invasion of Lebanon.

13 JUNE 1982
Siege of Beirut begins.

9-10 JUNE 1982
Israeli Air Force destroys Syrian missile batteries in Bekaa Valley, and inflicts defeat on Syrian Air Force in large-scale air battle.

11 JUNE 1982
Ceasefire agreed between Israel and Syria.

12 AUGUST 1982
Siege of Beirut ends when a ceasefire is agreed, and arrangements are made for PLO fighters to be evacuated from Lebanon.

JUNE 1985
Israel withdraws from most of Lebanon, maintaining a 8 km-wide security zone along border.

8 DECEMBER 1987
Start of first intifada.

NOVEMBER 1988
PLO recognizes the state of Israel.

2 AUGUST 1990
Saddam Hussein's Iraq invades Kuwait.

16 JANUARY 1991
Gulf War begins

JANUARY-FEBRUARY 1991
39 Scud missiles launched at Israel.

27 FEBRUARY 1991
Gulf War ends. Kuwait is liberated.

OCTOBER 1991
Middle East peace conference held in Madrid.

JULY 1992
Discussions begin in Oslo between Palestinian and Israeli delegations.

13 SEPTEMBER 1993
Oslo Accords signed in Washington. End of first intifada.

MAY 1994
Israel and the PLO sign the Gaza-Jericho agreement in Cairo.

OCTOBER 1994
Israeli forces begin phased withdrawal from most of the West Bank.

NOVEMBER 1995
Israeli prime minister Yitzhak Rabin is assassinated.

JANUARY 1996
Yasser Arafat elected president of the PA.

OCTOBER 1998
Wye Memorandum signed in Washington by Arafat and Netanyahu.

MAY 2000
Israeli forces withdraw completely from Lebanon.

JULY 2000
Barak and Arafat meet at Camp David for final status negotiations. Talks end in deadlock.

28 SEPTEMBER 2000
Second intifada begins when Ariel Sharon visits Temple Mount, sparking widespread protests.

DECEMBER 2001
Israeli tanks surround Arafat's headquarters in Ramallah, keeping him a virtual prisoner.

APRIL-JUNE 2002
Israeli forces invade and reoccupy seven West Bank towns in order to destroy terrorist infrastructure.

MARCH 2003
Mahmoud Abbas appointed Palestinian prime minister.

APRIL 2003
'Road map to peace' published, a new internationally backed plan to bring peace to the Middle East by 2005. Israel begins building its 'separation fence' between Palestinian-controlled areas and Jewish settlements on the West Bank.

6 SEPTEMBER 2003
Abbas resigns as prime minister.

STATISTICS CONCERNING COMBATANT NATIONS

Casualty Levels

Approximate numbers killed in all the wars fought since 1948:

Israel	12,000
Egypt	24,000
Syria	8,500
Jordan	7,000
Palestinians	7,000 (since 1982)

Distribution of the Palestinian Population and Jewish Settlers in the West Bank and Gaza Since 1967

Year	Palestinians		Jews
	West Bank	Gaza	West Bank & Gaza
1 Dec 1967	604,494	380,800	–
1979	791,000	447,700	3,176 (1976)
1984	896,000	509,900	16,119 (1981)
1988	977,000	588,500	60,500 (1986)
1990	1,075,531	622,016	98,750 (1991)
1997	1,873,476	1,022,207	165,000
2002	1,932,637	1,087,067	226,028

[Source: *Jerusalem Fund for Education and Community Development*; Israeli Central Bureau of Statistics; USAID West Bank and Gaza]

Global Distribution of Palestinian People (1986, 1990/1, 1995 and 2000)

Country	1986	1990/1	1995	2000
Jordan	1,398,050	1,824,179	2,170,101	2,596,986
West Bank/ East Jerusalem	951,530	1,075,531	1,227,545	1,383,415
Gaza	545,100	622,016	726,832	837,699
Israel	608,200	730,000	800,755	919,453
Lebanon	271,434	331,757	392,315	463,067
Syria	242,474	301,744	357,881	410,599
Remaining Arab States	582,894	445,195	516,724	599,389
Rest of World	280,846	450,000	500,000	550,000
Total	**4,880,518**	**5,780,422**	**6,692,153**	**7,760,608**

[Source: *Jerusalem Fund for Education and Community Development*]

Jewish Population Distribution in Palestine (1880-1947)

Year	**Population**	
	Palestinians Numbers (%)	Jews Numbers (%)
1880	300,000 (94)	24,000 (6)
1917	504,000 (90)	56,000 (10)
1922	666,000 (89)	84,000 (11)
1931	850,000 (83)	174,096 (17)
1936	916,061 (72)	384,078 (28)
1945/6	1,242,000 (69)	608,000 (31)
1947 UN Partition	1,300,000 (67)	640,298 (33)

Jewish Land Ownership in Palestine (1880-1947)

Year	**Land ownership (cumulative)**	
	dunums*	% of land
1880	n/a	n/a
1917	650,000	less than 3
1922	751,192	3
1931	1,171,529	4
1936	1,380,578	5
1945/6	1,588,365	6
1947 UN Partition	1,900,000	7

* 1 dunum = 1,000 square metres

[Source: *Facts and Figures on Palestine* (Washington, DC: Palestine Center, 1991), p.4]

Distribution of Palestinian Refugees Registered with UNRWA (2003)

Region	No. of Camps	Registered Refugees	Registered Refugees in Camps
Jordan	10	1,718,767	304,430
Lebanon	12	391,679	225,125
Syria	10	409,662	119,766
Gaza Strip	8	907,221	478,854
West Bank	19	654,971	176,514
Total	**59**	**4,082,300**	**1,301,689**

[Source: United Nations, *United Nations Relief and Works Agency for Palestine Refugees in the Near East*, 30 June 2003]

FURTHER INFORMATION

Note to parents and teachers

Every effort has been made by the publishers to ensure that the websites listed are suitable for children; that they are of the highest educational value; and that they contain no inappropriate or offensive material. However, because of the nature of the Internet, it is impossible to guarantee that the contents of these sites will not be altered. We strongly advise that Internet access is supervised by a responsible adult.

WORLD WAR I

RECOMMENDED BOOKS

Brendon, Vyvyen *The First World War, 1914-18* (Hodder & Stoughton Educational, 2000)
Brooman, J. *The Great War: The First World War 1914-18* (Longman, 1985)
Grant, Reg *Armistice, 1918* (Hodder Wayland, 2000)
Hansen, Ole Steen *The War in the Trenches* (Hodder Wayland, 2000)
Mair, Craig *Britain at War, 1914-1919* (John Murray, 1989)
Ross, Stewart *Battle of the Somme* (Hodder Wayland, 2003)
Ross, Stewart *Causes of the First World War* (Hodder Wayland, 2002)
Ross, Stewart *Leaders of the First World War* (Hodder Wayland, 2002)
Ross, Stewart *Technology of the First World War* (Hodder Wayland, 2003)
Wrenn, Andrew *The First World War* (CUP, 1997)

FIRST-HAND ACCOUNTS

Blunden, Edmund *Undertones of War* (London, 1928, and many further editions)
Britten, Vera *Testament of Youth* (Victor Gollancz, 1933)
Graves, Robert *Goodbye to All That* (Cassell, 1929, and many further editions)
Lewis, Cecil Sagittarius Rising (Peter Davies, 1936, and many further editions)
Manning, Frederick *The Middle Parts of Fortune* (privately published 1929, then Penguin 1990 and other editions)
Remarque, Erich Maria *All Quiet on the Western Front* (Putnam, 1929, and many further editions)
Sassoon, Siegfried *Memoirs of an Infantry Officer* (Faber, 1930, and many further editions)
For poetry see Jon Silkin, ed., *The Penguin Book of First World War Poetry* (Penguin, 1979)

SOURCES OF QUOTATIONS

A Farewell To Arms (Ernest Hemingway, Arrow edition, 1994)
All Quiet On the Western Front (Erich Remarque, Triad Panther edition, 1977)
Arab-Israeli Conflict and Conciliation: A Documentary History (edited by Bernard Reich, Praeger, 1995)
Great Issues in American History: From Reconstruction to the Present Day, 1864-1969 (edited by Richard Hofstadter, Vintage Books, 1969)
Somme, Lyn Macdonald (Penguin, 1983)
The Great War, edited by H.W. Wilson and J.A. Hammerton (Odhams, 1915)
The Imperial War Museum Book of the First World War, edited by Malcolm Brown (Sidgwick and Jackson, 1991)
They Called it Passchendaele, Lyn Macdonald (Penguin, 1993)
Twenty-five Years, 1892-1916, Viscount E. Grey (Hodder & Stoughton, 1925)

RECOMMENDED WEBSITES

Among the many:
http://www.schoolshistory.org.uk/firstworldwar.htm
http://www.schoolshistory.org.uk/firstworldwar.htm
http://www.worldwar1.com/bioindex.htm

PLACES TO VISIT

Imperial War Museum, London.
National Army Museum, London.
The site of the battlefield at Ieper (Ypres) in Belgium.
Battlefields, graveyards and war memorials of France, perhaps starting at Peronne and Albert.

WORLD WAR II: EUROPE

RECOMMENDED BOOKS

Of the many general single-volume histories of World War II, probably the best is John Keegan's *The Second World War*, first published in 1990. The war has given rise to many factual blockbusters, chunks of military history written to read like exciting action novels. Once the master of this genre was Cornelius Ryan, who in particular wrote *The Longest Day* (1959) on the D-Day landings and *A Bridge Too Far* (1974) on Operation Market Garden. Recently the leading author in this genre has been Anthony Beevor, whose *Stalingrad* (Viking, 1998) was an international bestseller, and was followed by *Berlin: the Downfall, 1945* (2002).

SOURCES OF QUOTATIONS

African Trilogy, Alan Moorhead (Cassell, 1998)
English History 1914-1945, A.J.P. Taylor (Oxford University Press, 1965)
Faber Book of Reportage, edited by John Carey (Faber and Faber, 1987)
History of the Second World War, B.H. Liddel Hart (Cassell, 1970)
Hitler, Joachim Fest (Weidenfeld & Nicholson, 1974)
Hitler Volume 2, Ian Kershaw (Penguin, 2000)
Russia's War, Richard Overy (Penguin, 1997)
The Holocaust, R.G. Grant (Wayland, 1997)

The Most Dangerous Enemy, S. Bungay (Aurum Press, 2000)
The Second World War: A Complete History (Martin Gilbert, Henry Holt & Co, 1991)
The Second World War, Henri Michel (Andre Deutsch, 1975)

RECOMMENDED FILMS

In some ways, the best films to watch on World War II are those made relatively soon after the war ended. They may be in black and white, but they capture the feel of the times. Such old movies to look out for include *The Dam Busters* (1954), *Dunkirk* (1958), and *The Longest Day* (1962), based on Cornelius Ryan's book mentioned above. As the war receded in time, movies about it tended to become gradually more cynical and harsh. Look out for *Patton: Lust for Glory* (1969), a biopic starring George C. Scott, *A Bridge Too Far* (1977) also based on Ryan's book, and director Sam Fuller's anti-heroic *The Big Red One* (1980), about the war as experienced by the US 1st Infantry Division. Recent movie-making on the war has been dominated by Steven Spielberg, with *Saving Private Ryan* (1998), which uses modern special effects to give an impression of the terror of landing on the Normandy beaches.

RECOMMENDED WEBSITES

The internet offers a vast archive of material both on the war in general and on every particular aspect of it. Starting points on the web might be:
http://www.historyplace.com/worldwar2
http://www.worldwar-2.net
http://www.bbc.co.uk/history/war/wwtwo/
http://www.angelfire.com/ct/ww2europe/
http://www.fordham.edu/halsall/mod/modsbook45.html

PLACES TO VISIT

Among places to visit connected to the war in Europe, top of the list must be the Normandy beaches. Apart from the beaches themselves, Normandy is dotted with World War II cemeteries and museums. Of the many museums partly or totally devoted to the war it is especially worth mentioning the Imperial War Museum in London. A National World War II Memorial opened to the public in Washington D.C. in 2004.

WORLD WAR II: THE PACIFIC

RECOMMENDED BOOKS

The following books look at the Pacific War as a whole or look at some of the key episodes in the Pacific War:

Chrisp, Peter, *The World Wars: the War in the Pacific* (London, 2003)
Denenberg, Barry, *Early Sunday Morning: The Pearl Harbor Diary of Amber Billows*, Hawaii, 1941 (New York, 2001)
Earle Jr., Rice, *Strategic Battles in the Pacific: World War II* (San Diego, 2000)
Grant, R.G., *Hiroshima and Nagasaki* (London, 1999)
Klam, Julie and Zimmerman, Dwight Jon, *Victory in the Pacific* (Mankato, Minnesota, 2003)
Nardo, Don, *World War II in the Pacific* (World History) (San Diego, 2002)
Stein, R. Conrad, *World War II in the Pacific* (Berkeley Heights, New Jersey, 2002)
Tames, Richard, *Turning Points in History: Pearl Harbor* (London, 2001)
Yep, Laurence, *Hiroshima* (New York, 1996)

The following books provide interesting and detailed accounts of particular battles or campaigns in the Pacific War:

Badsey, Stephen, ed., *Atlas of World War II Battle Plans* (Oxford, 2000)
Fuchida, Mitsuo and Okumiya, Masatake, *Midway: The Japanese Story* (London, 2002)
Grove, Eric, *Sea Battles in Close-Up: World War 2* (Shepperton, 1993)
Leasor, James, *Singapore: The Battle That Changed The War* (London, 2001)
Moran, Jim and Rottman, Gordon L., *Peleliu* (Oxford, 2002)
Warren, Alan, *Singapore* (London, 2002)
Wright, Derrick, *The Battle for Iwo Jima* (Stroud, 1999)
Wright, Derrick, *Tarawa – A Hell of a Way to Die* (Marlborough, 1997)
Wright, Derrick, *Tarawa 1943* (Oxford, 2000)

The following books provide fascinating first-hand accounts by people who experienced the Pacific War, either as combatants or civilians:

Cook, Haruko Taya and Cook, Theodore F., *Japan At War: An Oral History* (London, 2000)
Lewis, Jon E., ed., *How It Happened: World War II* (London, 2002)
Terkel, Studs, ed., *'The Good War': An Oral History of World War II* (London, 1984)

The following books all provide or include interesting accounts of the Pacific War as a whole, though sometimes there may be too much information for younger readers. In these cases the use of the contents page or index of each book is recommended as a way of finding out more about a particular battle or aspect of the war:

Bourke, Joanna, *The Second World War: A People's History* (Oxford, 2001)
Dear, I.C.B., ed., *The Oxford Companion to World War II* (Oxford, 2001)
Horner, David, *The Second World War: The Pacific* (Oxford, 2002)
Lewis, Jonathan and Steele, Ben, *Hell In The Pacific* (London, 2001)
Spector, Ronald H., *Eagle Against the Sun* (London, 2001)
Van Der Vat, Dan, *The Pacific Campaign* (Edinburgh, 2001)

SOURCES OF QUOTATIONS

Atlas of World War II Battle Plans, edited by Stephen Badsey (Oxford, 2000)
The Daily Express newspaper (London, 1941)
Hell In The Pacific, Jonathan Lewis and Ben Steele (London, 2001)

How It Happened: World War II, edited by Jon E. Lewis (London, 2002)
Japan At War: An Oral History, Haruko Taya Cook and Theodore F. Cook (London, 2000)
Singapore, Alan Warren (London, 2002)
Tarawa – A Hell of a Way to Die, Derrick Wright (Marlborough, 1997)
The Battle for Iwo Jima, Derrick Wright (Stroud, 1999)
'The Good War': An Oral History of World War II, edited by Studs Terkel (London, 1984)
The Oxford Companion to World War II, edited by I.C.B. Dear (Oxford, 2001)
The Pacific Campaign, Dan Van Der Vat (Edinburgh, 2001)
The Second World War: A People's History, Joanna Bourke (Oxford, 2001)

RECOMMENDED FILMS

The following films are set in the context of the Pacific War and are worth watching:
Empire of the Sun (1987)
Sands of Iwo Jima (1950)
The Bridge on the River Kwai (1957)
Tora! Tora! Tora! (1970)

The following documentaries about the Pacific War are also available:
Chronicles of World War II, with Walter Cronkite, Vol 2: The Pacific War Begins and Vol 7: The Pacific Campaign (20th Century Fox, 1981)
Hell in the Pacific (Carlton Visual Entertainment, 2001)
V is for Victory – America Goes to War – Guadalcanal and the Pacific Counterattack (Accord Media UK, 1998)
Battle Cry: Objective Burma – Operation Pacific (Warner Home Videos, 2003)

RECOMMENDED WEBSITES

http://www.combinedfleet.com/map.htm
http://www.historyplace.com
http://www.iwm.org.uk/
http://www.nimitz-museum.org/
http://www.spartacus.schoolnet.co.uk/2WWpacific.htm

PLACES TO VISIT

The National Museum of the Pacific War is the only institution in the continental United States dedicated exclusively to telling the story of the Pacific Theatre battles of World War II. It is located at The National Museum of the Pacific War, 340 East Main Street, Fredericksburg, Texas 78624. Two other important museums in the United States are The Naval Historical Center, Washington Naval Yard, Washington D.C. 20374 (www.history.navy.mil) and The *USS Arizona* Visitor Center, Pearl Harbor Naval Base, Hawaii. The Imperial War Museum, Lambeth Rd, London, SE1 6HZ, has lots of exhibits relating to World War II as a whole.

THE KOREAN WAR

RECOMMENDED BOOKS

There are many general histories of the Korean War, the best of which are listed below. While they may contain more information than younger readers can digest in their entirety, using the contents page or index of each book is a good way of finding out more about a particular battle or aspect of the war:
Catchpole, Brian, *The Korean War* (Constable, 2000)
Cumings, Bruce and Halliday, Jon, *Korea: The Unknown War* (Penguin, 1990)
Hastings, Max, *The Korean War* (Pan, 1988)
Hickey, Michael, *The Korean War: The West Confronts Communism 1950-53* (John Murray, 1999)
Kaufman, Burton I., *The Korean Conflict* (Greenwood Press, 1999)
Malkasian, Carter, *The Korean War 1950-53* (Fitzroy Dearborn, 2001)
Smith, Carter, *The Korean War* (Silver Burdett Press, 1991)
Stein, Richard Conrad, *The Korean War 'The Forgotten War'* (Enslow Publishers, 1994)

Also of interest are:
Ann Gaines, *Douglas MacArthur: Brilliant General, Controversial Leader* (Enslow Publishers, 2001)
Donald Knox, *The Korean War: Pusan to Chosin: An Oral History* (Harcourt, 1985)
Leckie, Richard, *March to Glory* (Simon & Schuster, 2002)
Rendall, Ivan, *Rolling Thunder: Jet Combat from World War II to the Gulf War* (New York, 1997)

Novels set in the Korean War include:
Griffen, W.E.B., *Retreat, Hell!* (Putnam's, 2004)
Griffen, W.E.B., *Under Fire* (Jove Books, 2003)

SOURCES OF QUOTATIONS

Korea: The Unknown War, Jon Halliday and Bruce Cumings (Penguin, 1990)
Office of the Press Secretary (The White House, October, 2003)
Rethinking the Korean War, William Stueck (Princeton University Press, 2002)
The *Guardian* newspaper, London and Manchester.
The Korean War, Brian Catchpole (Constable, 2000)
The Korean War, Michael Hickey (John Murray, 1999)
The War in Korea, Matthew B. Ridgway (Barrie & Rockliff, 1967)
War in Peace magazine (London, 1983)

RECOMMENDED FILMS

Korea has certainly been 'the Forgotten War' as far as filmmakers are concerned. There are no movies that can be unreservedly recommended as giving a true impression of the conflict. *M.A.S.H.* (1970) is the only well-known film set in the Korean War. However, it was made during the Vietnam War, and the attitudes expressed in it are much more typical of that conflict than of Korea. There is also a spin-off TV series of the same name. Both are based on Richard Hooker's comic novel for an adult audience, *M*A*S*H: A Novel About Three Army Doctors.*

The Manchurian Candidate (1962) is a thriller based on the idea of American prisoners of war in Korea being 'brainwashed' so that they act as communist agents after their return to the US.

The *Sergeant Bilko* black-and-white TV comedy series perhaps gives some impression of the kind of peacetime US Army that found it hard to adapt to war in Korea.

RECOMMENDED WEBSITES

http://www.korean-war.com/
http://korea50.army.mil/
http://www.usni.org
http://www.militaryhistory.about.com
http://www.nps.gov/kwvm/

PLACES TO VISIT

The Korean War Veterans Memorial, 900 Ohio Drive, SW Washington D.C. 20024, USA and the Korean War Museum, Yongsan-gu, Seoul, South Korea.

THE VIETNAM WAR

RECOMMENDED BOOKS

The most accessible fuller books on the war are:
Hall, Mitchel K., *The Vietnam War* (Longman, 1999)
Sanders, Vivienne, *The USA and Vietnam 1945-75* (Hodder Arnold, 2002)

Larger-scale historical, biographical and journalistic books about the war include the following titles. While they may contain more information than younger readers can digest in their entirety, using the contents page or index of each book is a good way of finding out more about a particular battle or aspect of the war:
Corbett, Robin, *Guerrilla Warfare* (London, 1986)
Currey, Cecil B., *Victory at Any Cost: the Genius of Viet Nam's General Vo Nguyen Giap* (London, 2000)
Fall, Bernard, *Street Without Joy* (London, 1961)
Fenn, Charles, *Ho Chi Minh* (London, 1973)
Karnow, Stanley, *Vietnam: A History* (New York, 1983)
Lewy, Guenter, *America in Vietnam* (Oxford, 1978)
Maclear, Michael, *Vietnam: The Ten Thousand Day War* (London, 1981)
Mann, Robert, *A Grand Delusion: America's Descent into Vietnam* (New York, 2001)
Scholl-Latour, Peter *Death in the Rice Fields* (New York, 1979)
Sheehan, Neil, *A Bright Shining Lie* (New York, 1988)
Summers Jr., Harry G., *Historical Atlas of the Vietnam War* (Boston, 1995)

There are many published first-hand accounts – or collections of first-hand accounts – of the Vietnam experience. Among the best are:
Barker, Mark, *Nam* (London, 1987)
Broyles Jr., William, *Brothers in Arms: A Journey from War to Peace* (New York, 1986)
Caputo, Philip, *A Rumor of War* (Pimlico, 1999)
Donovan, David, *Once a Warrior King: Memories of an Officer in Vietnam* (Corgi, 1981)
Mason, Robert, *Chickenhawk* (Corgi, 1984)
Moore, Harold G. and Galloway, Joseph L., *We Were Soldiers Once... and Young* (New York, 1992)
O'Brien, Tim, *If I Die in a Combat Zone* (Flamingo, 1989)

For a flavour of the anti-war movement, it is best to turn to books written at the time. Among the most readable still available are:
Mailer, Norman, *Miami Beach and the Siege of Chicago* (Penguin, 1971)
McCarthy, Mary, *Vietnam* (Penguin, 1968)

SOURCES OF QUOTATIONS

America in Vietnam, Guenter Lewy (Oxford, 1978)
Brothers in Arms: A Journey from War to Peace, William Broyles Jr. (New York, 1986)
Death in the Rice Fields, Peter Scholl-Latour (New York, 1979)
Guerrilla Warfare, Robin Corbett (London, 1986)
Historical Atlas of the Vietnam War, Harry G. Summers Jr. (Boston, 1995)
Vietnam: The Ten Thousand Day War, Michael Maclear (London, 1981)
War in Peace magazine (London, 1984)

RECOMMENDED FILMS AND TELEVISION

Many films have been set in the Vietnam War. Most contain strong language and, almost inevitably, extreme violence. So the following information is given on the understanding that younger readers would need to obtain parental permission before viewing these films. The movies are made from an American viewpoint and none can claim to present a balanced view of the Vietnam experience, but they are worth watching to gain an impression of what the war was like:
Apocalypse Now (1979)
The Deer Hunter (1978)
Good Morning, Vietnam (1987)
Platoon (1986)
Vietnam: A Television History (WGBH Boston Video, 1983) is also available to watch.

RECOMMENDED WEBSITES

http://www.spartacus.schoolnet.co.uk/vietnam.html
http://www.pbs.org/wgbh/amex/vietnam
http://www.lcweb.loc.gov/folklife/vets
http://www.WomenInVietnam.com
http://vietnam.vassar.edu/
http://hubcap.clemson.edu/~eemoise/bibliography.html

PLACES TO VISIT

The National Vietnam Veterans Memorial 900 Ohio Drive, SW (Near the base of the Lincoln Memorial and the Korean War memorial at the west end of the National Mall. Located near Henry Bacon Drive)
Washington D.C.
Tel: 202-426-6841
Website: http://www.nps.gov/vive/

The Vietnam Veteran's Memorial and The Vietnam Era Educational Center
Exit 116, Garden State Parkway
Holmdel, New Jersey
For group tours and additional information, see their website: http://www.njvvmf.org/

National Vietnam Veterans Art Museum
1801 South Indiana Avenue Chicago
Illinois 60616
Tel: 312-326-0270
Fax: 31-326-9767
Website: http://www.nvvam.org/

Gallery Vietnam
55 N. Moore Street
New York, NY 10013
Tel: 212-431-8889
Fax: 212-202-4737
Website: http://www.galleryvietnam.com

THE ARAB-ISRAELI CONFLICT

RECOMMENDED BOOKS

Harris, *Nathaniel, New Perspectives: Israel and the Arab Nations in Conflict* (Hodder Wayland, 1998)
Minnis, Ivan, *Troubled World: Arab-Israeli Conflict* (Heinemann Library, 2001)
Ross, Stewart, *Witness to History: The Arab-Israeli Conflict* (Heinemann Library, 2004)

SOURCES OF QUOTATIONS

Pages 4-5 Excerpts From Herzl's *The Jewish State* (Jewish Virtual Library, 2003)
Pages 6-7 Quoted in Ritchie Ovendale, *The Origins of the Arab-Israeli Wars* (third edition) (Longman, 1999)
Pages 10-11 Quoted in Bard, Mitchell, *Palestinian Refugees* (Jewish Virtual Library, 2003)
Pages 14-15 Israel Ministry of Foreign Affairs.
Pages 16-17 Quoted in Bregman, Ahron and El-Tahri, Jihan, *The Fifty Years War: Israel and the Arabs* (Penguin, 1998)
Pages 20-21 UN Security Council Resolution 242.
Pages 24-5 Quoted in Bregman and El-Tahri.
Pages 26-7 Quoted in Bregman and El-Tahri.
Pages 30-1 Quoted in Marcus, Yoel, *Camp David: The Door to Peace* (Tel Aviv, 1979)
Pages 34-5 Quoted in Wallach, John and Janet, *Arafat in the Eyes of the Beholder* (Random House, 1991)
Pages 38-9 Quoted in Bregman and El-Tahri.
Pages 40-1 Israel Ministry of Foreign Affairs.
Pages 48-9 Quoted on CNN.com: Inside Politics.
Pages 50-1 From an interview by Peter Beaumont, *The Observer* (13 July 2003)

RECOMMENDED FILMS

War and Peace in the Middle East (3k Media Ltd, 1995)
War Diary: Exodus - The Birth of Israel (Audiovisual Enterprises Ltd, 1989)
Wars in Peace: Six Day War/Yom Kippur War (K-Tel Entertainment, 1992)

RECOMMENDED WEBSITES

http://news.bbc.co.uk/hi/english/static/in_depth/world/2001/israel_and_palestinians/timeline/
http://www.merip.org/palestine-israel_primer/toc-pal-isr-primer.html
http://historyteacher.net/Arab-Israeli_Conflict.htm
http://www.mideastweb.org/briefhistory.htm
http://www.angliacampus.com/tour/sec/history/ariscon/index.htm

PLACES TO VISIT

Temple Mount/Haram Al-Sharif (known to Muslims as Haram Al-Sharif) is a hill in the eastern part of the Jerusalem's Old City, and is the site of two ancient Jewish temples. Since the seventh century, it has also been a place of Muslim worship. It is the world's holiest site for Jews, the third holiest site for Muslims, and also a place of special significance to Christians.

The Dome of the Rock is a famous Islamic mosque and was built between 687 and 691 CE. The rock in the centre of the dome is believed by Muslims to be the spot to which Muhammad was brought by night, and from which he ascended through the heavens to God.

The Western or Wailing Wall is all that remains of the second Jerusalem Temple, the holiest building in Judaism, destroyed by the Romans around 2,000 years ago. It is a traditional site of prayer for Jews.

The Al-Aqsa Mosque is the largest mosque in Jerusalem, and was completed in 710 CE. It is believed to have been built on the site of the original Jerusalem Temple. The mosque has been the target of attacks by Jewish extremists.

GLOSSARY

17th parallel Line of latitude 17 degrees north of the equator, chosen as dividing line between North and South Vietnam.
38th parallel Line of latitude 38 degrees north of the equator, this was the original dividing line between North and South Korea.
abdicate To choose to step down as a monarch.
activist Someone who acts in pursuit of a political aim.
AEF American Expeditionary Force.
air cavalry US troop formations using fleets of helicopters to advance to the battlefield.
air superiority Control of the skies during a military conflict.
aircraft carrier A large ship with a flight deck from which aircraft may take off and land.
airlift Delivery of supplies or troops by air.
airmobile Term used for US troops normally moving around by helicopter.
alliance An agreement between states for their mutual help in time of war.
Allies, the Countries at war against Germany, Japan and their supporters in the Pacific during World War II.
Allies, the Russia, France, Britain, Belgium, Italy, the USA and the countries that fought with them in World War I.
amphibious operation Military operation in which troops transported by sea make a landing in enemy-held territory.
annex To add territory to your country by conquering it.
anti-Semitism Prejudice against Jews.
Anzac Australia and New Zealand Army Corps.
appeasers Term used for British and French political leaders of the 1930s who believed that making concessions to Hitler would ensure peace.
Arab League A league of Arab states formed in 1944.
armistice A truce in a war to discuss terms for peace.
armoured columns Large formations of tanks and other armoured fighting vehicles.
arms race Two or more countries trying to outdo each other by building up their armed forces.
ARVN Army of the Republic of Vietnam.
Aryan race According to the racist theories embraced by the Nazis, Aryans were a superior race of human beings, of which the German people were part.
assassinate To murder a well-known figure, usually for political reasons.
atoll A ridge of coral rock and sand, just above the level of the sea, enclosing an area of sea.
atom bomb An extremely powerful bomb in which the explosion is caused by splitting atoms.
atrocity Massacre or other act of extreme brutality, especially against civilians in wartime.
attrition The wearing down of the enemy.
Austria-Hungary Empire of Austria and Hungary, joined in 1867.
authoritarian A government or ruler exercising power in a strict way with no regard for individual freedom.
autocratic All-powerful.
autonomy Political independence and self-government.
Balkans Region between the Black Sea and the Adriatic.
banzai A form of greeting, traditionally used by the Japanese to their emperor. Also used to describe the near-suicidal charge by Japanese soldiers against an enemy.
battalion A military formation, made up of around 750 men, under the command of a Lieutenant Colonel.
beachhead An area on an enemy beach or shoreline captured by an invasion force, where more troops and supplies can be landed.
BEF British Expeditionary Force, British troops on the Western Front.
besiege Surround a place such as a city with armed forces in order to bring about its capture or surrender.
bilateral negotiations Talks involving two parties or countries.
blitzkrieg In German literally 'lightning war' – a fast-moving offensive, especially using tanks and aircraft.
blockade To stop people and goods from going in or out of a town, port or country.
blockhouse Concrete shelter.
boycott To cease to deal with something, such as a country, or to stop buying certain goods, as a form of protest.
bridgehead A forward position seized by advancing troops in enemy territory which serves as a basis for more advances.
brigade A subdivision of an army, usually consisting of a small number of infantry battalions.
buffer zone A neutral area that lies between hostile forces and reduces the risk of conflict between them.
bureaucracy Civil service.
cabinet Leading members of a government campaign A series of military operations in a particular theatre of war.
capitalism Economic system based on a free market and private ownership of land and industry.
cavalry Soldiers who fight on horseback.
ceasefire Another word for an armistice (see above).
Central Powers Germany, Austria-Hungary, Turkey and Bulgaria.
charter The charter of the UN is the document that sets out what the organization is for, and how and when it is supposed to act.
chief of staff The senior officer in one of a country's armed forces.
CIA Central Intelligence Agency, the US organization dedicated to carry out espionage and covert operations abroad.
CIDGs Civilian Irregular Defense Groups – guerrilla forces organized by US Special Forces in remote areas of South Vietnam.
coalition Government in which more than one political party takes part and has a share in power.
Cold War The armed confrontation between the United States and its allies on one side and the Soviet Union and its allies on the other, which lasted from the late 1940s to the 1980s.
collaborate To co-operate, but in wartime used as a critical term meaning that a person has helped the enemy forces occupying his or her country.
colonial authorities People running a country – a colony – that is ruled by another country as part of its empire.
colony A country ruled by a foreign power as part of its empire.
Commonwealth troops Soldiers from one of the

independent states once ruled by Britain, including Australia, New Zealand, Canada, and South Africa.
communism A political and economic system, first established in the Soviet Union (which then spread to many other countries) involving rule by a single political party and control of industry and agriculture by the state.
communists People who believe in a state that is run by a single party that means to build a new society based on economic equality and the state ownership of property.
company In an army, a company is a unit made up of a number of platoons.
compatriot A person from the same country.
concentration camp A guarded enclosure in which people are imprisoned.
Congress US parliament.
conscripted Compelled to join the armed forces.
conservative Describing a political or religious outlook that desires to keep things as they are, and to preserve traditional ways of life and behaviour.
contingent Group of soldiers.
conventional warfare As opposed to guerrilla warfare, the use of regular armed forces fighting in the open with heavy arms and equipment.
CORDS Civil Operations and Revolutionary Development Support, an organization set up by the Americans in South Vietnam to encourage loyalty to the South Vietnamese government among the rural population.
corps A grouping of army formations brought together for a specific purpose in a war.
Cossacks Tribal cavalrymen from southern Russia.
counter-insurgency Operations to suppress a guerrilla movement.
coup The overthrow of one government and the setting up of another, usually by army officers.
CPV Chinese People's Volunteers – name given to the Chinese forces in the Korean War.
cruiser A warship that is less heavily armed than a battleship but which has greater speed.
Dardanelles The narrow strip of water between the Bosphorus and the Aegean.
defensive perimeter A line around an important place that an army sets out to hold against attacking enemy forces.
defoliants Chemicals that kill plants by destroying their leaves.
delegation A group of people who represent their side in negotiations.
demilitarized zone An area of land between two hostile states where – by mutual or international agreement – neither side is permitted to place its forces.
democracy Political system in which people freely elect their rulers.
Democrat A member of one of the United States' two major political parties (see also Republican).
democratic Having a government that is elected by the people and that allows a diversity of political movements and opinions.
depth charge Explosive device timed to go off at a pre-set depth to damage a submarine.
destroyer A warship used to attack enemy shipping with torpedoes and to protect its own fleet from attack by surface warships and submarines.
DFLP The Democratic Front for the Liberation of Palestine, a communist organization, set up in 1969 when it split from the PFLP. A member of the PLO, it believes that Palestinian national goals can only be achieved through a revolution of the masses.
dictator A ruler who has absolute power over the people in his country.
division A military formation made up of an average of around 12,000 men, although Japanese divisions were as large as 18,000, under a single command.
DMZ Demilitarized Zone, where military forces are not supposed to operate.
dog-fight One-to-one combat between fighter aircraft.
draft Compulsory military service.
dreadnought A fast, heavily armoured battleship.
Druze A member of a religious community similar to Islam and found mainly in Israel, Lebanon and Syria.
dynasty A succession of kings, queens or emperors belonging to the same family.
Eastern Front Battle front between the Central Powers and Russia.
empire A number of nations ruled by a single dominant power.
emplacement A platform for guns.
entente Informal agreement.
ethnic Relating to a group with distinctive cultural traits.
evacuate Withdraw from a place, like a scene of battle, often because the situation is considered too dangerous.
expeditionary force A term used in both World War I and World War II for the British troops sent to France at the start of the war.
Fatah A Palestinian nationalist group founded in 1957 by Yasser Arafat. Fatah became the PLO's leading faction in 1969. It maintains several espionage and terrorist groups within the occupied territories.
Filipinos People who come from the Philippines.
firebase A base where heavy artillery was stationed to provide supporting fire for infantry patrolling the surrounding countryside.
front The place where two opposing forces meet.
garrison A fortified position in which troops and their equipment are stationed.
Gaza Strip A narrow strip of land on the coast of the eastern Mediterranean, which has been occupied by Israel since 1967, although partial control has been handed over to the Palestinian Authority since 1994.
Geneva Convention An international agreement on how wars should be fought, including rules for the treatment of prisoners of war.
Grand Fleet Britain's main battle fleet in World War I.
guerrillas Fighters, not part of a regular government army, independently conducting military action.
gunships Fixed-wing aircraft or helicopters armed with guns and missiles, used to attack troops on the ground.
Haganah A Jewish underground militia that operated between 1920 and 1948, set up to defend Jewish settlements in Palestine from Arab attack.
High Seas Fleet Germany's main battle fleet in World War I.
Hindenburg Line German pre-prepared defensive line on the Western Front.
Holocaust The systematic extermination of nearly six million Jews by the Nazis during World War II.
IAF Israeli Air Force.
IDF Israeli Defence Force.
impeachment In the United States, putting the president on trial for crimes.
imperialism A belief in the value of acquiring control

over another country's resources and the establishment of colonies, often as part of the controlling country's empire.
incendiary bombs Bombs designed to create fires rather than to explode.
Indo-China A region of south-east Asia, including modern Vietnam, which was a colony of France before World War II.
indoctrination The process of drumming a set of beliefs into someone.
infantry Foot soldiers.
infrastructure The basic organization of a group which enables it to operate.
insurgency Revolt or rebellion against government authority.
intelligence In a military context, secret information about enemy movements or plans.
intifada The Palestinian popular uprising in the occupied territories that took place between 1987 and 1993. A second intifada began in September 2000.
Islamist Someone who follows a strict form of Islam based on a literal interpretation of the Koran and other holy Islamic scriptures.
kamikaze Japanese suicide pilots who undertook missions against enemy ships.
Khmer Rouge Communist guerrilla organization in Cambodia that ruled the country (as Kampuchea) 1975-9.
kibbutz A commune in Israel, especially for farming, and dedicated to the principle that production work and domestic work are of equal value.
Knesset The legislative assembly of Israel.
lend-lease program System by which the United States provided weapons and other supplies to its Allies in World War II without requiring immediate payment for them.
logistical support The supplies of ammunition, food, fuel etc. needed to keep an army in operation on the battlefield.
MACV Military Assistance Command, Vietnam – the US headquarters in South Vietnam.
Malaya Country in Asia, now called Malaysia, which was a British colony in 1941 when it was overrun by the Japanese.
Manchuria A Chinese state, a territory once disputed by China, Japan and the Soviet Union, occupied by the Japanese in 1931.
mandate An official command or instruction from an authority.
Maronite Christians Members of a Uniate church, based chiefly in Lebanon. Uniate churches belong to the Eastern Christian tradition, but submit to the authority of the Pope.
mediator Somebody who works with both sides in a dispute in an attempt to help them reach an agreement.
Middle East The region stretching from the eastern Mediterranean to the western side of the Indian subcontinent, including Egypt, the Arabian Peninsula, Israel, Jordan, Lebanon, Syria, Turkey, Iran and Iraq.
militant Extremely active in support of a cause, often to an extent that causes conflict with other people or institutions.
militia A group of armed people who carry out military operations on behalf of a cause or non-national organization.
mine Naval bomb, either floating on or under the surface of the sea.
multilateral negotiations Talks involving more than two parties or countries.
munitions Provisions of war, such as bullets and guns.
napalm Inflammable liquid, dropped from aircraft as firebombs (some 400,000 tons of napalm were dropped in the Vietnam War).
nationalism Belief in the right of one's people to exist as a nation, or belief in the status of one's nation above all others.
natural resources Sources of food and fuel, like wheat or oil for example, that belong to a country or region.
Nazi Germany Germany, between 1933 and 1945, when the country was governed by Adolf Hitler and members of his Nazi party.
Nazi Party The National Socialist Party that came to power in Germany under Adolf Hitler in 1933.
Nazism A system of government in Germany from 1933 to 1945, based on a belief in racial superiority and the rule of a strong and ruthless leader, Adolf Hitler.
Netherlands Country in western Europe, also called Holland and its people the Dutch, which lost control over its colonies in Asia after being defeated by Germany in 1940.
Netherlands East Indies Dutch colony in south-east Asia which became Indonesia after it achieved independence after World War II.
neutrality pact An agreement not to take part in a war.
Niitaka, Mount The highest mountain in Japan, the name of which was used as a code for the attack on Pearl Harbor in 1941.
NKPA North Korean People's Army.
NLF National Liberation Front – the South Vietnamese guerrilla movement.
no-man's-land The area between the front lines of two armies confronting one another.
NVA North Vietnamese Army.
Occupied Territories Those areas conquered by Israel in the 1967 Six Day War, including the West Bank and the Gaza Strip, the status of which remain disputed.
OSS The acronym for the Office of Strategic Services, set up by the United States in 1942 to gather intelligence and carry out secret operations.
Ottoman Empire A Turkish empire established in the late thirteenth century in Asia Minor, eventually extending through the Middle East, which came to an end in 1922.
outflank To advance around the side of an enemy position.
PA The Palestinian Authority is a Palestinian-run institution with limited powers of government over the Palestinians in the West Bank and Gaza Strip.
pacification Term used to describe the establishment of secure government control over areas where guerrillas have been active.
panzers German tanks and other armoured vehicles.
partisans Irregular troops fighting a guerrilla war.
partition The division of a country into two or more separate states.
peninsula A piece of land projecting into the sea and almost surrounded by water.
PFLP The Popular Front for the Liberation of Palestine is a left-wing Palestinian nationalist organization, founded in 1967, which joined the PLO in 1968.
Philippines The Philippines, made up of thousands of islands and with a population of 17 million in 1941, had been an American colony but was halfway to independence when the Pacific War broke out.
pincer movement An encircling movement by two wings of a force, closing in on the enemy.
platoon A small unit of soldiers.
PLO Originally founded in 1964, the Palestinian Liberation Organization is an organization of Palestinian Arabs dedicated to the establishment of an independent Palestinian state in the West Bank, Gaza and possibly parts or all of Israel.

politburo Short for 'political bureau', the ruling committee that in communist countries, such as North Vietnam, often held effective power.
power vacuum The situation in which, temporarily, no government is in control of a country.
PPP The Palestine People's Party, founded in 1947 as the National Liberation League before changing its name to the Palestine Communist Party and finally to the PPP. The party is a communist faction within the PLO.
pre-emptive strike An attack carried out on an enemy before the enemy has had a chance to strike first.
propaganda Information, often false or exaggerated, that is deliberately intended to promote a particular cause or to damage an enemy.
province Part of a country or empire.
Prussia Area of Eastern Germany around Berlin.
radar station A military installation employing radar – a method of identifying the position of distant objects using radio waves.
refugee Someone who is seeking refuge, especially from war or persecution, by going to a foreign country.
regime Government or system of government, especially one regarded as harsh or cruel.
regiment A large permanent army formation.
reparations Compensation payments.
repatriation Returning someone to their country of origin.
Republican A member of one of the United States' two major political parties (see also Democrat).
reservation Land set aside for a particular purpose.
resistance movements Groups organized to oppose the government or foreign occupation forces in their country.
resolution A formal proposal agreed by a vote.
reunification Joining together something that has been divided.
ROK Republic of Korea, usually known as South Korea.
rout To beat an enemy conclusively.
salient A place where a border or a front line sticks out or bulges into foreign or enemy-held territory.
salient-busting Eliminating bulges in the front line.
Schlieffen Plan German war plan, drawn up in 1905 and later modified, to defeat France before Russia.
Scud missile A type of surface-to-surface missile.
secular Not concerned with religious matters.
Security Council Part of the United Nations entrusted with maintaining international peace and security.
settlement A new community built in a place that is unpopulated or populated by people of a different race or ethnic group.
Shi'ite A follower of the Shia branch of Islam, which considers Ali, a relative of Muhammad, and his descendents to be Muhammad's true successors.
Siam Country in Asia, now called Thailand, invaded by the Japanese in 1941.
Slavs Inhabitants of countries in Eastern Europe, including Russia, Ukraine, Belorussia, Poland, Czechoslovakia, Bulgaria and Yugoslavia.
smart weapons Bombs or missiles with sophisticated guidance systems that give a high level of accuracy against a target.
SOE Special Operations Executive, an organization set up by Britain in 1940 to send secret agents into enemy-occupied Europe.
sorties Raids by those under siege against the besieging enemy.
sovereign territory An area or region legitimately controlled by a government.
Soviet Union Also known as the USSR (Union of Soviet Socialist Republics).
spotter aircraft Reconnaissance plane.
SS Schutzstaffeln, an elite unit in the Nazi party, which also had its own armed troops – the Waffen SS.
stalemate When no side appears to be able to win.
strafe Attack an enemy on the ground with machine-gun or cannon fire from a low-flying aircraft.
subversion Activities designed to undermine a government's authority.
tacit Understood or implied without being stated openly.
task force A unit of people and equipment brought together and organized for a special purpose.
terrorism The use of violence against civilians and political leaders in order to achieve political aims.
theatre of war A geographical area in which part of a war is fought, e.g. 'the Mediterranean theatre'.
tribunal A court of justice.
trusteeship In international affairs, an arrangement under which one country runs another for a limited period, until it is deemed fit to govern itself.
tsar Russian emperor.
U-boat German submarine.
umbrella organization A body that coordinates or protects a number of smaller organizations.
UN General Assembly The main debating body of the United Nations.
UN Resolution A decision of the UN reached after a vote of the General Assembly or Security Council.
UN Security Council The permanent committee of the United Nations that oversees its peacekeeping operations around the world.
United Nations An organization of nations, formed in 1945, to promote peace, security, and international cooperation.
UNLU The United National Leadership of the Uprising, an umbrella organization that coordinated the activities of the PLO groups during the first intifada (1987-93).
UNRWA The United Nations Relief and Works Agency, providing relief and human services to Palestinian refugees living in the Gaza Strip, the West Bank, Jordan, Lebanon and Syria.
USSR The Union of Soviet Socialist Republics (also the Soviet Union), of which Russia was the leading power. It was disbanded at the end of 1991.
VC Viet Cong – term used for communist guerrillas operating in South Vietnam.
veto The right to reject or block an action or proposal.
Vichy France After Germany's defeat of France in June 1940, the French government that was prepared to co-operate with Nazi Germany moved from Paris to the town of Vichy; the area of southern France that this government directly ruled was called Vichy France.
Wehrmacht The German armed forces.
West Bank The region between the Mediterranean Sea and the Jordan River, including the north-west quadrant of the Dead Sea, which does not belong to the state of Israel.
Western Front Front lines between the Allies and the Central Powers in France and Belgium.
wolf packs Groups of German submarines hunting together for ships to sink in the Atlantic.
Zeppelin German military airship.
Zionism A worldwide movement that sought to establish a Jewish nation in Palestine.

INDEX